AFRICAN BIBLICAL STUDIES

AFRICAN BIBLICAL STUDIES

Unmasking Embedded Racism and Colonialism in Biblical Studies

Andrew M. Mbuvi

t&t clark

LONDON • NEW YORK • OXFORD • NEW DELHI • SYDNEY

T&T CLARK
Bloomsbury Publishing Plc
50 Bedford Square, London, WC1B 3DP, UK
1385 Broadway, New York, NY 10018, USA
29 Earlsfort Terrace, Dublin 2, Ireland

BLOOMSBURY, T&T CLARK and the T&T Clark logo are trademarks of
Bloomsbury Publishing Plc

First published in Great Britain 2023

Cover design by Jade Barnett
Cover images: Apostolic Epistles manuscript f. 1v from the Robert Garrett Collection
of Ethiopic Manuscripts, Princeton University Library (top); © Heritage Image
Partnership Ltd/Alamy (bottom).

A catalogue record for this book is available from the British Library.

A catalog record for this book is available from the Library of Congress.

ISBN: HB: 978-0-5677-0771-0
ePDF: 978-0-5677-0772-7
eBook: 978-0-5677-0774-1

Typeset by Deanta Global Publishing Services, Chennai, India

To find out more about our authors and books visit www.bloomsbury.com and sign up
for our newsletters.

Dedicated to the recently transitioned "living-dead" ancestors:

John S. Mbiti (1931–2019)

Charles Nyamiti (1931–2020)

John S. Pobee (1937–2020)

David T. Adamo (1949–2022)

CONTENTS

Acknowledgments   x
Abbreviations   xiii

Part I
THE BIBLE, COLONIALISM, AND BIBLICAL STUDIES

Chapter 1
INTRODUCTION   3

Chapter 2
COLONIALISM AND THE EUROPEAN ENLIGHTENMENT   15
   2.1   The Enlightenment and the Bible   15
   2.2   The Bible, God, and Colonialism in Africa   20

Chapter 3
(WESTERN) BIBLICAL STUDIES AND AFRICAN COLONIALISM   25
   3.1   Introduction   25
   3.2   Albert Schweitzer: Biblical Scholar, Missionary, Colonialist   31

Part II
THE BIBLE, COLONIAL ENCOUNTERS, AND UNEXPECTED
OUTCOMES

Chapter 4
BIBLE TRANSLATION AS BIBLICAL INTERPRETATION: THE
COLONIAL BIBLE   61
   4.1   Introduction   61
   4.2   Vernacular Bible—The "Colonized" Bible   62
   4.3   Vernacular Bible and Vernacular Hermeneutics—Planting
       Seeds of Decolonization   70
   4.4   African Presence in the Bible: Whitewashing of a Text
       and a People   73

Chapter 5
THE BIBLE AND AFRICAN REALITY   79
   5.1   Concept of God in African Christianity   79
   5.2   Outline of African Religious Reality   81

Chapter 6

EMERGING AFRICAN POSTCOLONIAL BIBLICAL CRITICISM   84
   6.1   Introduction   84
   6.2   Négritude: Black Consciousness and Religion   86
   6.3   African Indigenous/Independent/Instituted/Initiated Churches
       (AICs)   89
   6.4   Hermeneutics of Rehabilitation: Post-Independence African
       Bible Scholarship   92

Part III
AFRICAN BIBLICAL STUDIES: SETTING A POSTCOLONIAL AGENDA

Chapter 7

DECOLONIZING THE BIBLE: A POSTCOLONIAL RESPONSE   103
   7.1   Definition of African Biblical Studies   103
   7.2   Scope of African Biblical Studies   104
   7.3   Exegesis versus Hermeneutics: Contemporary versus Historical   108

Chapter 8

THE BIBLE AND POSTCOLONIAL AFRICAN LITERATURE   111
   8.1   Introduction   111
   8.2   Dialogical Construct between Christianity and African
       Religion—Chinua Achebe   112
   8.3   Reconstituting Biblical Themes for a New Postcolonial
       Christianity—Ngũgĩ wa Thiong'o   117

Chapter 9

REWRITING THE BIBLE: RECASTING THE COLONIAL TEXT   125
   9.1   Introduction   125
   9.2   The Paradox of the Bible—Takatso Mofokeng   126
   9.3   Liberating the Bible—Itumeleng Mosala   127
   9.4   A "Supra-Bible" for All—Canaan Banana   129
   9.5   Reconstruction Hermeneutics: The Post-colonial/Post-
       Apartheid Bible   132
   9.6   Conclusion   133

Chapter 10

ESCHATOLOGY, COLONIALISM, AND MISSION: AN AFRICAN
CRITIQUE OF LINEAR ESCHATOLOGY   136
   10.1   Western Missionary Apocalypticism and Demonization of the
        African Religious Reality   136

10.2 John Mbiti's Critique of Western Eschatology   139
10.3 A South African Liberationist Eschatology: Allan Boesak   143
10.4 Ebussi Boualaga's "Christic Model"   145

Chapter 11
"ORDINARY READERS" AND THE BIBLE: NON-ACADEMIC BIBLICAL
INTERPRETATION   149
    11.1 Who Are "Ordinary Readers"?   149
    11.2 What Is Reading "With" versus Reading "For"?   150

Chapter 12
GENDER, SEXUALITY, AND THE BIBLE IN AFRICA   154
    12.1 Wälättä Peṭros: A Proto-Colonial Model of an African
          Christian Woman's Encounter with European Christianity   154
    12.2 Gender and Sexuality Discourse in African Biblical
          Studies Today   160

Chapter 13
CHRISTOLOGY IN AFRICA: "WHO DO YOU SAY THAT I AM?"   175
    13.1 Introduction   175
    13.2 Jesus in Africa   176
    13.3 Christology and Feminism   186
    13.4 Conclusion   188

Chapter 14
CONCLUSION: TOWARD A DECOLONIZED BIBLICAL STUDIES   191
    14.1 Transforming Biblical Studies   191
    14.2 Constructing a "Hermeneutic of Hope"   198
    14.3 A Final Thought   199

Bibliography   203
Name and Subject Index   220
Biblical Index   226

ACKNOWLEDGMENTS

The origins of this book go back to my graduate studies days, when, with fellow African doctoral students (Aanjov Aheneka from Nigeria, Peter Yimbu from Cameroon, Felix Asiedu from Ghana, and Bagudekia Alobeyo from DR Congo), we occasionally gathered for animated discussions about African biblical hermeneutics—interpretive approaches, distinctiveness, contributions, and so on. A commonly voiced concern in those sessions was the lack of a book volume (or volumes) that would critically synthesize the contributions of ABS scattered in hard-to-access journals and book essays. Such a volume would serve as an introduction for courses on African biblical interpretation.

Having taught for about two decades, served as the chair of the African Biblical Hermeneutics unit at the Society of Biblical Literature (2010–14), and published several works on African biblical interpretation, the need for a one-stop volume that encapsulates the innovative and varied interpretive approaches emanating from African biblical scholarship has become clear to me. While ideas in this volume started percolating over a decade before I put the proverbial "pen to paper," it was the invitation by Brad E. Kelle to publish an exploratory and introductory article on African Biblical Studies in 2017 for *Currents in Biblical Research* journal that provided the impetus for a full-blown book project. The positive reception of the article gave me the impression that a fully developed book-length volume needed to be produced. And so, here we are!

Sadly, while this book was in production, we witnessed the passing of some of the iconic pioneering figures of *African Biblical Studies* whose works are analyzed in this volume. John S. Mbiti, Charles Nyamiti, and John S. Pobee had joined the "cloud of witnesses" (Heb. 12:1) that are the "living-dead" ancestors. And, even as I was writing this tribute, news of David T. Adamo's passing reached me. Their significant foundational contributions to African Biblical Studies, and biblical studies in general, are critically analyzed in this work in a shared postcolonial hermeneutics that resists colonizing aspect of western Biblical Studies. Besides providing a distillation of the various methodological approaches represented in African biblical scholarship, this volume showcases how African biblical scholarship exposes and rebuffs the ingrained colonial and racist underpinnings that have, from its inception, shaped and continue to shape western Biblical Studies.

Research for this book took place during the period of 2016–20, which saw a devastating political period for people of African descent in America and the rise of the Black Lives Matter movement worldwide. White conservative Christians, primarily Evangelicals, were instrumental in electing the most openly racist and hate-mongering president in recent memory; the racialized nature of western Christianity was in the open. In this *zeitgeist* of this latest racial reckoning, and a world that is still reeling from the wake of the racially motivated killings of Black people, it was clear to me that one can only understand the present by fully comprehending the reality of the past, no matter how ugly. One cannot fully comprehend the murder of George Floyd on May 20, 2020, by a white police officer, in broad daylight, without understanding the history of policing and Black bodies in America. Similarly, one cannot fully grasp the motivations behind marginalizing of the so-called minoritized groups in the guild of Biblical Studies without a clear comprehension of the racist and colonialist convictions embodied by the pioneers of the discipline in western Europe.

There are many people I would like to thank. The initial draft was completed while I was faculty in the Religious Studies Department at the University of North Carolina at Greensboro (UNC-G), NC, with the final edits taking place as I transitioned to Albright College, Reading, PA. I want to express my sincere gratitude to my wonderful UNC-G colleagues whose collegiality developed into great friendships. I do want, however, to single out Dr. Greg Grieves, the Head of Department, for always going beyond the call of duty and for setting the tone for a work environment that was empowering to be part of. My colleague Ellen Haskell read the entire complete draft with enthusiasm and encouragement about what she saw as its significant value for Biblical Studies. UNC-G was a wonderful academic home, and I cherished my time there.

Several people read the manuscript at different stages with very helpful responses and suggestions. Duke University PhD student Mary D. Berry was the first to read and edit the entire manuscript draft with great care and precision. Dr. Felix Asiedu (King's College, Accra, Ghana) provided very helpful content critique and suggestions for improvement. Dr. Randall Bailey (Emeritus Distinguished Prof. Hebrew Bible at Interdenominational Theological Center), whose every conversation seems to simply detonate tones of new ideas and ways of seeing and reading texts in my head, has been a most cherished conversation partner throughout the writing process. David Horrell (University of Manchester) kindly read earlier drafts of the manuscript. Their responses greatly improved the final product, and any remaining shortcomings are entirely my own. A word of gratitude to the excellent Bloomsbury T&T Clark editorial team that helped to shepherd the book to its final form. Senior Editor Dominic Mattos believed in the project from the beginning, Jonathan Nash and Mohammed Raffi guided the manuscript through the editing process, and Jade Barnett and Lucy Davies helped design a splendid cover.

Finally, I would like to express my heartfelt appreciation to my family. We relocated amid the editing process for this book so that my wife, Amanda, could take up a new and well-deserved academic administration position in a new city. Our son Elijah and daughter Rachel had to adjust to a new home, new community, new schools, and new friends, all amid the Covid-19 pandemic. Through it all, I somehow managed to keep writing, editing, and reading proofs, and we managed to resettle. My wife's cousins, Carol and Betsy, were crucially instrumental in enabling the complicated task of both selling and purchasing homes in two distant states. My mother-in-law, Charlotte Beckenstain, together with her team of "prayer warriors," always a spiritual support of my scholarly endeavors, was no different this time. My father-in-law, Myron Beckenstein, has always been a source of encouragement. Teaching virtually, for me, proved to be a boon as it allowed me to work from home, making the adjustment to our new life much a bit smoother than anticipated.

ABBREVIATIONS

AA	African Affairs Journal
AAS	Asian and African Studies
Acta Theol.	Acta Theologica
ACS	African Christian Studies
AESTC	African Ethnographic Studies of the 20th Century
Aeth	Aethiopica: International Journal of Ethiopian and Eritrean Studies
AFAAS	French Association of Friends of Albert Schweitzer
AHR	The American Historical Review
AJBS	African Journal of Biblical Studies
ANE	Ancient Near East
Anth	Anthropos Journal
APSR	American Political Science Review
AQ	Australian Quarterly
BBh	Bible Bhashyam: An Indian Biblical Quarterly
BCB 1980	Biblical Criticism Before 1980 Series
BDV	Bulletin Dei Verbum
BiAS	Bible in African Series (Bamberg Univ.)
BIS	Biblical Studies Series
BTA	Bulletin de Théologie Africaine / Bulletin of African Theology
BZHT	Beiträge zur Historischen Theologie
CBR	Currents in Biblical Research
CC	The Christian Century
CI	Critical Inquiry
CJIA	The Commonwealth Journal of International Affairs
CR	The Contemporary Review
CUP	Cambridge University Press
EAJET	East African Journal of Evangelical Theology
Ed.	Edition
ed./eds.	Editor(s)
ET	Expository Times
FR	The French Review
FT	Feminist Theology Journal
GPBS	Global Perspective in Biblical Scholarship
HekR	Hekima Review
IAI	International African Institute
IJFM	International Journal of Frontier Missiology
IRM	International Review of Mission
HEI	History of European Ideas
HMC	Histoire et Missions Chrétiennes
HTS	Historiae Teologiese Studies/Historical Theological Studies
Huff Post	The Huffington Post

Hypa	Hypatia: Writing Against Heterosexism
IS	In die Skriflig
JAAS	Journal of Asian and African Studies
JAH	The Journal of African History
JBTSA	Journal of Black Theology in South Africa
JBL	Journal of Biblical Literature
JBS	Journal of Black Studies
JEH	Journal of Ecclesiastical History
JETS	Journal of Evangelical Theological Society
JGC	Journal of Global Christianity
JHI	Journal of the History of Ideas
JPS	Jewish Publication Society
JRER	Journal of Race, Ethnicity, and Religion
JSNT	Journal for the Study of the New Testament
JSOT	Journal for the Study of Old Testament
JSR	Journal for the Study of Religion
JRH	Journal of Religious History
JSP	The Journal of Speculative Philosophy
JTSA	Journal of Theology for Southern Africa
JWH	Journal of Women's History
Mill	Millennium Journal
NABIS	Nigerian Association of Biblical Studies
NAS	Northeast African Studies
Neot.	Neotestamentica
NYT	The New York Times
OUP	Oxford University Press
OTE	Old Testament Essays
POP	Patterns of Prejudice Journal
PQ	The Philosophical Quarterly
RAL	Research in African Literatures
RSR	Religious Studies Review
SBL	Society of Biblical Literature
SCM	Student Christian Movement Press
SCMEA	Some Contemporary Models of African Ecclesiology Series
SHE	Studia Historiae Ecclesiasticae
SHEB	Studia Historiae Ecclesiasticae Book Series
JESWTR	Journal of the European Society of Women in Theological Research
SPCK	Society for Promoting Christian Knowledge
STJ	Stellenbosch—Theological Journal
SUNY	State University of New York Press
THJ	The Historical Journal
TS	Theological Studies
URM	Ultimate Reality and Meaning Journal
WCC	World Council of Churches
WSJ	Washington Journal
WP	The Washington Post
YUP	Yale University Press

Part I

THE BIBLE, COLONIALISM, AND BIBLICAL STUDIES

Biblical Criticism is a very specialized endeavour. It involves observing meticulously every detail of a text, looking upon the finest nuance of an expression, comparing and dissecting, using seemingly objective methods. But one has to stress: *seemingly* . . . .

— H. G. Reventlow[1]

European theories themselves emerge from particular cultural traditions which are hidden by false notions of "the universal."

— *The Empire Writes Back*[2]

---

1. H. G. Reventlow, "Appendix: Conditions and Presuppositions of Biblical Criticism in Germany in the Period of the second Empire and Before: The Case of Heinrich Julius Holtzmann," in *Biblical Studies and the Shifting of Paradigms, 1850–1914*, ed. H. G. Reventlow and W. Farmer (JSOT Series 192: Sheffield: Sheffield academic, 1994), 272 (emphasis original).

2. B. Ashcroft, G. Griffiths, and H. Tiffin, *The Empire Writes Back*, 2nd ed. (Abingdon, Oxon and New York: Routledge, 1991), 11.

Chapter 1

INTRODUCTION

[A] Christianity of empire imposes itself only by tearing up its converts by the roots, out of where-they-live, out of their being-in-the-world, presenting them with the Faith only at the price of depriving them of their capacity to generate material and spiritual conditions of their existence.

— F. Ebousi Boulaga[1]

From a postcolonial perspective, canonical Scriptures are not the sole conveyors of truth. The suppressed Scriptures make it clear that competing claims and counter-claims were the characteristic features of early Christianity.

— R. S. Sugirtharajah[2]

When one speaks of the field of Biblical Studies, an unspoken assumption is that there is a "universal" Biblical Studies discipline that everyone adheres to and agrees upon, as Ashcroft, Griffiths, and Tiffin in the epigraph attest.[3] Such a standardized discipline is presumed to represent objective and unadulterated interpretations of the Bible. This view, that there is a pure discipline that reflects a universally representative reading of the Bible, has been around since the beginning of the emergence of Biblical Studies in Europe about one and a half centuries ago.[4] Its

---

1. Fabian Ebousi Boulaga, *Christianity Without Fetishes* (Maryknoll: Orbis, 1981), 17.

2. R. S. Sugirtharajah, "Postcolonial and Biblical Interpretation: The Next Phase," in *A Postcolonial Commentary of the New Testament*, ed. Fernando Segovia and R. S. Sugirtharajah (London and New York: T&T Clark, 2009), 455–66, 456.

3. I am aware of recent reception histories that have questioned the idea of a standardized Biblical Studies discipline, for example, Emma England and William John Lyons (eds.), *Reception History and Biblical Studies: Theory and Practice* (London and New York: Bloomsbury, 2015). However, I maintain the construct here because even reception history's challenge is based on the fact that most practitioners of Biblical Studies believe it is a standardized entity.

4. Warnings have been levied at the discipline on this issue, especially by minority groups including African American biblical scholars in Cain H. Felder (ed.), *Stony the Road we Trod* (Minneapolis: Fortress, 1991) and Randall Bailey (ed.), *Yet with a Steady Beat:*

emergence during the same period in which the European colonial project began meant that it would be both a beneficiary and an accomplice in Europe's political conquests and explorations of the world. Vincent Wimbush has made the case that the emergence of the Society of Biblical Literature (SBL) in 1880, just four years prior to the 1884 Berlin conference, which commenced the European colonization of Africa, is no coincidence.[5] Resultantly, the academic discipline manifests the same imperialistic and colonialist impulses of the European Empire. As Europe became the global power with the might to conquer, control, and name distant lands, it furnished both resources and language readily used by the academe to construct an interpretation of the Bible.[6]

With colonization, this process became solidified in the relationship between the colonizer and the colonized, between the "center" and the "periphery." The "center" could write the narrative of its establishment and expansion and of its subduing and possessing remote corners of the then known world.[7] The "center" could then establish what eventually the periphery would have to imbibe since the newly "discovered" distant worlds were to be run from the center—Europe. From the "center" would come weapons, militaries, administrators, explorers, and missionaries, and from the "periphery" would come natural resources (slaves, gold, ivory, timber; cash crops like cotton, spices, palm oil, coffee, cocoa, tea; sugar, etc.) and all the things that the center craved but did not have at home. The Empire would plunder and pilfer the periphery to feed the insatiable greed of the imperial economy. This is Fabian Eboussi Boulaga's lament in the epigraph at the beginning of the chapter.

With Europe controlling or occupying up to three-quarters of the world's lands and territories, confidence grew in a universal European outlook based on a biblical understanding of colonialism and imperialism as divine mandates,

---

Contemporary U. S. Afrocentric Biblical Interpretation (Atlanta: SBL, 2002). Just how much of an impact these have had in reshaping the discipline is yet to be determined, but they constitute part of the pushback to which this study contributes.

5. Vincent Wimbush, SBL's "#BlackScholarsMatter: Visions and Struggles," *Symposium*, August 13, 2020, Available online: https://sbl-site.org/meetings/blackscholarsmatter.aspx. For Wimbush, SBL was and still is fully embedded in the colonial project.

6. Though historical criticism goes as far back as the fourteenth through to the nineteenth centuries (including English Deists and continental rationalists such as Spinoza, etc.) and serves as the foundation for the formal construction of modern Biblical Studies, the actual establishment of academic Biblical Studies in the secular university in Europe happened in the nineteenth century. Cf. Magne Sæbø (ed.), *Hebrew Bible/Old Testament: The History of Its Interpretation, II: From the Renaissance to the Enlightenment* (Göttingen: Vandenhoeck & Ruprecht, 2008), 44–5.

7. J. C. Young, *Postcolonialism: A Very Short Introduction* (Oxford: Oxford University Press, 2003), 2. Colonialism was so widespread that in the nineteenth century "nine-tenths of the entire land surface of the globe was controlled by European or European derived powers."

and the discipline of Biblical Studies became a unifying construct of European supremacy.[8] The presumption that the universal perspective was what the "center" thought on any given subject matter gained currency. When it came to biblical interpretation and its relationship to Empire, the Bible was the *de facto* religious text of Europe, and it became the blueprint for the construction of the religious and moral justification of the colonial project. The Bible was not only a text that the Europeans had the sole mandate to interpret but also the source of political, social, economic, and theological arguments for the conquest of the rest of the world in the name of the Gospel.

At the heart of the colonial project was European hubris with its self-perception as the most advanced human civilization in the world. Europe and its peoples essentially became the chosen race, replacing biblical Israel, to be the torchbearer of the Bible's message of God's salvation to the world. The imperative to "go, and make disciples of the nations" in what came to be known as the "Great Commission" (Mt. 28:19-20) galvanized European Christian missions that gathered momentum in this period.[9] African scholars have critiqued this Matthean text by pointing out the colonialist and imperialistic impulses embedded therein, which European missionaries and colonizers fully embodied.[10] The conceptualization of the Christian mission beyond Europe became enmeshed with political and commercial ambitions to form a three-pronged attack commonly characterized as the three Cs—Commerce, Civilization, and Christianity.

If Europe was the center of civilization and progress, all non-European communities were in the periphery, both literally and figuratively, and in need of civilizing. The European self-perception crowned itself as the only authentic conveyor of the civilizing and Christianizing mission.[11] As envisioned by its early practitioners, Biblical Studies would construct a coherent narrative around this European framework, enabling both the religious and political establishments'

8. Edward Said, *Culture and Imperialism* (New York: Vintage, 1993), 8. "By 1914, the annual rate had risen to an astonishing 240,000 square miles, and Europe held a grand total of roughly 85 percent of the earth as colonies, protectorates, dependencies, dominions, and commonwealths."

9. R. S. Sugirtharajah, "Postcolonial Biblical Interpretation," in *Voices from the Margin: Interpreting the Bible in the Third World*, ed. idem (New York: Maryknoll, 2006), 64–84, 73. "A dormant text like Matthew 28:19 was reactivated to bolster the missionary enterprise . . . "

10. Musa W. Dube, "Boundaries and Bridges: Journeys of a Postcolonial Feminist Biblical Scholar," *JESWTR* 22 (2014): 139–56. "In this investigation I wanted to find out if the biblical text stood a better chance of providing a counter-colonial ideology. My findings were not encouraging. Mission texts constructed the Other negatively—as a blank slate awaiting divine teachers (Mt. 28:18-20), as ethically or morally lacking, and as women." (149).

11. "Colonialism," in *Stanford Encyclopedia of Philosophy*, Available online: https://plato.stanford.edu/entries/colonialism/.

interests of the Empire, by situating itself as part of the elite and the discipline as a superior "queen of sciences."[12] As one African scholar put it, "Christianity, Enlightenment, and colonial science witness a violence which posits itself as a condition for modernity."[13] Biblical Studies, thus influenced by Enlightenment thinking, not only set up parameters for what constituted the discipline but also sought to control who practiced it by insisting on the need to replicate whatever had been determined as the acceptable methods, presuppositions, and requirements of expertise.[14] It is this presumed comprehensiveness that postcolonial Biblical Studies puts to task, as reflected in the works of early pioneer R. S. Sugirtharajah and enshrined in the epigraph at the beginning of this chapter.

In fact, Biblical Studies in the West, as part of the colonial project has been instrumental in establishing parameters for the study of religion as a whole. For example, Dorothy Figueira makes the case that "[t]he comparisons of religious dogmas resulted in paradigms for practical analyses, most notably a form of biblical exegesis and a criticism of religious superstitions."[15] The result was a continuum of categories from superstition to advanced religion. When scholars applied these criteria to different geographical regions, they portrayed Asia, for example, as "a victim of prejudice and superstition" and yet a domain of "reason and virtue."[16] In contrast, they portrayed Africa only as the former, having no "reason or virtue" and therefore essentially having no religious, ethical, moral, or intellectual offerings of any kind to give. Consequently, the parameters of biblical exegesis deliberately omitted anything African. The contemporary eighteenth- and nineteenth-century theories of racial evolution of knowledge were corralled both to support the colonial project and to expound on theories in Biblical Studies which also made sure it was a discipline for only the "chosen few."[17] In Colin Kidd's

12. This phrase was used of Christian theology in the Middle Ages, but in the colonial project its use is in the German notion of *wissenschaftliche*—the study of the Bible as the source of truth, and therefore superior to all other forms of knowledge.

13. V. Y. Mudimbe, *Tales of Faith: Religion as Political Performance in Central Africa* (London and Atlantic Is.: Athlone, 1997), 61. Cf. also Kenneth Ngwa, "Postwar Hermeneutics: Bible and Colony-Related Necropolitics," in *Colonialism and the Bible*, ed. Tat-siong Benny Liew and Fernando Segovia (Lanham: Lexington Books, 2018), 43–74, 48.

14. Dorothy Figueira, *Aryans, Jews, Brahmins: Theorizing Authority through Myths of Identity* (New York: SUNY, 2002), 9.

15. Ibid., 10.

16. Ibid., 9.

17. According to David Theo Goldberg, *Racist Culture: Philosophy and the Politics of Meaning* (Cambridge: Blackwell, 1993), 11–13, a distinction can be made between "Racialism" (strictly embedded racism that is unacknowledged and remains invisible) and "Racism" (overt racial actions, speech, opinions, thought, etc.). In this construct, Biblical Studies and early practitioners of the discipline evidence both Racialism and Racism.

words, "The 'science' of biblical criticism was itself inflected with contemporary racialist assumptions."[18]

The European racialized conceptualization of the African peoples and their religio-cultural reality as devoid of reason and virtue also became the justification for the colonial project to civilize, commercialize, and Christianize the Other in the colonies. The European, as the sole bearer of "truth," was the morally justified emissary of God, the Bible, and the Empire. In this way, Biblical Studies embraced the imperializing mission while staking the claim to present a "universal" reading of the Bible that would speak on behalf of all peoples everywhere.[19]

This imposition of the western view as the "normative" one was a refusal to acknowledge Others' views as valid, let alone equal.[20] It reflects the colonial mindset that constructed the binary of the "center" as the source of all knowledge, power, and control, while the "periphery" or "margins" remained simply sources of raw materials, consumers, and subjects—not producers of knowledge—subjects of the center and objects of study, but not independent generators of ideas or thoughts! In an SBL presidential address given by J. H. Thayer in 1895, he acknowledged as much by thanking the missionaries for bringing archeological resources from the occupied region: "Thanks to the occasional generosity of a missionary or traveller, we have in this country here and there an embryonic museum of Biblical or Semitic antiquities."[21] What the missionaries procured was raw material for the

---

18. Colin Kidd, *The Forging of Races: Race and Scripture in the Protestant Atlantic World, 1600–2000* (Cambridge: Cambridge University Press, 2006), 203.

19. "Colonialism," May 9, 2006, Available online: https://plato.stanford.edu/entries/colonialism/.

20. The term "West"/"western" is, of course, itself a complicated obscuring nomenclature. I have used it to identify the set of European countries (and America), which colonized Africa or have had imperializing power over others from the nineteenth century onward. In this regard, it is a terminology of power and control resisted by Postcolonial African approaches. Yet, within the "West" are minority groups (e.g., African Americans, Native Americans, and Minority groups in Europe) that were not beneficiaries of the colonial infrastructure and power, and, in fact, themselves as much colonized as any of the African countries. Such groups are, as much victims of colonial oppression, as the Africans. So, the term "West" cannot include them as part of the power players. Instead, power players in this colonial and imperial context happen to be racially white Europeans/Euro-Americans. A similarly complex term is "Africa," which I use as a convenient umbrella term for different communities (Kenyan, Batswana, Nigerian, South African, etc.—themselves colonial constructs) that share a common historical experience as former European colonies. In that regard, the most basic way that these terminologies are used here basically reflects the power dynamics between oppressor (West) and oppressed (the rest).

21. J. Henry Thayer, "The Historical Element in the New Testament," *JBL* 14, no. 1–2 (1895): 1–18, 15. Concern for the local population did not drive Thayer's support of the opening of an American School for Oriental Study and Research in Palestine (British Occupied at this time). Instead, political maneuvering that decried the fact that the French

biblical scholar, the expert, to unpack and study. The missionary could identify and transport the raw material, but only the erudition and sophistry of the biblical scholar could discern its meaning. However, the end of imperial colonialism did not necessarily erase these colonial presuppositions, attitudes, and readings.[22]

With the turn of the twenty-first century, a major transition has characterized the makeup of the world of Judeo-Christianity.[23] In the "shift in Christianity's center of gravity," more Christians now live in the Southern hemisphere (south of the equator) than in the Northern for the first time in history.[24] This means that the face of Christianity has shifted from being predominantly Euro-American and white, to one increasingly reflecting a multiracial and multicultural religion. This shift has also witnessed Christian growth in cultures in the Global South, a region that has increasingly challenged, resisted, and struggled against the Europeanized form of Christianity. These communities of color—Africans, Latin Americans, Asians, Chinese, and others—have incessantly nudged their way into Christendom, changing the face of Christianity forever. While the immediate impact of this shift has yet to be felt fully realized in all spheres of life, especially in academia, there are indications that it is slowly encroaching on the predominant conversations in virtually all areas of the discipline.[25]

In the SBL, the preeminent and largest organization for the study of the Bible in the world with a current membership of over 8,000, these changes have become evident in the increased presence of previously unrepresented or underrepresented peoples. However, even as these non-white, non-Euro-American groups have become legitimate contributors to the changing face of the discipline and society, they remain largely confined to the margins. The pace

Catholic scholars had already beaten them to the punch in Jerusalem drove this support. On the role of SBL, Thayer asked, "Shall a Society, organized for the express purpose of stimulating and diffusing a scholarly knowledge of the Sacred Word, remain seated with folded hands, taking no part or lot in the matter?" (16)

22. R. S. Sugirtharajah, *The Bible and the Third World: Precolonial, Colonial and Postcolonial Encounters* (Cambridge: Cambridge University Press, 2001), 61.

23. Philip Jenkins, *The Next Christendom: The Coming Global Christianity* (Oxford and New York: Oxford University Press, 2011).

24. Kwame Bediako, *Christianity in Africa: The Renewal of a Non-Western Religion* (Edinburgh and Maryknoll: Edinburgh University Press and Orbis, 1995), 75; Jenkins, *The Next Christendom*, 1.

25. Phillip Jenkins, "The Power of the Bible in the Global South," *CC*, July 11, 2006, 22–6, Available online: http://www.religion-online.org/article/the-power-of-the-bible-in-the-global-south/. "Several factors contribute to a more literal interpretation of scripture in the global South. For one thing, the Bible has found a congenial home among communities that identify with the social and economic realities the Bible portrays. To quote Kenyan feminist theologian Musimbi Kanyoro, "cultures which are far removed from biblical culture risk reading the Bible as fiction." Conversely, societies that identify with the biblical world feel at home in the text." (23)

of change remains glacial, as the makeup of the society remains overwhelmingly white and male. The latest SBL Member Profile Report figures indicated that members of European or Caucasian background still make up 85 percent of the society while people of African descent make up only 5 percent. In terms of gender, percentages are better, but women still make up only 25 percent of the society.[26] SBL remains largely an enclosed white space that does not come anywhere close to reflecting the demographics of world Christianity where white Euro-Americans are no longer the majority.

This is a major disconnect between what, who, and whose interest SBL represents *vis-à-vis* the global Christian community. The presence in SBL, in the last four decades or so, of units such as African Biblical Hermeneutics, African American Biblical Hermeneutics, Asian and Asian-American Hermeneutics, Contextual Biblical Interpretation, Contextualizing North African Christianity, Latino/A and Latin American Biblical Interpretation, LGBTQI/Queer Hermeneutics, Minoritized Criticism and Biblical Interpretation, Postcolonial Studies and Biblical Studies, and Racism, Pedagogy, and Biblical Studies, signifies a shift in the conversation happening in the field of Biblical Studies, even as demographics significantly lag. Yet, the continued need to identify such approaches with modifiers (African, Asian, etc.) implies the continued underlying resistance of the discipline to incorporate them fully as genuine species of Biblical Studies.[27]

The question of how we get from the overt racism of yesteryear's scholarship that framed Biblical Studies to the persistent and invisible racialized system that continues to perpetuate imperialistic and colonizing biases in the discipline has received some scholarly analysis.[28] Galbraith, for instance, references David Theo Goldberg, who makes clear that suppressing racist language, behavior, or artifacts

---

26. These are figures from January 2019 and represent the most current figures posted by SBL. Available online: https://www.sbl-site.org/assets/pdfs/sblMemberProfile2019.pdf (accessed July 29, 2020). In the last five years, the population of people of African descent has grown by 1 percent, while that of European/Caucasian has fallen by 4 percent from 89 to 85 percent. (Cf. SBL Member Report figures in 2013. Available online: https://www.sbl -site.org/assets/pdfs/memberProfileReport2014.pdf

27. This holds true whether it is the practitioners of the so-called "new" approaches who choose to use the modifiers, or whether the modifiers are imposed from the outside. The recognition of the need for the modifier is an acknowledgment of the approach's ill fit within the traditional Biblical Studies discipline. Cf. also Wei Hsien Wan, "Re-examining the Master's Tools: Considerations on Biblical Studies' Race Problem," in *Ethnicity, Race and Religion: Identities and Ideologies, in Early Jewish and Christian Texts, and in Modern Biblical Interpretation*, ed. Katherine M. Hockey and David G. Horrell (London and New York: T&T Clark, 2018), 219–20, 226.

28. Deane Galbraith, "The Perpetuation of Racial Assumptions in Biblical Studies," in *History, Politics and the Bible from the Iron Age to the Media Age: Essays in Honour of Keith W. Whitelam*, ed. James G. Crossley and Jim West (London: Bloomsbury T&T Clark, 2017).

in a discipline like Biblical Studies without addressing the root cause simply renders invisible the racist structures without actually getting rid of them.

> So, institutionally, it is not that race has been made "absent" but that its presence has been rendered invisible and silenced (save to the sensitive eye and ear), purged of explicit terms of reference. The condition remains even where the terms of characterization and analysis, of condemnation (or for that matter of praise), of address and redress, have been removed. That there are no terms by which to mark it suggests that there is no condition to mark; but it doesn't rid the social of the condition even where the terms of target have been dimmed or quieted.[29]

According to Goldberg, racialized discourse began in the sixteenth century but retains direct implications in modern disciplines like Biblical Studies by retaining preconceptual elements like "classification, order, value, and hierarchy; differentiation and identity, discrimination and identification; exclusion, domination, subjection, and subjugation; as well as entitlement and restriction."[30] Similarly, writing on the pervasiveness of the privilege of "whiteness" and from the perspective of a white person, Peter McLaren asserts:

> The logics of empire are still with us, bound to our daily fabric of being in the world; woven into our posture toward others; connected to the muscles of our eyes; dipped in the chemical relations that excite and calm us; willed into the language of our perceptions. We cannot will our racist logics away. We need to work hard to eradicate them.[31]

In agreement, Galbraith posits that "racial distinctions remain embedded within contemporary conceptual frameworks [Biblical Studies] and academic institutions, even as [individual] scholars consciously adopt an explicit anti-racist posture."[32] And ultimately, he makes the indictment that "historical-critical scholarship is, in its origins and embedded structure, racialized scholarship. As a result, Biblical Studies continues in many ways to be complicit in, rather than a challenge to, modern forms of racial discrimination and oppression."[33]

Galbraith's analysis of the story of the spies in Numbers 13-14 reveals how this text that biblical scholars have perceived as being vital to understanding the entire Hexateuch (Genesis to Joshua as a single collection) is analyzed with "racial, social-evolutionary assumptions," as its category of "myth" renders the

---

29. David Theo Goldberg, "Call and Response," *POP* 44, no. 1 (2010): 89–106, 91.

30. Goldberg, *Racist Culture*, 49.

31. Joe L. Kincheloe, Shirley R. Steinberg, Nelson M. Rodriguez, Ronald E. Chennault (eds.), *White Reign: Deploying Whiteness in America* (New York: St. Martins Griffith, 1998), 63.

32. Galbraith, "The Perpetuation of Racial Assumptions in Biblical Studies," 119.

33. Ibid., 134.

narrative "primitive" and therefore earlier than the rest of the Hexateuch.[34] In such a reading, biblical material that cannot be mythical "reflect[s] an evolution from primitive to sophisticated thought."[35] Jeffery Tigay's 1996 commentary on Deuteronomy 1 connects the giants (*Anakim*—Deut. 2:10, 21; 9:2), just like those in Numbers (13:33), to the myth of the giant "Watusi" of East Africa (probably a corruption of the Tutsis), themselves constructs of racially-based anthropological studies, that influenced the Belgian installation of the Tutsis as a "superior" race to that of Hutus in Rwanda, setting in motion what would eventually result in the Rwandan genocide in 1994.[36] Yet, the Jewish Publication Society allowed Tigay's interpretation to stand, despite it being written after the genocide. Not only does this reading perpetuate the racial-based categories and evolutionary constructs, but it also fails to be cognizant of the insidiousness of such a racialized past.

The presence of previously unrepresented or underrepresented communities in SBL is only *a* beginning of the hoped-for erosion of the supremacy of white Euro-American male majority in the discipline. But presence alone is not enough to bring change. Like the tiny mosquito that incessantly buzzes at the ear and creates major discomfort for a person, these minoritized groups must be unwavering in pushing for changes in the types of conversations being had and the questions being posed to the Bible. They must also push for exposure to multiple approaches to reading the Bible while also holding a mirror to the dominant group's shortcomings. As such, it is important to note the contrast between the underpinnings of Biblical Studies' resistance to change and, say, African Biblical Studies' determination to decolonize both the interpretive space and its presuppositions. These sentiments are shared by the first Black president of SBL, Vincent Wimbush, who in his presidential address in 2010 called attention to the need of the society to engage "in persistent and protracted struggle, not symbolic or obfuscating games around methods and approaches, to come to terms with the construal of the modern ideologization of language, characterized by the meta-racism that marks the relationship between Europeans and Euro-Americans and peoples of color, especially black peoples."[37]

Put in this context, African Biblical Studies, as a postcolonial enterprise, "has been concerned with the elaboration of the theoretical structures that contest the dominant Western ways of seeing things."[38] An overwhelming desire to extricate the negative impact of colonization on the African reality—its peoples, cultures, religions, and so on—and to unmask readings that continue to impact this reality negatively, drives African Biblical Studies. Therefore, African Biblical Studies aims to decolonize colonial structures, colonized peoples, and colonized "texts" while

---

34. Ibid., 123–4.

35. Ibid., 129.

36. Ibid., 131–2. Cf. Jeffrey H. Tigay, "'Deuteronomy' and 'Debarim'" in *JPS Torah Commentary*, ed. J. H. Tigay (Philadelphia: Jewish Publication Society, 1996), 17.

37. Vincent L. Wimbush, "Interpreters—Enslaving/ Enslaved/Runagate," *JBL* 130, no. 1 (2011): 5–24, 9.

38. Young, *Postcolonialism*, 4.

being fully cognizant of the fact that part of the process may involve incorporating the colonialist's tools, such as education, to achieve this goal. It is the *use of the master's tools to bring down the master's house!*[39] The postcolonial African biblical scholar thus works to expose imperializing and oppressive elements of not only European imperialism in Biblical Studies, but also imperialistic elements of the biblical text itself.[40]

Furthermore, African Biblical Studies reads the biblical text to resist and expose the history of violent and dominating texts and practices that perpetuate imperialistic tendencies that have characterized the colonial enterprise.[41] Given the ubiquity of imperial Europe around the globe by the end of the nineteenth and the beginning of the twentieth century, its lasting impact is pervasive.[42] As part of this resistance, African Biblical Studies elevates the African cultures, peoples, languages, histories, and traditions as subjects and optics of interpretation while being fully cognizant that this is a limited and not a universal perspective. It also functions postcolonially by means of both the *historical* (having largely emerged in the postcolonial period) and the *postcolonial* (that seeks to prioritize marginalized and suppressed readings).[43]

---

39. C. Vander Stichele and T. C. Penner (eds.), *Her Master's Tools?: Feminist and Postcolonial Engagements of Historical-Critical Discourse* (Leiden: Brill, 2005); Lazare S. Rukundwa, "Postcolonial Theory as a Hermeneutical Tool for Biblical Reading," *HTS* 64, no. 1 (2008): 339–51; and K. Dickson, "Continuity and Discontinuity Between the Old Testament and African Life Thought," *BTA* 1, no. 2 (1979): 179–93, 106. For a critique of the use of the masters' tools, and their limits, see Audre Lorde, "The Master's Tools Will Never Dismantle the Master's House," in *Sister Outsider: Essays and Speeches* (Berkeley: Crossing Press, 1984), 110–13.

40. Throughout this work, I am following Edward Said's (Said, *Culture and Imperialism*, 9) distinction between imperialism—practice and theory attitudes of dominating metropolis over distant territories—and colonialism—actual occupation of distant colonies by imperial subject. European political powers identified with Christianity even as they colonized and subjugated Africans and others, using the gun.

41. M. W. Dube, "The Scramble for Africa as the Biblical Scramble for Africa: Postcolonial Perspectives," in *Postcolonial Perspectives in African Biblical Interpretations*, ed. M. W. Dube, A. M. Mbuvi, and D. R. Mbuwayesango (Atlanta: SBL, 2012), 1–28. African Biblical Studies works with the presuppositional starting point of serving a God who is decidedly on the side of the weak, the oppressed, the suffering, and the disempowered (Lk. 4:16-28).

42. Said, *Culture and Imperialism*, 8.

43. Spelling distinguishes between post-colonialism (with hyphen) and postcolonialism (without hyphen): The former is usually used in reference to the historical period that followed independence of African countries from colonialism, while the latter is an ideological stance that reflects resistance to colonial systems and imperializing structures without a specific historical time frame.

Therefore, as the resistance to presumed perch on which Biblical Studies in the West has placed itself takes hold, several responses have emerged: The *first* is to expose the ongoing sense of the universalism inherent in the way the discipline continues to function. The *second* is to establish the historical link of the imperialistic and colonial background from which Biblical Studies emerged and of which it was a full beneficiary and supporter. The *third* is to critique how the Bible became part of the colonial project and how it enabled imperializing readings as well as how it gave impetus to the construction of racially-based colonial Christianity that obliterated the religious heritages of the colonized. The *fourth* is to make plain the continued failure of Biblical Studies that, as a discipline, is an inheritor of a foundation built on racialized theories and presuppositions of its adherents and practitioners and that refuses to self-examine critically, resulting in a perpetuation of these theories and presuppositions. The *fifth* is to present a postcolonial response that not only seeks to undo the impact of colonialism but also seeks to present an alternative vision of Biblical Studies as a discipline. *Lastly*, it is to formulate a way forward so the postcolonial stance does not just remain embedded in resistance. So it is not simply seeking to replace the center with the periphery but undoing the very construct of the "center–periphery" binary by allowing the possibility of multiple centers.[44]

This book which hopes to add to the eroding of western hegemony in Biblical Studies studies, is divided into three parts. Part I establishes the relationship between colonialism, the Enlightenment, and Biblical Studies. It makes a case for Biblical Studies' deep entanglement with, and propagation of, the colonial project and its systemic impact on Biblical Studies in the West to the present day despite the failure to acknowledge or address, in any consistent or meaningful way, the still deeply entrenched racist foundations of the discipline. A close analysis of Albert Schweitzer, a twentieth-century western icon, follows; Schweitzer embodies the triple-nexus of colonialist, missionary, and biblical scholar, whose racist and white supremacist outlook drove his academic, medical, and missionary work. Though Schweitzer was a full and conscious participant in the dehumanization and colonization of the Africans, his celebration as one of the greatest biblical scholars of the twentieth century continues.

Part II begins by unveiling the unacknowledged negative impact of the colonial translation of the Bible into African vernacular as a means of unmasking the pretext of colonial benevolence as a mere charade of colonial imposition of meaning. It exposes the denigration of the African religious reality and the imposition of Eurocentric texts, translations, and perspectives through the

---

44. Sugirtharajah, *Voices from the Margin*, 9, asks, "Do we want to replicate the colonial game of occupation and capture the center in the name of the oppressed, or do we want to demolish the center itself and redraw its parameters? . . . . How many centers should we have? Who will provide the parameters?" I make the case here that African Biblical Studies responds to these questions by providing a template that not only resists the colonial structure but also offers decolonizing alternatives.

vernacular Bible translation. The last chapter in this section introduces emerging African postcolonial biblical criticism that not only calls the colonial vernacular translation project into question but also pushes back with its critical evaluation and hermeneutic of rehabilitation.[45]

Part III incorporates the basic framework of African Biblical Studies as a postcolonial approach that is, at its core, a response to the colonial project. Rejecting the narrow prescription of Biblical Studies proffered in the western academe, African Biblical Studies promotes an embrace of a broad spectrum of approaches to biblical interpretation. Divided into seven chapters, this section showcases the various tenets of African Biblical Studies, starting with its decolonizing of the Bible, creative literature's innovative approaches to reading the Bible, and finally, a rewriting of the Bible with an eye toward liberating and decolonizing the biblical text. Beyond resistance to the colonial imposition, approaches defined by a focus on "ordinary" readership, gender and sexuality, and African Christology showcase the innovative approaches that African biblical scholars have propounded in the last half-a-century, working from the "margins".

45. Over 100 years since its initial issue in 1906, his groundbreaking volume *Von Reimarus zu Wrede: Geschichte der Leben-Jesu-Forschung* (Tübingen: Mohr, 1906), trans. W. Montgomery as *The Quest of the Historical Jesus: A Critical Study of its Progress from Reimarus to Wrede* (London: Unwin Brothers, 1910), remains in print.

Chapter 2

COLONIALISM AND THE EUROPEAN ENLIGHTENMENT

> In the Enlightenment . . . the *truth* of the non-European Other is that
> he *manifests the false*, he makes manifest true ignorance and error, true
> unenlightenment. . . . The principle function and sign of the truth of
> Christianity is that it explains the falsity of the Other's difference.
>
> — Bernard McGrane[1]

> On the battlefield, the enemy had no religion. At the front lines of a context
> of religions, Christian missionaries adopted this strategy of denial.
>
> — David Chidester[2]

2.1 The Enlightenment and the Bible

Here, I start with the focus on the emergence of Biblical Studies as a discipline, both as a product of, and in response to, the Enlightenment's secularism. Jonathan Sheehan, in his recent important work titled *The Enlightenment Bible: Translation, Scholarship, Culture*, has argued that in the eighteenth century, Biblical Studies shifted the focus of the Bible from dogma to cultural reason by transforming the Bible from a theological into a "cultural Bible."[3] While this shift was vital in allowing Biblical Studies to emerge as a discipline, Sheehan's analysis overlooks a major factor in this process, which is the vital connection of the Enlightenment to the colonial project and the subsequent construction of what I will call the "Colonial Bible." The Enlightenment may have been the ideological foundation

---

1. Bernard McGrane, *Beyond Anthropology: Society and the Other* (New York: Columbia University Press, 1989), 52–3. (emphasis original)

2. D. Chidester, *Savage Systems: Colonialism and Comparative Religion in Southern Africa* (Charlottesville: University Press of Virginia, 1996), 94.

3. Jonathan Sheehan, *The Enlightenment Bible: Translation, Scholarship, Culture* (Princeton: Princeton University Press, 2013). The book jacket description notes that in response to the impulses of the Enlightenment in Europe, "the Bible was made into the cornerstone of Western heritage and invested with meaning, authority, and significance even for a secular age."

for European expansionism, but it was the colonial infrastructure that formed the social, economic, and religious crucible from which Biblical Studies as a discipline emerged and which unleashed the "Colonial Bible" onto the African continent.[4] This is an important claim to make and one that I believe bears elaborating. Modern Biblical Studies emerged out of religious upheaval in Europe that originated with the Protestant Reformation in the sixteenth century. Michael Legaspi, in his analysis titled *The Death of Scripture* and building on Sheehan's work, argues that rather than the Enlightenment, the Reformation caused the shift of the Bible from "scripture" to "text."[5] Biblical authority was no longer ecclesial but textual in the Bible itself, and its readers could engage that authority without ecclesial oversight. Commenting on the same, Wei Hsien Wan explains that "because the controversies of the age transformed the Bible into a heated site of theological contest, its textual purity and material integrity as an authoritative source became paramount."[6] As such, while in the Reformation period, "biblical teaching was conveyed through the enactment of liturgical rites," the post-Reformation era elevated the status of the Bible as the material artifact containing God's word.[7]

Clergy and non-clergy alike championed the Bible as an artifact of western civilization and an ally in European incursion into "ungodly" territories. To paraphrase David Chidester's forceful conclusion about the emergence of religious studies in the colonial encounter, "The discipline of [Biblical Studies] emerged, therefore, not only out of the Enlightenment heritage but also out of a violent history of colonial conquest and domination. Accordingly, the history of [Biblical Studies] is a story not only about knowledge but also about power."[8] And to justify incursions into foreign worlds necessitated a binary opposite of the Enlightened European, resulting in the construction of the non-European Other who, according to Bernard McGrane, became the manifestation of falsity.[9] On these grounds was justified the power to name, to set boundaries, to control discourse, to control participation, to determine the subject matter, and to define the limits of the discipline! The impact of this history remains within the discipline as these categories, labels, and boundaries remain intact, as Galbraith has convincingly shown in the aforementioned analysis of the perpetuation of racial assumptions in Biblical Studies.[10]

This shift in the prioritization of the Bible inspired ownership of the textual message as the premise of biblical authority, and it subsequently inspired the

---

4. Brian Stanley (ed.), *Christian Missions and the Enlightenment* (Grand Rapids: Eerdmans, 2001), 4; Cf. Hsien Wan, "Re-examining the Master's Tools," 222–3.

5. Michael Legaspi, *The Death of Scripture and the Rise of Biblical Studies* (New York: Oxford University Press, 2010), 9.

6. Hsien Wan, "Re-examining the Master's Tools," 221.

7. Sugirtharajah, *The Bible and the Third World*, 22.

8. Chidester, *Savage Systems*, xiii, 15.

9. McGrane, *Beyond Anthropology*, 52–3.

10. Galbraith, "The Perpetuation of Racial Assumptions in Biblical Studies," 116–34.

European Protestant missionary movement, which was driven as much by non-clergy missionaries as by clerical ones. These individuals, while supported by newly formed church mission organizations (e.g., CMS, LMS, Royal Danish College of Missions [under Dutch royal patronage], American Board of Commissioners for Foreign Missions, Netherlands Missionary Society, French Societas Missionum ad Afros [SMA], etc.), came to their missionary calling less from an ecclesial mandate than from a textual connection with the Bible. Among these organizations, the British and Foreign Bible Society (BFBS), established in 1804, stood out as it bucked the trend of its contemporary organizations that sent missionaries by prioritizing the free circulation of Bibles.[11]

The explosion of European exploration of previously unknown lands, between the fourteenth and nineteenth centuries, had opened previously unimagined opportunities to venture into the newly "discovered" worlds. Those who explored these lands armed themselves with the Bible, and they received financial support from private ventures that sought the economic potential in such worlds, such as the British American Tobacco company's financial support of David Livingstone's exploration of Africa and the East India Company's eventual support of missionary activity in India (1833 Charter).[12] Loyalty to these financial backers meant curtailing any criticism of their actions. So, while religious convictions and moral or ethical concerns, like the desire to see the abolition of slavery of Africans, may have motivated some missionaries, they often placed the blame for moral and ethical concerns not on their fellow European (or American) slave traders but on Africans themselves.[13] Even such abolitionists like Thomas F. Buxton still purported an explanation of African "greed," instead of western indulgences, and of a lack of moral intelligence as the culprits that necessitated that *"we raise the native mind."*[14]

Inevitably, as they carried the Bible along, these western missionaries indisputably also went forth as loyal citizens of Empire under the banner of their national flag, be it the Union Jack, the French *Tricolore*, or the Portuguese *Bandeira*, to claim souls and territories on behalf of their "Christian nations."[15]

11. Sugirtharajah, *The Bible and the Third World*, 54.

12. Stephen Neill, *The Story of the Indian Church in India and Pakistan, 1707–1858* (London: SPCK, 1970), 65–6.

13. Thomas F. Buxton, *The African Slave Trade and Its Remedy* (London: John Murray, 1840), 244. "The African will not have ceased to desire, and vehemently to crave, the spirits, ammunition and the articles of finery and commerce which Europe alone can supply: and these he can obtain by Slavery Trade and Slave Trade only, while he remains what he is. . . . But when the African nations shall emerge from their present state of darkness and debasement, they will require no arguments from us, to convince them of the monstrous impolicy of the Slave Trade."

14. Ibid. (emphasis original)

15. James Baldwin, "Letter from a Region in My Mind," *The New Yorker*, November 9, 1962, Available online: https://www.newyorker.com/magazine/1962/11/17/letter-from-a-region-in-my-mind

For, Christianity was also the *de facto* "official" religion of the major colonizing European empires like Great Britain, France, and the Netherlands. The head of the Church of England, for example, is the reigning King/Queen, who appointed (and still does) the Archbishop of Canterbury, the leader of the Anglican communion. In predominantly Catholic France, on the other hand, the Pope exercised indirect authority and influence over the political leadership.[16]

The pattern is evident in missionary examples, like the German Ludwig Krapf (1810–81) who explored in East Africa, leading to the German state's claims of the territory he traversed, or wherever the British/Scottish David Livingstone (1813–73) set his foot in Southern Africa, a claim being made for the British Empire. Some of the mission societies even modeled their organizational structures around the imperializing campaign of the colonial governments.[17] Political, economic, and religious pursuits were encapsulated in the missionary endeavor, as Pawliková-Vilhanová makes plain:

> The opening up of Africa to forces of change by the four Cs, namely by the introduction or the imposition of the so-called legitimate commerce and Christianity as a key to civilization and eventually colonization was seen by most abolitionists, humanitarians, philanthropists and missionaries as the only remedy.[18]

Furthermore, whether overtly or covertly, western missionaries exemplified the attitudes of the superiority of their European cultures.[19] The premise for such views was, of course, based on the assumption that European "Christianized" cultures were advanced civilizations and therefore superior to other cultures that did not measure up to their "God-given" power, knowledge, and privilege.

In this way, the Bible assumed its role as a tool for the defense of the colonial project. This attitude was congruous with the colonizing mission at the core of the colonial project's ideology and its religious justification of "conquest and subjugation."[20] As Cameroonian scholar F. Ebousi Boulaga puts it in his enigmatic

---

16. The *King James Bible* translation, dedicated to the translator's benefactor, King James VI (Scotland) and I (England), bears witness to this union.

17. Sugirtharajah, *The Bible and the Third World*, 60.

18. Viera Pawliková-Vilhanová, "Christian Missions in Africa and their Role in the Transformation of African Societies," *AAS* 16, no. 2 (2007): 249–60, 257.

19. Frantz Fanon, *The Wretched of the Earth*, trans. Richard Philcox (New York: Grove, 1963), 150. "And it is all too true the major responsibility for this racialization of thought, at least the way it is applied, lies with the Europeans who have never stopped placing *white* culture in opposition to the other *noncultures*." (Emphasis added)

20. Chidester, *Savage Systems*, xiv. "In southern Africa, for example, comparative religion was practiced, not by intellectuals aloof from the world, but by human beings engaged in religious conflicts on the ground. Principles of comparison were hammered out on frontier battlefields. Interpretive and explanatory strategies of comparative religion were inevitably entangled in the social, economic, and political conflicts of colonial situations."

but magisterial book *Christianisme sans Fetish* (trans. *Christianity without Fetishes*), "The pagan [African religious reality] has no value itself. The fullness of Christianity acknowledges its value by suppressing it."[21] Boulaga uses the colonialist derogatory language of "pagan" for African religious reality, not approvingly, but as a means of retaining the force of his critique. As he states further, for the western missionary, "It follows that paganism is not a neutral state, a lack to be made up. It is a state of guilt, of rebellion against God, and of fall beneath the threshold of humanity."[22]

The Bible then, not only became part of western literature which could distinguish between the enlightened Europeans and the unenlightened Other, but it also fit into an evolutionary structure that set the African in the furthest, most debased state, in the "dark continent." In such a setting, any native religious, social, and cultural practices encountered by missionaries would be classified as *un*-Christian, *un*civilized, and in need of conquest or eradication or transformation by impositions of a westernized Bible on the colonized. In such colonial thinking, it was more than just labeling, as it amounted to judgment and declaration of the African religious reality as wanting, and unredeemable. As the anti-colonial intellectual revolutionary, Frantz Fanon, puts it, "Colonialism is not content merely to impose its law upon the colonized country's present and future. . . . With some kind of perverted logic, it turns its attention to the past of the oppressed people, and distorts it, disfigures it, and destroys it."[23] Anything that did not conform to, or which could not be reconciled with, the western view of the Bible was to be excised, terminated.

Not surprisingly, language consistent with this mode of thinking became part of the missionary tool kit for fundraising as an expression of the dire need to bring the African communities from their "deep darkness" into the light. For example, in the *Proceedings of the Conference on Foreign Missions* held in Mildmay Park, London, October 5–7, 1886, in which Grattan Guinness in a section entitled "The Great Dark Continent" summarized religion in Africa thus: "As to religion they are mainly two—Mohammedanism and Heathenism."[24] And heathenism was most pervasive. In some instances, and reflecting the prolonged Reformation conflicts in Europe, Protestant missionaries equated African religions with the Catholic "paganism." As Chidester, focusing on the South African experience (but true also of the rest of the continent *mutatis mutandis*), reports, "In representing African superstition or religion, basic elements of a European Protestant polemic against Roman Catholics, which attacked pagano-papism as ignorance, fear, magic, the deification of objects, and the deification of the dead, were transposed onto indigenous people in Southern Africa. These forms defined the basic structure of

---

21. Boulaga, *Christianity without Fetishes*, 25.

22. Ibid., 21.

23. Fanon, *The Wretched of the Earth*, 149.

24. *Proceedings of the Conference on Foreign Missions* (London: Mildmay Park, October 5th to 7th, 1886).

African religions."[25] As an antidote, "The Bible was perceived as providing agency for purifying customs, habits, social institutions" of the receptor communities.[26]

On top of all that, the average competence of the missionary understanding and use of the Bible, in many cases, was suspect and the vast majority of missionaries sent (or who opted to go) to such places as Africa were also generally not of the highest academic pedigree.[27] Famous exceptions such as Dr. Albert Schweitzer, Dr. Ludwig Kraft, and Dr. David Livingstone, two of whom were trained physicians and accomplished academics, may skew views about the African missionary competency. However, these were the exception rather than the rule.[28] As a result, in contrast to what was happening in the "ivory tower" European academy with its Enlightenment foregrounding of the supremacy of European human reason, the missionaries sought to retain the precritical traditional authority of the Bible as Scripture, assuming the inability of the natives to comprehend complex discourses about the Bible.[29] Paradoxically, however, the same notions of the Enlightenment on rationality and skepticism shaped the missionary's negative presuppositions and evaluations of African sociocultural and religious realities.[30]

2.2 The Bible, God, and Colonialism in Africa

While Europe's global expansionism goes back at least to fourteenth-century Portuguese maritime exploits, the origins of Africa's colonial era are often traced back to the 1884/85 Berlin conference of European political leaders, organized by the incorrigible Belgian King Leopold IV (who deliberately did not attend) and hosted by Otto van Bismarck, where European countries are said to have met to stake their claims to different regions of Africa. This "Scramble for Africa" occasioned the dividing of the African continent like a pie/cake by the

---

25. Chidester, *Savage Systems*, 28.

26. Sugirtharajah, *The Bible and the Third World*, 148.

27. Albert Memmi, *The Colonizer and the Colonized* (Boston: Beacon, 1957), 48: "The constant removal of the best colonizers explains one of the most frequent characteristics of those who remain in the colony—their mediocrity."

28. John Mbiti, in *Christianity in Tropical Africa*, ed. C. C. Baëta (London: Oxford University Press, 1968), 329–43. See also Adam Hochschild, *King Leopold's Ghost* (New York: Houghton Mifflin Harcourt, 1998).

29. Philip Jenkins, *The New Faces of Christianity: Believing the Bible in the Global South* (Oxford: Oxford University Press, 2006), 17–21.

30. Stanley, *Christian Missions and the Enlightenment*, 3–4. Cf. Kidd, *The Forging of Races*, 120: "There is no single conclusion to be drawn from the study of racial ideas in the age of the Enlightenment. The Enlightenment did give birth to a de-Christianised form of scientific racism; but equally the moderate form of Enlightenment . . . was exported throughout the . . . [and] recycled as a sustaining ideology for Christian missions."

burgeoning European powers set to rule the world.[31] Yet, no African presence or representation was at the table in Berlin. With a giant map of the African continent before them, European leaders would proceed to stake claims on regions of the continent none of them had set foot on. While European missionaries and explorers had already been present in different parts of Africa starting in the fifteenth-century arrival of the Portuguese, the Berlin conference signaled the beginning of the political occupation that established the century-long colonial territorial occupation of the African continent by European powers.

Colonization, however, did not just involve the physical occupation of the African continent by Europe. As eminent DR Congolese philosopher V. Y. Mudimbe makes clear, Europe set out to "organize and transform non-European areas into fundamentally European constructs."[32] Colonizers enacted a systematic and gradual transformation not only of the colonized space itself but also of the meaning and explanation of that space to the detriment of the colonized's own perspective. The world would encounter Africa only through the eyes of the colonizer and not in its own right, its own voice, or its own construct.

And, inextricably bound to the colonizer was the missionary, who embodied the ideals of colonialism and couched them in biblical terminology. Commenting on the colonial English Christians, a pioneer of postcolonial biblical studies, R. S. Sugirtharajah, makes it clear that colonizers like England, "saw the circulation of the Bible as an important divine calling. This was supported by a belief that the secret of England's greatness was its reading of the Bible. They also believed that it was the reading of the Bible which preserved England from any political upheaval, and that the Bible could be a vehicle for training English values to the colonies."[33] Resultantly, European colonization of Africa ended up being described in biblical terms as the divine "mandate" of Europe to bring the light of the gospel to the "dark continent."[34]

This belief in a "God-given" directive became grounds to conquer lands and their peoples in the name of Christianity and occupy their territories under the pretext of Christianization and civilization. Without such biblical values, there would be no "moral" or "ethical" grounds on which the colonial project could stand. As the prolific New Testament scholar from Botswana, Musa W. Dube, puts it, "Unless the biblical values authorized coming into foreign lands and geographically dispossessing foreign people, such an expansionist program would

31. Hochschild, *King Leopold's Ghost*, 86: "Contrary to myth, the Berlin conference did not partition Africa; the spoils were too large, and it would take many more treaties to divide them all."

32. V. Y. Mudimbe, *The Idea of Africa* (Indianapolis: Indiana University Press, 1994), xiii.

33. Sugirtharajah, *The Bible and the Third World*, 53.

34. Memmi, *The Colonizer and the Colonized*. Cf. Henry W. Stanley, *Into the Dark Continent or The Sources of the Nile Around the Great Lakes of Equatorial Africa and Down the Livingstone River to the Atlantic Ocean*, Vols. 1 & 2 (New York: Harper & Brothers, 1878).

have been ethically inconsiderable for its Western readers."[35] So in this biblically sanctioned moral vision, the European missions became a new biblical "Israel" called to conquer "Canaan" (Africa). Further, missionaries marshaled the New Testament text of Mt. 28:19-20, and Christened the "Great Commission," to bolster the authority for political occupation in the name of religious proselytizing.[36] The ethical good of the Bible as a bringer of European values to the colonized, thus justified the invasion of foreign lands.[37]

And for this colonial construct to work, the African had to be the polar opposite of the Christianized European. The African had to become a godless idolatrous heathen, with no organized society, lacking in intellectual capacity, and essentially a blank slate on which Europe could imprint its own ideas of God, religion, the Bible, and Christianity.[38] The African was the quintessential anti-Christian, anti-civilization, and anti-progress that western Christianity had to reconstitute using the Bible. From such a point of view, there was no "noble savage." The Bible, as the religious talisman, contained the antidote to the poison of African heathenism. The true God was the God of the Bible, and the true religion was the religion of the Bible.

Such "heathenization" of the African starkly contrasts with the writings of an eighteenth-century former slave and renowned abolitionist Olaudah Equiano (a.k.a. Gustavus Vassa) whose report in his best-selling biography, first published in England in 1789 and then translated into Dutch, German, and Russian, presented an Africa with robust religious traditions and belief systems. Equiano saw evidence not only of this religious structure but also of its proximity to biblical religious practices so that he was able to opine, "We practiced circumcision like the Jews, and made offerings and feasts on that occasion in the same manner as they

---

35. M. W. Dube, *Postcolonial Feminist Interpretation of the Bible* (St. Louis: Chalice, 2000), 16.

36. Wolfgang Bruel, *Migration and Religion: Christian Transatlantic Missions, Islamic Migration To Germany* (Amsterdam and New York: Rodopi, 2012), 42, credits the first use of the term "Great Commission" to Justinian von Welz (1621–1668), who preached it at a missionary fundraiser for the Imperial Diet of Regensburg (*Corpus Evangelicorum*) in 1664. His argument was that it was not just Jesus's biblical disciples, but all Christians who received the mandate to preach the Gospel to other nations.

37. Greg Cuthbertson, "The English-Speaking Churches and Colonialism," in *Theology & Violence: The South African Debate*, ed. Charles Villa-Vicencio (Braamfontein, South Africa: Skotaville Publishers, 1987), 15–30, 16–17.

38. McGrane, *Beyond Anthropology*, 98, maintains that "the alien Other is not fundamentally pagan, savage, and demonic from a Christian frame of reference, nor fundamentally ignorant and superstitious from an Enlightenment frame of reference; rather the Other is more *fundamentally primitive* from a progress and evolution form of reference" (emphasis original). Without mentioning it in as many words, McGrane is pointing to the fact that this is a construct based on racist prejudice.

did. Like them, also our children were named for some event, some circumstance, or fancied foreboding at the time of their birth."[39] Further still, Equiano explained:

> As to religion, the [African] natives believe that there is one Creator of all things, and that he lives in the sun, and is girded round with a belt that he may never eat or drink; but, according to some, he smokes a pipe, which is our own favourite luxury. They believe he governs events, especially our deaths or captivity; but, as for the doctrine of eternity, I do not remember to have ever heard of it: some however believe in the transmigration of souls to a certain degree. Those spirits, which are not transmigrated, such as our dear friends or relations, they believe always attend them, and guard them from the bad spirits or their foes. For this reason, they always before eating, as I have observed, put some small portion of the meat, and pour some of their drink, on the ground for them; and they often make oblations of the blood of beasts or fowls at their graves.[40]

Not only were the African religious traditions that he wrote about clearly evident, but they also bore parallels to other religious traditions and could be well delineated and articulated. As such, even where Equiano noted differences, like the absence of ornate temples, he could still make the case that "though we had no places of public worship, we had priests and magicians, or wise men. I do not remember whether they had different offices, or whether they were united in the same persons, but they were held in great reverence by the people."[41] There was an organized religion that was recognized and practiced by the communities.

These observations by one who had been taken from his home in Benin at the young age of ten and who became a forceful abolitionist in England provide a very different picture from the one missionaries presented a century later. The colonial project needed to strip the African of these very elements that Equiano so clearly articulated and celebrated because it had to find a way of justifying its mission. To do so, it dehumanized and desacralized the African and the African religious reality, respectively. The African was declared godless, and so needed the European to introduce the "true religion and God." As Bernard McGrane put it, "They are only visible through Christianity as being the kind of beings that they are: a race of men bereft of God, hence extremely vulnerable to and also probably to a large extent ruled by Satanic forces."[42] In the colonial context, the African religious reality became the ideal anti-Christian conceptualization, and

---

39. Olaudah Equiano, *The Interesting Narrative of the Life of Olaudah Equiano, or Gustavus Vassa, The African* (London: Printed for and sold by the Author, No. 10, Union-Street, Middlesex Hospital, 1789), The Project Gutenberg E-Book, Ch. 1, 44.

40. Ibid.

41. Ibid.

42. McGrane, *Beyond Anthropology*, 53. The reference here is to Robinson Crusoe as emblematic of the colonial outlook.

the African god became the antithesis of the biblical god, with the latter having to vanquish the former.

However, the matter could not be that simple, as the missionary project again would produce unanticipated results. The attempt to erase the African religious reality or to depict it as incongruous with the Bible's message would prove difficult to enforce. First, the African converts noticed connections between their religious reality and some of the biblical elements as explained or translated to them by the missionaries. For example, the missionaries' apocalyptic eschatology envisioned mission as primarily converting the African so as to hasten the end of the days and bring back the venerated dead (1 Thess. 4:16), instead resonated with some of the African religious reality of a connection to the "living-dead." Second, the same apocalyptic outlook likely motivated many of the African converts who broke from the missionaries forming indigenous churches. As a result, many of the indigenous churches would end up having very strong foundational apocalyptic worldviews.

Chapter 3

(WESTERN) BIBLICAL STUDIES AND AFRICAN COLONIALISM

> Not coincidentally, the *great century* of Christian missionary expansion was in many ways also the *great century* of European colonialism.
>
> — Jaroslav Pelikan[1]

> Scholars of [western] Biblical Studies . . . have yet to address the relation between European expansionism and the rise of their own discipline.
>
> — R. S. Sugirtharajah[2]

3.1 Introduction

Having established the connection between the Bible, colonialism, and mission, I now turn to the emergence of Biblical Studies in Europe as a formal discipline in post-Enlightenment Europe of the nineteenth century. One may not see the connection initially, considering that the discipline of Biblical Studies emerged from academic institutions in Europe with no clear, direct connection either to missionary work or colonialism. This assumed disconnect may be the result of the failure, or unwillingness, by western biblical scholars to examine the role of the colonial enterprise in the discipline, as noted by R. S. Sugirtharajah in the epigraph. However, as I hope to show, Biblical Studies as a discipline was very much a supporter and beneficiary of the colonial project, making it complicit in the developments that related both to colonialism and European missions, as Pelikan earlier insinuates. In her analysis of the development of western disciplines of knowledge, such as Biblical Studies, Linda Tuhiwai Smith points out how such western disciplines are incontrovertibly related to the European colonial project

---

1. Jaroslav Pelikan, *Jesus Through the Centuries: His Place in the History of Culture* (New Haven: Yale University Press, 1985), 221. (emphasis added)

2. R. S. Sugirtharajah, *Postcolonial Criticism and Biblical Interpretation* (Oxford: Oxford University Press, 2002), 26.

because the discipline's content and methods were either derived from the colonized, or the ideas of the discipline were experimented upon the colonized.[3]

I have already mentioned that Sheehan, who views the Enlightenment as an ideological framing that encompassed a worldview, holds that the Bible became a cultural artifact in contrast to the "word of God" during the Enlightenment period.[4] This transformation allowed the Bible to become an object of study beyond its ecclesial settings, making its way into European universities. There, students studied the Bible as an ancient cultural text among other ancient texts, and professors who were not clergy, applied "scientific" approaches to its reading outside of ecclesial control.[5] In such a context, Biblical Studies appeared to offer itself as an alternative to the Enlightenment's eradication of religion, transforming and reconstructing it into an alternate vision of historical authority.[6]

Around this time also, growing expansionist interests in Europe were underway, and the colonial project was coalescing into a European vision of prosperity and power. Contributing ideologically and financially to these European expansionist efforts were the university scholars who were also involved in the formation of the discipline of Biblical Studies. This development of (western) Biblical Studies in the period of European colonial and imperial expansion coincided with the modern (re)introduction of the Bible in Africa through the European missionary enterprise, itself a beneficiary of the colonial enterprise. But the "ivory-tower" Biblical Studies contrasted itself with the missionary movement posing as a superior form of engagement with the Bible.

Not surprisingly then, central to the construction of Biblical Studies was the "exclusion, marginalization and denial" of indigenous ways of knowing as recounted by the European and missionary travelogues.[7] What's more, prevailing notions of race, gender, civilization, and religion greatly influenced the construction of Biblical Studies as an academic discipline.[8] Further still, connecting the discipline with the Enlightenment notion of "reason," a presumed preserve of an advanced western civilization, meant automatic elimination of non-western modes of knowledge that seemingly had not, or could not, attain to western Enlightenment reason.[9] In the words of Mudimbe, it is when, "Christian civilization discovers in its own

3. Linda Tuhiwai Smith, *Decolonizing Methodologies: Research and Indigenous People* (London and New York: Zed Books, 1999), 65.

4. Sheehan, *The Enlightenment Bible*.

5. W. Farmer, "State Interesse and Markan Primacy," in *Biblical Studies*, ed. Reventlow and Farmer, 15–49, 35. Writing on the development of the Markan Priority, Farmer notes that "it may be argued that no German scholar would have allowed himself to be influenced by non-scientific considerations."

6. Sheehan, *The Enlightenment Bible*, xi.

7. Smith, *Decolonizing Methodologies*, 68.

8. Ibid., 65.

9. Schweitzer, *Life*, 240: "Christianity cannot take the place of thinking, but it must be founded on it."

being and nature a form of conquest, . . . [that there is a] binding [of] reason to the ability to transform man through the diffusion of the Enlightenment."[10] It is not surprising then that (western) Biblical Studies as a discipline, from its inception to the present, has remained largely the domain of the western biblical scholars whose presuppositions, questions, concerns, methodologies, and theological interests continue to shape the discipline.

In Germany, in many ways, the birthplace of Biblical Studies, the connection between the church and the state, and therefore the colonial project, was incontrovertible. In a volume edited by H. G. Reventlow and W. Farmer, *Biblical Studies and the Shifting of Paradigms: 1850-1914*, which explores the emergence of Biblical Studies, several connections are laid bare about this relationship.

First, Reventlow and Farmer credit university scholars with the rise of academic biblical scholarship that at the time was at loggerheads with the church perspective. German scholars were essentially civil servants whom the government appointed and who worked at the behest of the government. According to Farmer, "Nineteenth-century Biblical criticism served German society well in enabling it to meet the pressing ideological needs. The state-supported universities facilitated the inevitable process of intellectual accommodation and/or assimilation."[11] The construction of ideologies (religious, political, ethical, etc.) that the government would subsequently diffuse among the people was done with the direct assistance of the universities. To ensure that the government was getting what it wanted from the universities, "all professors at German universities, Catholic and Protestant, were appointed by the state."[12]

Second, owing their careers to the state meant towing the government line if scholars wanted to keep their jobs. The government not only appointed the professors but also paid them.[13] Additionally, "the monarch regarded the university as his own institution, an attitude sometimes manifest in his desire to define the frame of reference of the university in terms of its loyalty and suitability to the court."[14] University professors, in particular, "played a decisive part . . . [as] leaders of political opinion outside the university as well."[15] So, when the German government sought to expand its Navy in 1897 (just three years after the Berlin conference of 1884/5) in preparation for the colonial project, it sought the support of university professors. According to Christian Simon, 270 professors wrote or spoke to support the effort, including "thirty-seven historians, twenty-nine theologians, twenty-three Protestant and six Catholic. . . . Their arguments were:

---

10. Mudimbe, *Tales of Faith*, 48.

11. Farmer, "State Interesse and Markan Primacy," 24.

12. Reventlow and Farmer, *Biblical Studies*, 34.

13. Christian Simon, "History of a Case-Study of the Relationship Between University Professors and the State in Germany," in *Biblical Studies*, ed. Reventlow and Farmer, 168–96, 170.

14. Ibid.

15. Ibid., 176.

'trade jealousy' of other nations, the necessity of a navy to *protect the colonies*, the external threat to Germany."[16] It was conscious support of the colonial project by the same scholars who would establish Biblical Studies.

Third, as a result of this link and their loyalty to the state, the professors classified themselves as the elite. These scholars despised other forms of academic education programs like technical schools. What is more, they perceived themselves as being in partnership with the state in governing society and therefore above the growing middle-class—the social category from which many missionaries would emerge.[17] They regarded their scholarship as an "autonomous moral and cultural force" that "social, economic, party-political or ecclesiastical" forces could not control, even as they remained ever loyal to the royal court.[18] Professors' loyalties were to God, king, and country, "which for them was above politics."[19]

Lastly, prejudice and anti-Semitism set on racist principles were prevalent in the universities. Scholars and students believed, for example, that Germans of Jewish descent could not comprehend "national patterns of thought" and that only Christians could understand German history, leading to the presence of a significant number of Jews in the intelligentsia to be investigated.[20] Sheehan points out that it was this perception of European heritage as "'an accumulated ineluctable racial memory' that undergirded the essential qualities of 'western civilization'" and provided the foundation for German and English universities' construction of the "cultural Bible."[21] It is out of this crucible of academic, social, political (colonial), and ecclesiastical admixture, laced with racist attitudes, that the discipline of Biblical Studies emerged. Legaspi, in his assessment of the transformation of European conceptualization of the Bible from the period of the Reformation to the emergence of modern Biblical Studies in the eighteenth century, states it this way:

> Scripture died a quiet death in Western Christendom sometime in the sixteenth century. The death of Scripture was attended by two ironies. First, those who brought the scriptural Bible to its death counted themselves among its defenders. Second, the power of revivifying a moribund scripture arose not from the churches but from the state. The first development was the Reformation, and the second was the rise, two hundred years later, of modern biblical scholarship.[22]

16. Ibid., 181–2. (emphasis added)
17. Ibid., 170.
18. Ibid., 175.
19. Ibid., 181.
20. Ibid., 190.
21. Sheehan, *The Enlightenment Bible*, 255. Reference to Franklin E. Court, *Institutionalizing English Literature: The Culture and Politics of Literary Study, 1750–1900* (Stanford: Stanford University Press, 1992), 78.
22. Legaspi, *The Death of Scripture and the Rise of Biblical Studies*, 3.

It was inevitable that the political, social, and economic realities of the colonial project would come to bear on the interpretation of the Bible as well. As R. S. Sugirtharajah explains:

> Without the support of the colonial apparatus, the Bible remained a minor text in the precolonial phase; it found its place among the religious texts of other traditions, one of the Books of the East, and it did so without threatening, surpassing or subsuming them.[23] . . . In [those] early days, the Church never subscribed to the belief that the only means of knowing God's word was through the written word. The Church had taught people to think about God, salvation, and grace in different ways, and inculcated the faith directly through non-textual means.[24]

European Christians saw the colonial project as a godsent opportunity for the Christianization of the "heathens" in the Global South.[25] Therefore, the earliest explorers from Europe were religious individuals (specifically Christian missionaries, the majority of whom were Protestants) who played multiple roles: explorers (government), missionaries (church), and agents of private prospectors (economic). Together, these three aspects would be defended as ultimately bringing the light of Christianity and western civilization to the "dark and primitive" world.[26]

Irrespective of any attempt to disconnect the religious from the economic and political, the interconnectedness of the three in the colonial project is undeniable, as I have illustrated in the example of Germany.[27] Indeed, in an effort to maximize their resources, missionary organizations even utilized business models *en vogue* within the colonial enterprise.[28] Just like the Apostle Paul was able to benefit from the roads and sea-faring developments that the Greco-Romans had established to preach the gospel, European Christians envisioned the colonial political project as opening opportunities of outreach for preaching the Bible to previously "unreached" parts of the world, which their political states were making accessible.[29]

23. Sugirtharajah, *The Bible and the Third World*, 5.

24. Ibid., 37.

25. Jürgen Osterhammel, *Colonialism: A Theoretical Overview*, trans. Shelly Frisch (Princeton: Marcus Weiner, 1997), 16.

26. *The Book of God's Kingdom: A Popular Illustrated Report of the British and Foreign Bible Society, 1901–2* (London: The Bible House, 1902), 7–11.

27. Cf. also Robert D. Woodberry, "The Missionary Roots of Liberal Democracy," *APSR* 106, no. 2 (May 2012): 244–74.

28. Sugirtharajah, *The Bible and the Third World*, 170. "The [Bible] Society was in essence a thoroughly Victorian colonial undertaking, successfully combining moral conviction and mercantile methods."

29. *Book of God's Kingdom*, 8–9.

What Legaspi does not explicitly point out, however, even as he recognizes the role of the European state, is the fact that the period of the rise of modern biblical scholarship coincides directly with the emergence of the colonial project in Europe with its concomitant violence.[30] While one must be careful not to demonize the entire European missionary enterprise (cf. Lamin Sanneh, Kwame Bediako, Joraslov Pelikan), there is no denying that it was heavily aided by the largesse and the army of the colonizing states. Mutual dependence between the interests of the European Church and those of the European State made the missionary enterprise in Africa possible and sustainable.

Jaroslav Pelikan, the famed Yale historian of Christianity, acknowledges as much noting that "although Jesus himself had lived in the Middle East, it was as a religion of Europe that his message came to the nations of the world . . . a religion of Europe both in the sense of a religion *from* Europe, and, often, a religion *about* Europe as well."[31] Pelikan then proceeds to give an *apologia* for the European mission, with its imperfections, as part of the successful spread of Christianity: "Although it has become part of the conventional wisdom in much of contemporary anti-colonialist literature, both Eastern and Western, it is an oversimplification to dismiss missions as nothing more than a cloak of imperialism."[32] A tacit acknowledgment of the missionary's collaborative role in imperialism, this statement still refuses to indict the missionary of any wrongdoing.

The epigraph from Pelikan at the beginning of this chapter characterizes the European mission and European colonialism as "great!" But great for whom? For the colonized or the colonizer? For the mission or the receptor community? Pelikan can only say this as a beneficiary of the colonial project and not as its victim. One can only posit greatness from the vantage point of the victor, not the victim—the colonizer, not the colonized! Putting things in a larger perspective, Pelikan, while acknowledging some atrocities of colonialism, seems too willing to excuse the dreadful impact of colonialization upon the colonized, simply because it also brought Christianity to these regions; a common *apologia* among colonizers and former colonizers. As James Stewart postulated while still exemplifying doubt in the Duff Missionary Lectures in New York in 1902, "The hot haste among nearly all the great European Powers to obtain the largest area of that hitherto neglected land [Africa], means belief in the Future of the African Continent, even though it is also true that they will not reap such immediate benefits as they probably expect."[33]

Defenders of the "positive" impact of the colonial project sought to uphold it by claiming that comprehending its negatives and positives required placing it in the larger scope of God's purpose in history. In such an argument, the "African

---

30. Mudimbe, *Tales of Faith*, 61.

31. Pelikan, *Jesus through the Centuries*, 222. (emphasis original)

32. Ibid., 222–4. 222.

33. James Stewart, *Dawn in the Dark Continent: Africa and Its Missions* (The Duff Missionary Lecture for 1902; New York: Young People's Missionary Movement, 1902), 357.

culture with its practice of witchcraft, ritual murder, and tribal warfare would not have prepared Africans to face the modern world."[34] Colonialism, in this mode of thinking, did Africa a great favor by dragging it into the modern world. Christianity was beneficial to the colonized, despite its cost. Similar complacency is evident in western biblical scholarship which refuses to acknowledge the historical negative impact of colonialism and racism, and the cultural and religious genocides that colonization wrought in its wake.

The impact of colonialism persists today in the postcolonial period and in the postcolonial space. The colonial encounter looms large, as the overarching background within which African Biblical Studies operates and the lens through which it interacts with the Bible, much in same the way that the Enlightenment loomed large in shaping western Biblical Studies.

3.2 Albert Schweitzer: Biblical Scholar, Missionary, Colonialist

As virtually every PhD student of Biblical Studies in western academic institutions discovers, the German language is the primary modern language requirement in the program. I had always wondered why degrees in Biblical Studies, Hebrew Bible/Old Testament, and the New Testament required this language. Why German? A quick glance at the history of western Biblical Studies makes clear the overwhelming influence German biblical scholars have had in creating and shaping the discipline. Associated with the emergence of the discipline are Julius Wellhausen, F. C. Baur, D. F. Strauss, and William Wrede in the nineteenth century and Rudolph Bultmann and Karl Barth in the twentieth century. These German scholars have had a supersized influence on the nature and form of Biblical and Theological Studies.

Among these names is that of Albert Schweitzer, whose works on Jesus and Paul completely transformed the discipline of Biblical Studies at the turn of the twentieth century.[35] I cannot imagine a more apt representation, who so thoroughly embodied the trifocal dimensions of a biblical scholar, a colonizer, and a missionary. As I will seek to demonstrate, the racial aspects and attitudes of Schweitzer's life did have significant bearings on his biblical scholarship, and its subsequent impact on the discipline.

Analyzing the three aspects of Schweitzer's life will allow us to see the interconnectedness and interdependence of Biblical Studies, missions, and

---

34. Sugirtharajah, *Postcolonial Criticism and Biblical Interpretation*, 27. Cf. also M. A. C. Warren, *Caesar the Beloved Enemy: Three Studies in the Relation of Church and State* (London: SCM Press/Chicago: Alec R. Allenson, 1955), 24–8.

35. *The Quest* (1906) and *The Mysticism of Paul the Apostle* (London: A. & C. Black, 1930). Cf. Andrew Pitt, "Albert Schweitzer: A Jewish-Apocalyptic Approach to Christian Origins," in *Pillars of Biblical Interpretation*, ed. Stanley E. Porter and Sean A. Adams, Vol. 1: Biblical Criticism Before 1980 (Eugene: Wipf and Stock, 2016), 211–38.

the colonial project. He becomes the classic embodiment of this multipronged approach as a biblical scholar, a medical missionary to Africa, and a Nobel Peace laureate (1952) who greatly affected western Christianity generally, and Biblical Studies, in particular.[36] Doubtless, Schweitzer, along with other European (and American) biblical scholars, bears responsibility for certain persistent problematic racial, academic, theological, and methodological idiosyncrasies in the discipline of Biblical Studies as evident in the western academe, as we will see below.

Schweitzer's racist and colonialist views were not unique, and even preceded him by as much as a century among Biblical Studies scholars.[37] Wei Hsien Wan has recently made a case for the continuing impact of the racist past on Biblical Studies.[38] He provided the example of the renowned German Hebrew Bible scholar Jonathan D. Michaelis (1717–91), who, a century before Schweitzer, rejected contemporary European Jewish scholarship as unreliable preferring, instead, contemporary Arabic-speaking communities, arguing on racial grounds of their "unpolluted evolutionary progress."[39] Michaelis would then go on to construct the "cultural Bible," where western civilization was the ultimate culture to which the Bible rightly belonged.[40] His contemporary French biblical scholar, Ernest Renan (1823–92) also denigrated Jews as a "Semitic race that "has neither mythology, nor epic, nor science nor philosophy, nor fiction, nor plastic arts, nor civil life."[41] No surprisingly, Renan was also a staunch supporter of African colonialism based on the right of the white race as "protectors of civilization" to dominate the inferior races.[42]

Michaelis's notion of a "foreign culture stuck in time" would become the stock colonial reasoning was proffered for justifying colonization of the "Other" in the framing of European mission to civilize the colonized.[43] Similar language was also evident in Schweitzer's paternalistic colonial and racist convictions. However, western biblical scholars have paid little attention to the impact of his racism

---

36. See M. W. Dube, "Reading for Decolonization: John 4:1-42," *Semeia* 75 (1996): 37–59.

37. Two other influential scholars, Jonathan Michaelis and Ernst Renan are discussed later. Cf. J. Cameron Carter, *Race: A Theological Account* (Oxford: Oxford University Press, 2008), esp. 40–81, who makes the case that the modern construction of race is essentially a theological one with Kantian roots that, in turn, get embedded into the colonial project. Cf. also, David G. Horrell, *Ethnicity and Inclusion: Religion, Race, Whiteness in the Constructions of Jewish and Christian Identities* (Grand Rapids: Eerdmans, 2020), 1–18, 299–345.

38. Hsien Wan, "Re-examining the Master's Tools," 217–29.

39. Ibid., 223.

40. Sheehan, *The Enlightenment Bible*, 255.

41. Quoted in Shawn Kelley, *Racializing Jesus: Race, Ideology and the Formation of Modern Biblical Scholarship* (London and New York: Routledge, 2002), 1.

42. Ernst Renan, *The Future of Science* (London: Chapman & Hall, 1891).

43. McGrane, *Beyond Anthropology*, 77, "In the nineteenth century, finally, it was *time*, geological time, evolutionary time, that came between the European and the non-European Other." (emphasis original)

and paternalism on his biblical hermeneutic.[44] A recent Schweitzer biographer Nils Ole Oermann, for example, understands Schweitzer as having been heavily entrenched in Enlightenment thinking in his approach to mission work in Africa and as taking great pride in his "occidental heritage" and its capacity to transform other cultures, but Oermann makes no attempt to relate the impact of such racist views to Schweitzer's academic writing.[45]

Like many European missionaries to Africa, Schweitzer exemplified inconsistent and conflicting attitudes toward Africans. On the one hand, he viewed the African as a potential recipient of the Bible capable of salvation while, on the other hand, he caricatured the African in crude racist terms as lower than white Europeans and even as less than human, exemplifying animal-like traits.[46] Chidester in his analysis of the origins of the study of religion in nineteenth-century Europe arrived at the following conclusion:

> By the nineteenth century, as the European colonization of Africa was underway, the denial of religion assumed another layer of significance by representing Africa paradoxically as both, empty space and also an obstacle to conquest, colonization, and conversion. Drawing upon earlier representations of indigenous people as animals with no rights to life or land, or as children out of touch with the real world because they could not evaluate objects, European comparativists added a third implication to the denial of religion by asserting that people who had no religion lacked industry.[47]

Africans were "humans" only in as far as the need to be evangelized, but less than humans when it came to intellectual capacity, religious practice, economic and political independence, and matters of property ownership.

There is no doubt that such attitudes filtered into biblical scholarly writing just like Michaelis's example given previously, but no serious effort has been made to critically examine Schweitzer's biblical works for this purpose, until now. As Musa Dube laments, "figures such as Albert Schweitzer, who acted as colony envoy and

---

44. Izak Spangenberg and Christina Landman (eds.), *The Legacies of Albert Schweitzer Reconsidered* (SHEB Series, 1; Cape Town: AOSIS, 2016). While reevaluating Schweitzer's contribution to Africa, this volume does very little with his racism. Even the section on the New Testament, when addressing Schweitzer's ethics, does not reflect on its connection to his worrisome racist perspectives about Africans, with the exception of the chapter by Menard Musendekwa ("Colonialism as an Obstacle to Civilization: A Critical Evaluation of Albert Schweitzer's Experiences and Observations," 81–107).

45. Nils Ole Oermann, *Albert Schweitzer, 1875–1965: Eine Biographie* (Munich: C. H. Beck, 2009). See review by James C. Paget, "Theologians Revisited: Albert Schweitzer," *Journal of Ecclesiastical History* 62, no. 1 (2011): 113–20.

46. Buxton, *The African Slave Trade and Its Remedy*, 244. See Sugirtharajah, *The Bible and the Third World*, 167.

47. Chidester, *Savage Systems*, 15.

influenced academic Biblical Studies in a big way, hardly exempt academic Biblical Studies, scholars, their interpretations, or, indeed, the texts themselves from the violence of imperialism."[48]

Schweitzer: A Brief Overview

After his publications on the eschatology of Jesus and Paul, Schweitzer completely abandoned the discipline and spent almost a decade training to get a medical degree that prepared him to spend the rest of his life as a medical missionary in Lambaréné (formerly in French Equatorial Africa, and modern-day Gabon), Africa. But not before these "earth-shattering" works convulsed the world of Biblical Studies, forcing a complete reevaluation of the discipline. His other writings, however, conjure very paternalistic and overtly racist attitudes toward the Africans whom he served as a physician for over fifty years. So loath was he of the African peoples and their cultures that, unlike other European missionaries of his time, he never learned a single African language.[49]

It is no surprise that Albert Schweitzer remains a controversial and enigmatic historical figure in the twentieth century. He is either lionized for his medical and humanitarian work or vilified as a paternalistic self-absorbed colonialist.[50] When, as a PhD candidate, I was required to read Schweitzer's *The Quest for the Historical Jesus* and *The Mysticism of Paul the Apostle* as part of my Biblical Studies exams, there was never a mention, in my predominantly white institution, of any controversial history of racism and bigotry concerning Schweitzer. No moral or ethical questioning. Nobody thought it unusual that, as an African, I should read this person's work approvingly, completely unaware that he would not have thought me capable of intellectual competence to comprehend his scholarship owing to my race. I was left to shockingly discover that for myself while researching Schweitzer's life for a different project.

A similar blind spot is evident in biblical scholarship, for example, in the article on Schweitzer and the New Testament by David Hawkin. While examining Schweitzer's influence on Biblical Studies, Hawkin is conscientious enough to include African Christianity in his discussion of methodologies that have addressed some of the implications of Schweitzer's work on Biblical Studies. However, at no point in his discussion does he broach the subject of Schweitzer's overt racism as to how that might play out for African scholars who encounter Schweitzer's works. In many respects, Hawkin's approach is representative of how the whole discipline of Biblical Studies in the West has chosen to turn a blind eye to Schweitzer's atrocious and overt racism and its concomitant implications, while choosing instead to celebrate his intellect, altruism, and humanitarian accomplishments.

---

48. Dube, "Reading for Decolonization: John 4:1-42," 303.

49. Ruth Harris, "Schweitzer and Africa," *THJ* 59, no. 4 (2016): 1107–32.

50. Cf. Nina Berman, *Impossible Missions? German Economic, Military, and Humanitarian Efforts in Africa* (Lincoln: University of Nebraska Press, 2004).

While Schweitzer's humanistic accomplishments reflected an unquestioned commitment to missionary work, his racist attitudes toward the same Africans whom he served (describing them in evolutionary terms as "my brother, but my brother by several centuries") represent the questionable nature of his commitment to Christian evangelism and "love for humanity." That attitude seems to have little bearing on his Christian morals or ethics, *vis-à-vis* the African.[51] His racist attitude, moreover, never seems to have significantly undermined his image in the eye of the western world, as he has been described as "one of the *foremost spiritual and ethical figures* of our time."[52]

I would, therefore, like to examine Schweitzer's writings more closely as a way of investigating the complex interconnectedness that he embodied, and explore \ how aspects of his colonialist and racist outlook, more likely than not, influenced his Biblical Studies works and by extension western Biblical Studies.[53] This would stand in contrast to the coy attitude typified by western scholars, for example, C. K. Barrett, who in his lecture celebrating Schweitzer's centenary in 1975 urged the need to "forget Lambarene and Goethe and the music" for a moment when dealing with Schweitzer's Biblical Studies. Why do they need to be sequestered?[54] Why would one do so, given that as readers we bring our whole being to bear upon the process of interpretation as interpreters of the Bible?[55] If nothing else, such a move only raises suspicion as to why Lambaréné and Goethe need to be temporarily sidelined. And as we will see, it obfuscates the otherwise damning racial verbiage and vitriol that undergirds a colonialist paternalism and racism that masks Schweitzer's unstated "love" for the African. By juxtaposing his overt racism in his other writings with Biblical Studies writings, we hope to tease out racialized readings in the latter.

a. Schweitzer's Impact on Biblical Studies So influential was Schweitzer's biblical scholarship that it continues to shape Biblical Studies, over a century since the publication of his major works.[56] While he published several works in Biblical Studies, it was perhaps Schweitzer's first book, *Von Reimarus zu Wrede: Geschichte der Leben-Jesu-Forschung*, published in 1906 (translated as *The Quest for the*

---

51. Albert Schweitzer, *On the Edge of the Primeval Forest: Experiences and Observations of a Doctor in Equatorial Africa* (London: A & C Black, 1924), 130–1.

52. Charles R. Joy, *The Spiritual Life: Selected Writings of Albert Schweitzer* (Boston: Beacon, 1947), xvii. (emphasis added)

53. Erich Grässer's *Albert Schweitzer als Theologe* (BZHT: Tübingen: Mohr Siebeck, 1979).

54. C. K. Barrett, "Albert Schweitzer and the New Testament: A Lecture Given in Atlanta on 10th April 1975 as Part of the Albert Schweitzer Centenary Celebration," *ET* (1975): 4–10.

55. Hans-Georg Gadamer, *Truth and Method* (London: Sheed and Ward, 1975).

56. Cf. Stephen Neill and Tom Wright (eds), *The Interpretation of the New Testament, 1861–1986*, 2nd ed. (Oxford: Oxford University Press, 1988).

Historical Jesus [1910]), that landed like dynamite in the field of Biblical Studies.[57] While some would argue that his *The Mysticism of Paul the Apostle* is the most profound of his Biblical Studies' writings,[58] I choose to highlight the tsunamic impact of *The Quest*, for now. Until the publication of *The Quest*, western Biblical Studies had essentially evolved into what was known as "liberal theology" whose emphasis was on human freedom, divinely ordained, and for service of humanity through love, resulting in the establishment of the Kingdom of God.[59] The recovery of "the historical Jesus" as the premise of this liberal theology was foundational.

First, Schweitzer argued that Jesus's commissioning of the twelve disciples in Matthew 10-11 did not produce the expected results—the disciples were not persecuted, the Son of Man did not return, and Jesus did not reveal the Kingdom as promised—and was dissatisfied with the silence in the rest of Matthew's Gospel about this failure. To Schweitzer, Jesus's failed prophecy did not stop Jesus from trying to bring about the Kingdom of God again by embarking on a journey to Jerusalem to die. In his words, Jesus

> in the knowledge that He is the coming Son of Man lays hold of the wheel of the world to set it moving on that last revolution which is to bring all ordinary history to a close. It refuses to turn, and he throws himself on it. Then it does turn; and crushes him . . . . The wheel rolls onward, and the mangled body of the one immeasurably great Man, who was strong enough to think of Himself as the spiritual ruler of mankind and to bend history to His purpose, is hanging upon it still. That is His victory and His reign.[60]

This was a distinctly different Jesus than his contemporary liberal theologians had constructed. It was a Jesus who could not be so easily transported into the modern world. Schweitzer's Jesus was so comprehensively a man of his first-century world as indicated by his apocalyptic convictions (believing the world was coming to an end in his lifetime) that led him to be a "world-denier," "a stranger[,] and an enigma" to the modern society.[61] Between Jesus and the modern person is such a huge chasm—a "hermeneutical gap"—that bridging it is simply not possible. Are Michaelis and Renan's anti-Semitic attitudes in the background here? As a result, Schweitzer's work effectively ended the study of historical Jesus in Biblical Studies for several decades.

---

57. Cf., among others, A. Schweitzer, *The Mystery of the Kingdom of God* (New York: Dodd, Mead & Co., 1914); idem, *The Mysticism of Paul the Apostle*, trans. W. Montgomery (New York: Macmillan, 1931); idem, *Christianity and Religions of the World* (New York: Henry Holt, 1939).

58. James C. Paget, "Schweitzer and Paul," *JNTS* 33, no. 3 (2011): 223–56.

59. Hawkin, "Albert Schweitzer," 297–314.

60. A. Schweitzer, *The Quest of the Historical Jesus: A Critical Study of its Progress from Reimarus to Wrede*, trans. W. Montgomery (London: Unwin Brothers, 1910), 370–1.

61. Ibid., 399; Hawkin, "Albert Schweitzer," 300.

Secondly, Schweitzer argued that Jesus had miscalculated the eschatological end of time which he assumed would accompany his own death, meaning Jesus's death had actually failed to accomplish the desired apocalyptic end. For Schweitzer's "thoroughgoing skepticism," the historical Jesus was a failure at his mission and died in a desperate suicide trying to transform the world. Did this contribute to Schweitzer finding greater purpose as a medical missionary other than the typical missionary preacher or teacher? The most then that modern Jesus followers could do is emulate Jesus's spirit and love of God and humanity, "not Jesus as historically known, but Jesus, as spiritually arisen within men, who is significant for our time and can help it. Not the historical Jesus, but the spirit which goes forth from him and in the spirits of men strives for new influence and rule . . . which overcomes the world."[62]

Thirdly, in contrast to the prevailing liberal theology's understanding of the Kingdom of God as something attainable on earth in the course of human history, Schweitzer's Kingdom of God was an eschatological future Kingdom. Only God could bring out this divine Kingdom, even though acts of love for humanity and God allowed its impact to be felt in the present. Because believers can orient themselves to this future Kingdom of God, it can transform their present actions. It is this "thoroughgoing eschatology" that allows followers to "experience" the spiritual Jesus in the present. And is this what motivates his idea of mission as simply "love of humanity"?

Fourthly, Biblical Studies after Schweitzer's work became preoccupied with the question that has dominated the discipline to the present—how to reconcile the "Jesus of history" with the "Christ of faith." According to David Hawkin,

> after Schweitzer's exegesis, the drawing out of the meaning of Biblical texts, is seen more clearly as a branch of the history of ideas. *Exegesis itself cannot adequately bridge the gap between then and now*. It *can* contextualize the message of Jesus and thus we can recapture what it meant for the people of the time. But to bring that meaning into the present requires more than exegesis. It requires hermeneutical creativity. . . . Before Schweitzer, it was assumed that exegesis *was* hermeneutics.[63]

He may not have introduced the dichotomy, but Schweitzer's work cemented the significance of the distinction between critical biblical analysis' "exegesis" (what the Bible meant in its context) and "hermeneutics" (application to the present reality), and the role that eschatological apocalypticism plays in shaping the understanding of the first-century Judeo-Christianity.[64] In essence, Scheistzer's arguments drew a line between what would become intellectual Christianity,

---

62. Schweitzer, *The Quest of the Historical Jesus*, 401.
63. Hawkin, "Albert Schweitzer," 301.
64. Ibid., 302.

exemplified by Schweitzer's own work, and the church praxis of faith, finding no compatibility between the two.[65]

So how did Schweitzer define Christianity? He described it this way: "The essential element in Christianity as it was preached by Jesus and comprehended in thought, is this, that it is only through *love* that we can attain communion with God."[66] Schweitzerian scholars have described him as either an agnostic or a devout Christian.[67] For Schweitzer, knowledge of the historical Jesus was virtually impossible due to insufficient evidence. In the Bible are mostly theological constructions of him and his teachings; but those are still vital in helping followers connect to this "spiritualized" Jesus.[68] Influenced by Kantian philosophy, Schweitzer understood Christianity primarily in terms of "ethics and free will" where love expressed in a hostile world was the paramount ethic. And what greater way to show love than through compassion for those suffering?—the "reverence for life" ethic! That is what physicians do. So why not become one?[69]

If the epitome of Christianity for Schweitzer was the *love* of God and humanity, then, by his own standard, he did not fare well in his long sojourn with Africans. He seemed only to tolerate them and often denigrated them, making it difficult to see how love applied with such an attitude. That he truly loved the African was not ever stated in *any* of his writings. So *apologias* for Schweitzer's racist attitudes toward Africans by western writers, like the one offered by Nils Oermann, which attempt to ameliorate Schweitzer's foibles only, end up sounding like cover-ups and become indictments of the apologists own tolerance for his colonialist and racist positions.[70] That Schweitzer had a close working relationship with his Gabonese workers does make him any less racist, much in the say way that benevolent slave owners in the American south could still be nice to their slaves. but were nevertheless still slave owners.

What of his medical and humanitarian work? Was this driven by a love of the African or his own selfish and stubborn convictions of what a heroic life, like that of Jesus, entailed? Schweitzer remained completely askance, and dismissive of

---

65. Schweitzer, *Life*, 192.

66. A. Schweitzer, *Out of My Life and Thought* (New York: Henry Holt & Co., 1948), 277. (emphasis added)

67. Ruth Harris, "The Allure of Albert Schweitzer," *HEI* 40 (2014): 804–25; Hawkin, "Albert Schweitzer," 301.

68. Schweitzer, *Life*, 90.

69. Ibid., 94: "I wanted to be a doctor that . . . this new form of activity I could not represent to myself as talking about the religion of love, but only as an actual putting it into practice."

70. Paget, "Theologians Revisited," 116. Oermann says of Schweitzer, "Many people, perhaps the majority, attribute to their own life the highest value without arriving at the conclusion that other lives must be of the highest worth" (107). I see this as representative of western attempts at excusing Schweitzer's inexcusable racism.

anything African cultures and religions could offer western Christian civilization.[71] While living in Africa, he instead opted to study Indian cultures and languages, and eventually premised his "reverence for life" theology on Jainism, Hinduism, and Chinese Confucianism.[72] To Schweitzer, the advanced western Christian civilization (at least his version of it) was what needed to be imposed upon Africa as the only hope for rescuing her from the deplorable primitive state and ushering her into "modern civilization".

Before exonerating Schweitzer as "a man his it is times" as some have done, it may be worth putting him side by side with a contemporaneous scholar-missionary in Africa. John W. Colenso, a British mathematician at Cambridge University turned priest, was appointed the first Anglican bishop of Natal province in South Africa (about fifty years before Schweitzer's sojourn in Africa). Within three months of his arrival in Natal in 1855, he had "produced a massive Zulu dictionary, a Zulu grammar, and a revised Zulu version of the Gospel of St. Matthew."[73] Working with African colleagues as equals, so productive was Colenso that he produced numerous Christian translations into *isi*Zulu (Zulu language) and produced writings on Zulu culture, language, astronomy, and history.[74] Besides that, he had so thoroughly familiarized himself with German biblical scholarship in a very short time, that he had aligned himself with moderate German biblical scholarship.[75]

However, it was in embracing the African and African reality fully that convinced Colenso in his commentary on the Pentateuch[76] (though hinted at in

---

71. Harris, "Schweitzer and Africa," 1108.

72. Ruth Harris, "Book Review: Albert Schweitzer in Thought and Action: A Life in Parts," *JEH* 69, no. 1 (2018): 215–17; idem, "Allure," 808. I honestly find the excuse given by James C. Paget and Michael J. Thate (*Albert Schweitzer in Thought and Action: A Life in Parts* [New York: Syracuse University Press, 2016], 14–16), that the Lambarene region had too many African languages to learn (the point is that he never bothered to learn even one!) and that "languages were never [Schweitzer's] strength—he never, for instance, learned English," to be rather insulting and consistent with the continued Western defense of Schweitzer's racist and colonialist attitudes. If he had worked in England, he most likely would have learned English. I agree with Harris's evaluation of this section of Paget and Thate's volume: "Schweitzer's judgements were haphazard, often ill-informed, and keen to reiterate the superiority of ethical monotheism as part of the developmental progression of Western civilization. Perhaps the chapters dealing with these subjects do not sufficiently deal with Schweitzer's blinkered evaluations."

73. Cf. Willie Jennings, *The Christian Imagination: Theology and the Origins of Race* (New Haven: Yale University Press, 2010), 132–3.

74. Ibid., 133.

75. Peter Hinchliff, "Ethics, Evolution and Biblical Criticism in the Thought of Benjamin Jowett and John William Colenso," *JEH* 37, no. 1 (1986): 91–110, 103.

76. J. W. Colenso, *The Pentateuch and Book of Joshua Critically Examined* (London: Longman, Green, Longman, Roberts & Green, 1862–79).

his earlier commentary on Paul's letter to the Romans)[77] of the divine presence within Zulu culture derived from its linguistic analysis. In Chidester's words, "If textual criticism of the Bible informed Colenso's construction of the Zulu religions, the reverse was also the case, as his reading of the Bible was apparently affected by his attempt to translate the Zulu idiom."[78] This affirmation of African religions and culture would prove to be the very grounds on which accusations of "heresy" would be levied against Bishop Colenso, eventually leading to his being deposed from church leadership.[79] While Schweitzer's racism was tolerated by his European supporters, Colenso's embrace of the African (though he still exhibited paternalistic tendencies) would be his own ministry's demise. For his convivial *bonhomie* with the African, Colenso had paid the ultimate ecclesial price: ostracism. In contrast, Schweitzer would continue to enjoy western church support for more than half a century. It is no coincidence then that Colenso's writings have remained essentially unknown and ignored in western Biblical Studies, a world in which Schweitzer remains a giant. Biblical Studies has been way more comfortable with Schweitzer's racist and paternalistic colonialist attitudes than it would ever be with Colenso's comparativist, culturally sensitive hermeneutics.[80]

b. Schweitzer on African Colonialism Schweitzer made his support of African colonization very clear. He declared, in his writing on race relations between whites and Blacks, and as a colonial agent, "We have, I hold, *the right to colonize* if we have the moral authority to exercise this influence."[81] Such a claim to a "right" is based on a racist and evolutionary construct that puts the white race at the apex of human progress, thus granting it the moral grounding to civilize non-European Others.[82] This is a relationship of domination that placed Schweitzer in the seat of power to diagnose the problem, prescribe a cure, and retain the authority to administer it. In medical terms, Africans could only be described as Schweitzer's subjects or "guinea pigs." He argued for a "civilized colonization" or "Christian civilization" that had the moral capacity to save the African from exploitation by others, both Europeans and Africans. How is this benevolence? How is this love?

---

77. J. W. Colenso, *St. Paul's Epistle to the Romans: Newly Translated, and Explained from a Missionary Point of View* (Bishopstowe: Natal, 1861).

78. Chidester, *Savage Systems*, 135. Chidester's focus is on Colenso's use of the comparativist method in the study of religion which would eventually prove influential in placing African religions on the same plane as Christianity.

79. Jennings, *The Christian Imagination*, 132.

80. Sugirtharajah, *The Bible and the Third World*, 126: "In his exegetical practice we see an early attempt at what has now come to be known as cultural exegesis."

81. A. Schweitzer, "The Relations of the White and Colored Races," *CR* CXXXIII, no. 745 (1928): 65–70.

82. McGrane, *Beyond Anthropology*, 85: In Darwinian terms, "The Others . . . are not so much different from as they are similar to Europeans in that they re-present stages that the Europeans have long since progressed beyond in the ever expanding space of 'history.'"

Indeed, he maintained that it was not only necessary to the spread of the godly western civilization, colonization was the only way to bring about the social and economic transformation of Africans.[83] For Schweitzer, such a process would take a specific form of "moral paternalism" that would have to last several generations.[84] In the words of Boulaga, "The proper pedagogy for the African, then, [would] be one of 'firmness.' It [would] inculcate obedience and gratitude. Firmness is necessary for taming the animal in the African. The Africans' obedience cannot be one that issues from the human 'rational will.'"[85] Boulaga's sarcastic comments inveigh against this dumbfounding rationality of "moral paternalism."

For Schweitzer, this "Christian" conviction to remake the African into a human in the image of the white European person, justified colonization.[86] Schweitzer's overall attitude toward the possibility of African "progress" involved the imposition of western civilization (the most advanced civilization), the imposition of an "ethical" western commerce, and a gradual "educational process" that would begin with rudimentary agriculture and labor-oriented instruction and gradually (though never stated how gradual) get to reading and writing, before culminating in intellectual and sophisticated subject matters. "Civilization," as Schweitzer understood it, was not simply a western invention, but, like western Christianity, was universal and universally transferable. It was the epitome of human ingenuity and development, and any rational person should desire it. That was never in doubt!

Appended to Schweitzer's conception of western civilization as superior to the African "primitive" culture that justified colonization, was the belief that the subjugation of Africa was necessary and "for her own good!" Simply put, the political colonization of Africa was necessary as a "corrective" of what Schweitzer saw as exploitative global commercial practices that started with slavery and continued to take place in Africa even after the end of slavery.[87]

So solve slavery with colonization? How is that a solution?

A person of no less stature than the African American Civil Rights stalwart, W. E. B. Du Bois, in a startlingly positive appraisal of Schweitzer's accomplishments, sought to excuse Schweitzer's view of the benefits of colonization due to his naïveté born of ignorance about the ills of colonialism elsewhere in the continent.[88] Yet,

83. Schweitzer, "The Relations of the White and Colored Races," 65.

84. Manuel M. Davenport, "The Moral Paternalism of Albert Schweitzer," *Ethics* 84, no. 2 (1974): 116–27.

85. Boulaga, *Christianity Without Fetishes*, 21.

86. Schweitzer, "The Relations of the White and Colored Races," 65.

87. Ibid.

88. W. E. B. Du Bois, "The Black Man and Albert Schweitzer," in *The Albert Schweitzer Jubilee Book*, ed. A. A. Roback (Cambridge: Sci-Art Publishers, 1945), 121–8, 127: "He had with all this no broad grasp of what modern exploitation means, of what imperial colonialism has done to the world. If he had he would probably have tried to heal the souls of white Europe rather than the bodies of black Africa." In subsequent communication between the

Schweitzer's explanation of the exploitative global commerce that was ravaging the Africans in Equatorial Africa makes it clear he was fully aware of its history, and of European culpability. And so, it's astounding that Schweitzer's response to this exploitation was not African independence but "benevolent colonialism," of which he was the embodiment.[89]

As has been pointed out, even the existence of mixed marriages between French men and Gabonese women in the region, of which he most likely was aware and which should have at least mitigated some of Schweitzer's extreme racial views, apparently did not do so.[90] Instead he exclaimed, "To do away with authority is to destroy your own intermediary between government and the people. In Europe, the intermediary between the government and the people is in the office. The *process is impossible with primitive peoples*."[91] In this case, the Africans are the "primitive" people. Schweitzer's overall attitude toward African peoples and cultures was that there was little of value for a white person in African social, commercial, or religious structures, a similar perspective to that of the historical Jesus whom Schweitzer also located in "primitive" Christianity. The only possible contributions Schweitzer envisioned from Africans were on "moral ethics," where his observed acts of kindness by Africans, even toward people with nefarious intentions against them, made Schweitzer marvel.[92]

But this was contribution within limits. For example, whenever a "westernized" African would make a claim to self-assertion based on attained western civilization, Schweitzer was quick to disparage those claims. In one instance, Schweitzer described a situation where on a rainy day he tried to get the help of an African "dressed in a white suit" to move some logs. The man replied, "I am an intellectual and don't drag wood about." To which Schweitzer quipped, "You're lucky! . . . I too wanted to become an intellectual, but I didn't succeed."[93] This is an obvious put-down of the African's claim, who paradoxically was in a waiting room of the hospital in which Schweitzer was the doctor. Knowing what we do about Schweitzer's conviction about African intelligence, that was not a mere sarcastic retort by the "good doctor."

two, DuBois made it clear that he abhorred Schweitzer's complicity in the colonial project, lack of reverence for African life, and failure to support African decolonization. (Cf. Michael J. Thate, "An Anachronism in the African Jungle? Reassessing Albert Schweitzer's African Legacy," in *Schweitzer in Thought and Action*, ed. Paget and Thate, 295–318, 305.

89. Schweitzer, "The Relations of the White and Colored Races," 66.

90. Rachel Jean-Baptiste, "'A Black Girl Should Not Be with a White Man': Sex, Race, and African Women's Social and Legal Status in Colonial Gabon, c. 1900–1946," *JWH* 22, no. 2 (2010): 56–82.

91. Schweitzer, "The Relations of the White and Colored Races," 70.

92. A. Schweitzer, *The Forest Hospital at Lambaréné*, trans. C. T. Campion (New York: Macmillan, 1948), 186; Idem, *My African Notebook*, trans. Mrs. C. E. B. Russell (London: George Allen & Unwin, 1939), 134.

93. Schweitzer, *The Forest Hospital at Lambaréné*, 119.

In a continued defense of colonization, Schweitzer opined, "Whatever the fundamental rights of men are, they can only be fully secured in a stable and well-ordered society. In a disordered society, the very well-being of man himself often demands his fundamental rights should be abridged."[94] In this concession of the difference in moral and ethical responsibilities that should govern the "stable and organized" society (Europe) as opposed to the "disordered" society (Africa), he implied the justification for "the use of authority" in imposing order that he mentioned previously. That biblical moral and ethical ideals (e.g., Matt 5-6) could be justifiably set aside when dealing with the Other who was not as "civilized" as oneself, puts to question the form of Christianity being advocated. It is essentially, in this context of Schweitzer's views on forced labor, we find a mind-boggling tacit endorsement of slavery: "I myself hold labor *compulsion* [of the African] to be *not wrong in principle*, but impossible to carry through in practice."[95]

How is this a "love of humanity" and "reverence for life" that are supposedly the hallmarks of his African missionary work? The similarity of these views of the African with those of Georg W. F. Hegel, a philosopher whose body of work on dialectics Schweitzer was closely familiar with, is telling. Hegel had favored a gradual abolition of slavery since slavery was a necessary "phase of education" for the hapless primitive Africans.[96] The only reason Schweitzer would thus promulgate for ending slavery was not morality but its *impracticality!*—not its being inhuman, unethical, or un-Christian! Simply astounding!

Since he considered himself to be living within the period of the most nascent stage of the African's development process, Schweitzer did not see the possibility either of teaching critical Biblical Studies to Africans or even expecting them to have any capacity to handle such intellectual matters. This paternalistic attitude never changed, even after half a century of life with Africans. To Schweitzer, "necessary progress" had yet place among Africans. An obvious contrast from aforementioned Colenso, who believed that the Africans "were capable of receiving at once and cherishing that advanced Christianity."[97] Even at his deathbed, in 1965, Schweitzer's conviction that Gabon's independence from the French in 1960 was premature, remained unaltered.

c. Schweitzer on Missionary Work and Biblical Studies Schweitzer's unapologetic conviction of western Christian civilization's superiority governed his approach to

---

94. Schweitzer, "The Relations of the White and Colored Races," 65.

95. Schweitzer, *On the Edge of the Primeval Forest*, 118 (emphasis added).

96. G. W. F. Hegel, *Philosophy of History* (Buffalo: Prometheus, 1991; Orig.1892): 117.

97. J. W. Colenso, *Ten Weeks in Natal: A Journal of a First Tour of Visitation among the Colonists and Zulu Kafirs of Natal* (Cambridge: Macmillan, 1855), 23–4. A little later in the journal, he provides a story of visiting a mission in his diocese where young and orphaned African children were, and he notes how "these children were under the instruction of a young lady, a niece of the Missionaries: and they did such credit to her teaching, that I was well pleased to leave with her a small donation for the purchase of books and slates." (66)

missionary work in Africa. He remained blind to how he was as much a subject of the same domineering egotistic impulses that he had accused his predecessors of reflecting. Schweitzer described his impetus for his mission to Africa in terms of the Lukan parable of the rich man and Lazarus (Lk. 16:19-31). The African is like Lazarus, and he, Schweitzer, is the rich man. Unlike the parables recrimination of the rich man, to Schweitzer, the African (Lazarus) is poor and helpless, and Schweitzer (and wealthy Europe) have the means and where-with-all to save them. Schweitzer determined that he must go forth and make sure that he does what the rich man in the parable never did while on earth—take care of the suffering! But what of Schweitzer's missionary life, and his reflections on missionary work? How then does he square his Biblical Studies work and his colonialist views with his missionary work on behalf of Africans for whom he seemed to care so little even as he proclaimed himself a savior, of sorts? It would seem that while his Biblical Studies work should have informed his missionary activities, instead his white supremacist and colonialist mentality supplanted all that.

Consistent with his racial ideology, Schweitzer never seemed to perceive any conflict between his notion of "love" and ethic of "reverence for life" on the one hand and his racist and colonialist outlook, toward the African and African cultures, on the other.[98] In his mind-bending reasoning, he perceived both as working in tandem. If "love," the ethical Kingdom of God preached by Jesus, was the essence of Christianity for Schweitzer, then his commitment to caring for the sick as a physician epitomized that divine expression of mission. To him, it was a "right" as a rich, intellectual, moral westerner to impose on the poor Africans! And for this to be accomplished, European colonizers had controlling political power that could order the chaos of the colony, enough to allow for the "good doctor" to function. His decision to leave the comforts of Europe, an assured career in academics or music, seen by colleagues simply as madness and a major loss to the discipline of Biblical Studies, was worth it, as it was a "right."[99] But also, in his mind, leaving Europe was escaping its cultural denouement, while fulfilling what serving God entailed.[100] And even though he described himself as a "slave" of Jesus, it was he who was in the mold of a "superhuman" Jesus, out to serve the neediest of humanity.

In his critical evaluation of the "Life of Jesus" studies in German biblical scholarship, Schweitzer concluded that the changing images of Jesus reflected the different authors' realities projected on the biblical image of Jesus.[101] Typically overlooked is how he arrived at this conclusion based on a methodology best described as a *racially based social-evolution approach*, an "idea that, if there was a teleological progression in nature, the principles by which it operated could also

---

98. A perspective missed by those who want to reclaim it as a useful concept in African Christianity. Cf. Spangenberg and Landman, *The Legacies of Albert Schweitzer Reconsidered.*

99. Harris, "Schweitzer and Africa," 1111.

100. Ibid., 1114.

101. Schweitzer, *The Quest of the Historical Jesus*, 7.

be used to define the extent of progress made by different human societies."[102] At the top of this ladder, of course, was the European, who for Schweitzer, was epitomized by the German thinker, openly acknowledged in his opening paragraph of *The Quest*.[103] This is because "[s]ocial evolutionism contained its own moral vision about chosenness and cultural superiority that religion had long implied."[104] Consequently, as a member of this superior race, Schweitzer could claim to better understand the biblical presentation of Jesus, penned by "primitive men," than they would have understood it themselves: "Jesus stands much more immediately before us, because He was depicted by *simple Christians without literary gift*."[105]

Schweitzer was confident that he could decipher falsity from truth, in a way that ancient uncivilized authors, clouded by superstitions, could not. This he held to also be true of his recent predecessors, who he argued could not, given their lack of "scientific" rigor, arrive at the correct answers.[106] To Schweitzer, each recent past scholar was looking into the Bible, and rather than seeing the first-century Jesus, they superimposed their self-images onto that of Jesus.[107] Resultantly, the Jesus they ended up constructing was merely a reflection of their European reality, rather than an accurate image of a first-century Jesus. This "European Jesus" was not the Jesus of the Bible. Instead, Schweitzer argued, Jesus must be understood in light of his historical context, which was his first-century "Jewish eschatological context."[108]

Schweitzer's reproach of the lack of self-awareness and self-critique by the preceding European biblical scholars in their interpretation of the Bible, however, did not seem to translate into his perception of missionary work in Africa where he seemed completely blind to his own critique. Just like the European biblical scholars had presented a Europeanized Jesus made in their own image, Schweitzer presented a "white Jesus" created in Schweitzer's own image governed by his racist and prejudiced evolutionary position as a member of an advanced race. Africans

102. John P. Burris, *Exhibiting Religion: Colonialism and Spectacle at International Expositions, 1851–1893* (Charlottesville: University of Virginia Press, 2001), xviii.

103. Schweitzer, *The Quest of the Historical Jesus*, 1: "For *nowhere save in the German temperament* can there be found in the same perfection the living complex of conditions and factors—of philosophic thought, critical acumen, historical insight, and religious feeling—without which no deep theology is possible." (emphasis added)

104. Burris, *Exhibiting Religion*, xviii.

105. Schweitzer, *The Quest of the Historical Jesus*, 6 (emphasis added). He classifies Johann G. Herder as a "primitive rationalist" for continuing to believe in Jesus' miracles (36).

106. Ibid., 4–5: They advanced the science, but only Schweitzer has the complete set of tools: "But for the offence which they gave, the science of historical theology would not have stood where it does today."

107. Schweitzer, *The Quest of the Historical Jesus*, 4. "But it was not only each epoch that found its reflection in Jesus; each individual created Him in accordance with his own character. There is no historical task which so reveals a man's true self as the writing of a Life of Jesus."

108. Schweitzer, *The Quest of the Historical Jesus*, 23. Cf. also Pitts, "Albert Schweitzer."

remained trapped in their "superstitious ideas," unless, of course, they embraced Jesus's "higher moral ideas of religion," essentially, western Christianity.[109]

Not surprisingly, Schweitzer would then perceive himself as an embodiment of Jesus exemplifying "love of God and neighbor" to the African.[110] As we have seen, however, his unverbalized "love," was contradicted by his racist and colonialist views of the Africans. His African mission could be more accurately characterized in terms of a "white savior" mentality rather than as a "servant/slave" of Jesus. He believed that he had the right and moral capacity to save the Africans from themselves and from the exploitative world of commerce that was corrupting and decimating them. So, rather than view his mission in the *au courant* "Great Commission" (Mt. 28:19-20), Schweitzer rejected this text as a late addition to the Matthean Gospel, and having nothing to do with Jesus.[111]

Once again, a quick comparison with Colenso would put Schweitzer in a certain relief. Colenso's positive attitude toward Africans and their religio-cultural reality, even when expressed within colonialist and imperialist frameworks, was in the minority among European missionaries.[112] Colenso's analysis of the Bible side by side with African culture was reinventing world religions, setting in place the comparativist approach as a new methodology. As Willie Jennings describes Colenso's approach, "Ngidi [the Zulu] takes the role of the intellectual provocateur in Colenso's theological project. It is noteworthy that the African becomes an intellectual dialogue partner, someone whose thoughts, even if expressed only in question, make real his humanity."[113] Yet, Colenzo's significant contributions remain overshadowed by Schweitzer's oversized oversize presence in Biblical Studies.

d. Schweitzer—White Supremacy, Racism, and the Bible Projecting his notion of white supremacy, Schweitzer's view of Africans remained essentially racist throughout most of his life. What primitive Africans needed was not formal education but manual labor: "Taken by itself, a thorough school education is, in my opinion, by no means necessary for these *primitive* people. The beginning of civilization for them is not knowledge, but industry and agriculture."[114] African religious and cultural reality, a form of superstition, needed to be gradually replaced with the rationality of "western Christian civilization." This dread of curses, taboos, and juju/fetish needed to be wiped out:

109. Schweitzer, *On the Edge of the Primeval Forest*, 155.

110. Schweitzer, *Life*, 249.

111. Schweitzer, *The Quest of the Historical Jesus*, 18: "In the first place the genuineness of the command to baptize in Matt. xxviii. 19 is questionable, not only as a saying ascribed to the risen Jesus, but also because it is universalistic in outlook, and because it implies the doctrine of the Trinity and, consequently, the metaphysical Divine Sonship of Jesus."

112. Colenso continued to utilize colonialist terms in reference to Africans such as Kaffir, heathen, and even reference to them as "childlike." So, while he did show great strides in humanizing the African, he remained firmly an imperialist and a colonialist.

113. Jennings, *The Christian Imagination*, 152.

114. Schweitzer, *On the Edge of the Primeval Forest*, 122.

Anyone who has once penetrated into the *imaginary world* of primitive man, and knows something of the state of fear in which people may live when they believe in taboos, unavoidable curses and active ju-jus [fetishes], can no longer doubt that it is *our duty* to endeavor *to liberate them from these superstitions . . . .* These conceptions have such deep roots in the world-view and traditions of primitive people that they are not easy to eradicate.[115]

Similar arguments were posited against "primitive Christianity," filled with its superstitious miracles. And just how was this eradication to be achieved? According to Schweitzer, this was the role of western Christianity (devoid of primitive elements).

For the African, Christianity is *the light which shines in the darkness of fear.* It assures him that he is not under the control of nature-spirits, ancestral gods, or fetishes. It testifies that no man exercises any uncanny power over another. It signifies that only God's will is sovereign in all events.[116]

To justify the annihilation of African religious reality in the name of western Christianity, African religion was suddenly categorized as "imaginary," "nature-spirit," "fetish," and a "superstition." By situating African religious reality outside the realm of "the real" (a view in keeping with influential philosopher Hegel's notion that "only the rational is real"), Schweitzer could eliminate any sense of guilt that may have accompanied the religio-cultural bulldozing that he (and fellow colonialists) endorsed.

This attitude aligns with the colonization strategy that sought to justify lording over the Other, by declaring the Other as nonexistent—as a people, as a society, as a religion, as a civilization[117]—a *tabula rasa* that was waiting for the arrival of the European to put its imprimatur upon, and save it! While Schweitzer may have lost faith in aspects of European capitalism, he nevertheless remained a western thinker, philosopher, theologian, and colonialist.[118] His was a version of a "benevolent western colonizer" who was doing his best to Christianize and civilize the African.

---

115. Schweitzer, *My African Notebook*, iv.

116. Schweitzer, *On the Edge of the Primeval Forest*, 122.

117. While endorsing human rights (Races, 65), the list he offers contradicts the things he has said elsewhere about the African. "The fundamental rights of man are, first, the right to habitation; secondly right to move freely; thirdly, the right to the soil and subsoil, and to the use of it; fourthly, the right to freedom of labor and of exchange; fifthly, the right to justice; sixthly, the right live within a natural, national organization; and, seventhly, the right to education." Since Africans were not fully human, or were lesser humans, these rights did not seem to apply to them as they were denied their land by colonialism, lost freedom, lost ownership of land and its produce, and the like, as colonization was a moral right for the colonizer.

118. , "Theologians Revisited," 119.

For Schweitzer, biblical analysis as the preserve of the rational human was beyond fathoming for the less evolved African.[119] In such a racist imperialistic stance, the "Bible and church are substituted for intelligence and conscience" which the African does not quite possess.[120] As Schweitzer explained, the need for any complicated education for Africans was simply aiming "higher than is natural."[121] Paradoxically, in the very next line, he concedes that many natives did have "astounding" intellectual abilities, and, as an example, he recounted an incident of a "native government clerk" who was able to handle the most sophisticated statistical assignments "faultlessly."[122] It would seem that for Schweitzer, such individual achievement reflected the exception rather that the rule, since even such an intelligent African lacked the moral constitution to be considered an equal. Exceptions did not negate the general rule!

Given this general assessment of the African, then, the most useful preaching of the Bible that Africans could comprehend, according to Schweitzer, was the beatitudes of Jesus (Matthew 5–7).[123] Being the most basic and "primitive" teachings of the gospel, they could be understood by these most primitive of peoples. The teachings are practical and not doctrinal, and so could be understood even by a child, and the African, according to Schweitzer, was a "child." In his racist evolutionary human scale, the African (blacks) was the polar opposite of the sophisticated and "adult" European (whites).

> A word . . . about the relations between the *whites and blacks*. What must be the general character of the intercourse between them? *Am I to treat the black man as my equal or my inferior?* I must show him that I can respect the dignity of human personality in every one, and this attitude in me he must be able to see for himself; but the essential thing is that there shall be a real feeling of brotherliness. How far this is to find complete expression in the sayings and doings of daily life must be *settled by circumstances*. The *negro is a child, and with children nothing can be done without the use of authority*. We must, therefore, so arrange the circumstances of daily life that *my natural authority can find expression*. With regard to the negroes, then, I have coined the formula: "*I am your brother, it is true, but your elder brother.*"[124] (emphasis added)

What pompous proclamations! Several things can be extrapolated from this extraordinary quote: 1) the African is inferior to the European; 2) Schweitzer retains a colonialist view of his authority as natural (divinely or racially ordained?) over the African; 3) the African has no intellectual capacity to comprehend

---

119. Schweitzer, *On the Edge of the Primeval Forest*, 122.
120. Boulaga, *Christianity Without Fetishes*, 9.
121. Schweitzer, *On the Edge of the Primeval Forest*, 122.
122. Ibid.
123. Harris, "Schweitzer and Africa," 1113.
124. Schweitzer, *On the Edge of the Primeval Forest*, 130–1.

complicated issues (e.g., Biblical Studies?) fully, for the African is a "child."[125] Showing love to the African versus applying "my natural authority" over her depends on "circumstances." Such racist constructs, typical among colonialists, according to Albert Memmi, serve to stifle any social mobility or freedom of the colonized, and to effect the suppressing of any potential resistance or revolt. And so, this "racism appears not as an incidental detail, but as a consubstantial part of colonialism . . . [its] highest expression, [which] lays the foundation for the immutability of this life."[126]

This was a fundamental belief of Schweitzer for, according to historian Ruth Harris, visitors to his Lambaréné hospital "found it difficult to square the myth of the benevolent 'grand Docteur' with the hospital's less appealing reality. They were disturbed by Schweitzer's authoritarianism, [and] disquieted by his refusal to train local physicians."[127] Boulaga's statement adroitly critiques Schweitzer's colonialist attitudes, alluding to the notion of the "child":

> whatever their merits, the new [African] Christians cannot be placed on an equal footing with Western colonials; and those colonials, be they the most vicious miscreants, will be more deserving of respect and consideration than their protégés. Why? Because in either, there an inalienable substratum that changes the meaning of visible, surface manifestations. The black is still a pagan, and rather a child, despite baptism; the white Occidental is still a Christian, a rational, reasonable being, despite transgressions and straying. The Christianity of the former is a veneer, something adventitious, an accident. The Christianity of the latter is substrate and substance.[128]

What Cameroonian Buolaga excoriates, Tunisian Memmi perceives as an inevitable phenomenon in the colonizer–colonized relationship: "Racism sums up and symbolizes the fundamental relation which unites colonialist and colonized."[129] He explains further that "colonial racism is built from three major ideological components: 1) the gulf between the culture of the colonialist and the colonized; 2) the exploitation of these differences for the benefit of the colonialist; 3) the use of these supposed differences as standards of absolute fact."[130] It is therefore rather perplexing and somewhat disconcerting to see a prominent African historian like

---

125. The same language of describing an African as a child is also found in the German philosopher Hegel (*Philosophy*) whose work was very familiar to Schweitzer. After distinguishing Africa into three parts—Egypt (advanced), European Africa (north of Sahara), and Africa proper (South of the Sahara), he described Africa proper as "the land of childhood." (91)

126. Memmi, *The Colonizer and the Colonized*, 74.

127. Harris, "Schweitzer and Africa," 1108.

128. Boulaga, *Christianity Without Fetishes*, 21.

129. Memmi, *The Colonizer and the Colonized*, 70.

130. Ibid., 71.

Ali Mazrui of Kenya who, in an effort to rehabilitate or even vanish this "dark stain" on Schweitzer's image, declared him a "benevolent racist" (as opposed to a "malignant racist" or a "benign racist"), as though racism could be mitigated somehow by simply placing an adjective before it.[131] At the very least, it would seem Mazrui, at the time the Albert Schweitzer Professor in the Humanities, State University of New York, had bought into Schweitzer's own colonial justification of the notion of "moral paternalism."[132]

It is difficult not to, once again, want to juxtapose John Colenso for comparison here. Colenso was so confident in the African's intellectual capacity that he encouraged his African students to write their own books, resulting in some of the earliest writings by Zulu authors.[133] His African students and counterparts also forced him to reevaluate his own western (and German informed) readings of the Bible, as their questions challenged his Eurocentric hermeneutic. These African questions undergirded the intellectual and investigative impulse of his biblical commentaries on the Pentateuch and the Book of Joshua, which would eventually form the basis of Colenso's accusation of "heresy."[134] His willingness to take those questions from the "margins" seriously, enabled him to arrive at a different hermeneutic than those of his contemporaries in Europe within the emergent Biblical Studies, a new vision of salvation, for which his body of work, unlike that of the "benevolent racist" Schweitzer, remain ignored the discipline.[135]

e. Schweitzer in Missionary Context   Schweitzer was not unique among European missionaries to Africa in his racist attitude toward Africans. Even for those who may have sympathized with the African cultural and social reality and advocated for culturally sensitive interpretations of the Bible, western missionaries remained "products of their empire and believed that the best of the European values

---

131. Ali A. Mazrui, "Review: Dr. Schweitzer's Racism," *Transition* 53 (1991): 96–102. I find Mazrui's attempt at rehabilitating Schweitzer's racist perspective rather befuddling, and it seems to me an attempt to excuse the racist foundation of the colonial project. Racism cannot be benign or benevolent. Racism is essentially the rejection of the Other as an equal. Though, perhaps, a racist person can still be benevolent.

132. Davenport, "The Moral Paternalism of Albert Schweitzer," 126.

133. *Three Native Accounts of the Visit of the Bishop of Natal in September and October, 1859, To Umpande, King of the Zulus*, ed. and trans. J. W. Colenso (Pietermaritzburg: University of Natal, 1901) and Magema Magwaza Fuze (c. 1840–1922); *Abantu Abamnyama Lapa Bavela Ngakona (The Black People and Whence They Came)*, ed. A. T. Cope and trans. H. C. Lugg (Pietermaritzburg: University of Natal, 1979).

134. Sugirtharajah, *The Bible and the Third World*, 113–14; Jennings, *The Christian Imagination*, 132–4.

135. Jennings, *The Christian Imagination*, 145, reminds us that as radical as Colenso's arguments were, they remained embedded in the colonial project, so that "[w]hat looks like a radical anti-racist, anti-ethnocentric vision of Christian faith is in fact profoundly imperialistic. Colenso's universalism undermines all forms of identity except that of the colonialist."

and customs blended effortlessly with egalitarian religious concepts and robust indigenous social institutions. In their minds European rule was social reality, never a political imposition."[136] This blind optimism on the part of the European Christians was based on a deliberate ignoring of the atrocities of the colonial project of which they were beneficiaries.[137]

For example, in a somewhat confusing statement, Schweitzer seems to hold the view of gradual education of the African from the crafts to the more "commercial and intellectual" education.[138] That was why he made the argument that African colonialism should last "for several generations" before African nations received independence.[139] While conceding the intellectual capacity of some, Schweitzer, nevertheless, saw no long-term value in the thorough formal education of the African *per se*. So Schweitzer indicated the potential for progress but found no clear way to justify the connection between the African's formal education and the reception of the gospel message.

And while some European missionaries, like Colenso, whom we mentioned before, in Africa espoused confidence in African intellectual capacity busy with translations of the Bible into native African languages and building schools for Africans, Schweitzer retained his racist construction of Africans' anemic aptitude and indolence.[140] Placide Tempels, for example, a missionary in Belgian Congo beginning in 1933, made the case for complexity and sophistication in African religions and cultures in his *Philosophie Bantoue*.[141] Schweitzer, however, not

---

136. Sugirtharajah, *Postcolonial Criticism and Biblical Interpretation*, 52.

137. M. De Secondat Baron De Montesquieu, *The Spirit of Laws*, Vol. 11, trans. Thomas Nugent (Cincinnati: Robert and Clarke, 1863), 238. In the name of Christianity, one Charles De Secondat, Baron of Montesquieu, postulated a defense of African slavery that seemed to reflect pervasive racist and dehumanizing claims about Africans:

Were I to vindicate our right to make slaves of the Negroes, these should be my arguments:

- These *creatures* are all over black, and with such a flat nose that they can scarcely be pitied . . .
- It is hardly to be believed that God, who is a wise Being, should place a soul, especially a good soul, in such a *black ugly body* . . .

It is *impossible for us to suppose these creatures to be men, because, allowing them to be men, a suspicion would follow that we ourselves are not Christians.* (emphasis added)

138. Schweitzer, *Life*, 194.

139. A. Schweitzer, "Our Task in Colonial Africa," in *The Africa of Albert Schweitzer*, ed. C. K. Joy and Melvin Arnold (New York: Harper & Bros., 1948), 145–50.

140. "Theologians Revisited," 118. On this point, I am in disagreement with Oeermann who believes that Schweitzer's attitude toward Africans had improved.

141. Cf. Placide Tempels's *La Philosophie Bantoue* (Paris: Presence Africaine, 1945), 11: "To declare on *a priori* grounds that primitive peoples have no ideas on the nature of beings, that they have no ontology that they are completely lacking in logic, is simply to turn one's back on reality." Unfortunately, even Tempels's attempts at affirming African intelligence

only retained a very paternalistic and purely racist attitude toward the African,[142] in exasperation, he would denigrate and dehumanize them as "savages," "semi-primitive," "primitive," and even "monkeys."[143]

Not only did Schweitzer question the African capacity to comprehend the Bible, but he also brought their very humanity into doubt. While reflecting on his lifelong work in Africa, Schweitzer seemed to arrive at a premise of regret by questioning the essence of the African's humanity.

> I have given my life to try to alleviate the sufferings of Africa. There is something that all white men who have lived here like I must learn and know: *that these individuals are a sub-race. They have neither the intellectual, mental, or emotional abilities to equate or to share equally with white men* in any function of our civilization. I have given my life to try to bring them the advantages which *our civilization* must offer, but I have become well aware that we must retain this status: *we the superior and they the inferior.*[144]

A sub-race, is what he called the Africans, after half a century of living with them. In contrast, for example, in the *Proceedings of the Conference on Foreign Missions*, Mr. Guinness, perhaps addressing prejudice in his audience, had this to say about Africans:

> Let me tell you the last news from the Congo, I wanted to have had one of our dear Congo natives here to-night, but he could not come . . . I meant to put him on this platform before you that you may see he has hands, and eyes and feet just like you. He has *mind, intelligence, conscience* and *affection* just as we have.[145] (emphasis added)

If racism is the denial of the Other's humanity, then Guinness's is an ardent anti-racist statement that makes clear that Schweitzer's racist views were ever present in every aspect of his academic work, even when not overtly referenced. Guinness's equation of European and African mental and emotional capacities stands in stark contrast to Schweitzer's racist and prejudiced assessments of the African. What possibly could one attribute to Schweitzer's unyielding racist attitudes and views about the African then? The answer may lie in his academic affiliations, with the

---

remained within a racialized framework and could only do so within the westernized thought matrix.

142. Schweitzer, *The Forest Hospital at Lambaréné*, 186: "How many beautiful traits of character that we can discover in them, if we refuse to let the many and varied follies of the child of nature prevent us from *looking for the man in him.*" (emphasis added)

143. Schweitzer, *Life*, 147–52.

144. Schweitzer, *My African Notebook*.

145. *Proceedings of the Conference on Foreign Missions*, 142.

works of certain German philosophers who continue to be influential in (western) Biblical Studies and theology, even today.

f. Schweitzer in European Academic Context The racist ideas and language espoused by Schweitzer especially correspond with those of three philosophers, two German and one Scottish, considered giants in both western philosophy and theology—David Hume, Emmanuel Kant, and Georg Hegel. Their racist arguments about Africans, in the development of what was considered scientific evolutionary human taxonomies, may have laid the ground for Schweitzer's.[146] These three European philosophers, whose own writings have greatly influenced the discipline of Biblical Studies in the West over the years, share the white supremacist and racist attitudes espoused by Schweitzer.[147]

While I may not be able to prove direct influence on Schweitzer's racism comprehensively, David Hume, whose works Schweitzer knew; Emmanuel Kant, on whom Schweitzer had written a doctoral thesis; and Georg F. Hegel, whose work on dialectics impacted Schweitzer's thinking, had earlier expressed quite similar racist attitude toward Africans.[148] Hume, in a now-infamous footnote, exclaimed:

I am apt to suspect the Negroes, and in general, all other species of men (for there are four or five different kinds), to be *naturally inferior to the whites*. There never was a civilized nation of any other complexion than white, nor even any individual eminent either in action or speculation. No ingenious manufactures amongst them, no arts, no science.[149]

146. Henry Paget, "Between Hume and Cugoano: Race, Ethnicity and Philosophical Entrapment," *JSP* 18, no. 2 (2004): 129–48: "On this basis, Native Americans were ineducable because they lacked passion and affect. Africans had sufficient passion and affect to be trained as slaves and servants. For Kant, all inhabitants of the tropical zone were without exception idle. Thus, along with his suggestion for their training, there were also instructions for *flogging Africans*. Finally, Hindus could be educated to the highest degree but only in the arts. The sciences and abstract thinking were beyond their reach. To *achieve these one had to be a member of the white race*." (136) (emphasis added)

147. Albert Schweitzer, *Die Religionsphilosophie Kants: Von der Kritik der reinen Vernunft bis zur Religion innerhalb der Grenzen der bloßen Vernunft* (Leipzig and Tubingen: J. C. B. Mohr [Paul Siebeck], 1899), trans. *Kant's Philosophy of Religion: From the Critique of Pure Reason to Religion within the Limits of Reason*.

148. A. Schweitzer, "Religion and Modern Civilization," *CC* (1934): 1519. Schweitzer thinks Hume's philosophy of values is "dangerous" and also directs arguments against Hume's skepticism in religion.

149. T. H. Green and T. H. Grose (eds.), *The Philosophical Works* (London, 1882; repr. Darmstadt, 1964), III, 253. Subsequent revisions of the quote by Hume did little to change his racist perspective (Cf. John Immerwahr, "Hume's Revised Racism," *JHI* 53, no. 3 [1992]: 481–6 [483]).

While the Scottish Hume based his argument regarding the inferiority of the Africans (Negroes) on their lack of "civilization," Kant connected inferiority to race. In referencing the color of an African carpenter, he stated, "In short, this fellow was very black from head to foot, a clear proof that what he said was stupid."[150] He offers the carpenter's blackness as the basis for his stupidity. Further, Kant makes this explicit: "The Negroes of Africa have by nature no feeling that rises above the trifling . . . [but] among the whites some continually rise aloft from the lowest rabble, and through superior gifts earn respect in the world. So fundamental is the difference between these two races of man [black and white], and it appears to be *as great in regard to mental capacities as in color*."[151] Hegel's *Philosophy of History* equivocates on Africans and their environment:

> [The African] exhibits the natural man in his completely wild and untamed state . . . [Africa] is no historical part of the world; it has no movement or development to exhibit . . . [the African] has "no sense of personality; their spirit sleeps, remains sunk in itself, makes no advance, and thus parallels the compact, undifferentiated mass of the African continent."[152]

In these three influential western thinkers are racist notions of the apparent inferiority of African intelligence, humanity and identity comprehensively articulated. One African historian's comment on Hegel is applicable to the other two; "Hegel denies rationality to Africans, implying racial considerations, the effect of the milieu, and African social structure."[153] To do so, Hegel strangely singled out Egypt for its ancient intelligence that thrived "in the vicinity of African stupidity."[154]

In their constructions of global human history framed around categories of race, Kant and Hegel found no room for Africans. Africans stood "beyond the pale of history (pre-historic)," literally outside the system, and their civilizations had "no intrinsic value" to contribute to "global civilization" that, for Kant and Hegel, had at its pinnacle western Christian civilization.[155] In Hegel's words, "At this point we leave Africa never to mention it again. For it is no historical part of the World. . . . What we properly understand as African is the Unhistorical, Undeveloped spirit, still involved in the condition of mere nature."[156]

---

150. Emmanuel Kant, *Observations on the Feeling of the Beautiful and Sublime and Other Writings*, trans. John T. Goldthwait (Berkeley: University of California Press, 1981), 111.

151. Ibid., 110–11.

152. Hegel, *Philosophy of History*, 111.

153. Babacar Camara, "The Falsity of Hegel's Theses on Africa," *JBS* 36, no. 1 (2005): 82–96; 94.

154. Hegel, *Philosophy of History*, 223.

155. Justin E. H. Smith, "The Enlightenment's 'Race' Problem, and Ours," *NYT Opinionator*, February 10, 2013, Available online: https://opinionator.blogs.nytimes.com /2013/02/10/why-has-race-survived/ (accessed July 11, 2019).

156. Hegel, *Philosophy of History*, 117.

In the Hegelian dialectic, for the European civilization to exist as the nexus of human advancement, it required an antithesis, the primitive African "non-civilization, even when evidence suggested otherwise." To sustain the notion of the rational European, the construction of the "primitive African" had to happen. This is the same principle that guided Schweitzer's beliefs about Africans. While Hume, Kant, and Hegel never set foot in Africa, Schweitzer's half a century sojourn there never altered his racist views.[157] He may have been physically situated in Africa, but intellectually, he never departed from his European Enlightenment thinking where African intellectual interlocutors were non-existent.

While this may sound baffling, it is entirely in keeping with Schweitzer's personality. His stubbornness and his unwillingness to change certain fundamental views he held on, took him to Africa when others thought he should stay in Europe. It is not surprising then that his very own writings bear witness to this apparently lacking African intelligence, even as he refused to acknowledge it. For Schweitzer, just as for Hume, Kant, and Hegel, there was no possibility in their evolutionary taxonomy, for the African attaining the capacity of a "rational being".[158]

In later interviews, Schweitzer is said to have remarked that "the time for speaking of older and younger brothers has passed."[159] What may sound as contrition, nonetheless, is not. This was not an apology or reversal of his position on the African. Only a few lines later, he maintained his initial justification that "we had *the right* to regard ourselves as elder brothers of the natives; elder brothers who were well disposed toward the younger brothers, and at the same time sufficiently experienced and knowledgeable to be able to *judge what was best for their true advancement*, and able to act accordingly."[160] At least he was consistent to the end!

---

157. Emmanuel C. Eze, *Race and the Enlightenment* (Malden and Oxford: Blackwell, 1997). Eze's brief anthology makes it clear that these three influential philosophers shared and probably built on each other's racial construction. In the cases of Hume and Kant, their defense of their racist views in light of opposition—Hume against James Beattie, Kant against Herder—indicates that this was a deliberate choice. In the case of Hegel, European racial supremacy undergirds his justification of African slavery, imperialism, and colonialism.

158. See, however, Pauline Kleingeld, "Kant's Second Thoughts on Race," *PQ* 57, no. 229 (2007): 573–92, who mounts a substantive argument that "later Kant" may have toned down, or even reversed his racist ideas. about hierarchies of race. However, as Jasmine Gani, "The Erasure of Race: Cosmopolitanism and the Illusion of Kantian Hospitality," *Mill* 45, no. 3 (2017): 425–46, 446, who argues this is an erasure of the Other, rather than a reversal of view: "By excavating his works on geography and anthropology, it is possible to identify the constitutive effects of an erasure of race from Kant's legal–political theory on the one hand, and a simultaneous project of racist codification in his natural history on the other."

159. Cf. Lachlan Forrow's "Foreword" to Schweitzer's *African Notebook*.

160. Preface of Schweitzer's *On the Edge of the Primeval Forest*, French ed., 1952, trans. Fitzgerald, 1964), 160–1. (Emphasis added)

g. Conclusion and Implications for Biblical Studies The celebration of Schweitzer by the West completely ignores, plays down, or tries to whitewash his racist beliefs about Africans and others.[161] In comparison, Colenso's writings are nowhere to be seen in western Biblical Studies, significant as they are in critiquing the Eurocentric nature of interpretation, its racist and dehumanizing stance, and its colonialist underpinnings. Instead, the spotlight has remained on Schweitzer's "superhuman" accomplishments in Biblical Studies, music, medicine, and missionary work.[162] As we have seen these excuses are unwarranted and dangerous, as they reflect the discipline's unwillingness to deal with its dark past while perpetuating and sanctioning the embedded racism that undergirds his works. Western biblical scholars seem to retain a mistaken notion that Schweitzer's racist and paternalistic tendencies had no direct influence on his works in Biblical Studies.

The *passé* concept of "objective reading," in which the reader's context does not affect the interpretive meaning of the Bible, and which characterized western Biblical Studies through the mid-twentieth century but has convincingly been debunked by literary criticism, and postcolonial studies. The presupposition of the necessity to separate a scholar's personal life and opinions from their academic work creates a false dichotomy between one's religious praxis and one's academic work. Postmodern, literary, and postcolonial studies have challenged this dichotomy of conceptualization of meaning, undermining the presumed objectivity of the "uninterested" reader.[163] Yet, the continued failure of critical introspection within western Biblical Studies has allowed racist and paternalistic attitudes not only to persist, but dominate unhindered in the discipline. Silence on the racist underpinnings of the discipline's foundations is the complacency of western Biblical Studies' acceptance of such perspectives or the choice to cast a blind eye toward them since the collective "good" in the founders, like Schweitzer, far surpasses their foibles.

Schweitzer's racial ideas and paternalism continue to shape, who gets to access and interpret the Bible. The dichotomy between the academic (intellectual) and the practical (non-academic) within Biblical Studies perpetuate the racist structures. Challenges from outside the discipline like those from cultural studies, postmodern and postcolonial readings have only had a minor impact on western Biblical Studies as they remain largely on the margins of the discipline. Even as critics have challenged its preponderance of universalism, western Biblical Studies has not fully yielded. Schweitzer's position that Biblical Studies would remain the domain of the "superior race," and therefore would not be for groups like Africans, remains the unstated default position of the discipline that remains over 85 percent

---

161. Note, for example, how Pelikan, *Jesus through the Centuries*, 2, approvingly quotes from Schweitzer but never raises the issue of his racist opinions.

162. For example, Reventlow and Farmer, *Biblical Studies*.

163. George Aichelle et al. (eds.), *The Postmodern Bible*, Bible and Culture Collective (New Haven: Yale University Press, 1997); R. S. Sugirtharajah (ed.), *The Postcolonial Bible* (Bible and Postcolonialism; Sheffield: Sheffield Academic, 1998).

white, and male. Consequently, the continued labeling of certain aspects of African biblical scholarship as "unscholarly" persists within this racialized paradigm that does not recognize intelligence beyond Eurocentric approaches.

Changes in Biblical Studies that started appearing in the second half of the twentieth century, with the emergence of literary approaches in the late 1960s and dissolution of former European colonies, continue to compel minor disciplinary self-interrogation, but not major transformations. Literary studies that have shown the importance of the reader's location as vital in the construction of meaning, have made it clear that all reading is subjective. The reader's context has a direct bearing on her interpretation of the Bible. Taken more seriously in Biblical Studies, the implication of this would be transformative for the discipline.

That Schweitzer represented a mode of thinking that characterized many European missionaries is exemplified in Mudimbe's claim that "If the movement, or more exactly, the missionary activity, finds its unique purpose, this seems to be so only because of an exterior or more general purpose: the necessity of converting the backward cultures and introducing them in the Hegelian perspective of history."[164] Consistent with the colonial *dictum*, Schweitzer's language is clear in declaring that he believed that the European knew exactly what the African needed and had the "right" to "judge" what that was and to implement it. In essence, the missionary was playing god. And, western Biblical Studies, in many respects perpetuates that by playing the gatekeeper's role.

---

164. Mudimbe, *Tales of Faith*, 40–1.

Part II

THE BIBLE, COLONIAL ENCOUNTERS, AND UNEXPECTED OUTCOMES

In order to triumph, colonization wanted to serve only its own interests. But by pushing aside the colonized man, through whom it could have exalted the colony, it condemned itself to remain foreign to it and thus of necessity transitory.

—Albert Memmi[1]

In sum, decolonization is a very complex battle over the course of different destinies, different histories and geographies, and it is replete with works of the *imagination, scholarship and counter-scholarship.*

—Edward Said[2]

1. Memmi, *The Colonizer and the Colonized*, 111–12.
2. Said, *Culture and Imperialism*, 219 (emphasis added).

Chapter 4

BIBLE TRANSLATION AS BIBLICAL INTERPRETATION

THE COLONIAL BIBLE

Language becomes the medium through which a hierarchical structure is perpetuated, and the medium through which conceptions of "truth," "order," and "reality" become established.

— *The Empire Writes Back*[1]

In the colonial context, translation acted as a mediating agency between conquest and conversion.

— R. S. Sugirtharajah[2]

4.1 Introduction

Beyond overt racism and colonialism, other subtler modes of subjugation of the natives were part of the colonial projects' arsenal. Perhaps none more important than translation of the Bible. Commenting on the colonial English Christians, Sugirtharajah makes it clear that European translators "saw the circulation of the Bible as an important divine calling. This was supported by a belief that the secret of England's [and Europe's] greatness was its reading of the Bible. They also believed that it was the reading of the Bible which preserved England [and Europe's] from any political upheaval, and that the Bible could be a vehicle for training English (and European] values to the colonies."[3] So translation was less about the religious benevolence to the colonized, though that may have been part of it, and more of the colonizers' self-serving purpose. As Albert Memmi notes in the epigraph virtually every aspect of the colonizer's action was a means of imposition of control over the colonized.[4] The vernacular Bible translation then, was the Trojan horse through which the colonizers' "English or European values" infiltrated local languages and communities according to Ashcroft, Griffiths, and Tiffin, in their vital work *The Empire Writes Back*. The New Testament scholars from Botswana, Musa Dube,

---

1. Ashcroft, Griffiths, Tiffin, *The Empire Writes Back*, 7.
2. Sugirtharajah, *Biblical Criticism*, 156.
3. Sugirtharajah, *The Bible and the Third World*, 53.
4. Memmi, *The Colonizer and the Colonized*, 111–12.

has shown in her essay, "Scramble for Africa as the Scramble for the Bible," that at the center of the scramble for spoils of the African continent was the struggle for the Bible itself—the scramble to lay claim on the Bible, in order to justify the European colonial project's divine imprimatur. [5] It follows, then, in Said's words, mentioned earlier, that it would necessitate a complex decolonizing process to reexamine and re-present the impact of the translation project. Yet, as we will see, some unexpected and unintended outcomes of the vernacular translations lent impetus to local communities' liberative impulses and independent constructions of biblical interpretations eventually undermining the colonizer's project.[6]

4.2 Vernacular Bible—The "Colonized" Bible

Initial European missionary efforts in Africa saw minimal results until the translation of the Bible into African vernacular began.[7] While the earliest translation of the Bible can, indeed, be traced to Africa (Egypt) between the second or third century BCE with the translation of the *Septuagint* (the Greek translation of the Hebrew Bible), our focus here is on the "re-introduction" of the Bible in Africa with European imperialism.[8] Where prior interaction with the "white man's" book acquired an aura of talismanic reputation among the Africans, it was European nineteenth- and twentieth-century translation projects that produced the Bible in the African vernacular.[9] Following the Bible's vernacular translation, local African converts became the backbone of spreading its teachings to their communities, resulting in an explosion of conversions to Christianity.[10] This vernacular spread, however, was not always in ways envisioned by the European translators.[11]

---

5. Dube, Mbuvi, Mbuwayesango, *Postcolonial Perspectives*, 1–28.

6. Lamin Sanneh, *Translating the Message: The Missionary Impact on Culture* (Maryknoll: Orbis, 1989), 203: "It is one of the interesting ironies of the Western missionary enterprise that the evangelical motive actually helped to shield indigenous populations from the unmitigated assault of the West and that through the elevation of the vernacular in translation, missions furnished the critical language for evaluating the West in its secular and religious impact."

7. Sanneh, *Translating the Message*, 205; W. A. Smalley, *Translation as Mission: Bible Translation in the Modern Missionary Movement* (Macon: Mercer University Press, 1991); P. Stine (ed.), *Bible Translation and the Spread of the Church: The Last 200 Years* (Leiden: Brill, 1990).

8. See H. St. J. Thackeray, *The Letter of Aristeas* (London: SPCK, 1917).

9. G. West, "The Beginning of African Biblical Interpretation: The Bible among the BaTlhaping," *Acta Theol* 12, no. 1 (2009): 33–47.

10. Matthias Gerner, "Why Worldwide Bible Translation Grows Exponentially," *JRH* 42, no. 2 (2018): 145–80; Cf. also Paul Jenkins (ed.), *The Recovery of the West African Past: African Pastors and African History in the Nineteenth Century: C. C. Reindorf & Samuel Johnson* (Basel, Switzerland: Basler Afrika Bibliographien, 1998).

11. Sanneh, *Translating the Message*, 208.

While zeal to Christianize the natives may have motivated missionary translators, translations also provided a means to pacify the natives through what Sugirtharajah calls "Scriptural imperialism".[12] First, translation became a way of bifurcating the European "cultural Bible" that would remain in the hands of Europeans, from a "tribal Bible" for the native Africans. As Sheehan puts it, "Translations were tools for consolidating biblical authority and wresting it from opponents."[13] For if missionaries were to continue teaching the Bible to the natives in the European languages, it would eventually result in the assimilation of the native and bring the colonial project to a halt.[14] Second, translation, however, was also as much about distancing the colonizer from the colonized, by denying the colonized the colonizer's language and authority.

Thus, what looked on the surface like benevolence turned out to have also been a cloak of self-interest worn by mission organizations in their self-perceived notion as chosen conduits of God's authority and mission, as we say with Schweitzer's views.[15] Ideological struggles and competing concerns of race and Empire plagued translation projects, as they simultaneously championed translation and denigrated the African reality.[16] I am acutely aware of Lamin Sanneh's spirited defense of the missionary translation enterprise, in his vitally important *Translating the Message*, as a source of vernacular revitalization and social transformation of the African communities and cultures. However, this is a retrospective analysis with the benefit of hindsight that can see only these positive side effects of the European translation project without its exoneration.[17] European prejudices and the sense of cultural and linguistic superiority were evident in the reactions of European translators of the non-European vernacular. The reports make it clear that they presumed non-European languages were

12. Sugirtharajah, *The Bible and the Third World*, 56–7.

13. Sheehan, *The Enlightenment Bible*, xiii.

14. Memmi, *The Colonizer and the Colonized*, 72–3.

15. Buxton, *The African Slave Trade and Its Remedy*, 414. Sugirtharajah, *The Bible and the Third World*, 56.

16. M. W. Dube, "The Bible in the Bush: The First 'Literate' Batswana Bible Readers," in *Ethnicity, Race, Religion: Identities and Ideologies in Early Jewish and Christian Texts, and in Modern Biblical Interpretation*, ed. Katherine Hockey and David Horrell (London and New York: T&T Clark, 2018), 168–82, 181.

17. Sanneh, *Translating the Message*, 206. Cf. also idem, "Christian Missions and the Western Guilt Complex," *Christian Century* 104, no. 24 (1987): 331–4, 33: "Often the outcome of vernacular translation was that the missionary lost the position of being the expert. But the significance of translation went beyond that. Armed with a written vernacular Scripture, converts to Christianity invariably called into question the legitimacy of all schemes of foreign domination—cultural, political, and religious. Here was an acute paradox: the vernacular Scriptures and the wider cultural and linguistic enterprise on which translation rested provided the means and occasion for arousing a sense of national pride, yet it was the missionaries—foreign agents—who were the creators of that entire process."

inadequate to communicate God's truth.[18] Colored by their own racial, cultural, social, and religious prejudices, translators blamed the inadequacy of these receptor languages to convey the message of the Bible, rather than their own inability to comprehend the receptor languages.

In the evolutionary linguistic schema, colonizers considered oral cultures like those found in most of Africa south of the Sahara to be a reflection of the "primitiveness" of African cultures, thought to be devoid of historical value, civilization, complex religious thought, or philosophical comprehension.[19] The same racial attitudes exemplified by Schweitzer. Literacy became a measure of a society's advancement on the evolutionary scale and a necessary vehicle to attain civilization into which colonizers had to drag African oral communities. And so the translation of the vernacular Bible was not only the primary means to communicate the Bible's message to the African, but it was also, more significantly, an aid to achieving both conversion and civilization as desired by the colonial agenda. This was vernacular translation's ultimate goal.

This aim is captured well in the *British and Foreign Bible Society* (BFBS) Report (1908–09) on the colonial attitude of the western missionary in juxtaposing the need to translate the Bible for peoples, with the description of the missionary's role in military terms as a "conquest."

> Now if the Bible is to come home to all nations, kindreds and tribes, it must become naturalized in each country, it must learn to speak to each man in his own tongue in which he was born. The *missionary conquest of the world* involves an immense task in the mere translation of the Scriptures. . . . The declaration is made that the translations into the vernacular would mean . . . out of the mouths of *savages* come testimony to the wonderful Word of God."[20]

Additionally, while pronouncing that there is "no such thing as a perfect translation," the BFBS Report still makes the claim that "the finest translation in the world is the English Authorized Version of the Scriptures [which] *expresses the religious emotions of the English people* as they were inspired by the original."[21]

To excuse the inadequacy of the western translator, the BFBS Report declares that "[e]ven in a faulty translation, with many inadequate terms, the word of God is far more pure and holy than anything else in a heathen tribe."[22] Even

---

18. Sugirtharajah, *The Bible and the Third World*, 58: "In translating biblical truth into vernacular languages, the Report made clear the inadequacy of the local languages to convey the truth of God. The fact that the translator could not find verbal counterparts in indigenous languages was taken as proof that these languages were incapable of expressing the Christian message."

19. Buxton, *The African Slave Trade and Its Remedy*, 404ff.

20. *The Book above Every Book: A Popular Illustrated Report of the British and Foreign Bible Society, 1908–1909* (London: The Bible House, 1909), 18, 23. (emphasis added)

21. Ibid., 20. (emphasis added)

22. Ibid., 24. (emphasis added)

an incompetent translation is better than what they have—false religions. The statement disparages the receptor languages, including "anything else" that those communities embody. And so, while Bible translation into the receptor language is vital for conversion nothing in the receptor community—person, possession, thought—can sufficiently or adequately harbor the word of God. Such paradoxical statements betray the "real" purpose of vernacular Bible translations.

The effort then was not only to provide the translation of the Bible in vernacular but to "Christianize" the receptor languages themselves: "Not only the heathen, but the speech of the heathen, must be Christianized. Their language itself needs to be born again."[23] Translation of the Bible was simply a proxy for the imposition of European cultural norms in receptor communities through linguistic manipulation, manipulation of receptor cultures and languages, or even outright falsifications.[24] Even the methodology reflected this. Culturally, western missionaries, influenced by western individualism, presented the interpretation of the Bible as a private enterprise undertaken in solitude—a "minimalist hermeneutic," undermining the corporate cultural process of production and dissemination of religious knowledge within African communities.[25]

Through all of this, while the colonizer deliberately, and inadvertently, denigrated the agency of the African in the translation process, African readers found in the translations forms of resistance that allowed them to maintain some agency. For example, South African biblical scholar, Gerald West, has shown that the African translation agents were careful not to fully expose their communities to the European translators, revealing only what they wanted the missionaries and colonizers to see and thereby undermining the European translation project.[26] To give a sense of some of these interpretive encounters, I will now turn to specific examples of African vernacular Bible translations that exemplify the issues noted so far.

a. Translating *Daimonia* in Mt. 8:28-34; 15:22; 10:8

This first example reflects a possible deliberate European translator's linguistic manipulation. In her article "Consuming a Colonial Cultural Bomb," Musa Dube explains her shock and dismay at the discovery of the missionary translation of the biblical *daimonia* ("demons," "unclean spirits"), which equated *daimonia* and *badimo*—"ancestors" or "high ones" in the Setswana language of Bostwana.[27] Missionary translators transformed the otherwise sacred personalities of the precolonial Batswana people into evil spirits or devils in the translated Bible.

23. Ibid., 23.

24. Sugirtharajah, *The Bible and the Third World*, 63–5.

25. Ibid., 156–7.

26. G. West, *The Stolen Bible: From Tool of Imperialism to African Icon* (Leiden: Brill and Pietermaritzburg: Cluster, 2016), 120, 178–215.

27. M. W. Dube, "Consuming a Colonial Cultural Bomb: Translating *Badimo* into 'Demons' in the Setswana1 Bible (Matthew 8.28-34; 15.22; 10.8)," *JSNT* 73 (1999): 33–59.

As Mudimbe puts it, "[T]wo conflicting paradigms meet here and conflict with each other: a negative one equals Africans to an absolute evil—*furca, furax, infamis, iners, furiosa ruina* . . . ; and a positive one, which assigns itself the ambiguous role of translating the negative symbolized by the evil into the ineffable delight of God's children."[28] Turning to Mt. 8:28-34, the story of the two Gadarene men possessed by unclean spirits, Dube finds to her horror, in the Setswana translation, the demoniac possessed by the spirits of the ancestors, *badimo*, who were essentially the embodiment of evil in this interpretive translation.[29] Suddenly, to Dube, it was the African ancestors begging Jesus not to destroy them.

Dube is aghast that "Christian tradition hardly lost anything central to its faith in this translation, while the Setswana tradition lost its very center. The translation is, therefore, a structural device of alienating natives from their cultures."[30] For Dube, this text was transformed into a "text of terror."[31] The wholesale lumping together of the African religious traditions as devoid of emancipatory efficacy meant there was a willingness by European missionary translators to undermine linguistic structures and meanings of the Setswana receptor language.

Rejection of the African religious ontology was driven by the racially-based denigration of the African reality and religions. This resulted in a failure to comprehend Setswana linguistic sacred language and its religious lexicon in its true religious and cultural contexts. It meant a failure to grasp that there was a continuous, uninterrupted relationship between the unborn, the living, the dead, and the "living-dead."[32] This translation has uprooted, misconstrued, and effectively destroyed the religious fabric of the Setswana converts. The colonial translation had become for the Setswana, a "colonized Bible."[33] Beloved ancestors had become indelibly marked in the text as evil from that point on, for every Motswana who encountered this Setswana translation. Like a virus invading a body, this missionary translation had cavalierly introduced into the cultural, linguistic, religious, and social fabric of the Batswana, a violent extermination of the religio-cultural nexus of existence.[34]

b. Translating Hebrew *Navi* (Prophet) into Shona Language

From a slightly different angle of colonial linguistic imposition, Zimbabwean biblical scholar, Lovemore Togarasei, shows how missionary translations also

---

28. Mudimbe, *Tales of Faith*, 44.

29. Dube, "Consuming a Colonial Cultural Bomb," 40–1.

30. Ibid., 42.

31. Dube, "Boundaries and Bridges," 152.

32. J. S. Mbiti, *African Religions and Philosophy* (London: Heinemann, 1969), 25.

33. Dube, "Boundaries and Bridges," 152.

34. Musa forcefully responded to a translator who defended the colonialist *badimo* translation in, "What I have Written, I have Written," in *Interpreting the New Testament in Africa*, ed. M. Getui, T. S. Maluleke, J. Ukpong (Nairobi: Acton Publishers, 2001), 145–63. Shockingly (or maybe not!), the translator, Eric Hermanson, a white South African, essentially espoused the same misplaced colonialist conceit that Dube was critiquing in her argument.

made deliberate decisions to transliterate certain key vocabulary rather than translating them, seeking to shield the translated biblical text from invasions of native meanings.[35] The example that Togarasei references has to do with the vocabulary of "prophet" that was transliterated in the Shona Bible as the jumbled anglicized nonsense, "*muporofita*."[36] It is noteworthy that missionary misgivings regarding the Shona language resulted in impositions of alien vocabulary despite Shona having sufficient vocabulary to capture the essence of the word "prophet"; still, it is even more remarkable and ridiculous that the transliteration came from the English translation rather than the original Hebrew "*navi*."[37] The colonizers' English Bible had become the basis of the translation of the Shona Bible, imposing the colonizers' colonial rejection of the Shona cultural reality.

In tandem with Dube's and Togarasei's exposés, Sugirtharajah explains that

> The effort of missionaries to reach the natives in their own language might conjure up a compassionate and benevolent face of the colonial project. The flip side was the domestication of languages. Rather than harmlessly retrieving vanishing languages, missionaries aided by the colonial apparatus reconfigured the vernacular lexicon, molding the thinking of indigenous people to fit with [western] Christian thought patterns, and thus prescribing alien ways of conceptualizing language and displacing native religious and linguistic conventions.[38]

Gradually, after independence, in most African countries, trained national native speaking translators have taken over many Bible translation projects; this shift has given native speakers greater ownership of the translation project and positioned them with better understandings of receptor languages in making translation decisions. This practice is not without its challenges, one of which includes a very limited number of technically trained African biblical translators.[39] So, the advantage of familiarity with the local language has not completely insulated the African Bible

---

35. Evidence that this was not unique to Africa and that it was a widespread *modus operandi* of European missionaries everywhere is reflected in C. Trevelyan's writing. He was a missionary to India who reasoned that replacing the Indian alphabets, such as Sanskrit, with the Roman letters for Bible translation would be better for Christianization of Indians: "But the greatest advantage of all the use of these [Roman] letters is that it will cut up the existing [Indian] literature by the roots, and give rise to a new and purified literature, unconnected with the abominations of idolatry, and impregnated by the Spirit of Christ." (C. Trevelyan, *The 35th Report of the British and Foreign Bible Society*, 1939: 59)

36. Lovemore Togarasei, "The Prophet and Divine Manifestation: On the Translation of the Word 'Prophet' in the Shona Union Bible," *OTE* 30, no. 33 (2017): 821–34, 823.

37. Ibid., 825–6.

38. Sugirtharajah, *Postcolonial Criticism and Biblical Interpretation*, 157.

39. Emmanuel Obeng, "Use of Biblical Critical Methods in Rooting the Scripture in Africa," in *The Bible in African Christianity*, ed. Hannah Kinoti and John Waliggo (Nairobi: Acton, 1997), 21.

translator from the challenges of translation. As will see below, some of the challenges encountered have required more than just skillful linguistic maneuvering.

c. Translating Deut. 6:5 into Rendille (Kenya)

I happened to have been present when the inaugural presentation of the Kenyan, pastoralist community's, Rendille Bible took place at the Nairobi Pentecostal Church, Valley Road, in Kenya in 1990. To illustrate some of the challenges the interpreters faced, the lead interpreter shared a story about the struggle to translate the passage in Deut. 6:5—"You shall love the Lord your God with all your heart, and with all your soul, and with all your might" (NRSV)—into Rendille idiom.

The issue was not with the receptor vocabulary sufficiency, since the Rendille language had the necessary words for translation. The initial reading of the draft translation to the community elder elicited bewilderment. As it turned out, among the Rendille, there are different versions of "love," all derived from different parts of the human body, akin to the Hebrew language, but with quite different meanings. There is the "love of the stomach," "the love of the kidneys," the "love of the heart," and the "love of the intestines." They all have different values or levels of intensity, from the most pedestrian to the most revered form. In Deut. 6:5, the command is to love God with one's *heart*, which in the Hebrew context, is the greatest form of love, as it identifies the seat of human identity. As it turns out, for the Rendille, of the four forms of love, the "love of the heart" expresses the least amount of commitment. So, a literal and accurate translation of Hebrew had unintentionally rendered the command as "love God with the *least* amount of love." The exact opposite meaning the Hebrew text intended to convey. So, the translators had to make a challenging decision.

For the Rendille, the expression that captures the most intense form of love is the "love of the stomach." The translators then had to determine whether to stick with the literal text as it stood in the original Hebrew or translate the meaning into the local idiom, shifting around the receptor vocabulary. On the one hand, rendering the translation using the preferred Rendille "love of the stomach" would convey the accurate meaning, but would change the wording of the Hebrew text.

This conundrum typifies calculations all translators have to make every time a text is translated from one language to another. As in the movie title, something is usually "Lost in Translation."

Comparatively, an example I use while teaching Greek, is the paucity of the English word "love" compared to the rich expression of Greek vocabulary. The Greek language has various words that express multiple "types" of "love" (*agape*—communal love, Jn 3:16; *philios*—deep friendship, Mt. 6:5, Jn 21:15-17; *eros*—sexual love, implied in 1 Corinthians 7; and *storge*—familial love, Rom. 12:10), the inadequacy of the English language means it has only one word to translate all these different Greek words. This means that when the English translator translates the different forms of love simply as "love," the reader of the English Bible misses the nuances expressed in the Greek language. English must then employ adjectives to differentiate these forms of love.

Ultimately, for the Rendille Bible translators, in consultation with the elders, to ensure the least confusion in the meaning of Deut. 6:5 was to use the "love of the stomach." A footnote would subsequently explain the difference in the language of love between the Hebrew text and Rendille and would include the expression found in the original language.

In agreement with Dube and Togarasei, the Rendille Bible translators' stance and guiding principles contrast with those employed by the European translators, whose racialized denigration of local idioms meant that their translations only introduce colonizing readings and with insidious ideology into the receptor communities.

d. Translating Isa. 11:3 as Spirit or Smell?

In tandem with the introduction of colonizing foreign constructions, European translations also rejected possible cultural affinities in the receptor languages. R. S. Sugirtharajah provides an example of translation within the African context which was overlooked or explained away by western interpreters: olfaction as a rite of passage.[40] Using Isa. 11:3—"His delight shall be in the fear of the Lord. He shall not judge by what his eyes see or decide by what his ears hear" (NRSV)— as an example, Sugirtharajah begins by exploring the connection of the first two lines, finding the first line to seem out of context. The second line references sight, while the third line references audibility. One would expect, then, that the first line would indulge the third line's sense: "smell." However, English translations instead prefer to use "delight" which has nothing to do with the other two body senses.

A look at the Hebrew text underlying the English translations reveals that, indeed, the first line should be read in connection to smell. At stake is whether the root for the *hiphil* infinitive construct וַהֲרִיחוֹ (*wahărîḥōw*) is "Spirit" (*ruah*) or "smell"/"scent" (*re'ha*)—"He shall smell in the Lord."[41] The tendency of English translators is to either expunge the word ("and he will fear the Lord"), explain it away as a copyist error, or provide emendations.[42] Explaining why "smell" makes the most sense in Isa. 11:3, Sugirtharajah states:

> The importance of olfaction as a rite of passage and transition, in some African cultures, could also open up some of the difficult biblical passages which exegetes, raised in Enlightenment mode of thinking, try to expurgate or explain away . . . . Such a translation causes uneasiness among cultures which fail to see a potential link between odour and discriminatory powers. God discerns through the senses of smell and taste just as much as through the oral and the visual. In African traditional religions this is a common practice. . . . The Hebrew Bible is full of olfactory images, olfactory language, and olfactory metaphors

---

40. Sugirtharajah, *Postcolonial Criticism and Biblical Interpretation*, 167–8.

41. Arie Shifman, "'A Scent' of the Spirit: Exegesis of an Enigmatic Verse (Isa. 11:3)," *JBL* 131, no. 2 (2012): 241–9, 250.

42. Ibid., 150.

of knowledge. The current Western hermeneutical paradigm is heavily biased towards a visual mode of knowledge and equates seeing, especially seeing of the text, with knowing. African culture, like the Hebrew [culture], is free of this exclusive textualist and visualist paradigm and it is an advantageous position to appreciate the Isaian and similar passages.[43]

Similarly, Arie Shifman arrived at a similar conclusion regarding the olfactory translation of Isa. 11:3, though he seems quite unaware of Sugirtharajah's earlier study.[44] Evan Mwangi explains this phenomenon well in his discussion of creative African literature in translation, noting the guidance of the receptor community: "I have also argued that post-independence African-language translators seem more interested in communicating with the target audiences than in reproducing the original in a different language."[45] As Sugirtharajah puts it, since "the history of the battle for the Bible translation has demonstrated that truth questions are eventually settled not on the intrinsic authority of the text but by extra-biblical factors," both the world and language of the text, as much as that of the receptor culture and language, should be open for interrogation.[46]

4.3 Vernacular Bible and Vernacular Hermeneutics— Planting Seeds of Decolonization

Despite the racialized colonizing and corrupting effects of European Bible translations in Africa, unexpected and unintended positive outcomes would emerge. Instead of the anticipated infiltration of western Christian religion, African readers of the vernacular translation meant the biblical God's ability "to speak in our language." Reading the vernacular translation unmediated by missionary thinking created a sense of ownership of the biblical text in ways that infused African religious and cultural content creating distinct African readings.[47] Translation into the vernacular provided a whole new way of seeing things for the African reader by incorporating the African socio-religious outlook into the Bible, resulting in a "counter-reading," (a "vernacular hermeneutic," if you will) in the spirit of Edward Said's decolonization notion of counter-scholarship.[48]

Gambian, and Yale University historian, Lamin Sanneh, while maintaining that European missions must be understood as a continuation of the early church mission, argues that they were nonetheless dogged by "the contradiction between

---

43. Sugirtharajah, *Postcolonial Criticism and Biblical Interpretation*, 167–8.

44. Shifman, "'A Scent' of the Spirit," 150–68.

45. E. Maina Mwangi, *Translation in African Contexts: Postcolonial Texts, Queer Sexuality, and Cosmopolitan Fluency* (Kent: The Kent State University Press, 2017), 224.

46. Sugirtharajah, *Postcolonial Criticism and Biblical Interpretation*, 164.

47. Sugirtharajah, *The Bible and the Third World*, 167.

48. Said, *Culture and Imperialism*, 219.

translation and cultural diffusion."[49] Unlike, say, the *Qu'ran*, according to Sanneh, "Christianity is remarkable for the relative ease with which it enters living cultures. In becoming translatable it renders itself compatible with all cultures. It may be welcomed or rejected in its western garb, but it is not itself uncongenial in other garbs."[50] This, translatability of Christianity, is what undermined the colonizing process since, as Sanneh argues, it cannot be simply the preserve of one community. Vernacular hermeneutics were not part of European missionaries' calculus with the translation project. Their haughty assumption that the vernacular translations would simply reproduce the colonial religion in the vernacular and nothing more, had failed.

Earlier in their history, Europeans themselves had embraced the "cultural Bible," with European cultures becoming the lens through which to read the Bible.[51] It is this hypocrisy, that the vernacular hermeneutics emerging in the postcolonial period aimed to critique. Consciously decentering and legitimizing "culture" as a component of the vernacular, and as a vital part of biblical hermeneutics, vernacular hermeneutics undermined the Europeans' claim to superior agency.[52] "Culture" was not the preserve of the European society to be imposed on others.

Conclusion: Vernacular Hermeneutics

So, while Bible translation and academic biblical scholarship, both emerged around the same time within the colonial project, and were beneficiaries of the colonial enterprise, they came to represent two essentially disconnected ventures. While the latter coalesced around European (and American) universities—increasingly becoming an esoteric venture full of methodological, linguistic, and theological theories—the former increasingly became the preserve of the missionaries and natives.[53] And, although the origins of the modern vernacular Bible hearken back to the Protestant Reformation in the sixteenth century with German and English vernacular translations being part of the academic revolution in Europe, a wedge developed between what was classified as biblical scholarship and the vernacular

---

49. Sanneh, *Translating the Message*, 90.

50. Ibid., 50.

51. Sheehan, *The Enlightenment Bible*, 254–5: "And so the English idea of culture, like the German, was never merely an anthropological descriptor. It also had a strong normative dimension—it was fundamentally better to have culture than mere technology and better to have Christian culture than any other—which was what made it so attractive to a generation worried about moral decline. Culture represented that 'heritage of an accumulated ineluctable racial memory' that undergirded the essential qualities of Western civilization."

52. Sugirtharajah, *The Bible and the Third World*, 182, 190–1.

53. Sheehan, *The Enlightenment Bible*, 49. Referencing Bentley's *Greek New Testament*, Sheehan explains that "scholarship of the New Testament was, in other words, to stay rigorously distinct from the public Bible as consumed in more ordinary churches and households."

Bible by the nineteenth century.[54] Thus, Biblical translation, like that into African vernaculars, was never quite part of the academic enterprise; instead, it served only to provide the "uneducated masses," access to the text.[55]

Unfortunately, his dichotomy whose origins also were race-driven, has persisted throughout biblical scholarship. For example, western biblical scholars consistently classify non-western hermeneutical endeavors (often based on vernacular Bibles) as "*un*scholarly" or outside the realm of *real* Biblical Studies. It is partly in response to this denigration of the vernacular Bible and hermeneutics that has prompted non-western biblical scholarship to rigorously challenge the assumed authority and legitimacy of western biblical scholarship. A sentiment shared by Edward Said when he explained how, "Such a perception reinforces the orientalist notion of the 'other' being emotional and sentimental and does a grave injustice to the analytic and logical traditions developed [in the receptor communities]."[56]

That the discipline of Biblical Studies stubbornly remains the domain of white Euro-American male scholars, even as there is a sea change in the makeup of the Global Christian community, attests to this persistent racialized colonial classifications of preference that undergird. the discipline. According to Sugirtharajah, "There are two great dangers within the field [of Biblical Studies]. One is an uncritical acceptance of the principle tenets of the discipline [with their racist underpinning], and the other is its failure to relate it to the society in which its work is done."[57]

That vernacular hermeneutics finds itself struggling against the core of western Biblical Studies discipline, is because, in the words of Sugirtharajah,

> Vernacular hermeneutics is not a discrete movement, but part of the ongoing intellectual and critical movement of our time. It is postmodern in its renunciation of the Enlightenment meta-narratives and its elevation of the local as a site of creativity, and it is postcolonial in its battle against the invasion of foreign and universalist modes of interpretation.[58]

Vernacular hermeneutics, thus, forces open a postcolonial space where encounters with ideas unmitigated by the imperial hermeneutical enterprise can germinate and bloom. Those practicing vernacular hermeneutics, therefore, seek the freedom to chart a course devoid of the imperial agenda while remaining acutely self-conscious about the pitfalls of colonialist hubris. Sugirtharajah further explains that "If vernacularism is held to mean the hermeneutical cleansing of imported elements extraneous to one's culture, then surely it is bound to be a disaster. But

---

54. Sheehan, *The Enlightenment Bible*, 53.

55. Ibid., 50.

56. Sugirtharajah, *Postcolonial Reconfigurations*, 3: ". . . 'spiritual,' 'practical,' and non-rational."

57. Sugirtharajah, *Postcolonial Criticism and Biblical Interpretation*, 26.

58. Sugirtharajah, *The Bible and the Third World*, 177–8.

on the other hand, if it means critical freedom to resist cultural imperialism and challenge ideologies, then it will continue to be an important hermeneutical category."[59]

A freeing of the discipline from its western constraints and framing is the objective of vernacular hermeneutics! In this new space, fluency of translation does not mean capitulation to hegemonizing structures but incorporating resistance to imperializing tendencies that would seek to limit the freedom of expression in Biblical Studies.[60] This, however, is not simply a quest to replace one domineering approach with another. No biblical interpretation is without shortcomings for there is "[n]othing . . . axiomatically admirable because it is indigenous and local . . . . Vernacularism can easily degenerate into chauvinism, jingoism, or narrow-minded communalism."[61] Similarly, "using an African language as the language of composition or translation does not, in itself, liberate one from colonialism; neither does using English make one cosmopolitan. What is important is the way a particular language is used in writing and translation"[62]—either to liberate or to colonize.

Resistance must include an eye toward something new, something wholesome. In this regard, the "prime concern for the interpreter must be to facilitate communal harmony rather than to resuscitate a projected, invented or imagined hypothetical identity or a past entombed in a bygone age."[63] This does not mean simply a return to the pre-missionary world, as though it were an unadulterated space.[64] Rather, it should be a careful articulation of an indigenous-inspired reading of the biblical text with the intent to fully actualize the biblical message to the local reality of the reader, while at the same time being conscious of its own shortcomings.[65]

4.4 *African Presence in the Bible: Whitewashing of a Text and a People*

The vernacular translation project in the colonies had a parallel in the translation of the European Bible with its racialized effacing of peoples of African descent

59. Ibid., 198–9.

60. Mwangi, *Translation in African Contexts*, 230.

61. Sugirtharajah, *The Bible and the Third World*, 195.

62. Mwangi, *Translation in African Contexts*, 229.

63. Sugirtharajah, *The Bible and the Third World*, 200.

64. Ibid., 202: "It is also tempting to freeze part of the indigene's life as if it represented the whole, and confine him or her to the local. Such an indigene may be no more than a creature of the hermeneutical imagination."

65. Musimbi Kanyoro, "Interpreting Old Testament Polygamy Through African Eyes," in *Will to Arise*, ed. Oduyoye and Kanyoro, 99: "The dilemma of Bible translations and interpretation hinges on whether to mold a text to conform to [the recipient's] cultural value system, or whether to translate a passage literally at the expense of not being understood or creating confusion."

from their translations. As we have noted, language is vital as a tool for either colonization or liberation. Language not only communicates ideas and thoughts, but it also reflects aspects of sociocultural and religious presuppositions and biases, power dynamics between the controller and the controlled, and unspoken aspects of dominance and subordination, among other elements. When it comes to colonial discourse, language plays a vital role in imposing the colonizer's ideas and perspectives on the colonized. And when it came to the Bible, translations were not neutral or impervious to the translators' worldviews, positive or negative.[66]

Nigerian scholar David T. Adamo interrogates issues of translation regarding the "erasure of the African" from the European Bible. Studying the naming of peoples and geographical locations in the European Bible translations produced during the Enlightenment, especially the KJV, Adamo exposes how they deliberately obscured African identities in the Bible. Adamo raises pertinent questions about European Bible translations that exemplify ideological and racial parallels to the vernacular translations projects, when it comes to the identity of the Africans in the Bible: How accurate are these translations when it comes to identifying Africa and Africans in the Bible? Why are Africans often, instead, given an Eastern or Middle Eastern identity? Is Egypt in Africa or the Middle East? What of Ethiopia and Sudan?[67] Adamo argues that these European translation choices reflect the same racial biases evident in European Enlightenment thinking analyzed in the last chapter.

In two volumes, *Africa and Africans in the Old Testament* and *Africa and Africans in the New Testament*, and in a third *Explorations in African Biblical Studies* defending the first two, Adamo maintains that modern western Europe systematically sought to "de-Africanize" the Bible by inserting non-African names in place of references that readers would otherwise rightly understand as African.[68] For Adamo, the translation of the Bible in the West throughout the Enlightenment period became a means of expunging African identity from the biblical text by Eurocentric translators in two ways: First, by choosing to transliterate African related names rather than translating them, obscuring any connections to the peoples of the continent. In this way, even Egypt became a distinct entity from the rest of Africa, with Egyptian power, civilization, and influence divorced from any African contributions. Second, by denying or minimizing Africa's contributions in the biblical stories and writings.

---

66. Sanneh, *Translating the Message*, 229.

67. Western biblical scholarship challenging predominant positions gets limited attention, for example, Edith Sanders's "The Hamitic Hypothesis; Its Origin and Functions in Time Perspective," *JAH* 10, no. 4 (1969): 521–32.

68. David T. Adamo, *Africa and Africans in the Old Testament* (San Francisco: International Scholars Publications, 1998); idem, *Africa and Africans in the New Testament* (Washington: University Press of America, 2006); idem, *Explorations in African Biblical Studies* (Eugene: Wipf and Stock, 2001).

Adamo understands his task as the need to "*re*-Africanize" the text, or more accurately, to provide a corrective to the western obfuscation of the African presence and contributions in the Bible: "I have tried not only to argue for the presence of Africans in the Old Testament but to highlight their substantial contribution to the culture, religion, civilization, economic, military and political life of ancient Israel."[69] By stripping the biblical text of African presence and contributions, the western translations essentially leave the false impression that there were no African connections in the Bible.

Adamo is aware that the name "Africa" with its ancient Roman provincial origins only finds its full continental expression in European expansionism, led by the Portuguese explorations and raced-based enslavement of Africans, between the fourteenth and seventeenth centuries. And so, this continental version comes into the Enlightenment and the European colonial project as a construct laden with racial prejudices. By the time European nations gathered in Berlin, in 1884, to begin apportioning themselves chunks of the African continent, the name "Africa" had been firmly entrenched in European cartography.

In biblical times, conversely, there existed different references to peoples originating from the African continent, south of Egypt. Adamo lists six words (from biblical and non-biblical sources) that Bible readers should understand and interpret as relating to or representing Africa and Africans. These include four Egyptian names, *Wawat, Kush (Cush), Punt, Nehesi,* and three names of Greek origin, *Magan, Meluhha,* and *Ethiopia.*[70] Kush, for example, translated as "Ethiopia" in the King James Bible, does not refer to the modern country of Ethiopia. Instead, it comes from the Greek word *Aethiopia,* meaning "dark skin or burnt face," and may have racialized *Kush,* though not in the modern hierarchical racial construct.[71] So *Aethiopia* functioned in at least two distinct ways: as a reference to a specific region called "Ethiopia," but also as a reference to all darker-hued peoples from Africa, south of Egypt.

In the Hebrew Bible, therefore, *Kush* implies a much broader identity than the modern concept of Ethiopia permits. In Isa. 18:1-6 and Zeph. 3:10, for example, the geographical reference implies a wide scope of land beyond Egypt, while its use in Jer. 13:23 implies skin color. In Ps. 68:31, however, Egypt and *Kush* are distinct but related. *Kush* has both a people identity (that may also be a political one) and a geographical identity as an unspecified location beyond Egypt. Modern translations, such as the *New International Version,* choose to revert to the transliteration of *Cush,* but this too obscures the embedded African identity, as

---

69. Adamo, *Africa and Africans in the Old Testament,* 5.

70. Ibid., 6.

71. In the hands of Greek writers like Claudius Ptolemy (90–168 CE), for example, in his *Terabiblos (Quadrapartite): Being Four Books of the Influence of the Stars,* Ethiopians are contrasted to other peoples of the world by their physical features, and the term is generalized to include all dark-skinned people.

there is no modern place or people called Cush.[72] To a person reading the English text, nothing gives the impression that Cush has anything to do with the modern iteration of Africa, even though it should.

For Adamo, European translators deliberately made these decisions based on their racist prejudices, essentially refusing to acknowledge the African identity embedded in *Kush*. Adamo argues that if translators can render *Mitzrayim* as "Egypt" in English translations, "There is no reason why Cush cannot be translated into African/Africans."[73] Instead, European translators erased the otherwise clearly present African identity from the Bible by alternatively identifying *Kush* with Mesopotamia, Arabia, or India.[74] Consequently, the vernacular Bible (often based on the European Bible) had remained a foreign book, with no African presence in it, by the time the colonizers reintroduced it to the African continent south of the Sahara, as part of the colonial project. European translators had excised what could have served as a vital identity link for African converts with the Bible.

On occasion, however, Adamo overplays his hand, not only making unfounded proclamations about the superiority of African intelligence but also overgeneralizing about the ubiquity of the use of "Africa" to translate every reference to *Kush* in the Bible.[75] Nevertheless, his work serves as an important corrective and response to the colonizing Bible exposing the racist and prejudiced underpinnings in western translations. Adamo's resistance to the racist appropriation of the biblical translation stands in direct opposition and in response to such racist interpretations as the misdirected "Curse of Ham" that appealed to the reference of Cush in Genesis 9-10, to conclude that Europeans (sons of Japheth) rightfully enslaved people of African descent (sons of Ham) as a result of the Noahic Curse.

What of the connection of Cush, Put, and Canaan in Genesis 10? Scholars often connect the place of Egypt as a historical referent to people of African descent to Ethiopia in the Hebrew Bible (cf. Ezek. 30:4; Isa. 20:3-5, 43:3, 45:14; Ps. 68:31; Nah. 3:9). Cush's son Nimrod established the Assyrian and Babylonians, yet elsewhere, Cush is a term that from time to time seems to indicate the people of African descent. At other times, however, Cush may refer to peoples or places that are not African (e.g., Isa. 37:9, Ezek. 38:5). On the other hand, Put and Canaan are hardly ever associated with the African peoples or lands. So, if this "table of nations" in Genesis 10 is to indicate the origins of humanity after the Noahic flood, the names may be less of geographical reference points and more of an attempt at a peoplehood construction that assigns them identity based on their perceived origins.

This interpretation was not accidental. As Ebussi Boulaga has pointed out, the colonial project, driven by Enlightenment philosophy, sought to distinguish between the ancient historical model, which simply assumed classical Greek

---

72. Adamo, *Africa and Africans in the Old Testament*, 35–7.

73. Adamo, *Explorations in African Biblical Studies*, 81.

74. Ibid., 80. Note, for example, that Est. 1:1 and 8:9 clearly delineate between India and Cush, as the polar opposites of the reaches of the Persian Empire: "from India to Kush."

75. Cf. Adamo, *Explorations in African Biblical Studies*, 79.

civilization's deep indebtedness to both African (Egyptian and Ethiopian) and Semitic (Hebraic and Phoenician) civilizations, and the "Aryan model," which developed in the wake of slavery and colonialism.[76] The Aryan model had to perform ingenious hermeneutical acrobatics to "purify" classical Greece of all African and Asian "contaminants."[77]

If the Exodus story, for example, presents Egypt in a negative light as the enslavers of God's elect people, does that give Africa a negative image? Not necessarily! Exodus tells the story from the perspective of Israel and not Egypt, yet there is the tacit acknowledgment of Egypt as an ANE superpower. In the biblical story, the aim is to show the power of the Israelite God over that of the otherwise immensely powerful entity that was the Pharaonic empire, over its gods, and especially over the divine–human Pharaoh. But then in complicating the story, Exodus portrays the Israelite hero, Moses, whose name is of Egyptian provenance, as a beneficiary of the Egyptian largesse, having grown up in Pharaoh's court as Pharaoh's son. Egyptian education, military training, and understanding of leadership were all benefits that Moses would utilize in leading Israelites out of Egypt.

Egyptian Hebrew Bible scholar, Safwat Marzouk, has recently addressed this aspect of Egypt's depiction in the Bible, focusing on Hagar and Ishmael. For Marzouk, the suffering of Hagar, Sarah's Egyptian maidservant, "deconstructs the tendency to essentialize the portrayal of Egypt and the Egyptians as the oppressors."[78] Marzouk eschews the simple binaries of oppressor/oppressed, dominant/dominated, by, instead, pointing to the complex relations that Hagar and Ishmael have with Abraham and Sarah as a microcosm of the complex portrayal of Egypt and its relations in the Hebrew Bible. As such, the hybrid identity of Ishmael offers a more promising avenue to grapple with the multivalent portrayal of Egypt in the Bible.

Unfortunately, in the received tradition, the negative portrayal is so overwhelming that it conceals any existing ambivalence in the text. According to Marzouk, "The negative portrayal in Hebrew scriptures as the house of slavery (Exod. 20:2; Deut. 8:14), embodying it as a monster of chaos in Ezekiel 29 and 32 or representing it as a threat to the Israelite identity as in Jeremiah 40-42, overshadows the blessing of Egypt (Isa. 19:25) and Egypt's role as a place of refuge for the ancestors (Gen. 12:37-50) and Jeroboam (1 Kings 11)."[79] The general

---

76. Boulaga's reliance on the controversial and intriguing work by Martin Bernal, *Black Athena* (Rutgers University Press, 1987), is evident here.

77. Boulaga, *Christianity Without Fetishes*, 45.

78. Safwat Marzouk, "Interrogating Identity: A Christian Egyptian Reading of the Hagar-Ishmael Traditions," in *Colonialism and the Bible: Contemporary Reflections from the Global South*, ed. T. Benny Liew and F. Segovia (Lanham: Lexington, 2018), 3–30, 3.

79. Ibid., 5. The African American community faces a similar dilemma with the embrace of the Exodus motif as the hermeneutical matrix for interpreting their hope of redemption from slavery with the identification of white America with Egypt. This reading clashed with their other favorite Hebrew Bible text (Isa. 63:1), the desire to look to Africa, as a metonymy

tendency of Egyptian Christians is to either ignore the troubling texts (subsume it to history and not the religious aspect) or allegorize the negative aspects (e.g., Paul in Gal 4).[80] Marzouk suggests a third optic—a hybrid identity that can uphold the conflicting perspectives. Juxtaposed, Sarah and Abraham were as much oppressors and enslavers of Egyptians Hagar and Ishmael, as Egypt was of Israelites.[81] In this ambivalence, Israel and Egypt are both oppressors and oppressed.

Put in this perspective, Adamo's, Boulaga's, and Marzouk's works provide a significant point of departure for the text for the African reader, exposing and undermining European racialized translations and transmissions of the Bible that deliberately obscured, ignored, or changed biblical content. Recognition that Abraham's concubine Hagar and Moses's wife Zipporah may have been of African descent (Gen. 16, 41:45; Num. 12:1) or that the prophet Zephaniah (Zeph. 1:1) was of African descent, may have allowed the African reader to identify and embrace the Bible as an "African" book, rather than a "white man's" book.[82] For example, the distinct connection of the Ethiopian church, both in history and identity, comes from the textual links like that of the Ethiopian Eunuch, the first African baptized into Christianity (Acts 8:26-39).[83] Thus, to the Ethiopian Christians and Jews, the Bible is not a foreign history or identity; it is *their* story, and they have claimed it as such, for the last two thousand years.

in Ethiopia in Ps. 68:31(KJV): "Princes shall come out of Egypt; Ethiopia shall soon stretch out her hands unto God." Prioritizing the Ethiopia part as an oracle for African American return to Africa, the Egyptian reference was completely ignored. Cf. A. D. Callahan, *The Talking Book: African Americans and the Bible* (New Haven: Yale University Press, 2006), 138–84.

80. Marzouk, "Interrogating Identity," 6.

81. Ibid., 13.

82. Dora Mbuwayesango, "Childlessness and Woman-to-Woman Relationships in Genesis and in African Patriarchal Society: Sarah and Hagar from a Zimbabwean Woman's Perspective (Gen. 16:1-16; 21:8-21)," *Semeia* (1997): 27–36. Mbuwayesango shows that reading Hagar's status as "concubine" instead of "wife" (KJV) is a misnomer that originated with the European translator who failed to understand a culture where polygamy was functional, and it served to denigrate Hagar's status. Comparing the story to that of Ndebele women in Southern Africa, Dora highlights this inaccuracy in the translation.

83. I am aware of the complexity of the identity of the Eunuch in Acts 8 (Cf. A. Mbuvi, "Revisiting Translation and Interpretation Issues in the Story of the African Royal Official ["Ethiopian Eunuch"] in Acts 8:26-40: The Hebrew Bible (LXX) Background," *OTE* 34, no. 2 (2021): 474–84.), but it does not change my point. See also, Edwin Yamauchi, *The Bible and Africa* (Grand Rapids: Baker Academic, 2006), especially ch. 6: "Why the Ethiopian Eunuch was not from Ethiopia." In fact, going by Yamauchi's argument, the Eunuch would have been from the ancient kingdom of Meroe that occupied what is part of modern Sudan.

Chapter 5

THE BIBLE AND AFRICAN REALITY

Africans are notoriously religious . . . Religion permeates into all the departments of life so fully.

— John S. Mbiti[1]

5.1 Concept of God in African Christianity

In the wake of the European racially inspired evisceration of the African religious reality as a viable medium through which to communicate the Bible, there arose postcolonial African scholarly determined to prove otherwise. I will refer to it here as "rehabilitation hermeneutics." Two writings that did a masterful job of rehabilitating the notion of God in the African reality which European missionaries had otherwise tarnished were Kenyan biblical scholar John S. Mbiti's *Concepts of God in Africa* and Nigerian theologian, Bolaji Idowu's *Olodumare: God in Yoruba Belief*.[2] In the African religious reality, no distinction exists between the sacred and profane, between the spiritual and the physical—everything has a religious provenance. In perhaps his most famous work on African religion Mbiti's opening sentence, quoted above, succinctly captures this sentiment. While Mbiti's writing focused on multiple communities in Africa, Idowu's looked only at the Yoruba community in West Africa. In both their writings, research led them to a unified construct of a monotheistic deity that had a central, if somewhat removed (*deus absconditus*), place in African religious structure. Analysis of the names of God in African communities led both to conclude that the God whom Africans worshiped was essentially the same creator and almighty God revealed in the Bible. This was, of course, anathema to the European missionarys' conceptualizations. But both Mbiti and Idowu's proffered evidence of continuity, additional cultural affinities between the African world and the world of the Bible, especially the Hebrew Bible, and brought to light aspects that enabled the juxtaposition of the African religious reality with that of the Hebrew Bible. Where missionaries had seen no God (reference to Africans as "heathens"), the African scholars revealed a fairly unified concept of

1. Mbiti, *African Religions and Philosophy*, 1.
2. John S. Mbiti, *The Concepts of God in Africa* (London: S. P. C. K., 1970); Bolaji Idowu, *Olodumare: God in Yoruba Belief* (London: Longmans, 1962).

One supreme being; where missionaries saw only demons, these African scholars revealed a complexity religious reality of ancestors, the living-dead, spirits, and so on, all beholden to the One supreme being; where missionaries saw idols, these African scholars presented divinities serving the One supreme being. The African religious reality thus constructed, ultimately was not incompatible with the Bible.[3]

The initial arrival of the European in Africa is encapsulated in an image of white people armed with the Bible, the gun, and a sense of mission, as reflected in the classic African novel discussed later, *Things Fall Apart*. Such Europeans' relentless focus on the Christian mission meant an essential eradication of African religious reality, so that the center could not hold. Notwithstanding the onslaught, the matter could not be that simple, as once again the colonial missionary project would experience unexpected encounters that produced unintended results. The attempt to erase the African religious reality because of its supposed incongruity with the biblical message would prove difficult to enforce.[4] African converts, just as in the translation project, would prove to be the initial stumbling block. They were first to notice the cultural–religious connections of some biblical elements as explained or translated to them by the European missionaries. The missionary could not police the African ideological–cultural perspective from which converts would read the Bible, especially in the vernacular translation. Their familiarity with the local religio-cultural "terrain" granted the colonized converts unexpected avenues of resistance. No colonial effort at suppressing the African religious reality could stop it from informing these early African readers of the Bible and shaping their interaction with the biblical text.

For example, the missionaries' apocalyptic eschatology—envisioning the mission primarily as the conversion of the African in order to "hasten the end the days" (1 Thess. 4:16)—instead resonated with the African religious reality concept of the "living-dead," in the reference to Jesus bring with him the dead relatives. And, instead of African converts uncritically embracing this missionary apocalypticism into submission, it motivated many to break with the European missionaries to establish their own indigenous churches. Not only were their religious movements independent, they were decidedly anti-imperialist and anti-colonialist.[5]

The colonialist mentality had been that anything the western missionary could not reasonably fit into western Christianity had effectively to be demythologized or excised. This way, the biblical text was adjudged as having no room for the "mystical" in the African reality. Classifying the African religio-cultural reality as

3. Kwesi Dickson, *Uncompleted Mission: Christianity and Exclusivism* (Nairobi: Acton, 2000), 149–50.

4. Paolo Freire, *Pedagogy of the Oppressed* (New York: Continuum, 1988), 60–1. As Freire puts it, in the relationship between the oppressor and the oppressed, "The interest of the oppressors lie in the 'changing consciousness of the oppressed, not in the situation which oppresses them' . . . [t]he truth is, however, that the oppressed are not 'marginals' . . . they have always been 'inside.'"

5. David Barrett, *Schism and Renewals: Analysis of Six Thousand Contemporary Religious Movements* (Nairobi: Oxford University Press, 1968), 83–91.

evil was not simply a result of racially motivated classifications on the part of the European missionary, it was a decided epistemological construction of the African religious reality as *contra* Christianity as a whole and devoid of any redeeming possibilities. No effort, for example, was made to distinguish between herbalist (medical practitioner) from, say a shaman (spiritual healer), or spirits of ancestors (venerated) and malevolent spirits (feared). All were lumped together as evil.[6] But African resistance could not be suppressed.

5.2 Outline of African Religious Reality

Ultimately, then, with independence from Europe, African scholars were quick to (re)turn to the African cultural and religious reality to construct an African expression of Christianity devoid of western colonial encumbrances and which took seriously its African religio-cultural setting. It is within this epistemological reassessment and reconstitution process that Nigerian New Testament scholar, Justin Ukpong delineates elements of what would emerge as central guiding tenets for African biblical interpretation.[7] With my added commentary, the list is as follows.

1. Interpretation constructed within an African Cosmic view that envisions a unified cosmos with no distinctions between the physical and the spiritual. Paralleling the three-tier biblical worldview, perceptions of the physical and the spiritual worlds as co-existent realities, allows for a seamless connection between them in a porous divide that evidences constant interaction between the spiritual and physical worlds.[8]
2. Belief in the Divine origin of the universe. Again, finding parallels and connections in the Bible's creation myth, African communities value find no contradiction in their creation myths that attribute the origins of the universe to a creator God.
3. Significance of "communality" in defining both individuals and society. This is not simply a recognition of the core value of community in African identity formation, but, in distinct contrast to the prevalent individualism that governs the western societal outlook. A context where personal worth and value are inextricably tied to the welfare of the community.
4. Emphasis on the "concrete" rather than "theoretical." I am not sure I agree with Ukpong on this one since I do believe that Africans have a strong interest in theory, especially in genres like proverbs and poetry. I understand that, for Ukpong, the need is to distinguish between African interpretations that arrive at concrete application or praxis versus western interpretations

---

6. It is true the distinctions were not that clear since the herbalist could also be playing the role of the shamans, while ancestral spirits could also be malevolent.

7. Justin S. Ukpong, "Rereading the Bible with African Eyes: Inculturation and Hermeneutics," *JTSA* 91 (1995), 3–14.

8. Similarly, Dickson, *Uncompleted Mission*, 142: "The African does not separate religion and life."

that tend to value interpretation "for interpretation's sake" is the point, but I do not think he states his case as clearly.

5. Recognition of the supernatural as a "given" in African cosmology, much in the same way the biblical narratives do. This point stands in contrast to the western "scientific approach" that has essentially rejected the supernatural or "demythologized" it, providing instead a "rational explanation" for things like miracles or spirits in the biblical text.

6. Allowing a place for rituals, such as initiations and sacrificial ceremonies within its hermeneutic, especially given the presence of the same in the Bible, provides cultural and religious connection points that mutually inform and critique one another.

7. Paying attention to the important spiritual role of ancestors (both ancient and the recent "living-dead") in the life of the African communities, gives new meaning to such passages as Hebrews 12:1, with its reference to the heavenly "cloud of witnesses."

A reading of the Bible that takes these presuppositions seriously would result in interpretations that look quite distinct from those produced in the West. Especially in the context where, as read-response hermeneutics has enlightened us, the interpreters' background is vital in creation of the interpretive meaning of a text like the Bible. Taking the context of the reader seriously does not mean ignoring historical questions, however, but it does mean prioritizing the implication of interpretations for the interpreting community. Taking seriously questions that the African reality poses to the biblical text allows for the possibility of constructing genuinely African biblical interpretations that contribute to the richness of biblical scholarship. Therefore, Ghanaian Kwesi Dickson's warning is apropos at this juncture:

> Any biblical interpretation which fails to endorse a person's or a people's inherent dignity hardly deserves to be taken seriously. In this regard one might mention discrimination (racial, on grounds of religion, color, and so forth), the denial of one's cultural identity and worth, educational and other policies which cause alienation, all forms of exploitation, and starvation.[9]

For Dickson, not only are such interpretations "not Christian," but they are also in direct violation of God's creative will that includes diversity (Heb. 1:1-2).[10] Having outlined the principles of African biblical interpretation, it seems useful to provide an example that highlights some of these key elements.

An Interpretive Sample: 1 Cor. 11:27-34: The Lord's Supper as an African Communal Meal

In this example, Nigerian biblical scholar Ayodeji Adewuya provocatively argues that western cultural individualism, which closely aligns with the very

---

9. Dickson, *Uncompleted Mission*, 148–9.
10. Ibid., 149.

individualistic aspects challenged by Paul in his letter to the Corinthians, as ill-equipped to comprehend Paul's instructions on the Last Supper.[11] For Adewuya, the entire letter of 1 Corinthians militates against the individualism that results in the abuse of the Lord's Supper in its Corinthian observance.[12] The Corinthians had allowed cultural sensibilities and social stratifications to continue dominating their Christian practices. Shifting the conversation from the western tendency to analyze 1 Corinthians 11 "theologically or ethically," Adewuya chooses to read the passage in tandem with African communal meals, in order to bring out what he believes to be a reading more attuned to Paul's focus—"communal well-being": "The African communitarian sense, when expressed through the Lord's Supper, may afford the churches of Christ a new way of working toward unity, without which the church's voice is nothing but a discordant noise to the rest of the world."[13]

While initially utilizing the historical–grammatical approach of interpretation, Adewuya illustrates the significance of taking seriously a reader's cultural perspective when interpreting a text. But utilizing African communality model, Adewuya argues that "[e]ven in one's individuality, one is never truly separated from his or her fundamental communal connection. Therefore, to be human is possible only when one is in community."[14] Communal goals supersede individual interests and goals—hence the African adage "I am because we are." With communal meals at the epicenter of African communal life, individual eating is anathema—it only draws suspicions negative assessment.

Secondly, since African meals have attached to them sacral meanings, and they often serve as seals of covenantal agreements. This function makes great sense of Paul's understanding of the Lord's Supper as a sacred meal that ought to establish a sacred bond among the participants. As vital contexts for reconciling feuds, African meals play a vital role in resolving conflict. When two warring parties agree to a meal, there is, in essence, a nod toward peace, which would make Paul's appeal for peace that much more meaningful. Whatever communal differences may exist (e.g., 1 Corinthians 5 and 6), Paul expects the Lord's Supper to be a meal that dissolves, rather than perpetuates, community divisions. Similarly, the sacredness of the Lord's Supper and the rituals of drinking Jesus's blood (wine) and partaking of his body (bread) are properly expressed only if the participants are in communal harmony. Similarly, present in African meals is the communion of the departed, recognized via libations and food offerings, exemplifying the mystical nature of African meals. In such a context, what Paul intones, of the Lord's Supper being more than a meal (1 Cor. 11:20-22), but also an invocation of the presence of the risen Lord, gains a whole new meaning.

11. J. Ayodeji Adewuya, "Revisiting 1 Corinthians 11.27–34: Paul's Discussion of the Lord's Supper and African Meals," *JSNT* 30, no. 1 (2007): 95–112.

12. Ibid., 97.

13. Ibid., 109.

14. Ibid., 103.

Chapter 6

EMERGING AFRICAN POSTCOLONIAL BIBLICAL CRITICISM

Whether I am a Christian or not is none of your business. . . . The Bible is not the property of one nation or of one group of people, it can be quoted by anyone, even you.

— Jomo Kenyatta[1]

One way for the Bible to gain its respectability in a post-missionary and postcolonial context is to shed its Western protection and its imperialistic intentions.

— R. S. Sugirtharajah[2]

6.1 Introduction

As we have seen so far, in spite of what the western missionaries thought, Africans were never really passive receptacles of the Bible but engaged active participants eventually constructing counter-narratives that problematized the assumptions and presuppositions of Eurocentric readings of the Bible being imposed on them.[3] European emphasis on the Bible as a sacred text led to its objectification by the Africans, resulting in the appropriation of the Bible in unexpected ways, included fetishizing the text, maintaining suspicion of it as a colonial artifact, and applying it to questions never anticipated by the European missionary.[4] Jomo Kenyatta's testy exchange with a white British journalist, quoted in the epigraph, captures the form of pushback on the presumed European sense of ownership of the Bible.

---

1. Kenyatta's response to the question on the floor "Are you a Christian?"—*Kenya National Assembly House of Representatives Report*, "Kenya National Committee Minutes: Motion—Kenya National Funds," Column 1475 (July 30, 1963).

2. Sugirtharajah, *The Bible and the Third World*, 282.

3. Pawlikov101-Vilhanov101, "Christian Missions," 258; Sugirtharajah, *The Bible and the Third World*, 6–7, 105, 164.

4. Sugirtharajah, *The Bible and the Third World*, 161; Boulaga, *Christianity Without Fetishes*.

African postcolonial analyses, especially, have pushed back on the colonizing appropriation of the Bible in western interpretations. As explained by a leading proponent, R. S. Sugirtharajah,

> The purpose of Postcolonial reading is not to invest texts with properties which no longer have relevance to our context, or with excessive and exclusive theological claims which invalidate other claims. It seeks to puncture the Christian Bible's Western protection and pretensions, and to help reposition it in relation to its oriental roots and Eastern heritage.[5]

To do this, postcolonial readings encompass a variety of approaches that are essentially undergirded by a colonial experience (past or current) which has shaped or continues to shape, the life or literary experience of the colonized or formerly colonized reader. The colonial system's goal is to control, manipulate, and impose its colonial agenda on its subjects. The Bible, subsumed in western garb, must be resisted, investigated, interrogated, evaluated and eventually rejected. From the vantage point of the colonized or formerly colonized, its use as part of the colonial tool kit means it has to be rehabilitated to be of value. What started in the colonial context, continues today. I shall analyze three responses to colonial vilification of the African religious reality, *Négritude*, African Instituted Churches, and Hermeneutics of Rehabilitation, to showcase the variety of ways this has taken place.

A popular aphorism attributed to the first president of the Republic of Kenya, Jomo Kenyatta, who was an anthropologist captures this aspect aptly: "When the missionaries arrived, the Africans had the land and the missionaries had the Bible. They taught us how to pray with our eyes closed. When we opened our eyes, they had the land and we had the Bible." A later postcolonial version of the saying adds the second tool of colonialism to the maxim, the gun: "When the white man came to our land, he had a Bible on one hand *and a gun on the other*. He asked us to close our eyes in prayer and when we opened our eyes, he had the land *and the gun*, and we had the Bible." This composite makes it clear that the introduction of the Bible in Africa was fraught with its connection to oppressive and authoritarian colonial power.

In the eyes of the African, distinguishing the Bible-toting *mzungu* ("white man") missionary from the gun-slinging white colonizer was not that obvious. They all arrived in the same boat, from the same place, spoke the same language, spoke about their country where Christianity was the only religion (even the kings or queens were Christians), and demanded that Africans convert to the God of the Bible, who loves them. However, any African resistance was not met with love, but promptly by means of the gun.[6]

---

5. Sugirtharajah, *The Bible and the Third World*, 257–8.

6. James Baldwin, "Letter from a Region in My Mind": "The Africans put it another way: When the white man came to Africa, the white man had the Bible and the African had the land, but now it is the white man who is being, reluctantly and bloodily, separated

Therefore, for the African Bible interpreter, there was a need to wrest the Bible from its colonial moorings and set it as a source of justice, liberation and freedom. To accomplish this, a "hermeneutic of recovery" dominated the earliest postcolonial African biblical scholarship. A determined effort not only to authenticate the elements of "truth" in the precolonial African religious reality, but also fully embrace and articulate the Bible's coherence within the African context.

6.2 Négritude: Black Consciousness and Religion

This phase of African Biblical Studies which coincided with the period of African nations' independence from colonial rule in the late 1950s to 1960s reflected the optimism of the Pan-African movement (the movement that began in the 1950s and articulated the self-determination of the African peoples in African and in the Diaspora). The concept of *négritude (Black consciousness)*, coined by the Martinican poet, playwright, and politician Aimé Césaire, who, in conjunction with the Senegalese philosopher, and independent Senegal's first president, Léopold Sédar Senghor, formed the Négritude movement while students in France in the 1930s. Négritude catalyzed the rehabilitation of the African reality as a response to racialized colonial discourse on Africa.[7]

Especially among (the largely Catholic) Francophone African scholars, the notion of *négritude*—as "Black consciousness" or "self-affirmation of Black people"—represented a reaction against the colonizing "Christian" claims of the colonial project. Senghor is said to have made the following realization:

> In his revolt against his teachers at College Libermann high school in Dakar, he had discovered "négritude" before having the concept: he refused to accept their claim that through their education they were building Christianity and civilization in his soul where there was nothing but paganism and barbarism before.[8]

from the land, and the African who is still attempting to digest or to vomit up the Bible. The struggle, therefore, that now begins in the world is extremely complex, involving the historical role of Christianity in the realm of power—that is, politics—and in the realm of morals. *In the realm of power, Christianity has operated with an unmitigated arrogance and cruelty*—necessarily, since a religion ordinarily imposes on those who have discovered the true faith the spiritual duty of liberating the infidels." (emphasis added)

7. Attribution to influence by Harlem Renaissance through the Nardal sisters, Paulette and Jane. Fanon, *The Wretched of the Earth*, 150, noted as much: "The concept of negritude for example was the affective if not the logical antithesis of that insult which the white man had leveled at the rest of humanity."

8. Souleymane Bachir Diagne, "Négritude," in *The Stanford Encyclopedia of Philosophy*, ed. Edward N. Zalta, Summer 2018 ed., Available online: https://plato.stanford.edu/archives /sum2018/entries/negritude/.

Senghor, who had attended a Catholic seminary in Dakar in preparation for the priesthood before changing his mind, articulates an African cognition of the colonial agenda that was to be the driving force for the independence of African states. Senghor, however, asserts more than political independence; he also recognizes that the missionary's apocalyptic zeal retained a myopic view of the purpose of formal education—as simply, to read the Bible and nothing else. Such a view, by establishing the binaries mentioned earlier, failed to envision (or as we saw earlier were deliberately curtailed on racist grounds) other possibilities that education and the Bible could produce for the African. It is no surprise that missionary schools trained many of the African leaders, like Senghor intending to use education to pacify them, but who instead, turned around and led their countries to independence, using the "master's tools to bring down the master's house."[9]

Babacar Camara makes the case that *négritude* responds to the Hegelian dialectic that sought to erase the African from history (see Chapter 2 of this study). A certain inversion of the Hegelian construct accomplishes this: "What Hegel proposes as an absolute lack is considered as an absolute asset by Negritude. With Senghor, Negritude becomes a general theory of the African. It is a coherent and systematic ensemble of ideas that first reflects a reaction to the colonial past and, second, a Human-ism that transcends racial particularisms to reach the Civilization the Universal."[10]

A gifted poet, Biblical psalms seem to have influenced Senghor's poetry. This is especially the case in his introductions that echo the psalmist setting his work to specific musical instruments. For example, Senghor dedicates his poem to his beloved uncle Tokô'Waly and entitles it *Que m'accompagnent Koras et Balafong* ("To the accompaniment of the Kora and Balafon"), echoing the Davidic psalms set to musical instruments, for example, a Psalm of David to the stringed instruments. Of course, the Kora is a stringed instrument too.[11] This was not just parallelism, but also an assertion of the African ability to match the biblical text with a culture equally sophisticated and robust.[12]

---

9. Jomo Kenyatta of Kenya, Julius Nyerere of Tanzania, Kenneth Kaunda of Zambia, Kamuzu Banda of Malawi, to name just a few, were all products of missionary education with its intended emphasis on Christianization.

10. Camara, "The Falsity of Hegel's Theses on Africa," 82–96, 83.

11. Janis L. Pallister, "Leopold Sedar Senghor: A Catholic Sensibility?" *FR* LIII, no. 5 (1980): 670–9, 672. "We must, thus, observe that Senghor himself regards African religion as the foundation, and Catholicism as a type of reinforcement, or superstructure."

12. Unfortunately, the withering critique of *négritude* was that it adopted the colonizer's stereotypes in its critique of colonialism. For example, it made claims that Black culture is emotional (aesthetic) rather than rational, that it emphasized wholeness in contrast to dissection and analysis, that it operated in distinctive African time and space, and suchlike. (See Ashcroft, Griffiths, Tiffin, *The Empire Writes Back*, 20). This notwithstanding, the main point I want to stress is that *négritude* was the first comprehensive articulation of Black consciousness, not just African culture and religion, as a heuristic starting point for

Within Francophone Africa, and particularly among African Catholic priests and scholars, *négritude* would find full religious and biblical expression in one of the earliest Africentric Christian documents produced by African Christians, *Des Pretres Noirs S'interrogent* [*Black Priests Wonder (or Question Themselves)*] in 1956. Before Liberation theology would become a theological movement in the late 1960s and early 1970s, the African priests in this document had explicated a form of liberationist hermeneutics that focused on issues of race and racism.

Identifying themselves as *Des Pretres Noirs* or "Black Priests," rather than, say, "African or Africana Priests" in the title of their document was a bold proclamation of their conviction that racial issues were central to biblical interpretation in the African continent. To prove them right, there was immediate blowback from some of their European Fathers Superior who immediately bemoaned this "Africanization" of the Bible as degrading, both to the Bible and the French language.[13] The echo of Schweitzer's and European missionary attitudes toward African intellectual capability is obvious, but here the Fathers Superior turn around and levy the accusation of denigration on the African intellectual critique. The African priests' self-description as "wondering" or "questioning themselves" (i.e., processing of thought) attests to their erudite intellectual "counter-reading" presumed incapable by Africans.

By creatively utilizing the concept of *négritude* to expose western weaponization of the Bible as a colonizing tool, these African priests, while critiquing the nature of the western church, the issue of race in western Christianity, and the need for an African theology, and expanding the reach of theological discourse beyond European missionary constrictions set in motion some of the fundamental ideas upon which later African theologians and biblical interpreters would build. As Pierre Diarra explains,

> In writing their book, the black priests were anxious to lay the foundation for liberation, while remaining in communion with their superiors. They focused their efforts on welcoming the Gospel, a source of gentleness, refusing to approach the political domain, believing that it is not the jurisdiction of the priests and that it is violent. They proposed a kind of "liberated theology," apart from the philosophical tendencies inspired by Nietzsche and Marx, to create a space for dialogue that allowed black priests to reflect and work together.[14]

a uniquely African interpretive process. This is especially so in the way the Black priests utilized the interpretation of the Bible.

13. Elizabeth A. Foster, *African Catholic: Decolonization and the Transformation of the Church* (Cambridge, MA: Harvard University Press, 2019), 152–5: Some of the French missionaries ". . . worried that this would lead to an 'Africanization' of the church as a whole, which would debase its rites and chase French language from its African schools. Moreover, some missionaries, particularly older ones, simply could not stomach the idea of white priests having to obey a black bishop." (153)

14. Pierre Diarra, "Des Prêtres Noirs S'interrogent," *HMC* 1, no. 1 (2007): 156–60. "En écrivant leur livre, les prêtres noirs étaient soucieux de poser les jalons d'une libération, tout

In many ways, these African priests were way ahead of their time, for example, in advocating liberationist readings long before Liberation theology would enter the lores of western academy in the late 1960s. Or the case for foregrounding the interpreter's social location and recognizing the African cultural and religious reality as an authentic starting point for the interpretation of the Bible, long before it would become *de rigueur* in Vatican II (1962–65) and later Postcolonial Studies.[15]

6.3 African Indigenous/Independent/Instituted/Initiated Churches (AICs)

The AICs reflect two tensions of the Bible and colonialism for the Africans—the embrace of the Bible and the rejection of the presumed western missionary ecclesial authority of it. As we noted earlier, the vernacular precipitated this indigenous revolution. The European missionary expectation was that the African would be able to read the "Word of God" in his/her own language, and hear God speak in his/her mother tongue in uniformity with the missionary. However, the African readers formulated independent biblical interpretations that led them to question the accuracy of the missionary's interpretations. The unmediated interpretation unleashed a profoundly distinct African hermeneutic relevant to the African reality. For one scholar, "the [African] Independent Churches (speaking broadly) are more realistic and practical when it comes to taking the African situation seriously."[16]

Emergence of AICs preceded political independence in Africa and in some cases, may have instigated the anti-colonialism fight. In general, the AICs revolted against western colonialist impositions. In the hands of such AIC pioneers like Isaiah Shembe (South Africa) and Simon Kimbangu (Congo), among others, the vernacular Bible became an "African Bible," read through an unfiltered African experience and interpreted to address African concerns.[17] The Bible without missionary mediation undermined the presupposed authority of colonial missionary.[18] Not surprisingly, then, the condemnation of AICs by the western

---

en restant en communion avec leurs supérieurs hiérarchiques. Ils focalisaient leur effort sur l'accueil de l'Évangile, source de douceur, refusant d'aborder le domaine politique, estimant que celui-ci n'est pas du ressort des prêtres et qu'il est violent. Ils proposèrent une sorte de « théologie libérée », en dehors des tendances philosophiques inspirées de Nietzsche et de Marx, pour créer un espace de dialogue qui permette aux prêtres noirs de réfléchir et de travailler ensemble" (my translation).

15. See Andrew M. Mbuvi, "An African Biblical Scholar Explores the Broadening of the Biblical Studies Landscape," *JTSA* 168 (2020): 41–63.

16. J. S. Mbiti, "Christianity and Traditional Religions in Africa," *IRM* 59, no. 236 (1970): 430–40,

17. Bengt G. M. Sundkler, *Bantu Prophets in South Africa* (Cambridge: James Clarke & Co., 1948, 2004). Cf. West, *The Stolen Bible*, especially chapters 5–6 on Isaiah Shembe.

18. C. M. Pauw, "African Independent Churches as a 'People's Response' to the Christian Message," *JSR* 8, no. 1 (1995): 3–25. AICs have to be understood not only as

missionaries and accusations of producing illegitimate, dangerous, corrupt, and syncretistic interpretations of the Bible was par for the course. The feared "denigration of the Bible" had begun.

A common theme among AIC pioneers was a "prophetic hermeneutic" that drew inspiration from the biblical prophets and African religious authority figures like seers.[19] This was not accidental. Many African communities had pre-Christian prophetic traditions, and parallels with biblical prophets enabled AIC leaders to tap into both traditions indiscriminately. The colonial experience brought to bear on the colonized had made clear the power of the "white man." And because divine power, greater than that of earthly rulers, had been attributed to the Bible, it made sense that AIC leaders perceived utilizations of both traditions would yield a potent combination. If the God of the Bible was as powerful as the European claimed, and interested in all peoples, then surely this God could be persuaded (or manipulated) to serve the African communities' needs and interests.

AIC leaders were wise in recognizing that embedded in African religious practices were elements that made the God the Bible palatable for the African in ways the western missionary could not envision. Because they found these "African" traditions *in* the Bible! This is not what some western critics may label "*eis*egesis" (to read ideas into the text), as opposed to "*ex*egesis" (to draw meaning out the text), but rather a more basic comparativist approach. The issue of polygamy was probably one of the most rife among AIC concerns. So the fact that many key figures in the Bible, Abraham, Isaac, Jacob, David, etc., had multiple wives and concubines, directly contradicted the western missionary insistence on monogamy for African converts. Polygamous African converts to Christianity were required to get rid of all their wives, except the first one, who was considered the legitimate wife.

Another aspect was that of sacrifices. In a practice similar to those in African religious traditions, worshippers offered sacrifices to God in the Bible. Nevertheless, the missionaries insisted that not only were religious sacrifices unnecessary (Jesus's sacrifice having nullified all sacrifices) but also that African sacrifices were, in fact, offerings to demons and Satan, not to God as Africans supposed. It is these sorts of contradictions that AIC leaders found they could not abide by.

So the AIC pioneers, as Christian converts, found that they either had to be silenced or forced out of the missionary planted churches. So, forced out or voluntarily departing, the pioneer AIC leaders established their religious communities where pertinent African religious and cultural traditions could find expression guided by a Christianity that willingly merged them with the Bible. So, the inability to conform the missionary interpretation of the Bible message to the African reality engendered the emergence of the AICs seeking to rectify the perceived anomaly.

---

reactive (negative—to western interpretations) but also as *responsive* (positive—to the Gospel message).

19. Bengt Sundkler, *Bantu Prophets in South Africa*; Cf. José Antunes da Silva, "African Independent Churches: Origin and Development," *Anth* 88, no. 4/6 (1993): 393–402.

Caught unprepared by this outcome, the initial western missionary reaction was to fall back to the same old colonial tool bag—reject such interpretation as corrupt, unsophisticated, uneducated, and heretical.[20] Corrupt because AICs did not align with the "orthodox" missionary readings; unsophisticated and uneducated because most of these African individuals were not formally theologically trained; and, heretical because of the attempt to connect the Bible to the irredeemably Satanic African religious reality, rendered any such interpretations as dangerous falsehood. This colonial attitude, well articulated by John Mbiti in his appeal to Peter's prejudiced position in Acts 10, persists in western biblical scholarship:

> When Peter was called by God to go and take the Gospel to Cornelius and his household, Peter objected that he had "never eaten anything that is common or unclean." To this God told him that "what God has cleansed, you must not call common" (Acts 10:14-16). This happened three times, we are told. I wonder whether for too long (Western) Christianity in Africa has taken Peter's attitude towards the African background. My plea is that whether that background is common or clean, we should first of all understand it, experiment with it, and pray for God's careful guidance. I know that there are those who are ready to shout "Syncretism! Syncretism!" in order to dismiss this concern; but who of us is free from syncretism, pride, prejudice and sheer obstinacy?[21]

Essentially, what Postcolonial Studies has labeled *hybridity* can subsume what Mbiti calls syncretism.[22] What Mbiti is castigating, then, is the West's interpretive hypocrisy of exclaiming the corruption of non-western interpretations while ignoring their own centuries of westernizing Christianity. For Indian critical theorist Homi Bhabha, hybridity becomes a form of subversive resistance to dominating authority: "Hybridity is a problematic of colonial representation and individuation that reverses the effects of the colonialist disavowal, so that other 'denied' knowledges enter upon the dominant discourse and estrange the basis of its authority—its rules of recognition."[23] This means, according to Dube, "Hybridity becomes a form of resistance, for it dispenses with dualistic and hierarchical constructions of cultures, which are used to claim the superiority of colonizing cultures, and shows that culture grows and is dependent on borrowing from each other."[24] What, in the colonialist's construct, had been the premise for

---

20. David Barrett, *Schism and Renewal in Africa*, was one of the earliest western scholars to see AICs as reformation and renewal, rather than "heretical and undisciplined."

21. Mbiti, "Christianity and Traditional Religions in Africa," 430–40.

22. Young, *Postcolonialism*, 79: "Hybridity works in different ways at the same time, according to the cultural, economic and political demands of specific situations. It involves the processes of interaction that create new social spaces to which new meanings are given."

23. H. Bhabha, "Signs Taken for Wonders: Questions of Ambivalence and Authority under a Tree Outside Delhi, May 1817," *CI* 12 (1985): 144–65, 156.

24. Dube, *Postcolonial Feminist Interpretation of the Bible*, 51.

an "Othering" terminology, in postcolonial discourse it becomes defanged: "The native questions quite literally turn the origin of the book [Bible] into an enigma."[25]

This is the acknowledgment that encounters between two cultures, religions, and peoples produces, a third entity that is neither of the two, but a legitimate and distinct "Third"—neither a negative nor a corruption of the former. When it comes to Christian encounters, Sugirtharajah explains that ancient Christianity was itself a hybrid religion that sought to redefine its Jewish heritage in light of the new teachings of Jesus: "The Jewish Christians were the original hybridizers who wished to remain within the Jewish religious parameters and reconfigured their faith in light of the teachings of Jesus."[26]

Returning to AICs, it can then be argued that the western missionary's negative assessment of heresy has, as its basis of response, the colonialist denigration of the African religious reality. If they had achieved their desired result of imposing western tenets, the result would have simply been colonial mimicry that would have engrained colonialist attitudes and perspectives into the African interpretation.[27] Instead, the AIC revolt occurred and the fear of "corrupting" western Christianity, the supposed "true" or "authentic" expression of Christianity, with African religio-cultural reality propagated gave way to the renunciation of any possible African Christianity. Yet, this very hybridity of the AICs has provided to be one of the most innovative religious spaces for biblical interpretation in African Christianity.

6.4 Hermeneutics of Rehabilitation: Post-Independence African Bible Scholarship

I begin this section with an extended quotation from Hegel. This Hegelian assessment of the African peoples and reality, misconstrued as the assessment is, remained quite influential throughout the colonial period. Even when its details were refuted, the overall assessment of the godlessness of the African—the *tabula rasa* of the African mind and the "man of nature" or the primitive being—continued to exercise the European view of the African.

> The peculiarly African character is difficult to comprehend, for the very reason that in reference to it, we must quite give up the principle which naturally accompanies all *our* ideas—the category of Universality. In Negro life the characteristic point is the fact that consciousness has not yet attained to the realization of any substantial objective existence —as for example, God, or Law—in which the interest of man's volition is involved and in which he realizes his own being. This distinction between himself as an individual and the universality of his essential being, the African in the uniform, undeveloped oneness of his existence has not yet attained; so that the

---

25. Bhabha, "Signs Taken for Wonders," 158.
26. Sugirtharajah, "Postcolonial Biblical Interpretation: Next Phase," 457.
27. Memmi, *The Colonizer and the Colonized*, 119–21.

Knowledge of an absolute Being, an Other and a Higher than his individual self, is entirely wanting. . . . But even Herodotus called the Negroes sorcerers:—now in Sorcery we have not the idea of a God, of a moral faith; it exhibits man as the highest power, regarding him as alone occupying a position of command over the power of Nature . . . For the soul of man, God must be more than a thunderer, whereas among the Negroes this is not the case. Although they are necessarily conscious of dependence upon nature—for they need the beneficial influence of storm, rain, cessation of the rainy period, and so on—yet this does not conduct them to the consciousness of a Higher Power.[28]

It is no surprise then that post-independence African Christian academics inclined toward a "hermeneutic of rehabilitation." At its core, it is an "anti-Hegelian" stance aimed at confronting the European denigration of the African reality. It's determination was to salvage the African religious and cultural reality by showing its greater affinity to the biblical world view than even the western worldview.

This "hermeneutic of rehabilitation"—rehabilitation of the African religio-cultural reality—sought to establish the African reality as a viable premise for articulating the biblical message, and various titles have been proffered by its proponents including "heritage hermeneutics," "Africanization," "Indigenization," "Adaptation," "*Authenticité*," among others. One of the earliest products of these efforts was the post-independence volume edited by Ghanaian biblical theologian, Christian Baëta, *Christianity in Tropical Africa*.[29] In his introductory chapter, Baëta decries the effects of the neglect of the African reality by missionaries:

> The story of the Christian influence in Africa should consider not only the effects of evangelization on a people but also those of the people and their religion on the character and growth of the Christian communities which come into being among them. . . . In Africa, however, a distinguishing mark of missions has been their almost unanimous refusal to incorporate elements of the local traditional cults in any shape or form within the Christian system of religious thought and practice.[30]

In a *New York Times* interview in 1971, some of the African contributors to the volume were emphatic about its significance as the beginnings of the "Africanization" of the Bible: "The days are over when we will be carbon copies of European Christians," said the Rev. John Mbiti, a Cambridge-educated Anglican theologian at Makerere University College in Kampala, Uganda. "Europe and America Westernized Christianity. The Orthodox Easternized it. Now it's our turn to Africanize it."[31] As an example, the Nigerian scholar Idowu noted that, while

---

28. Hegel, *Philosophy of History*, 111.

29. Baëta, *Tropical Africa*.

30. Ibid., 6.

31. Edward B. Fiske, "African Christians are Developing their Own Distinctive Theologies," *NYT* (March 12, 1971): 10.

the African Christian found it difficult to understand the concept of a "bodily resurrection" described in 1 Corinthians 15, the alternative image of the deceased entering "a building from God, a house not made with hands, eternal in the heavens" in 2 Corinthians 5 was quite in keeping with an African outlook.[32]

For these African scholars, Africanization of the biblical text and message was the key function of African biblical scholarship, to create a distinctly African hermeneutical path for African concerns.[33] They perceived it, not simply as self-serving, but as a means of making a distinct contribution to the vibrancy of Bible readers worldwide: "African theologians talk quite frankly about the potential contributions that African Christians can make to Christians elsewhere based on their particular experience."[34] This contribution would emanate not simply from the situations of the African interpreter, this "their particular experience," but from the acknowledgment of such situations as necessary to derive meaning from the text. In a sense, African biblical scholars were already practicing a form of reader response hermeneutics even before it was *en vogue* in Biblical Studies.

The African religious past, the contributors to the volume reckoned, was not as alien to the biblical reality as the western missionary had purported. They argued that any perceived chasm was only a figment of the western missionaries' imagination driven by racial prejudice against the African reality. The African reality bore an even closer connection to the biblical world than the western culture could claim, with its notion of a Supreme Being (a person, not an entity) who created the world and interacts with humans, and who has the power to intervene in human affairs. Additionally, African believers do not question God's goodness, and human parties (living or dead) or spiritual entities, since in this worldview it is witchcraft, evil eye, curse, spells, spirits (ancestral and otherwise), and the like are responsible for misfortunes. This bears similarity to the biblical worldview, where Satan, fallen angels and demons are often to blame for human misfortunes. Even while the idea of the devil may not have been that developed in the Hebrew Bible, human misfortune rests squarely on the shoulders of both humans and other entities e.g., the serpent in Eden (the serpent is not Satan in Genesis) or on the God, as in the book of Job. Failure of the humans to adhere to the regulations that God outlined in Eden which commenced human misfortune, was instigated by the Serpent (Gen. 2–3). However, it is God whom human disobedience offends and who banishes the humans from Eden, ending unmediated interaction with humans.

In African myths, human action also leads to God's ultimate separation from humanity. In a myth prevalent in various forms in several West and Central African

---

32. Ibid.

33. Aylward Shorter, *African Christian Theology—Adaptation or Incarnation* (Maryknoll: Orbis, 1977), 132, echoes the sentiment: "The talk of 'Black Theology' or 'African Theology' is excellent, but it must mean a contribution to other theologies. If it is exclusive, then it ceases to be theology. No single culture has a monopoly of God, just as no single culture has a monopoly of human experience."

34. Fiske, "African Christians," 10.

communities, God's dwelling (the sky, referred to as the "floor of the divine") used to hang so low that humans could touch it. Over time, the woman kept annoying God by using a pestle and mortar to pound food, rhythmically lifting the pestle above her head and pounding what was in the motor, and continually knocking onto God's sky. And so, God eventually moved the dwelling higher up, farther away from the humans.[35] Three points of connection emerge. In both the Genesis and the African myth, (i) the woman receives the blame for human separation from the divine, (ii) the separation is essentially connected with food consumption, and (iii) divine judgment ensues for all humans.[36]

For some African scholars, such alignment of the African and biblical worldviews is so close that an argument could be made, and was indeed made, that the African religious reality could serve as a form of *praeparatio evangelica* (preparation for the gospel or Christian message), much in the same way that the Hebrew Bible/OT, with its origins in oral tradition, served to prepare the Jewish community for the arrival of the Messiah.[37] In a 1938 SBL presidential address entitled "The Primitive Christian Message," William P. Hatch made the argument, following Macgregor and Purdy, that Hellenistic culture was a prime *praeparatio evangelica*.[38] The case for proximity, African scholars, argued, had closer affinity to African religio-cultural reality than that of Hellenistic culture, making the African *praeparatio evangelica* claim that much more profound.

This bold claim, however, has not gone without its detractors![39] The parallels between the African reality and the Hebrew biblical culture, often close enough to warrant their comparison, does not equate one with the other. Yet, if the biblical claim that God created humans in God's own image (Genesis 1–2), then African scholars have countered that perhaps vestiges of this image of god-ness, would be what the African religious parallels have retained. This would be true for the African religious reality as it would be for any other peoples, if *all* humans have this divine image. As Congolese theologian Bénézet Bujo puts it, "It is not a question of replacing the God of the Africans but rather of enthroning the God of Jesus Christ, not as a rival of the God of ancestors, but as identical with [the African] God."[40]

Indeed, this is not such a radical perspective. The difference is that western missionaries had insisted on converting Africans to a cultural Christianity that

---

35. Thomson Gale, "African Religions: Mythic Themes," *Encyclopedia of Religion*, 2005, Available online: Encyclopedia.com (accessed June 24, 2019).

36. Hugo Huber, "Anthropological Approaches to the Study of Myth: African Variants of the Separation of Heaven and Earth," *URM* 10, no. 1 (1987): 54–66.

37. Mbiti, "Christianity and Traditional Religions in Africa," 435–40. While Mbiti is credited with being the first African biblical scholar to arrive at this formulation, Bishop Colenso (mentioned earlier) in the mid-nineteenth century had already presaged it.

38. William P. Hatch, "The Primitive Christian Message," *JBL* 58, no. 1 (1939): 1–13, 11.

39. Robert S. Heaney, *From Historical to Critical Post-Colonial Theology: The Contribution of John S. Mbiti and Jesse N. K. Mugambi* (Oregon: Pickwick, 2015), 105–8.

40. Bénézet Bujo, *African Theology in Its Social Context* (Maryknoll: Orbis, 1992), 16.

turned out to be "western culture in Christian garb." The western missionary refused to acknowledge or was completely blind to the influence of his/her western culture that shaped his/her form of Christianity through the "cultural Bible." Western Christianity is just as "cultural" as African Christianity, yet this fact went unacknowledged.

The overall response to Baëta's volume was mixed. Groundbreaking as C. C. Baëta's volume on the Bible's encounter with African realities was, two significant reactions exemplify its reception.[41] The first is a scathing book review written by Nigerian scholar E. A. Ayandele who at the time, taught at the University of Ibadan, Nigeria.[42] His complaint about the volume was that, in its critiques of the western missionary enterprise, it exercised the very same high-handed attitude that the European missionaries employed, spewing judgment instead of constructively criticizing the missionary enterprise.[43] Ayandele's response evidences the robust and varied perspectives that exist among African scholars, even when they agree on basic premises. Ayandele's critique also betrays his own alignment with the western missionary perspective, making him a faithful proponent of the negative European appraisal of the African reality.

The second response was a book review by American anthropologist Helen Codere, who taught at Brandeis University at the time. In an interesting twist, Codere praised the volume for its sophistication, yet when she went on to highlight what she considered the four best papers in the volume, all written by white authors.[44] Codere preferred and legitimated white scholars' views of Africans over those of African scholars in the same volume. While Baëta's volume gave pride of place to African reality as sufficient in constructing an African Christianity, colonial mentality was still embedded in it, especially in Fr. Laroche's essay that contrasted the Catholic veneration of Saints with the African veneration of ancestors. His clear denigration of the latter, and defense of the former, is a reflection of the colonial mentality that persisted and persists today. Years later, Ghanaian biblical theologian Kwame Bediako, contra Laroche, would use the passage of Hebrews 12 to make a persuasive case of the African veneration of ancestors as in-keeping with the biblical understanding of the afterlife.[45]

Ayandele's views, representing those who remained wedded to the missionary agenda, was not alone. Fully enmeshed in the western evangelistic perspective, they reject their own African cultural and religious realities, as the only way to

41. Baëta, *Tropical Africa*.

42. E. A. Ayandele, "Review: *Christianity in Tropical Africa* (Edited by C. C. Baëta. Oxford University Press, 1968)," *JAH* 10, no. 2 (1969): 336–40.

43. Takatso Mofokeng, "Black Christians, the Bible and Liberation," *JBTSA* 2 (1988): 34–42.

44. Helen Codere, "Book Review: C. C. Baëta (ed.), *Christianity in Tropical Africa*," *JAAS* 4, no. 3 (July 1969): 233–4.

45. William Dyrness (ed.), *Emerging Voices in Global Christian Theology* (Grand Rapids: Zondervan, 1999), 112–19.

fully embrace "true Christianity," the western form of missionary Christianity.[46] Nigerian theologian Byang Kato's *Theological Pitfalls in Africa,* in alignment with Yendele's position, spells out more of the dangers envisioned by those embracing the African reality as the starting point of biblical interpretation. But the, arguments, built on uncritical conceptualizations of "syncretism" are moot, given our earlier conclusion that all religions, including the Judeo-Christian religion, are essentially syncretistic.[47]

Perhaps it is Jean-Marc Ela of Cameroon, a priest, theologian and sociologist, who has made one of the most consistent and withering attacks on the Africanization process. He warns that "the preoccupation with what is 'typically African' runs the danger of ignoring the historical factors that condition the production of theological knowledge itself."[48] For Ela, the concern is that the focus on Africanization within African biblical scholarship may result in a myopic stance that fails to recognize and address larger issues, such as the continued abuse of political power, the oppression of the poor by the rich, and other forms of systemic tyrannies that have continued to assail individuals and communities. Ultimately, for Ela, focus on Africanization fails to bring the needed liberation of communities and individuals because its focus on theological concerns obscures its responsibility to the "real life" needs of the community. However, I do believe that Ela's concerns find a corrective in the more recent postcolonial approaches in African biblical scholarship with their emphasis on liberative readings which address issues of power dynamics and social justice.

On the heels of Baëta's edited volume, Mbiti and Idowu produced monographs that would prove quite influential in the hermeneutic of rehabilitation. These volumes, Mbiti's *African Religions and Philosophy* and *The Concepts of God in Africa* and Idowu's *Olodumare,* were crucial, especially in establishing the presence of a monotheistic core in African religions, which European missionaries and scholars of religion had dismissed.[49] That African religions had at their heart the notion of a supreme deity was a vital case in subsequently equating of this supreme African deity with the Judeo-Christian God. From these arguments, other African scholars would proceed with the rehabilitation of other aspects of African religious reality.

---

46. Memmi, *The Colonizer and the Colonized,* 72: "To be sure the church has greatly assisted the colonialist: backing his ventures, helping his conscience, contributing to the acceptance of colonization—even by the colonized."

47. H. L. Richard, "Religious Syncretism as a Syncretistic Concept: The Inadequacy of the 'World Religions' Paradigm in Cross-Cultural Encounter," *IJFM* 31, no. 4 (2014): 209–15. Sanneh, *Translating the Message,* 36–9.

48. Jean-Marc Ela, *My Faith as an African* (Maryknoll: Orbis, 1988), 173. See also idem, *Cri de l'homme Africain* (Paris: L'Harmattan, 1980)—English translation *African Cry!* (Maryknoll: Orbis, 1986).

49. Mbiti, *African Religions and Philosophy;* idem, *The Concepts of God in Africa;* Idowu, *Olodumare.*

Later generations of African scholars, such as Nigerian New Testament professor, Justin Ukpong, while using a different terminology of "inculturation" or "intercultural" hermeneutics, retained and further expanded on the hermeneutic of rehabilitation.[50] Inculturation terminology is primarily a reserve of the Catholic Church, as the interpretive approach that is rooted in Vatican II (1962-65), the papal document that authorized the use of vernacular language in Catholic Mass, in place of the colonial European language of Latin. Ukpong, himself a Catholic priest, claims to have invented the term "inculturation hermeneutics" in the 1990s, to identify an interpretive methodology in which "the African context is seen as providing the critical resources for biblical interpretation."[51] With the primary goal of "social-cultural transformation," this interpretive method maintains a "holistic" view of culture, utilizing an "African conceptual frame of reference" that prioritizes the African reality in interpretation.[52] Explaining inculturation's distinctiveness from western approaches, Ukpong notes:

> For example, within the African conceptual frame of reference, the reality of the interaction between the supernatural and natural worlds, the spirit world and the world of the physical human existence, and the interconnectedness of all these, are taken for granted while that is not the case in the Western conceptual frame of reference.[53]

The interaction of the biblical text and the reader's social-cultural reality thus produces interpretive meaning. Such a reading fuses the horizons of *exegesis* (objective historical exercise) and *hermeneutics* (subjective contextual application), with the present receiving precedence in constructing an understanding of the biblical text.[54] In this way, inculturation readings are in line with recent literary biblical interpretations that understand every interpretive process culturally bound, making all interpretation essentially "existential and pragmatic" rather than "objective and universal."

---

50. Ukachukwu Cris Manus, *Intercultural Hermeneutics in Africa: Methods and Approaches* (Nairobi: Acton, 2003), 32. "*Intercultural Hermeneutics* is one way of describing the process of doing contextual exegesis and theology for contemporary culturally renaissant persons, such as those in Africa today. By using the term *Intercultural Hermeneutics*, I intend to assert, *inter alia*, that there is no universal hermeneutics which is ready-made and applicable to every country or situation in the world." (Italics original)

51. J. Ukpong et al., *Reading the Bible in the Global Village: Cape Town* (Atlanta: SBL, 2002), 11.

52. Ibid., 12–13.

53. Ibid., 15.

54. Ibid., 18.

An Interpretive Sample: Noah's Curse (Genesis 9–10) through an African Cultural Optic

To illustrate the rehabilitation hermeneutic, let's take a look at a passage in Genesis that has had controversial interpretive history. In the story of Noah, the text means for its readers to understand that the offspring of Noah's three sons, Japheth, Shem, and Ham, would constitute the new generation of humanity after the flood destroyed the rest of the world. When the "Table of Nations" (Gen. 10:1-10) lists their progeny, it identifies what is referred to as Egypt, together with Cush, Put, and Canaan, as the descendants of Ham. In the earlier chapter of Genesis 9, Noah had cursed Ham's son, Canaan, for gazing onto drunken Noah's nakedness. As a result, many interpretations, going all the way to rabbinical times, sought to connect this curse to whatever negative attitudes people held toward Africa (and Africans), attributing them to this divinely sanctioned curse.[55] The early link between Noah's sons and the ancients' conceptualization of the "three races" of the world aligned Noah's curse with peoples of African descent. The most obvious problem with this connection is that it misreads the text; Canaan, rather than Ham, Egypt, or Cush, receives the curse. Yet, reasoned arguments can do little to topple stereotypes once established.

Historically, interpreters have also struggled to understand the reason and the nature of Noah's curse since what seems to have transpired does not seem to warrant such a dire response on Noah's part. What is it about simple nakedness that would result in a curse? Jewish interpreters in history have struggled with this issue and postulated several possibilities.[56] First, Ham may not have simply gazed at his father's nakedness but may have committed a more heinous offense by possibly having raped his father. Such a reading comes from Gen. 9:24 which states that, after Noah had woken up from his drunken stupor, "he knew" (Heb. *yada*) what Ham had done to him. Noah could know, so the argument goes, because he could "feel something was wrong" and so deduced that something had been *done to him*. Since the last person he saw was Ham, he concluded that Ham had committed the wrong. Japheth and Shem, on the other hand, had walked backward with the blanket to cover their naked father, who was already asleep.

Second, the text simply notes that Ham's action dishonors his father by exposing his nakedness. While the term "exposing his nakedness" can euphemistically refer to sexual intercourse (cf. Lev. 18:7-16, 20:11-21), here it may refer to his failure to do the honorable thing, namely covering his dad. Kenyan theologian, Johnson Kimuhu, analyzes the pivotal terminology of "uncover" (Heb. *gillah*) and "see" (Heb. *ra'ah*) in Leviticus and finds it significant that the Genesis story lacks the former. As such, the classification of Ham's action as sexual contact is doubtful.[57]

---

55. Yamauchi, *Bible and Africa*, ch.1.

56. Ibid., "The Curse of Ham."

57. Johnson M. Kimuhu, *Leviticus: The Priestly Laws and Prohibitions from the Perspective of Ancient Near East and Africa* (New York: Peter Lang, 2008), 70–2. Kimuhu, however, does not broach the comparison with his Gikuyu customs on curses and nakedness even as he investigates aspects of taboo.

Instead, Ham acted dishonorably in telling others of his father's naked state without attempting to do anything about it.

A third possibility comes from an African community and centers on the understanding of curses and nakedness in certain communities. Among some of the Bantu tribes of East and Central Africa, the curse is a potent instrument of social control.[58] Members of these communities typically understand curses to work based on the relationship between the person issuing the curse and its target. The closer the blood relationship of those involved the more potent the curse. Therefore, parental curses are some of the most powerful and feared in these communities.[59]

Among Bantu communities of Africa, exposure to one's parents' nakedness is taboo.[60] Even accidental exposure to one's parents' nakedness would require some form of cleansing ritual to ensure no ill befalling on you. Therefore, it is no surprise that one means of a curse among the Bantu is the exposure of parental genitalia coupled with the pronouncement of the curse upon the child.[61] The exposure of the parental genitalia, which is a taboo in normal circumstances, is here a signification of the child's failure to honor "from whence they came"; thus, exposure that is a most dishonorable and shameful act in and of itself becomes a virtual death sentence.

When reading the story of Noah in such a context, the meaning and impact of Noah's actions suddenly make sense and do not require explanations beyond the face value of the story. If the basic exposure of the parental genitalia in and of itself constitutes a curse, then Ham's act elicited the appropriate response from Noah, especially considering Ham's seeming lack of repentance or recognition of the gravity of his act. Such an interpretation eliminates any need to try and find a reason aside from the nakedness to which the text refers to explain the harsh consequence.

But why curse Canaan and not Ham himself? Here the explanation may also come from the Bantu notion of inheritance of curses. One can inherit a curse that his or her parents have. This view is familiar in the biblical worldview, as seen in Ezekiel's reversal of such teaching while inaugurating the "new covenant" with Israel: "The person who sins shall die. A child shall not suffer for the iniquity of a parent, nor a parent suffer for the iniquity of a child; the righteousness of the righteous shall be his own, and the wickedness of the wicked shall be his own" (Ezek. 18:20). What Noah may be doing in this situation is making Ham suffer by cursing his own grandson, Canaan, just as Noah's own son, Ham, made Noah suffer the humiliation Ham had brought upon him.

58. Adda Bruemmer Bozeman, *Conflict in Africa: Concepts and Realities* (Princeton: Princeton University Press, 1976): 161.

59. Gunter Wagner, *The Bantu of North Kavirondo, Volume 1: African Ethnographic Studies of the 20th Century* (Oxford: Oxford University Press, 1949; Abingdon, Oxon: Routledge, 2018).

60. P. N. Wachege, "Curses and Cursing among the Agĩkũyũ: Socio-Cultural and Religious Benefits," unpublished article available on author's website https://profiles.uonbi.ac.ke/patrickwachege/ (accessed July 28, 2020).

61. Ibid.

Part III

AFRICAN BIBLICAL STUDIES

SETTING A POSTCOLONIAL AGENDA

Decolonization, we know, is an historical process: In other words, it can only be understood, it can only find its significance and become self-coherent insofar as we can discern the history-making movement which gives it form and substance.

— Franz Fanon[1]

Postcolonialism examines the role of narratives in colonizing, decolonizing and nation-building. It is concerned about economic, political, cultural and social justice in the world. But above all, postcolonialism proposes many different ways to co-exist on earth without having to suppress and exploit the other.

— Musa W. Dube[2]

Applied to Biblical Studies, [postcolonialism] seeks to uncover colonial designs in both biblical texts and their interpretations, and endeavors to read the text from such colonial concerns as identity, hybridity and diaspora.

— R. S. Sugirthrarajah[3]

1. Fanon, *The Wretched of the Earth*, 2.
2. M. W. Dube and J. Staley (eds.), *John and Postcolonialism: Travel, Space, and Power* (Sheffield: Sheffield Academic Press, 2002), 3.
3. Sugirtharajah, *Postcolonial Reconfigurations*, 4.

Chapter 7

DECOLONIZING THE BIBLE

A POSTCOLONIAL RESPONSE

There cannot and should not be such a thing as 'African Biblical Scholarship' if this is envisaged in terms akin to that produced by Western-type training.

—Tinyiko Maluleke[1]

7.1 Definition of African Biblical Studies

As Franz Fanon, makes clear about decolonization, understanding the colonial process is vital for a successful decolonizing process. Biblical interpretation in Africa, to one extent, can viably claim its origins in the works of early church luminaries in North Africa, such as Origen or Augustine, or in fourth-century Ethiopia.[2] Interesting and informative as such connections may be, though, they are not the focus of this study. Instead, the focus in this study is on the more recent historical incarnation of the Bible's encounter with Africa South of the Sahara, via the European mission and colonial experience. African biblical scholarship, with a postcolonial bent has been classified under several titles, including African Biblical Hermeneutics, African Biblical Interpretations, African Inculturation/Intercultural Hermeneutics, and African biblical scholarship, etc.

My classification of "African Biblical Studies" aims at solidifying the relationship that I seek to emphasize, the historical connection that inextricably binds African interpretive endeavors, for better or worse, to the larger discipline of Biblical Studies. I seek to emphasize the case for African Biblical Studies' rightful place in the larger scheme of things. The first time, as far as I can tell, the phrase "African

1. Tinyiko Maluleke, "The Bible among Africans: A Missiological Perspective," in *To Cast First upon the Earth: Bible and Mission Collaborating in Today's Multicultural Global Context*, ed. Teresa Okure (Pietermaritzburg: Cluster, 2000), 87–112, 94–5.

2. Keith A. Burton, *The Blessing of Africa: The Bible and African Christianity* (Downers Grove: InterVarsity, 2007).

Biblical Studies" appears as a reference to a distinct discipline seems to be from South African biblical scholar Gerald West, in a 1991 article.[3] More recently, biblical scholars David T. Adamo, Mbengu Nyjawung, Andrew Mbuvi, and Berekiah Olusegun have defended and used the title African Biblical Studies to define a form of biblical interpretation that is decidedly both biblical and African.[4] However, as South African theologian Tiniyiko Maluleke rightly observes, such a discipline of African biblical scholarship cannot be limited to the established confines of the discipline as envisioned in the West.

7.2 Scope of African Biblical Studies

Works by African scholars going back more than half a century can be rightly classified within the rubric of African Biblical Studies.[5] In an earlier study, I postulated what I see as fundamental foci of African Biblical Studies, outlined in one of the earliest complete monographs to substantiate a framework for a distinct African Biblical Studies; John S. Mbiti's *New Testament Eschatology in an African Background* (1971).[6] The analysis that follows includes most of the key elements highlighted in the study, albeit in a different order and detail.

From the very beginning, African biblical scholars have held that any aspect of biblical interpretation carried out within the context of Africa, by African scholars, and/or addressing African concerns should be independent of any direct

---

3. Gerald O. West, "The Relationship between Different Modes of Reading (the Bible) and the Ordinary Reader," *Scriptura* 9 (1991): 87–110.

4. Andrew M. Mbuvi, "African Biblical Studies: An Introduction to an Emerging Discipline," *CBR* 15, no. 2 (2017): 149–78; O. Olusegun Berekiah, "African Biblical Studies in Retrospect and Prospect: A Reflection on the Practice and Praxis of Biblical Studies in Africa," in *The Present State and the Future of Biblical Studies in Africa: Essays in Honour of Samuel O. Abogunrin*, ed. J. D. Gwamna, A. O. Dada, and Hope Amolo (Ibadan, Nigeria: NABIS, 2017), 70–87. Adamo, *Explorations in African Biblical Studies*. Though titled *African Biblical Studies*, this article is less of an attempt at constructing a discipline and more of a sampling of one perspective of African Biblical Studies. It is primarily a collection and defense of positions on Africans in the Bible, a topic he has championed for the last two decades.

5. Mbengu D. Nyiawung, "Contextualising Biblical Exegesis: What is the African Biblical Hermeneutic Approach?", *HTS* 69, no. 1 (2013): Art. #2011, 9 pages. Also, as a point of interest, the Nigerian Association of Biblical Studies (NABIS) formed in 1985 and began publishing its journal *AJBS* (formerly *Nigerian Association of Biblical Studies Journal*) in 1986.

6. (London: OUP, 1971). Cf. Mbuvi, "An African Biblical Scholar Explores the Broadening of the Biblical Studies Landscape," 150.

imposition of presuppositions governing Biblical Studies in the West.[7] Maluleke's *dictum*, quoted above, represents the prevailing sentiment among African biblical scholars about their interpretive occupation and the need to chart a course that addresses African concerns and interests, without necessarily becoming provincial or parochial.[8] Gerald West is as emphatic as Maluleke when he urges that "the separation of Biblical Studies from other theological disciplines, so common elsewhere, cannot be allowed to happen in an African Biblical Studies."[9] With a predominant postcolonial inclination from its beginning, African Biblical Studies has sought to shape the interpretive process through critique and innovation. So the different facets of biblical interpretation in Africa—*négritude*, inculturation, rehabilitation hermeneutics, comparative hermeneutics, cultural hermeneutics— all have a decidedly postcolonial dynamic that unites them.

The following then are the key factors that contribute toward the construction of such postcolonialist African Biblical Studies outlook. First, and most obvious, neither Euro-American questions nor categories that have been dogmatized in the western (Global North) should define such a discipline. Any acquiescence and conformity would simply evidence the continued imposition and domination of the colonial agenda upon the African subject matter and scholarship.[10] Such approaches have to be creative by not limiting themselves within established parameters and categories, keeping their eye on the relevance of their readings to their immediate contexts, and drawing from questions relevant to their contexts.[11] In this regard, for example, as much of the western biblical scholarship has remain

---

7. I am aware I am painting with a very broad brush here given the breadth of perspectives present in African Biblical interpretations. For example, most Evangelical interpretations in Africa remain rooted in uncritical adoption of western methodologies of biblical interpretations, distinguishing only their African applications from what they consider "objective exegesis." A good sample of this approach is the *African Bible Commentary* (Grand Rapids: Zondervan, 2010), edited by Tokunboh Adeyemo. Single-volume commentaries written by Samuel Ngewa and others in the Hippo/Africa Bible Commentary Series follow the same trajectory. It is also true that most of the scholars mentioned earlier were trained in western institutions or in institutions where they were engaged in the western methodology of biblical interpretation.

8. Mbuvi, "An African Biblical Scholar Explores the Broadening of the Biblical Studies Landscape," 152–4.

9. Gerald West, "On the Eve of an African Biblical Studies: Trajectories and Trends," *JTSA* 99 (1997): 99–115, 101. Cf. also T. Maluleke, "Half a Century of African Christian Theologies: Elements of the Emerging Agenda for the Twenty-First Century," *JTSA* 99 (1997): 4–23.

10. Sugirtharajah, *The Bible and the Third World*, 61.

11. Maluleke, "Half a Century of African Christian Theologies"; Ukpong, "Popular Reading"; G. West, "On the Eve"; Mbuvi, "An African Biblical Scholar Explores the Broadening of the Biblical Studies Landscape"; and Adamo, *Explorations in African Biblical Studies*.

largely dominated by historical-critical concerns, African Biblical Studies tends to focus on the biblical relevance for the present.

Second, such a discipline should be free to interrogate concerns relevant to interpreters' contexts and allow for the possibility that new methodologies and interpretive questions may emerge from reading the Bible in non-western contexts. A plurality of approaches would mean that the Biblical Studies discipline, as currently constructed in the West, would need to cede its domination, as new entries reconfigure the discipline.

Third, in utilizing the postcolonial optic, African Biblical Studies unapologetically reads from the point of view of colonized or formerly colonized; it prioritizes readings from the vantage point of the poor, the oppressed, the dominated, the suffering, and the marginalized. This of course is an implicit critic of Biblical Studies in the West, which have been the preserve of the colonizer and former colonizer. However, as South African biblical scholar Jeremy Punt warns, this does not mean "romanticis[ing] or idealis[ing] the poor, but . . . *refus[ing] to blame the victims.* [African Biblical Studies] is, rather, concerned with such social or other structures and institutions which foster and contribute to victimhood."[12] It is a means of giving voice to the silenced *and the ostracized.* As Dube explains, "Clearly, rereading the Bible for social justice demands that one should read both the text and the society. Since society is dynamic, *a reader for social justice never arrives.* One cannot say, I am a narrative critic, a feminist reader, a postcolonial reader, period. Rather, one is constantly forced to delve into completely new reading strategies in search for social justice."[13]

Fourth, at the base of African Biblical Studies' critique would be issues of power dynamics, dominance and control at play within western Biblical Studies' historical role in colonialism and imperialism. It critically examines both western interpretations and biblical texts themselves to expose the dynamics of power and oppression, seeking to undermine and subvert the imperializing aspects of such readings. According to Dube and Staley, such an approach "seeks to examine how the colonizer constructs and justifies domination of the other in various places and periods of history; how the colonized collaborate, resist, and assert their rights to be free in various places and periods of history; and how both parties travel and cross boundaries."[14]

Overall, then, to maintain that all African Biblical Studies is postcolonial, as I do, is not necessarily to disagree with Gerald West, who makes the case for African Biblical Studies as being three-pronged—"tri-polar," he calls it. According to Gerald West, African Biblical Studies can be divided into three distinct groupings.

12. Jeremy Punt, "Postcolonial Biblical Criticism in South Africa: Some Mind and Road Mapping," *Neot* 37, no. 1 (2003): 66.

13. M. W. Dube, "Rereading the Bible: Biblical Hermeneutics and Social Justice," in *African Theology Today*, ed. Emmanuel Katongole (Scranton: University of Scranton Press, 2002), 57–68, 65. (emphasis added)

14. Dube and Staley, *John and Postcolonialism*, 3.

So, besides the inculturation and the liberation models, a third, "ideological appropriation," can be distinguished which, he maintains, serves to provide the needed link to the contemporary reader, especially the oppressed and the marginalized reader.[15] This distinction, to me, does not preclude that even the inculturation and liberationist models are postcolonial in nature as they also focus on the oppressed and marginalized. Gerald West, however, rightly points out that "postcolonial interpretation is not a technique, a 'method' to be applied to the biblical text. For those of us who inhabit a post-colony, post-colonial interpretation is a way of life before it is an interpretive tool. Post-colonial interpretation is a way of being (African)."[16] Essentially, Gerald West agrees that postcoloniality encompasses the whole African Biblical Studies interpretive process, and not simply methodologically, a perspective also shared by a pioneer of Postcolonial Biblical Criticism, Sugirtharajah in the quote at the beginning of this chapter.

The African biblical scholar, therefore, must continue to make the case for the relevance and legitimacy of the readings of the Bible addressing the plight of the oppressed and silenced, as a conscious presupposition. And given that the oppressed and silenced are in every culture and community, the implications of African Biblical Studies' readings go beyond the African setting. Therefore, African Biblical Studies can play several primary roles: First, is to introduce different questions to Biblical Studies, necessitating a rethinking of the discipline's focus as it currently stands. Second, is to challenge the established disciplinary categories and boundary lines that Biblical Studies in the West has established, as they have mainly served to keep out non-western and non-white perspectives— for example, the role of the "theologically untrained 'ordinary' readers," or so-called grassroots readings of the Bible, challenges the long-held notion that biblical interpretation is the preserve of the biblical expert.[17] Third, addressing historical atrocities (religious, political, ideological or interpretive) perpetuated within western Biblical Studies, e.g., in support of colonialism or enslavement of Africans, etc.) as a way of moving forward with oneness of purpose, as a justice-seeking interpretive community. Fourth, to address the resultant impact of inequality and oppression that scholars of non-western origins have endured in their ostracization, marginalization, denigration and suppression, whether as teachers (when they can't find jobs), researchers (when the academy deems their research not erudite and sophisticated enough), or as members of society who have negotiated matters of racism, colonialism, and other forms of oppression.

15. Gerald West, "African Biblical Scholarship as Post-colonial, Tri-Polar, and a Site-of-Struggle," in *Present and Future of Biblical Studies: Celebrating 25 Years of Brill's Biblical Interpretation*, ed. Tat-siong Benny Liew (Leiden and Boston: Brill, 2018), 240–73.

16. Ibid., 247.

17. G. West, "Constructing Critical and Contextual Readings with Ordinary Readers: Mark 5:21-6:1," *JTSA* (1995): 60–9.

7.3 Exegesis versus Hermeneutics: Contemporary versus Historical

It is clear, so far, that African Biblical Studies reflects distinct aspects from the dominant western approaches in Biblical Studies. A vital distinction in the interpretation of the Bible between its western and African readings is the former's proclivity toward historical issues in contrast to the latter's inclination toward the use of the Bible to address present concerns.[18] I have highlighted earlier how Schweitzer's works, and those of other European biblical scholars within Enlightenment thinking, orchestrated the western penchant for the historical. African biblical interpretations' is markedly distinct as it resists the colonizing and imperializing impulses that western Biblical Studies continues to not only perpetuate, but also defend.

Initially, the western focus on what was at some point categorized as "scientific approaches" to the interpretation of the Bible led to the distinction between *exegesis* (understanding the Bible in its ancient setting) and *hermeneutics* (application of the exegetical findings to the present reality). While western Biblical Studies held both as vital to the interpretive process, exegesis continued to receive priority, especially in European academic institutions, as it provided the hope of getting at the biblical authors' intended meanings and at approximating the "original" texts. These readers presumed that the so-called scientific methods could be objective and thus reliable in determining not only accurate, but universal meanings of ancient biblical texts.

This led to the study of subdisciplines or related disciplines like biblical languages, philology, and archeology, eventually dominating western Biblical Studies. The ground for the dominance of the grammatical-historical methods of biblical interpretation had been set for Biblical Studies in the West. Thus, with gradual dominance of "scientific approaches", a separation of scholarly study of the Bible from the "everyday" readership and Church Bible study was established. What subsequently developed, was an increased bifurcation of what was deemed "scholarly" (and therefore academically reliable because it could be rationally defended) versus "popular" (unscholarly, non-rational, and therefore unreliable?) readings of the Bible. In the second half of the twentieth century, the emergence of "new" literary methods of reading the Bible would eventually challenge the grammatical-historical dominance. Central to this new shift in interpretation was a growing awareness of the need to approach the Bible as literature rather than a source of historical interrogation.

At around the same time that Baëta's *Tropical African Christianity* was published, James Muilenburg read a discipline-shifting presidential address at the Society of Biblical Studies meeting, which he entitled "Form Criticism and Beyond."[19] This address would engender what would come to be known as Literary Criticism

---

18. Mbuvi, "An African Biblical Scholar Explores the Broadening of the Biblical Studies Landscape," 149–78.

19. James Muilenburg, "Form Criticism and Beyond," *JBL* 88, no. 1 (1969): 1–18.

of the Bible (he called it "rhetorical criticism") in Biblical Studies.[20] *Contra* the grammatical-historical approach, Literary Criticism moved the discipline from studying the biblical text like an archeological dig, always trying to reach behind the text to arrive at possible contributors to the text's meaning (historical approaches); instead, it shifted the focus to the biblical text in its "final form" (the biblical text as it is). The introduction of literary criticism also brought into question the idea that grammatical-historical approaches had a level of objectivity that would lead to more reliable readings of the Bible. Only with this introduction did Biblical Studies in the West start looking at the roles that methods of interpretation, types of questions asked, and readers' role in arriving at meaning played in biblical interpretation.

While Muilenburg was shaking the foundations of the staid grammatical-historical dominance in western Biblical Studies, African biblical scholars from the newly independent African countries were already engaging in post-colonial/postcolonial discourses of the Bible that already was focused less on the historical–grammatical and more on the final form of the text. Then and now, African scholars have found that the final form of the text provides a sufficient starting point for the interpretive process without necessarily denigrating historical analysis. The focus is *less* on "what the biblical text meant for its ancient settings," and *more* on "what the text means for the current reader." As a result, African interpreters pose fundamentally different questions to the text, which inevitably leads to fairly different analytical approaches and results.

So laden was the Bible with encumbrances of the colonial project that it could never simply be relegated to its ancient status. For the African biblical scholar, because the Bible is not simply an ancient text, but one that essentially finds its full expression in the reader's present, the need to understand how it applies to the contemporary realities precludes (but does not ignore) its historical provenance. For the African, the Bible has always been about the present, as the expectation is that it ably addresses the reader's current concerns. Because African readers received and experienced the Bible as a component of the colonizer's tool bag, the Bible was always about current affairs (dynamics of authority, power, subjugation, and oppression), and not ancient history. In the parlance of the enslaved Africans in America, the Bible had become in the hands of the European, the "talking book" whose colonial manifestation had revealed it as "the white man's book."[21] As long as the European missionary could hold the Bible aloft and proclaim "the Bible says . . ." it had attained a living, breathing, talking book dynamic.

It is not surprising then that New Testament scholar Musa Dube has questioned the focus on the Greco-Roman world for New Testament studies, especially with the tendency to bracket questions about modern implications of reading the Bible in oppressive contexts like colonialism. While she believes in the value of historical

---

20. Joe Sprinkle, "Literary Approaches to the Old Testament: A Survey of Recent Scholarship," *JETS* 32, no. 3 (1989): 299–310.

21. Callahan, *The Talking Book.*

analysis of the biblical background, she holds that the focus on the historical often becomes an excuse to avoid present concerns on the pretext of situating the text in its "original context."[22] As we noted earlier, for the African, the Bible stopped being "the white man's book" to the "word of God" only when it spoke in the local African vernacular. The mediation of the "white man" had become unnecessary and so the articulation of liberated African thought directly from the pages of the Bible to one's cultural and religious reality was instantaneous. The African could understand the Bible in local idiom using cultural imagery.[23] When, thus, the African could *hear* the Bible in his/her mother tongue and African idiom, it ceased to be the colonialist's book and became, almost instantly, an anti-colonial manifesto. Contained in the Bible were aspects unengaged before by the Africans that resonated with the African reality in ways that made them question what the European missionaries' intent was in choosing what was presented or not.

Since the Bible was already connected to the plight of the colonized African as a component of the colonial project, its relevance in the day-to-day affairs of the African as a people has remained crucial. The Kenyan novelist Ngũgĩ affirms this relevance while reflecting on his political detention. In a reporting on a chat with a Kenyan warden while in prison, Ngũgĩ exclaims: "He would refer to biblical passages which talked of faith, sin, salvation, grace, life to come; I would, in turn, refer him to alternative passages where God is cited as having sent his prophets to denounce earthly misrule and oppression of innocents."[24]

With this preference for the present, African biblical approaches refuse to remain simply esoteric academic exercises but seek to engage social realities such sickness (e.g., HIV/AIDS pandemic) or violence (colonialism, terrorism, wars, etc.) with an intent of proclaiming justice, freedom, hope. Elsewhere, I have made the same argument that

> Overall . . . A[frican] B[iblical] S[tudies] refuses to deal with the Bible simply as an ancient text and demands that it be engaged to deal with present concerns, addressing issues that resonate with African (and world) realities. Accordingly, A[frican] B[iblical] S[tudies] embraces more than just exegetical interests but privileges hermeneutical concerns.[25]

Content that resonates with the African experience and present reality fills the Bible, and the biblical events serve as commentary on readers' contemporary experiences in multiple ways.

---

22. Dube, "Boundaries and Bridges," 152–6.

23. Kwame Bediako, "Jesus in African Culture: A Ghanaian Perspective," in *Emerging Voices in Global Christian Theology*, ed. William Dyrness (Grand Rapids: Zondervan, 1994), 93–121.

24. Ngũgĩ wa Thiong'o, *Detained*, A Writer's Prison Diary (London: Heinemann, 1981), 25.

25. A. Mbuvi, "African Biblical Studies: An Introduction to an Emerging Discipline," *Currents in Biblical Research* 15, no. 2 (2017): 149–78, 154.

Chapter 8

THE BIBLE AND POSTCOLONIAL AFRICAN LITERATURE

I would be quite satisfied if my novels (especially those set in the past) do no more than teach my [African] readers that their past—with all its imperfections—was not one long night of savagery from which the Europeans acting on God's behalf delivered them.

— Chinua Achebe[1]

Postcolonial literature echoes and mirrors the realities of the postcolonial world, but it also attempts to awaken its audience, asking—both in its thematic concerns as well as in its very existence—for greater justice.

— Susan V. Gallagher[2]

8.1 Introduction

Creative literature in Africa has been in the vanguard of postcolonial writing. African novelists have not shied away from injecting their own interpretive voice in response to the impact of colonialism and Christianity on the African community. African novels thus posit the challenges that reading the Bible in the African context encounters. For the African novelist, the Bible is a socially engaged writing that is both a challenge to, and challenged by, its cultural encounter with the African reality.[3] Offering no easy answers, African novels present readings outside the ecclesial tradition and therefore have greater freedom to engage the Bible and its presuppositions, exposing its complicity in both the colonial and postcolonial political structures in Africa. These novels, whose authors' role is defined by the preeminent African novelist Chinua Achebe as "teachers" to African readers, also provide avenues for interpreting the Bible in the African context which

---

1. Chinua Achebe, "The Novelist as a Teacher," *New Statesman*, London, January 29, 1965: 40–6, 45.

2. Susan v. Gallagher, *Postcolonial Literature and the Biblical Call for Justice* (Jackson: University Press of Mississippi, 1994), 20.

3. Andrew Mbuvi, "African Novels as Resource for Socially Engaged Gospel?" *SBL Forum*, 2006, Available online: https://www.sbl-site.org/publications/article.aspx?ArticleId =527 (accessed June 23, 2020).

take seriously Christianity's complicity with the powerful and the wealthy in the precolonial and postcolonial. This complicity has rendered Christianity unable to be the voice of justice when necessary, as Susan Gallagher points out, such as in the case of the Rwandan genocide where the number of people killed and buried in churches elucidated the complicity of the Church.[4]

Some of the vital voices in the construction of Postcolonialism as a discipline in literary theory have included such luminaries as Nigerian Chinua Achebe and Kenyan Ngũgĩ wa Thiong'o. Achebe's and Ngũgĩ's writings have been especially pointed in their critique of the colonial project and in formulating a way forward in constructive formulations of literary analysis.[5] Their significance for us, however, is their exhilarating engagement of the Bible in their writings. The Bible, as the "white man's book," has carried with it religious, literary, cultural, political, social, and economic significance for these authors as a foil for grappling with the impact of imperialism and colonialism on the African community.

Because these novelists are not theologically trained, their biblical engagement is not strictly guided by ecclesial or academic religious discourses. Their medium of creative writing frees them from ecclesial constraints and allows them to employ imagination in their engagement with the history of the Bible and Christianity in Africa. Yet, the Christian experience in Africa and an acute awareness of the complicated relationship of the Bible, colonialism, and the African reality and postcolonialism, informs their commentary. Their views, consequently, are as valuable as those of the trained biblical scholar and have a significant impact on the understanding and interpretation of the Bible in the postcolonial African reality.

8.2 Dialogical Construct between Christianity and African Religion—Chinua Achebe

African biblical scholars have been keen to show how African creative writers contribute to the interpretation of the Bible by exploring African novels' engagement with the Bible. In many of these novels, the authors interrogate and critique the Bible's role in the colonial enterprise, encapsulation of local biblical interpretations, and political engagement. For example, Ashton Nichols has pointed out that even before Backhtinian dialogism gained currency in western Biblical Studies, Achebe's fiction already utilized fictional dialogical models by presenting competing religious definitions and beliefs.[6] An analysis of Achebe's

---

4. C. Rittner (ed.), *Genocide in Rwanda: Complicity of the Churches* (Paragon House Books on Genocide and the Holocaust; St. Paul: Paragon House, 2004).

5. C. Achebe, *Home and Exile* (New York: Anchor, 2000); Cf. Ngũgĩ wa Thiong'o, *Decolonising the Mind: The Politics of Language in African Literature* (London: Heinemann, 1986).

6. Ashton Nichols, "'If there is One God, Fine there will be Others': Dialogical Theology in the Novels of Chinua Achebe," in *And the Birds Began to Sing: Religion and Literature in Post-colonial Cultures*, ed. Jamie S. Scott (Amsterdam and Atlanta: Rodopi, 1996), 159–69.

early novels—*Things Fall Apart* (1958), *No Longer at Ease* (1960), *The Arrow of God* (1964), and *A Man of the People* (1966)—evidences "dialogical interactions between religious beliefs and social action," and the resultant progress.[7]

Achebe's various inspirations to write his novels included response to the colonial caricature of the Africans and the African reality, collusion of the European mission and colonialism, and the political corruption and failure of postcolonial African leadership. Western colonial depictions of Africa made it clear to Achebe that these were foreign perspectives grossly misrepresenting the African reality. Books like Joseph Conrad's *In the Heart of Darkness* portrayed the colonial gaze of the European author who failed to comprehend the cultures, religions, and social reality of the African.[8] So Achebe envisioned his novels as reminders to the Africans "that their past—with all its imperfections—was not one long night of savagery from which the first Europeans acting on God's behalf delivered them."[9] This perspective aligns with African biblical scholars' hermeneutic of rehabilitation that advocates for a more accurate articulation of the African reality and challenges the racist views that missionaries such as Schweitzer maintained about Africans. Achebe believed this was the role of the African writer, who could not "be excused from the task of re-education and regeneration."[10]

Arguably, the most celebrated of African novels, Achebe's *Things Fall Apart*, provides two points of analysis of the colonial encounter. The story is about an African community's encounter with the encroaching missionary and colonial infrastructure that slowly undermines the core values which hold the community together, eventually tearing it apart between those who convert to the "white man's" religion, and those who resist. Presentation of the biblical-theological teachings of an "Only God," who has a son but not a wife, is simply confounding for the Umuofia villagers. This is not intellectual incapability on their part, but a logical inconsistency within the constructs of their worldview that does not allow them to accept such an unusual setup.

Conversely, in the conversation between a wise villager called Akunna and the British missionary, Mr. Brown, failure to comprehend the system of the Umuofia gods depicts a western failure to comprehend the African religious reality. Akunna's claim that the missionary and the villagers worship the same Supreme Being, albeit with different names, prompts Mr. Brown to disagree by pointing out the "worship of idols" by the villagers. In a witty response, Akunna explains that the so-called idols are God's emissaries, just like the leader of the Church of England is God's emissary. Unlike Schweitzer and missionaries like him, it occurs

---

7. Ibid., 160.

8. Andrew M. Mbuvi, "Missionary Acts, Things Fall Apart: Modeling Mission in Acts 17:15–34 and a Concern for Dialogue in Chinua Achebe's *Things Fall Apart*," *Ex Auditu* 23 (2007): 140–56.

9. C. Achebe, *Morning Yet on Creation Day* (London: Heinemann, 1977), 45.

10. Ibid.

to Mr. Brown that he had errantly prejudged the Igbo religious reality, before fully understanding it, and he had underestimated his counterpart's intelligence.[11]

In *Things Fall Apart*, Umuofia community members, with the exception of those marginalized within the community, meet colonial encroachment with resistance. They describe colonial encroachment in terms of the specific order of religion, government, and education. But the dialogs offer multivalent voices within the community in response to this arrival of the white man—from the resistance of the protagonist Okwonko to the total embrace by his son, Nwoye, who put a "knife" in the family and ruptured it with his conversion to Christianity. In the voice of the disappointed resisters:

> Does the white man understand our custom about land? How can he when he does not even speak our tongue? But he says that our customs are bad; and our own brothers who have taken up his religion also say that our customs are bad. How do you think we can fight when our own brothers have turned against us?[12]

Note the echoes of what we discussed earlier concerning missionary attitudes toward the African reality in the first two questions, and the subsequent response. All the questions anticipate negative answers and highlight the destruction of colonial imposition on the community's religio-cultural center.

Seen from the vantage of the Umuofia's experience, what the missionary assumed was "the good news" turned out to be bad news indeed. It became the wreaking of social, cultural, and religious fabric that held it together. Conversion of some members of the community to the white man's religion, had created a major conundrum for Umuofia as it could not fight back, since that would entail fighting against their own brothers and sisters.

Skillfully portrayed, even as there is a blanket characterization of the colonial project in the novel, its dialogic construct does not succumb to sanctimonious portrayals of the African religion. There is nothing as poignant as the death of Ikemefuna, the protagonist Okwonko's adoptive "peace child," who must eventually be sacrificed to appease the Umuofia Oracle lest judgment falls upon the community. Ikemefuna's sacrificial killing in the hands of his "adoptive" father, Okwonko, fulfills the religious requirements of the Oracle, but leaves a clear sense of confounding loss for everyone else involved.

The lingering question becomes whether this death was necessary. Even for those who may see a Christological parallel in Ikemefuna's death (a "beloved son" given over to death by his "father" to avoid judgment on the community), the unwarranted violence prompts the community to question its own traditions. Similarly, the infanticide of newly born twins among the Igbo, a tradition Christianity pushed against by rescuing those children and showing that no harm came from the Igbo deities("idols") to those who did so.

---

11. John A. Anonby, "Achebe's Novels and their Implications for Christians in Africa," *AJET* 9, no. 1 (1990): 14–23; 16.

12. Achebe, "Missionary Acts, Things Fall Apart," 157.

Ultimately, the community succumbs to the "trickery of the white man":

> The white man is very clever. He came quietly and peaceably with his religion. We were amused at his foolishness and allowed him to stay. Now he has won our brothers, and our clan can no longer act like one. He has put a knife on the things that held us together and we have fallen apart.[13]

In the section that gives the novel its title, Achebe holds the mirror to the European missionary project's callousness. The story is now told from the Africans' point of view, and it reflects the sense of deception the Africans felt when what they thought was an extension of their hospitality had turned out to be a "trojan horse" infiltration with its resultant social destruction. Notice how the arrival of the European religion is "quiet and peaceable," but in the end the impact is "violence"— it puts a "knife" into the social, religious, and cultural world of Umuofia.

This could describe Mr. Brown, the missionary who arrived while Okonkwo was in exile. He was a peaceable man, uninterested in forcing Umuofians into Christianity, willing to learn the language and culture of the community and yet remained part of the imperial power. His replacement, however, is the stereotypical hard-charging and uncompromising colonialist, Rev. Smith, determined to get converts at whatever cost. I do think it is not coincidental that Brown is referred to as "Mr." and Smith as "Rev." They represent two types of missionaries—the ecclesial-backed and conservative reverends, and the more open-minded and usually not church-ordained missionaries with a sense of respect for recipient communities. While the novel's dialogic reflects the multivalent nature of the European encounter, Mr. Brown was still essentially a part of the imperial powers, whose knowledge of the community's culture may have been used to undermine it.

The novel ends with the suicide of the protagonist Okonkwo, who, after failed attempts to rally the community against the "white man" and his followers (Christian converts), realizes resistance is futile, and chooses an ignoble suicide death rather than succumb to the "white man." Okonkwo is the epitome of the anti-colonial resistance that sought to reclaim what was being lost to colonization. Achebe, in analyzing the novel three decades after its publication, described Okonkwo's suicide in theological terms as "eschatological defiance."[14]

In the follow-up novel *No Longer at Ease*, the story jumps one generation to Okonkwo's grandson Obi, the son of Nwoye who left home after his conversion to Christianity led to a falling out with his father. With Obi, the reader now encounters the first generation of Igbos born into postcolonial Christian families. Unlike their parents who abandoned everything African in their Christian conversion, Obi's generation is eager to embrace again their African reality, as a means to

---

13. Ibid., 176.

14. C. Achebe, *The Education of a British-Protected Child: Essays* (New York: Alfred A. Knopf, 2009), 129.

contextualize or Africanize their Christian faith. It is a rejection of the "all-or-nothing" religious attitudes of their fathers and an embrace of religious hybridity.[15]

The novel also expresses disappointment with the imposition of western religious structures of worship where the hierarchical model of authority leaves the priest or pastor no room for dialogue with the congregation. In a culture where everything, even religion, is always a negotiable proposition, this led to a feeling of unwarranted constriction. Echoing the reference to divine consultation at creation in Gen. 1:26-28, Achebe intones that Chukwu, the name of the Supreme Being among the Igbo, "did not make the world by fiat. He held conversations with mankind [. . .] to make the earth firm and productive."[16]

In the third novel, a critique of the post-independence political leadership in Africa, religion in *The Man of the People* becomes a form of political discourse devoid of any depth of commitment or conscience. Religion becomes a pawn in political power games. In a searing critique of the postcolonial political elite, most of whom were products of missionary schools, religious phrases become platitudes for endearing oneself to the community to gain votes for political office. Religion simply becomes a tool or device for power and control. To a certain degree, the African leader turns out to be just like the colonizer, with a thirst for power and control, with religion simply a useful means to attain the latter.

One encounters a more direct critique of religious orthodoxy in *Anthills of the Savannah*. Gender issues are also highlighted in considering the role of women in religion. Comparison is made between the myth of the women's pounding of the mortar and pestle which prompts the distancing of the Supreme Being, to the story of Eve. And in language reminiscent of the African biblical scholars who advocated for African religions as *praeparatio evangelica*, the protagonist Ikem exclaims, "Our ancestors, without the benefit of hearing about the Old Testament, made the very same story differing only in local colour."[17] He goes on to cite what he sees as a contradiction, that "man . . . turn[s] his spouse into the very mother of God" in the New Testament, but he also notes parallels with the African tradition that teaches "mother is supreme."[18] In this regard, Igbo religion and Christianity essentially independently arrive at a congruent teaching.

Achebe, ultimately, expresses dismay with the postcolonial moral decline among the African leaders and elite, partly an indictment of western Christianity's dissolution of pre-colonial African institutions. Regarding religious orthodoxy, which he castigates, "Achebe's conviction that integrity is more basic than orthodoxy is both attractive and compelling, especially on a continent as politically and ideologically fragmented as Africa . . . .[since] [f]or Achebe, true worship transcends religion or creed."[19]

---

15. Nichols, "If there is One God, fine, there will be Others," 163.
16. Ibid.
17. Ibid., 167.
18. Ibid.
19. Anonby, "Achebe's Novels and their Implications for Christians in Africa," 22.

8.3 Reconstituting Biblical Themes for a New Postcolonial Christianity—Ngũgĩ wa Thiong'o

There is hardly any other African novelist and literary critic who engages the Bible as thoroughly as Ngũgĩ wa Thiong'o of Kenya. His novels follow the trajectory of his religious transformation, from his earlier conservative Christian conversion (having been baptized "James," a name he would later reject as a colonial nomenclature) to his transformation as a Marxist socialist.[20] His novels and plays, which include *Weep not, Child* (1964), *The River Between* (1967), *A Grain of Wheat* (1967), *I Will Marry When I Want* (1977), *Petals of Blood* (1977), *Caitaani Mutharabaini* (*Devil on the Cross*, 1982), *Matigari* (1998), *Murogi was Kagogo* (*Wizard of the Crow*, 2006), not only heavily employ biblical imagery and allusions, as some titles suggest, but also engage in biblical interpretation that provides a transgressive articulation of the Bible as an anti-colonial text.[21]

He wrote his first three novels during his Christian phase in classic realist form, and they display a certain optimism about Christian religion, in an almost utopian framework. This is especially true of a form of Christianity that incorporates the Gikuyu community's culture and idioms. But beginning with his fourth novel, *Petals of Blood*, there is a significant shift in the tone of his *oeuvre* as Ngũgĩ shows increasing dismay at the emergence of neocolonialism in post-independence Kenya, and the ecclesial collusion with post-colonial African political leadership. Not only was the political neocolonial class corrupt and inept at leadership, but it was also aping the colonial predecessors' violence in suppressing the masses (average citizens) while creating a cabal of classist political society. The religious community is not exempt, and Ngũgĩ vilifies the failure of the African Christian ethic to transform post-independence Kenyan churches into a voice of justice. He exposes Christian leaders as willing tools of the political oppressors, not unlike colonial missionaries' connivance with colonizers.

20. Peter Mwikisa, "Politics and the Religious Unconscious in Ngugi wa Thiong'o's *A Grain of Wheat* and his other Works," *Scriptura* 92 (2006): 248–64, esp. 249, where he argues that "Ngugi's oppositional stance or resistance against the cultural imperialism of the Bible and Christianity should not be thought of exclusively in terms of an invasive decolonization strategy launched from the standpoint of a secular ideology, that is, Marxism. It should, instead, be seen also as a product of the internal dynamics of the Christian faith in the postcolonial epoch, which leads believers to problematize the major tenets of their faith, without necessarily rejecting it."

21. Michael Valdez Moses, "Caliban and his Precursors: The Poetics of Literary History and the Third World," in *Theoretical Issues in Literary History*, ed. David Perkins (Cambridge, MA: Harvard University Press, 1991), 206–26, 211—"By means of a deliberate recontextualising of passages from the Old and New Testament, Ngugi transforms a text which was used ideologically to subdue the Gikuyu people, into one which serves as a vehicle for their liberation from British imperial rule."

Set in the periods just preceding and following Kenya's independence from British colonial rule, the first three novels portray a clash of religions between Kenyan Christian converts and those who did not convert; between the colonial and the African. For Ngũgĩ, Christianity and African cultures can co-exist, as long as Christianity is first stripped of its western garments, and allowed to enmesh itself within African culture to produce an African Christianity. Ngũgĩ remarks in *The River Between* that

> not all of the ways of the white man were bad. Even his religion was not essentially bad. Some good, some true shone through it. But the religion, the faith, needed washing, clearing away all the dirt, leaving the eternal. And that eternal that was the truth had to be reconciled to the traditions of the people.[22]

It is not clear what the "eternal" kernel of Christianity stripped of its western "dirt" is. Ultimately, though, this "eternal kernel" would have to reconcile with the Gikuyu (African) traditions to arrive at an authentic Gikuyu Christianity. The novels also depict how the Christian religion, by Africanizing, can become an anti-colonialist weapon in antithesis to its use as a colonial weapon.

The title of the second novel, *A Grain of Wheat*, comes from Jn 12:24, "Very truly, I tell you, unless a grain of wheat falls into the earth and dies, it remains just a single grain; but if it dies, it bears much fruit." In it, Ngũgĩ depicts Kenyan freedom fighters as co-opting the biblical ethic of sacrificing one (or few), for the benefit of the many (the community). The protagonist Waiyaki, the "Moses" of the people, keeps a copy of his Bible in his pocket even as he leads the anti-colonial fight, and he becomes the first native "martyr" in the fight for freedom. Ngũgĩ portrays Waiyaki as a "type" of Jesus, as both "are . . . betrayed by friends [and] . . . both [are] judged and found guilty by their adversaries."[23] Ngũgĩ's vision of Waiyaki as messianic, "expressed in overwhelming biblical terms," deliberately disarms the colonial framing of the Bible as western, by legitimizing his actions in biblical terms.[24] Additionally, Kihika's elusive betrayer is referred to throughout the book, as "Judas." So what emerges is a form of liberationist African Christianity that envisions the fight for independence as a fight for justice.

Just like Achebe bemoans the community's destruction by Christianity, Ngũgĩ portrays social disintegration squarely placing the blame on African Christian characters Rev. Jackson Kigondu and Rev. Morris King'ori. The former, for example, was initially willing to incorporate African religious concepts into Christianity when he explained that "Ngai, the Gikuyu God, is the same One God who sent Christ, the son, to come and lead the way from darkness to the light'"

---

22. Wa Thiong'o, *The River Between*, 141.

23. John A. Anonby, *The Kenyan Epic Novelist Ngugi: His Secular Reconfiguration of Biblical Themes* (Lewiston: Edwin Mellen, 2006), 9.

24. Lupenga Mphande, "Ngugi and the World of Christianity: A Dialectic," *JAAS* 39, no. 5 (2004): 357–67, 360.

(*Grain*: 73). But after being drawn into the revivalist movement with its emphasis on personal salvation, Rev. Kigondu does an about-turn and rejects everything to do with African religious reality, politics, and culture. His religious focus turned "other-worldly!" Unsurprisingly, "for all his unworldliness, Jackson [became] . . . an ally of the colonial regime, calling on Christians to fight side by side with the white man, 'their brother in Christ.'"[25]

The utopian optimism in the first three novels gives way to an unrelenting critique of the postcolonial leadership, both political and religious. The adoption of a different literary form, allegory, accompanies this set of novels. The realist novel is gone and, in its place, allegory offers an alternative sacred history.[26] Even the novel titles, *Petals of Blood* and *Devil on the Cross*, exude a brooding and darkening pessimism absent in the first three novels. The gruesome violence and depiction of the corruption, ungodliness, and hypocrisy that characterizes the leadership of the country, subsumes complicity of the Church as partakers in the bloodbath of the innocent lives.

Another vital change at this stage of Ngũgĩ's writing was his permanent switch from writing in English to using his mother tongue, the Gikuyu instead. Just as Christianity had to become African, language too had to be decolonized, freeing himself and his reading community to access his writings without the mediation of the oppressor's language.[27] In so doing, Ngũgĩ put the politics of language at the center of the neocolonial project. European colonizers had introduced their languages (English, German, French, Dutch, Spanish, and Portuguese)as colonizing tools in the civilizing of the native whose language was gibberish. The local vernacular, for Ngũgĩ, is the most authentic means of articulating African thought and expression. This coheres with the aspects noted earlier regarding the vernacular Bible.

In Ngũgĩ's transition to allegorical writing, Christian imagery becomes more malleable in exposing the Colonial/Bible confluence that culminated in the ravaging of African communities, the loss of their land, and the uprooting of their religious traditions. In contrast to the positive application of the Bible in *A Grain of Wheat*, for example, the *Devil on the Cross* constructs a counter-reading of Jesus's crucifixion story by depicting the rich and powerful rescuing the Devil (neocolonial African leaders). As Mphande put it, "By employing Christianity in terms of its orality, prophecy, and style, Ngũgĩ's aim is thus to use Christianity through its own imagery to expose it as a capitalist arm of exploitation."[28]

---

25. Marijke van Vuuren, "Kihika's Bible: The Recontextualisation of the Gospel in Ngugi's *A Grain of Wheat*," *Koers* 65, no. 1 (2000): 1–16, 7.

26. Oliver Lovesey, "The Postcolonial 'Crisis of Reception' and Ngugi wa Thiong'o's Religious Allegory," in *And the Birds Began to Sing: Religion and Literature in Post-colonial Cultures*, ed. Jamie S. Scott (Amsterdam and Atlanta: Rodopi, 1996), 184.

27. Ngũgĩ wa Thiong'o, *Decolonizing the Mind: The Politics of Language in African Literature* (Nairobi, 1986), 27.

28. Mphande, "Ngugi and the World of Christianity," 361.

Ngũgĩ's utilization of Christian imagery and language serves only as familiar starting points as he transitions beyond their biblical familiarity surreal metaphysical images, drawn from the roots of their transformative potential.[29] For example, the resurrection in the novel *Matigari*, which has been christened the "Gospel according to Ngũgĩ," becomes a metaphor for political and cultural liberation.[30] The entire novel is an allegory that portrays the construction of the community's struggle with neocolonialism in terms of a parable that portrays the protagonist, Matigari, in Christ-like elusive mysterious appearances (cf. Jesus's appearance on the road to Emmaus in Luke 24 and at the seaside in John 21) to his faithful followers.

When John Anonby compares Ngũgĩ's novels to Bunyan's *The Pilgrim's Progress* and concludes that the primary distinction in their orientations is that Ngũgĩ's work is temporal and terrestrial while Bunyan's is eschatological, I think it is a misapprehension of Ngũgĩ's eschatological thinking.[31] Ngũgĩ's works are essentially eschatological, especially *Matigari*. The utopian expectation of the first three novels, which gives way to the more communitarian critique of neocolonialism, is in every sense eschatological in its outlook. Ngũgĩ's expectation of an outcome that transforms the downtrodden and gives them freedom and control of their destinies, is every bit as eschatological as Bunyan's journey to the Celestial City.

Ngũgĩ's is a radical liberationist eschatology that foresees not a "pie in the sky, by and by" theology espoused by European missionaries (the colonial eschatology that misdirected the colonized's gaze from the material world, allowing the colonizer to acquire the land and establish empire), but a form of "realized eschatology," where the hopes of the future shape the present reality.[32] Ngũgĩ's radicalized eschatology utilizes Marxian socialism to articulate, in congruence with Gustavo Guttierez's *Liberation Theology*, a "political eschatology" that can formulate a means of resisting the oppressive capitalist and colonialist/neocolonialist political systems that continue to ravage the African poor and vulnerable masses. As Mahfoud explains, "While eschatology opened the door for a more just world in the life to come, Marxism offered that reality in this one."[33] This radical eschatology is reflected in Ngũgĩ's reading of the messianic Ps. 72:4, 12, which he referenced in *A Grain of Wheat*:

He shall judge the *poor of the people*, he *shall save the children of the needy*, and shall *break in pieces the oppressor*.

For he shall *deliver the needy* when he cries; the *poor* also, and him that has no helper.

29. Lovesey, "The Postcolonial 'Crisis of Reception' and Ngugi wa Thiongo's Religious Allegory," 188.

30. Anonby, *The Kenyan Epic Novelist Ngugi*, 13.

31. Ibid.

32. See Sebastian Mahfood, *Radical Eschatologies: Embracing the Eschaton in the Works of Ngugi Wa Thiongo, Nuruddin Farah, and Ayi Kwei Armah* (Lambert Academic Publishing, 2009).

33. Ibid., 3.

The reader could understand this passage as a summation of Ngũgĩ's novels, as they consistently present the struggles of the community against the imposition of colonial and neocolonial authority. He finds his resistance and means of liberation in the same text that had been used to justify colonialism.

In conclusion, African creative writers anticipated major approaches that would later shape Biblical Studies in the West, and in Africa. African biblical scholars have highlighted African creative writing's engagement with the Bible and pointed out its unique contribution to the interpretation of the Bible, e.g., Postcolonial interpretation. While Biblical Studies in the West was still trying to look for the author's intent in interpreting the Bible in the 1960s, African creative writers were already paving the way for what would come to be understood in Biblical Studies as reader-response criticism. They were displaying awareness that the Bible's readers could use the text to undergird their presuppositions, assumptions, prejudices, political views, sexual views, and even scientific beliefs. It is a form of reader-response hermeneutics that one scholar has called the "resisting reader" approach, as it pushes back on presuppositions imposed on the African reader.[34]

Under the presumption of "objective" reading of the text, western scholars presented their interpretation of the Bible as *the* way to read the Bible. These readers resisted any interpretations that disagreed or failed to align with their perspectives, deeming them unscientific or unsophisticated, and therefore unreliable. The idea of classifying Biblical Studies in the West as a scientific discipline was another way of keeping it as a preserve of the privileged and sophisticated western biblical scholar, who alone could understand science.

African novelists, seeing through this veneer of self-importance, rendered meaningless the western readings by exposing their complicity in the colonial project and their inadequacy within the African context. By turning the same Bible against those who had used it as a tool of colonization and oppression, African novelists brought to light this unholy colonial marriage and put a spotlight on western exploitation of the Africans in the name of proselytization. Even preceding the liberation movement, African creative writers had articulated a liberationist reading of the Bible and advocated for the poor and oppressed, using the same Bible that was used to colonize them. To recover the colonial Bible for Africans, African novelists understood that they had to challenge the colonial and neocolonial projects, conform it to the African context, address African concerns, make it meaningful to the African audience, and liberated it from its western constraints. The Bible had to be decolonized.

---

34. Judith Fetterley, *Resisting Reader: A Feminist Approach to American Fiction* (Bloomington and London: Indiana Univ. Press, 1978). Though focused on feminism in America, the types of issues addressed align very closely with the colonial experience and its aftermath in Africa as addressed by African fiction.

An Interpretative Sample: Acts 17—Paul in Athens and Redefining Mission

Creative African literature's decolonization of the Bible intersects with decolonizing Bible interpretations. A recent volume that critically analyzed the Great Commission (Mt. 28:19-20) in light of its connection to the colonial project concluded that the passage lay "dormant" prior to the colonial project and gained prominence only as a fully actuated colonial mission text.[35] The colonial project provided the impetus for this passage to overshadow all other models of mission, like the one found in Acts 17, in the Bible. This interpretation fit well with the sense of the missionary's authority over the Other. It was the perfect colonizing text—go, every nation, make converts, baptize them—since it does not permit the recognition of the Other. It encourages neither negotiation nor dialog. It places the "right" to "go and do" solely on the sent.

In contrast, the mission encounter between Paul and the Athenians at the Areopagus in Acts 17 provides a different model of mission to which several African scholars have pointed as a viable alternative to the European mission model.[36] On his second missionary journey, Paul makes a stop in Athens where, after a couple of days of orienting himself to the city and its religious ethos, he decides to engage the leading thinkers of the community at the famed Areopagus. Respect for the Other, gathering knowledge of the Other, and preference for dialog with the Other, shows deference while persuading regarding the teachings of the *euangelion*, characterizes Paul's rhetoric.

Elsewhere, I have argued that the dialogical form of engagement reflected in Acts 17 better suits a Christian mission that does not presuppose the religio-cultures of the Other as unredeemably evil.[37] In that piece, I read Acts 17 in tandem with Chinua Achebe's novel *Things Fall Apart* and its portrayal of a dialogical encounter between Christianity and European mission. In the following analysis, I will not juxtapose Acts 17 with the novel, but my previous research and that of Chidi D. Izisoh's PhD dissertation on Acts 17 will guide me.[38]

First, Paul does not begin his speech with condemnation, as the European missionaries' predisposition did with declaring African religions "heathenish" or even "Satanic." Rather, he opens with affirmation: "In every way you are a religious people" (v. 22). This sounds uncannily similar to Mbiti's assertion about African

35. Mitzi J. Smith, and Jayachitra Lalitha (eds.), *Teaching All Nations: Interrogating the Matthean Great Commission* (Minneapolis: Fortress, 2014).

36. Chidi Denis Isizoh, "African Traditional Religious Perspective of the 'Areopagus Speech' (Acts 17, 22-31)," *ACS* (1998): 1–25; Manus, *Intercultural Hermeneutics in Africa*, 67–83; and David A. Reed, "Acts 17:16–34 in an African Context (An Assessment from a N. Atlantic/Western Perspective," *AJET* 22, no. 1 (2003): 87–101.

37. Mbuvi, "Missionary Acts, Things Fall Apart."

38. Chidi Denis Isizoh, "The Resurrected Jesus Preached in Athens: The Areopagus Speech (Acts 17, 16-34)— An Inquiry into the Reasons for the Greek Reaction to the Speech and a Reading of the Text from the African Traditional Religious Perspective," (PhD Diss., Rome: Pontificia Universitas Gregoriana, 1996).

peoples as "notoriously religious."[39] If European missionaries had begun their conversations with Africans in this way, a very different experience of mission in Africa could have been envisioned. Paul is not pretending or ignoring the religious form that the Athenians practice, but he is aware that any conversation that begins with condemnation elicits only resistance and pushback. While Paul stands before what all Christians, including Paul, would classify as idols (cf. 1 Cor. 10:15-22, Gal. 4:8-11, 1 Thess. 1:9, etc.), Paul is here measured in his assessment of the Athenian religion and establishes a point of contact to enable dialog to flourish.

Second, Paul shows his familiarity with their religious tradition by acknowledging their religious shrines (v. 23). Again, most scholars acknowledge the presence of shrines in most African religions.[40] This Pauline recognition legitimizes the Athenian religion and does not make it a demon-filled satanic playfield. Instead, Paul makes an astounding capitulation to the Athenian religion's capacity as a receptacle of God's truth. Paul must be well aware of the Hellenistic religion with its myriad deities and the need for adherents to make sure no deity is left out or forgotten as the reason for the altar to the "unknown god" (v. 24). But Paul is willing to put his arguments for the gospel in terms of the Athenian religion. He is willing to co-opt the religion's elements to make the gospel message palatable to those hearing it for the first time. This would certainly fit with his mission ethos stated elsewhere as "I have become all things to all, to save at least some" (1 Cor. 9:22; cf. Rom. 15:2).

Third, by relating the God of Jesus to the "unknown god," Paul universalizes the otherwise Jewish and local Palestinian God. Just like the Gospel of John would eventually Hellenize Jesus by interpreting his Jewish identity of Messiah into the Hellenistic notion of *Logos* (Jn 1:1-4), Paul converts the Jewish God into a transcendent God beyond the confines of the Judeo-Christian religion. The African reality also includes the presence of such a God with the accepted attribute of unknowability—the *"mysterium tremendum."*[41] God was simply awaiting revelation to be discovered and embraced by the African.

Fourth, scholars have suggested that Paul overstated his case to appeal to the Athenian thirst for novelty.[42] While that is admissible, it does not negate the fact that Paul makes claims he believes to be theologically in line with his Judeo-Christian beliefs, and that he is not involved in any form of ideological trickery or duplicity. At stake is the message of the gospel, and Paul is aware of the implications of any ethical compromise. Joshua Jipp, providing a constructive analysis of the passage, states it this way:

---

39. Mbiti, *African Religions and Philosophy*, 1.

40. Mbiti, *The Concepts of God in Africa*.

41. Ibid., 27.

42. W. Jipp Joshua, "Paul's Areopagus Speech of Acts 17:16–34 as Both Critique and Propaganda," *JBL* 131, no. 3 (2012): 567–88, 574.

Paul engages in critique of his audience with respect to superstition and idolatry by using Hellenistic philosophical tools and by hellenizing biblical traditions. In so doing, he demonstrates that his movement's beliefs about God not only *demonstrate it to be legitimate* but even *prove it to be a superior* form of religion. The Christian movement embodies the philosophically elite's ideals better and more consistently than do the Athenians.[43] (emphasis added)

Essentially, Paul engages in a form of mimicry that utilizes the Hellenistic philosophical worldview to claim its fit with Christianity while also retaining foundational elements of the worldview. While I agree with Jipp regarding the aspect of legitimacy as applied by Paul, I disagree that Paul uses the language of superiority in this speech. It is more a speech of improvement and transformation of Hellenistic religious and philosophical claims which affirms that, all along, the guiding presence of God was among the Athenians (v. 34).

Nigerian New Testament scholar, Ukachukwu Manus, rejects the tendency of the western biblical scholars to characterize Paul's Athenian speech as a "juridical" exchange and, instead, advocates understanding it as a sermon.[44] It is the tendency to characterize it as a juridical exchange that leads to the misplaced opinion that it was a failed mission encounter, evidenced by only the handful of converts (v. 34). Turning to an Igbo translation of the speech and a comparable folk narrative, Manus demonstrates how it blends into an Igbo religious worldview. His inculturation interpretation results in his conclusion that Paul's speech "succeeds in establishing the fact that the proclamation of divine creation, glorification of God the Father and, the call to repentance and to seek God in obedient fellowship should be the hallmarks of missionary sermons especially in the African missionlands."[45] So convinced also of the speech's rhetorical and religious fit within an African religious worldview is Isizoh that he writes, "If the speech had been addressed originally to the Africans of the African Traditional Religious worldview, it would have been well received by an appreciative audience."[46]

The point is important given that the Lukan purpose in Acts is mission—from Jerusalem to Rome (Acts 1:8). While Paul elsewhere engages Empire by utilizing its benefits, in Acts 17, he acquiesces to the employment of a dialogical approach that grants epistemological equality and dignity to the Other. In so doing, he makes possible the creation of a space for a genuine exchange of ideas with no notion of domination or imposition. It is an anti-colonialist move on the part of Paul, even as he also enjoys the benefits of being a card-carrying citizen of the Roman Empire who can traverse its horizons unhindered (Acts 22:22–23:11).

43. Ibid., 569.
44. Manus, *Intercultural Hermeneutics in Africa*, 70–1.
45. Ibid., 81.
46. Isizoh, "The Resurrected Jesus Preached in Athens," 22.

Chapter 9

REWRITING THE BIBLE

RECASTING THE COLONIAL TEXT

It is through an appropriation of the power invested in writing that
this discourse can take hold of the marginality imposed on it and make
hybridity and syncrecity the source of literary and cultural redefinition.

— *The Empire Writes Back*[1]

Decolonization, therefore, implies the urgent need to thoroughly challenge
the colonial situation. Its definition can, if we want to describe it accurately,
be summed up in the well-known words: "The last shall be first."

— Franz Fanon[2]

9.1 Introduction

Decolonization of the Bible in African Biblical Studies has taken several different
forms as different attempts have been made to legitimate the Bible within the
African context and to rid it of any perceived colonial overtones. Two trajectories
have arisen in this process: the first is made up of those who believe the colonial
Bible was the product of the European justification of the colonial process, and
exposing the western presuppositions, would be sufficient in letting the Bible
find an interpretive home in the African context. From this perspective, the main
point entails highlighting the fact that African readings of the Bible are just as
acceptable as European readings, and even more relevant and meaningful to
the African context. The second, and more radical approach, is to find fault not
just with western interpretations of the Bible, but also with the biblical text itself
since it harbors the kinds of readings that perpetuated the colonial mentality.
This approach calls for a reconfiguring of the biblical text by either rewriting it or

---

1. Ashcroft, Griffiths, and Tiffin, *The Empire Writes Back*, 77.
2. Fanon, *The Wretched of the Earth*, 2.

rejecting it.[3] Both these sentiments, captured in the epigraphs at the beginning of this chapter, push back against the western fetishization of the Bible as an object of power and control.

9.2 *The Paradox of the Bible—Takatso Mofokeng*

Writing in the context of racialized apartheid South Africa, Mofokeng points out that both the oppressive white supremacist apartheid government and the oppressed people appealed to the Bible as the basis for their diametrical opposition. The oppressor used the Bible to justify the racist apartheid system that set the white race as superior and divinely chosen to rule over the Black Africans. On the other hand, Africans presumed the Bible to be primarily a liberationist text and accused the white South Africans of "misusing the Bible."[4] For Mofokeng, both groups misread the Bible. Because, in the Bible, there are texts amenable to the oppressor's position and, any arguments pitted against them would only go to serve the oppressor's position. The alternative, Mofokeng argues, is to find texts in the Bible that resist dehumanization. For example, Jesus's teachings of empowerment that promote human enfranchisement and dignity would provide the antidote to oppressive texts used to justify violence against the African subjects.

Inevitably, a struggle for the Bible would ensue. For Mofokeng, "What is within reach as a viable option is to insist on finding and controlling the tools of opening and interpreting the Bible as well as participating in the process of interpretation itself."[5] Identifying with the oppressed in the Bible would be the best way to galvanize the oppressed Black South Africans to find liberative elements in the Bible which would empower them to encounter apartheid and overcome it.

3. What these African biblical scholars are calling for here bears resemblance to works of a minority of western biblical scholars who have challenged the notion of the "Bible canon" as a closed unit, building especially on the Hungarian Geza Vermes's notion of the "re-written Bible" (*Scripture and Tradition in Judaism* [Leiden: Brill, 1961]). A recent fascinating study by Eva Mrozcek, *The Literary Imagination in Jewish Antiquity* (Oxford: Oxford University Press, 2016), 4–6, bemoans the fact that the study of the Bible is "constrained by two forms of anachronism: a religious one—Bible"—and a "bibliographic one—book." That the late development of the Bible as an iconic corpus "normative for human behaviour and religious practice . . . ," must give way to the possibility of the "idea of different kinds of textual authority." Though focused on the Second Temple Period, Mrozcek's study has vital implications for contemporary biblical interpretation.

4. Mofokeng, "Black Christians, the Bible and Liberation," 37.

5. Ibid., 39.

9.3 Liberating the Bible—Itumeleng Mosala

For South African biblical scholar Itumeleng Mosala, the "oppressed and exploited people must liberate the gospel so that the gospel may liberate them."[6] Rooted in Black Theology, Mosala's "black biblical hermeneutics of liberation," like Mofokeng's, is a response to the oppression and exploitation of Black people in the South African context of apartheid.[7] However, for Itumeleng, the problem with Black theology is that it has remained an elitist preserve based on its linkage to the "bourgeois biblical-hermeneutical assumptions" and thus has not made inroads into the lives of the oppressed masses and their struggles.[8]

Open declaration of ideological and theoretical stances is a must if this approach is to succeed. And in Mosala's case, a clear break from the ideology and theory of "dominant practices and discourses is necessary if a biblical hermeneutics of Black theology is to emerge."[9] His aversion to "dominant practices and discourse," by which he means the dominant western approaches to biblical interpretation, comes from the belief that they created the oppressive colonial system and are, therefore, unlikely to offer a resolution to its problems. Instead, Mosala chooses what he calls a "historical-materialist" reading based on Marxian approaches to history. In this regard, the reader must answer the following questions when analyzing biblical texts:

> What is the nature of these texts? Whose class, gender and race interest does this challenge exist to serve? Who is making the challenge? Where and where? What are the ideological and literary mechanisms whereby the challenge is formulated? . . . What effects, then and now, are these texts having on the social classes, genders, and races on whose behalf they were *not* produced?[10]

Mosala's critique includes interrogation of the concept of the Bible as the "Word of God" which he concludes "leads to a false notion the Bible is nonideological" by which he means the Bible is not neutral or lacking in agenda.[11] This misconception, in turn, leads to a failure to integrate issues of class, race, gender, and ideology comprehensively when interpreting the Bible.

An honest engagement with the text, according to Mosala, should have the potential for either a positive or negative outcome since the Bible itself "is the product and record of historical, cultural, gender, racial and social-class struggles."[12]

---

6. Itumeleng Mosala, *Biblical Hermeneutics and Black Theology in South Africa* (Grand Rapids: Wm. B. Eerdmans, 1989), 172.

7. Ibid., 131.

8. Ibid., 3.

9. Ibid., 4.

10. Ibid., 131. (emphasis original)

11. Ibid., 6.

12. Ibid., 8, 9.

To build his case, Mosala offers a historical-materialist analysis of the biblical texts of Micah and Luke 1-2, utilizing the experience of struggle as a "hermeneutical key" since the "biblical texts are products of contradictory and struggle-ridden conditions of production."[13] What Mosala essentially does is preclude the notion of biblical authority and, in true enlightenment fashion, read the biblical text as a human product.

Mosala's analysis of Micah and Luke 1-2, concludes that the biblical text favors the oppressors. Following his analysis of Micah, Mosala concludes that the prophetic writing fails to highlight the struggles of the downtrodden and, instead, hides the actual plight and struggles of the oppressed within an ideological construction that favors the oppressor's view.[14] In his analysis of the Gospel of Luke 1-2, a gospel traditionally touted by interpreters as a gospel for the poor due to its numerous mentions of their plight and Jesus's concern for them (e.g., Luke 4), Mosala finds that such a reading of Luke 1-2 does not represent the Gospel's overall position. In Mosala's eyes, while Luke may seem to present a picture of a subversive movement, he actually aims to contain it.[15] He elaborates further,

> Luke's ideological production of the history of Jesus within the historical context of first-century Palestine has made available a gospel that is acceptable to the rich and the poor of Luke's community, but in which the struggles and contradictions of the lives of poor and exploited are conspicuous in their absence. By turning the experiences of the poor into the moral virtues of the rich, Luke has effectively eliminated the poor from the Gospel.[16]

As Mosala argues, the construct of the Bible as the "Word of God" is itself an "ideological maneuver" by the ruling class (e.g., Luke's audience, Theophilus) which curtails human agency and excuses divine responsibility.[17] An example is how Luke co-opts the genealogies through Joseph, simply to connect Jesus to royalty.[18] Similarly, in his context of South Africa, the elite too co-opted the biblical text against Black South Africans, Black women in particular. As a concept that operates on the presumption of universal authority, it has laid claim to being the only way one can interpret and apply the Bible, while it has continued to benefit only the oppressor (bourgeois, both white and Black South Africans) over the oppressed (Black South Africans). Any questioning of this designation of the Bible leads one to be labeled adversarial, and liable to discipline.

Given that colonizers used the Bible as a tool to claim African land ownership, Mosala wants to use the same Bible "to get the land back and to get the land back

---

13. Ibid., 10.
14. Ibid., 153.
15. Ibid., 175.
16. Ibid., 163.
17. Ibid., 18.
18. Ibid., 170.

without losing the Bible."[19] Such a process must start with liberating the Bible itself by confronting "the class and ideological position and commitment of the text and the reader."[20] For, the reader's role in determining meaning is key. That notwithstanding, the most appropriate context for reading the Bible is that of the oppressed, the poor, and the suffering. Reading the Bible uncritically, as the "Word of God," has, for too long, been a tool of oppression and suppression. For liberative reading to happen, Mosala advocates appropriation of the biblical text with a "materialist reading," even if the "silences" of the texts remain problematic.

9.4 A "Supra-Bible" for All—Canaan Banana

Canaan Banana, the first Black president of Zimbabwe, a Methodist priest, and a professor of theology, presented an even more radical response to the Bible than Mosala's, following his discontent with both the violent history of the Bible and its co-opting as colonialism's imperializing tool. To Banana, the Church in pre- and post-independent Zimbabwe failed to "attack problems of racism, inequality, and socioeconomic realities."[21] Banana's solution was not a new interpretation, but a complete re-writing of the Bible in favor of the oppressed, which he personally undertook. It was not enough that sections of the text advocated for justice for the oppressed, the widow, and the poor. The whole text needed to be overhauled from the vantage point of the marginalized and downtrodden. As an example, this is how he rewrote the beginning of the Lord's prayer:

Our father who art in the ghetto
Teach us to demand our share of the gold
Forgive us our docility
As we demand our share of justice.[22]

Banana's intense frustration with the continued escalation of hostility in the Middle Eastern standoff between Israel and Palestine, where the appeal to scriptural authority on both sides (the Bible and the Qur'an, respectively) played a major role in justifying the continued conflict, propelled his action. He envisioned a "supra-Bible," "which is above all contemporary religions, in which the voices and experiences of all peoples of the world are condensed into a single universal collection of sacred writings for a universal religion."[23]

---

19. Ibid., 153.

20. Ibid.

21. Canaan Banana, *The Gospel According to the Ghetto* (Gwelo, Zimbabwe: Mambo Press, 1981), 1.

22. Ibid.

23. Masiiwa R. Gunda, "'Rewriting' the Bible or De-biblifying the Public Sphere? Proposals and Proposition on the Usage of the Bible in the Public Square in Zimbabwe,"

Though this may seem naïve and overreaction, Banana was not the first (nor, I suspect, will he be the last) to recommend the emendation or excising of the biblical text following frustrations with its content. His controversial "solution" to what he saw as the problem with the biblical text had precedence in at least two influential figures in western history. Thomas Jefferson, the third president of the United States, also took to literally excising entire sections of the Bible he disagreed with, and pasting them in a different order creating a "new" redacted Bible.[24] Similarly, the prominent twentieth-century New Testament German scholar, Rudolph Bultmann, essentially did away with major parts of the New Testament (e.g., miracles of Jesus or any supposed unnatural occurrences) which he labeled "myth." Bultmann believed that such materials reflected flights of fancy among prescientific "primitive" Christians since they could not be scientifically or historically verified.[25] While he did not literally excise them from the Bible, like Jefferson, Bultmann's project of *demythologizing* the Bible achieved similar results of rendering parts of the Bible inadmissible.

For Banana, instead of presenting the story of only one community, Israel, his rewritten Bible would take into consideration the experiences of other religious communities as well. As he explained, "Attempts should be made through rewriting to universalize God. Revelation is not for Jews alone. Our God is discernable in all nations."[26] So, while Banana's Bible would include the Qur'an, the Bhagavad Gita, and so on, a biblical text like Genesis 1 with its notion of a creator God from whom all humanity originates he would keep. However, the divine call of Abraham (Gen. 17:7-8) to establish a special and distinct group of humans he would eliminate.

So Banana found Deut. 13:6-10, for example, to be "one of the most notorious passages in the Bible" for its concession to the killing of those who were not worshippers of the God of Israel." 1 Cor. 14:34-35 he found to be a "terrible impasse for women."[27] Banana then advocated for uprooting such verses because they undermined the universal divine–human relationship by positing the special

---

in *The Bible and Politics in Africa*, ed. Masiiwa R. Gunda and Joachim Kügler (BiAS 7; Bamberg, Germany: University of Bamberg Press, 2012), 27–8. Cf. also, Masiiwa R. Gunda, *On the Public Role of the Bible in Zimbabwe: Unpacking Banana's "Re-writing" Call for a Socially and Contextually Relevant Biblical Studies*. BiAS 18 (Bamberg: University of Bamberg Press, 2015).

24. Stephen Prothero, "Thomas Jefferson's Cut-and-Paste Bible: Our Third President Sought to Separate the Words of Jesus from the 'Corruptions' of his Followers," *WSJ Opinion*, March 25, 2011.

25. Rudolph Bultmann, *New Testament & Mythology and Other Basic Writings* (Philadelphia: Fortress, 1984).

26. Canaan S. Banana, *The Case for a New Bible*, in *"Rewriting" the Bible: The Real Issues: Perspectives from within Biblical and Religious Studies in Zimbabwe*, ed. Isabel Mukonyora, James L. Cox, and Frans J. Verstraelen (Gweru, Malawi: Mambo Press, 1993), 17–32, Kindle Edition, 166.

27. Ibid., 167.

privilege of one group. In Banana's words, "The fact of the matter is that this is the same God the Israelites are trying to possess tenaciously. It paints the picture of a *hooligan* God who loves punishing, destroying and annihilating. Our God is a God of mercy and kindness and compassion."[28]

Anyone familiar with Christian history will no doubt hear echoes of Marcion (c. 144) the second-century bishop condemned for his "heretical beliefs" in Rev. Banana's words. Marcion believed that the God of the Hebrew Bible or "the Jewish God" (a God of violence and revenge and blood) was not the same God preached by Jesus (a God of mercy, forgiveness, "turning the other cheek," and kindness). Marcion's Bible too, was distinct from what would eventually be approved by the Church. Unsurprisingly, Banana too was accused of heresy by the Church.[29]

Canaan Banana's struggle was with an immense ethical issue that has vexed biblical readers over the centuries—reconciling how a just God would ever permit or orchestrate human atrocities in God's name. At the heart of Banana's discomfort with the Bible was this textual support for violence and injustice, and for the notion of "chosenness" present in the three Abrahamic religions (Judaism, Christianity, Islam), also relied upon to defend modern colonialism.[30] To Banana, these texts reflected human corruption projected as God's justification for human greed, injustice, and violence.[31] A "colonized Bible"! Thus, to Banana it was not violating God's moral standard to rid the Bible of such texts. His desire was for an equal footing for all religious traditions of the world, as *God's revelation.*

This notion of an omnipresent God, who, nevertheless, has multi-local presences, also prompts Boulaga to share a similar expectation when he asks:

Shall we ever commonly see Taoist Christians, Hindu Christians, Buddhist Christians, Animist Christians? When we dream fondly of an African Christianity, we have to be willing to dare to think this far. When we wonder whether Africans, conscious of their identity, their continuities and solidarities, can be Christians, we are asking the question about Christianity's original meaning.[32]

28. Ibid. (emphasis added)

29. Archford Musodza, "'Rewriting' The Bible: Its Canonical Implications and Meaning for Anglicans in the City of Harare," (Unpublished M.Phil. Thesis, University of Zimbabwe, 2003).

30. Banana, *The Case for a New Bible*, 39.

31. Isabel Mukonyora, James L. Cox, and F. J. Verstraelen (eds.), *Rewriting the Bible: The Real Issues: Perspectives from Within Biblical and Religious Studies in Zimbabwe* (Gweru, Zimbabwe: Mambo Press, 1993). Virtually all respondents to Banana's proposal, both African and western, essentially offered alternative answers to the issue of making the Bible address the injustices committed in its name.

32. Boulaga, *Christianity Without Fetishes*, 161.

Banana's controversial solution is driven by a desire to end the violence and intolerance that is embedded in the Bible, and is wrought by western Christian dogma of the universality of Christianity.[33]

9.5 Reconstruction Hermeneutics: The Post-colonial/Post-Apartheid Bible

Some perceived the end of apartheid in South Africa in the early 1990s as a watershed moment for the liberationist interpretations of the Bible in Africa to reconstitute themselves to address new concerns. Liberation had been accomplished, so society now needed a new uniting focus. Enter Reconstruction hermeneutics, which envisioned replacing the combative stance of Liberation struggle, with a rebuilding model. Reconstruction hermeneutic presented itself as a counterpoint to the "reactionary" nature of other approaches in African Biblical Studies, projecting a proactive and constructive approach.[34] Primary proponents included South African theologian C. Villa-Vicencio,[35] Kenyan philosopher and theologian J. N. K. Mugambi,[36] and Congolese (DRC) theologian K. Kä Mana.[37]

Reconstruction hermeneutics moved the interpretive focus from liberationists' appeal to the book Exodus, to the rebuilding and reconstruction texts of Ezra-Nehemiah. This move beyond the Exodus liberation model envisioned a different biblical model relevant to the post-apartheid *zeitgeist*. Ezra-Nehemiah's reconstruction of Jerusalem, and its temple following the return from Babylonian exile offered a perfect model. This post-apartheid era should usher in a period of religious, social, cultural, economic, and political reconstruction.[38]

Several shortcomings however hampered Reconstruction hermeneutic's usefulness. First, it assumes that there was something that needed to be rebuilt. What exactly this was remained quite unclear. Was it calling for going back to the reconstitution of societies in the precolonial model? That would be regressing and would be impossible anyway, since doing so would ignore the encounter of the colonial experience. Secondly, Ezra-Nehemiah indicates that the rebuilding of the temple in Jerusalem elicited mixed results, with those who beheld the glory

---

33. Ibid., 209.

34. J. N. K. Mugambi, *Christian Theology and Social Reconstruction* (Nairobi: Acton, 2003). See especially ch.3, "Liberation and Reconstruction as Consecutive Processes."

35. Charles Villa-Vicencio, *A Theology of Reconstruction: Nation-building and Human Rights* (Cambridge: Cambridge University Press, 1992).

36. J. N. K. Mugambi, *From Liberation to Reconstruction: African Christian Theology After the Cold War* (Nairobi: East African Publishing House, 1995).

37. K. Kä Mana, *Eglises Africaines et Théologie de la Reconstruction* (Genève: Protestant, 1994). Cf. also Valentin Deji, *Reconstruction and Renewal in Africa in Christian Theology* (Nairobi: Acton Publishers, 2003).

38. Villa-Vicencio, *A Theology of Reconstruction* and Mugambi's *Christian Theology and Social Reconstruction*, 36–60.

of Solomon's temple rejecting this second temple, for its structure's inadequacy in comparison to the first. Even the spirit of God did not appear at its dedication like in the first temple's dedication (1 Kings 8). Thirdly, the rebuilt temple resulted in conflict as it glorified the accomplishments of the returned Babylonian exiles while ignoring their colonial discrimination and oppression of the *am ha'aretz* ("people of the land") who had remained in Palestine.[39] These critiques dealt a fatal blow to Reconstruction hermeneutics.

Rather than "*reconstruction*," perhaps what is needed is a "new construction" that moves beyond the colonial impact and is not beholden to the precolonial reality. It is one that imagines a new way of being, that resists colonial impulses, and respects difference, and embraces plurality.

9.6 Conclusion

Decolonization is reflected in diverse ways in the dealings with the Bible in the African context. As the overarching concern of the writers analyzed in this section shows, the role of the reader is vital. And, consistent throughout these approaches, is the critique of both the dominant interpretive methods, and the complicity of the Bible as well, in historically enabling colonialist agendas. Alternative interpretive approaches are offered and a reconstitution of the biblical text itself is not shied away from. Not only are there challenges to colonizing oppressive interpretations, but there are also critiques of the biblical text itself which includes the same oppressive tendencies that have historically enabled domineering communities. Recommendations, which challenge the presuppositions of western biblical interpretations and interpretive methods, are offered. And if all else fails, a "rewrite" of the Bible is presented as a drastic, but necessary, option.

An Interpretative Sample: Lk. 16:1-13—"Parable of the Shrewd Manager"

Justin Ukpong utilizes "inculturation biblical hermeneutics," to interpret Jesus's parable of the shrewd manager in Luke 16.[40] He defines it as "an approach that consciously and explicitly seeks to interpret the biblical text from socio-cultural perspectives of different people."[41] This, however, is not a simple correlation of elements from the biblical text with contemporary contexts but must involve

---

39. Elelwani Farisani, 'The use of Ezra-Nehemiah in a Quest for a Theology of Renewal, Transformation and Reconstruction in the (South) African Context', (Unpublished PhD Thesis, University of Natal, Durban, 2002). Cf. also, idem, "The Ideologically Biased use of Ezra-Nehemiah in a Quest for an African Theology of Reconstruction," in *Postcolonial Perspectives*, ed. Dube, Mbuvi, and Mbuwayesango, 331–48.

40. Justin S. Ukpong, "The Parable of the Shrewd Manager (Luke 16:1-13: An Essay in Inculturation Biblical Hermeneutic," *Semeia* (1996): 189–210.

41. Ibid., 190.

conscious critical interpretive questions. The biblical text, and especially parables, is assumed to be "plurivalent" (the ability to be comprehended differently by readers in different contexts) but within certain interpretive parameters. And while not ignoring historical issues, the end goal is the "actualization of the text within today's context."[42]

A short survey analyzes the interpretive history of the parable and concludes that the passage has historically been a challenge to interpreters. Yet, Ukpong is optimistic that reading the passage from the perspective of "ordinary readers," namely West Africa (Nigerian) peasant farmers, can allay some of the historical concerns, especially those unsettling western interpreters. With the arrival of colonialism, traditional economic structures in Nigeria were upended, creating a money-oriented economy in place of the traditional barter trade that existed before. The result was an explosion of poverty levels previously unknown, as small farmers lost land (usually ancestral land) to large international corporations, to ill-advised loans with their farms as collateral, or by being squeezed out by "middlemen" in the new economic structure. This is the context in which Ukpong reads this Lukan parable.

Most western interpretations of Lk. 16:1-13, according to Ukpong, tend to focus on the farm manager in the parable. Negatively, some see him as a fraudulent person (even though he is praised for this, v. 8a) or as an outright criminal. Positively, others perceive him as prudent in utilizing his position to serve the poor and gain favor from God. One critic of these western interpretations attacks the interpretation offered by J. Jeremias, a notable German biblical scholar, as being "more in keeping with tabloid journalism than the sober judgment of a dispassionate biblical scholar. (In Jeremias's view, this debt-fixing was because people in the East had no knowledge of accounting or bookkeeping)."[43]

While Ukpong understands that his is only one among many possible interpretations, he feels that it is more in keeping with the world of the parable and thus closer to its representative meaning. For Ukpong, the western line of thinking inadvertently (or maybe advertently?) identifies with the rich man's harsh judgment of the manager. As a result, the western interpretations of the parable fail to critique the rich man or the economic system.

Even for those interpreters who use ancient Near Eastern cultural content to interpret the manager's action as a viable part of the system of farm management, the interpretive focus comes from the vantage point of the rich man. Connecting this parable to Luke 15 and making it about forgiveness, as others have done, is commendable, but fails to pay attention to other aspects of the parable, especially the fact that the rich man did not forgive the manager. This creates a significant problem for those who like to understand the rich man as representing God.

However, reading the parable from the vantage point of the peasant farmers, as Ukpong proposes, offers a distinctly different understanding of the parable.

---

42. Ibid., 192.
43. Sugirtharajah, "Postcolonial Biblical Interpretation," 73.

Readers must also understand the parable in light of Luke's larger context (Lk. 9:25–19:27) where Luke focuses on "discipleship, God's mercy and forgiveness" with three parables and two narratives focused on riches (12:13-41, the rich fool, and the folly of hoarding; 16:19-31, the rich man's lack of concern for poor Lazarus; 18:18-30, the rich young ruler; 19:1-10, Zacchaeus).[44] These Lukan parables and narratives critique the failure of the rich to show compassion for, or care about, the poor and needy around them.

Read in light of the ancient Palestinian practice of land use, usury, and exploitative loans, Ukpong argues that this parable becomes one where the rich man is an exploitative landowner, making the manager's action one of restoring justice to the exploited farmers. Yet, the manager's unforgiving attitude, though impressive, only registers economic loss and shows little concern for the farm-workers or the master. In the same way that the African farmer (and African countries) are laden with unfair debt from the rich corporations in the west and rich western countries, they are like the farmers in need of a liberator like the manager. Initially, while working for the rich man, the manager had been part of the exploitative system. Only after the system turned against him did he undermine the system, making him a hero to the peasant farmers. His personal crisis turned him into a resister against the system and a champion for a new system that was just. In Ukpong's words, the "parable challenges Christians to be committed to working towards the *reversal* of oppressive structures of contemporary economic systems."[45]

---

44. Ukpong, "The Parable of the Shrewd Manager," 196.
45. Ibid., 208. (emphasis original)

Chapter 10

ESCHATOLOGY, COLONIALISM, AND MISSION

AN AFRICAN CRITIQUE OF LINEAR ESCHATOLOGY

The Bible brought to its African readers the idea of history as progress, the concept of linear rather than cyclical time, and with this was linked a liberating yet frightening emphasis on the individual.

—Richard Gray[1]

10.1 Western Missionary Apocalypticism and Demonization of the African Religious Reality

A binary outlook that viewed the world in terms of good versus evil, godly versus satanic, civilized versus primitive, advanced versus backward, Black versus white, African versus European, and so on, characterized the form of Christianity that western missionaries practiced and brought to the colonies. This perspective was essentially the product of the colonial project that conceived its Christian mission in binary format too, as a struggle against Satan's kingdom (religions of the colonized)![2] The Evangelical awakenings in Europe and America in the eighteenth and nineteenth centuries, with their strong apocalyptic dynamic, may also have influenced this interpretive understanding.[3] As Paul Gifford puts it, "Given [western] missionaries' perception of Africa as a battleground for the souls of Africans, there was an added stress on the millenarian aspects of Christian theology. Indeed, a core element of evangelical thought was the desire to convert all the heathens so that Jesus could return from heaven and bring

---

1. Richard Gray, "Christianity and Religious Change in Africa," *AA* 77, no. 306 (1978): 89–100, 98.

2. This is also reminiscent of the Hegelian dialectic.

3. Cf. Paul Gifford, "The Vanguard of Colonialism: Missionaries and the Frontier in Southern Africa in the Nineteenth Century," *Constellations* 3, no. 2 (2012): 165–74; Available online: https://journals.library.ualberta.ca/constellations/index.php/constellations/article/view/17204 (accessed June 20, 2019).

all good Christians back to life in the end of days."[4] If the Lord's return was to happen following the conversion of all peoples (Mt. 24:4), there was little room for tolerance of the recipient communities' religious and cultural structures. The result was the imposition of foreign ideological concepts into receptor communities together with divergent or contradictory ideological frameworks. For example, the imposition of the idea of linear time into contexts where time has cyclical frameworks, as referenced by Richard Gray, in the epigraph.

Apocalyptic urgency and fervor necessitated a simple eradication of everything deemed not "Christian," which just happened to be everything non-western. Thus, western missionaries' apocalyptic convictions and racist notions of the superiority of European cultures that Schweitzer called "Christian civilization," drove their blindness toward (or deliberate rejection of) any biblical affinities to the African reality.[5] Schweitzer's *The Quest for the Historical Jesus* and *The Mystery of the Kingdom*, among other writings, had elevated the role of eschatology within the Bible from a fringe subject to the central hermeneutical lens for interpreting the New Testament.

John Mbiti, acknowledging the importance of Schweitzer's employment of eschatology in understanding the life and teaching of Jesus and Pauline theology, notes that ". . . in spite of its weakness, Schweitzer's study of the Gospels marked a turning point from the liberal studies of the life of our Lord in the nineteenth century."[6] The significance of eschatology influenced the European missionary movement by constructing mission as part of the eschatological process of bringing the Kingdom of God to the whole world, which would trigger the return of the Son of Man to earth. The urgency of the coming *eschaton* meant a need for a decisive and pointed message that paid attention only to salvation of *souls*.

If the goal was to quicken the eschaton, then European missionaries saw little purpose in giving attention to African cultures or religions, as these were already outside the scope of Christian teachings and would only be a stumbling block to salvation. Instead, the aim of the colonial Christianization project was to eradicate these "heathen" religions and cultures and bring converts into "Christian civilization." Appealing also to pseudo-sciences (including aspects of biology, anthropology, archeology, physical sciences, etc.) that espoused an evolutionary continuum, western Christian apocalypticism envisioned itself at the apex of human evolution and at the cusp of a divine eschatological timeline.[7]

---

4. Ibid., 169.

5. Schweitzer, "The Relations of the White and Colored Races," 65.

6. John S. Mbiti, *New Testament Eschatology in an African Background: A Study of the Encounter between New Testament Theology and African Traditional Concepts* (London: Oxford, 1971), 34: "But, in spite of its weakness, Schweitzer's study of the Gospels marked a turning point from the liberal studies of the life of our Lord in the nineteenth century."

7. The subject of anthropology, for example, owes its origins to the study of "primitive" peoples such as the African communities (e.g., E. E. Pritchard published on the Nuer after a total of only twelve months of living among them [Cf. David Fiensy, "Using the Nuer Culture

Based on such eschatological reasoning, European missionaries would feel fully justified in declaring native religions and cultures, anti-Christian and unredeemable. In such a world of intensified binaries, Africans converted to Christianity would have to give up everything African, to salvage their admittance into the Kingdom of God. In a worldview where the Kingdom of God was already breaking through, urgency called for a strict demarcation between things "of the world" (destined for eternal damnation) and things of God's Kingdom (destined for eternal salvation). And African "pagan" or "heathenish" religions, belonged to "this world" as ungodly, demonic, and satanic.

Essentially, the western missionary perspective was constructing its own sense of eschatological mission in diametric opposition to the native religious reality. Both could not be right or even hold shared truths. In this construction, European missionaries reasoned that they had to declare war against the African religious and cultural realities for, essentially, the African would need to fully adopt western Christian religion and values to be "authentically Christian." There was no time to dilly dally!

It is no wonder that in this eschatological framing, the articulation of the African reality served no particular interest for most western missionaries. So even what may have seemed like exceptions, like the Belgian missionary to Congo, Placide Tempels' eagerness to invest value in African religious and cultural reality, the end goal remained the same, a rapid conversion of the native. It did not change the fact that even for Tempels, only by subsuming African realities into racialized western categories of knowledge and pedagogical systems with its eschatological outlook, could he envision a more fitting way of converting the Africans.[8] Such thinking fit well within the colonial project, enhancing also the speed of colonization. While colonial administration envisioned colonizing Africa by means of the gun, they could count on subdued Africans under "civilized" western systems of governance, grounded on eschatologically motivated missionary activity. In the midst of it all, the Bible, serving both as an impetus for the missionary (Mt. 28:19-20) and as the "prize" presented to the native.

---

of Africa in Understanding the Old Testament: An Evaluation," *JSOT* 38 (1987): 73–83, 74], and yet his writing became *the* authoritative work on the Nuer. This is the power of the colonial project: to name and to define, to explain and to control knowledge, identity, and reality. This control rested on political, literary, scholarly, and geographical power. Based on such studies, others sought to find parallels between the "primitive" ANE religions of the Bible and the "primitive" African religions, for example, E. A. McFall, *Approaching the Nuer of Africa through the Old Testament* (South Pasadena: William Carey Library, 1970). These studies relied on evolutionary—and racially-based presuppositions—and focused on the comparison of both cultures' "primitiveness." However, their primitiveness was not equal; biblical primitiveness was the product of an ancient text or literary fixity and was not a negative evaluation, but African primitiveness was the product of its "backwardness" in comparison to modern society—a continuum into the "exotic" past of modern civilization.

8. See opposing responses to P. Tempels's *Bantoue Philosophie* by L. Senghor (positive) and Aimé Césaire (mixed—rejection of its perpetuation of the colonial agenda). Available online: https://plato.stanford.edu/archives/spr2014/entries/negritude/

10.2 *John Mbiti's Critique of Western Eschatology*

a. Time and Eschatology

John S. Mbiti's *New Testament Eschatology in an African Background* offers the first comprehensive postcolonial African response to eschatologically driven western missionary activity in Africa. Mbiti's work sets out to show how the interpretive presuppositions of western eschatology failed to comprehend an already existent and distinct African eschatological outlook, before imposing the western eschatological Christianity that conflicted with the African religious reality.[9] In a review of Mbiti's book, G. Wesley Johnson of UC Santa Barbara characterized it as an attempt to "Africanize the Church," but this was a failure to fully comprehend the argument.[10] It was much more than that.

Mbiti understood the deeply eschatological nature of western Christianity to be what drove a fairly eschatological missionary movement in Africa. The intent to attain an eschatological transformation of the African communities drove the evangelization of the African continent.[11] So, distinguishing between biblical eschatological models, which he maintains are multiple, and the singular western *linear* eschatology, Mbiti faults the western selective application that ignored other eschatological possibilities present in the Bible: "It is false to suggest only a single biblical conception of Time, and this false basis must undermine the whole theory and interpretation [of the Bible]."[12]

As Mbiti points out, the Jewish eschatology that forms the background for the New Testament contains two ages, "this age" and "the age to come."[13] The new age of peace and God's reign to come would replace "this age" with its suffering and pain. It is also important to note that the Jewish notion of time emphasizes events, and not chronology.[14] With Christianity, the Incarnation (birth of the Son of God into the world) interrupts this linear timeline; the future ages of God's reign (or Kingdom) become part of the "this age" because of Jesus's arrival. The arrival of Jesus inaugurates the "age to come" in "this age," meaning that Jesus's arrival sets in motion the journey toward the end of *all* time.[15]

---

9. I am aware of the heavy critique Mbiti's work received, especially from African philosophers, for its extrapolation from a single African community and concept of Time to a generalization for all of Africa (Cf, especially, Kwame Gyekye, *An Essay on African Philosophical Thought: The Akan Conceptual Scheme* (Cambridge: Cambridge University Press, 1987) and D. A. Masolo, *African Philosophy in Search of Identity* (Nairobi: General Printers, 1994). Despite the perceived weaknesses of Mbiti's concept of Time, the significance of this book as a postcolonial rebuttal of western imposition on African religious reality is often overlooked.

10. G. Wesley Johnson, "Book Review," *AMR* 78, no. 2 (1973): 469.

11. Ibid.

12. Mbiti, *New Testament Eschatology in an African Background*, 37–8.

13. Ibid., 32.

14. Ibid., 39.

15. Ibid., 33.

At this juncture, Mbiti makes it clear that he disagrees with Schweitzer's wheel analogy about Jesus: "It is Jesus who sets in motion the great eschatological wheel. But this is not the wheel in terms of Albert Schweitzer's contention [that it crashes him]."[16] In contrast to the linear eschatology, Mbiti posits the existence of a "cyclical eschatology" in the Hebrew Bible/Old Testament (e.g., Eccl. 1:4-11, 3:1-8, etc.), where "what has been, will be again." Similarly, in the fourth gospel, one encounters another nonlinear "supra-temporal" eschatology where the notion of eternity "lends new dimensions in the themes of Life, Light, Knowledge, Belief, Judgement and the like."[17] This says to Mbiti that the Bible offers multiple notions of time, and so the exclusive emphasis by the West on the linear chronological construct has obscured other ways of engaging chronology within the Bible.

On these grounds, Mbiti critiqued western missionary eschatology as simply misrepresenting what could be considered biblical concept of time, by emphasizing only the "futuristic" linear timeline. What is obscured is the "cyclical chronology" which would better fit within the Akamba (African) mythological notion of a "cyclical eschatology" with no future but is oriented toward a "never-ending past." The western missionary's failure to understand the African concept of time meant imposing a linear eschatology which conflicted with the Akamba's notion of cyclical time, that had only a "present" and a "never-ending past." This made it difficult for the Akamba (Africans') understanding of concepts such as the end of the world, resurrection, and future/last judgment.[18] As Bénézet Bujo, a Congolese theologian, extrapolates from Mbiti's conclusion, it meant that the "new" future concept "becomes over-valued and exaggerated, and is easily exploited by Messianic figures proclaiming the end of the world."[19]

Attacking western missionary emphasis on a "soon-to-return Christ" as the primary catechetical message brought to the Akamba (Africans), Mbiti warned of the danger of a false spirituality or despondency unleashed when the soon expected return of Christ fails to materialize. It is this myopic western reading and application of the biblical text that Mbiti feels reflects the missionaries' failure to comprehend and apply a symbolic interpretation of the Bible to make it relevant to the Akamba (Africans). For Mbiti, western missionaries set up the Akamba to fail, like some in the early church who misunderstood the timeline of the return of Jesus (*Parousia*) and fell from the faith when the expected return of Jesus failed to occur (1 Thess. 5:1-11).

The encounter between western linear eschatology and African cyclical chronology "produced an area of conceptual inversion," for both geography and time.[20] The African concept of a "never-ending past" was transformed into an

16. Ibid.
17. Ibid., 50, 39.
18. Ibid., 56-7.
19. Bujo, *African Theology in Its Social Context*, 29.
20. Mbiti, *New Testament Eschatology in an African Background*, 63.

eschatologically driven future, while the perpetual "hereafter" moved from "earth to the sky or heaven above."[21] Yet, for Mbiti, the materialistic conceptualization of the "hereafter" within African cyclical eschatological reality coheres better with the New Testament's own construction of life after death. Such "an African language can [sufficiently] contain biblical concepts" like the resurrection.[22]

For Mbiti, the western missionaries' failure to understand the Akamba (African) concept of life and death meant a failed opportunity to articulate the Christian message, especially the story of Jesus' resurrection, in ways relevant to the African concept of the "living-dead." At stake for the African converts to Christianity was the question of the fate of those who had died before hearing the gospel message. Within the Akamba (African) cosmology, death is not a total rupture of a person from the realm of the living but simply a transition to an alternate invisible world adjacent to this world, from where the dead may still emerge or communicate with the living. It is not where God dwells, and so not heaven as such, "but . . . [it] is almost an exact replica of this land from which they come—with fields, rivers, mountains, and so on."[23] For this reason, the Akamba recognize the departed "living-dead" as still present members of the community, and are consulted on important family or community matters.

So, in contrast to the individualism that characterizes western Christianity, Mbiti promulgates an African notion of resurrection that embodies a "corporate eschatology."[24] Embedded in community myth and folk tales, the notion of resurrection among the Akamba is not a future event but an "ever-present possibility" that involves a battle with those in the spiritual world; both spirits and the "living-dead." It does not include divine intervention as such, but is brought about by human victory over the inhabitants of the spirit world, freeing the dead to come back to life. This meant that the notion of resurrection among the Akamba predated Christianity itself and Mbiti postulates a similar transformation within Judeo-Christian eschatology, arguing that Christianity itself moved from a futuristic Jewish expectation (of the Messiah) to a present reality in the person of Jesus Christ (realized eschatology). The mysterious workings of the Holy Spirit unite the resurrected Jesus and his followers, resulting in their individual and collective resurrection.[25]

b. Critique of Mbiti's Concept of Time

The greatest pushback on Mbiti's analysis of an African eschatological conceptualization has come mainly from African philosophers such as Congolese

---

21. Ibid.
22. Ibid., 64.
23. Ibid., 79.
24. Ibid., 155ff.
25. Ibid., 165.

V. Y. Mudimbe, who have heavily critiqued his concept of time.[26] Simply put, most critics found the conclusions he drew from his Akamba community to be overgeneralized to the rest of Africa without sufficient support, and were not as universal as Mbiti claimed. But some African theologians, such as Bénézet Bujo, have defended Mbiti's position with their own emendations. For example, on the primacy of the past and present for the African, Bujo maintains that such an emphasis makes sense only if placed outside of their significance in influencing the present and the future. Using the setting of ancestor veneration, as an example, Bujo surmises that, "Certainly the African cherishes the traditions of the ancestors, but this is so not for the sake of the past, but uniquely for the sake of the present and future, which it is hoped in this way to render better."[27] However, John Parratt, building on the premise that African religions are governed by the idea of the "celebration of the fullness of life," points out that such acknowledgment of life's fullness or the continued presence of the living-dead implies the existence of "a future beyond death," one that is eschatological in nature.[28]

An Interpretive Sample: Lk. 16:19-31—Lazarus and the Rich Man

Turning to Jesus' parable of "Lazarus and the Rich Man" (Lk. 16:19-31)—the same one to which Schweitzer appealed in explaining his call to medical mission in Africa—we find that it contains all the elements of African (Akamba) cosmology identified by Mbiti.[29] In the parable, following his death, the angels took Lazarus to the mythical Abraham's side (or bosom). This does not seem to be heaven, because the angels do not take him to God but to the resting place of his Jewish grand ancestor, "father" Abraham. This aligns with the African notion of a "hereafter" in which one joins one's ancestors in the realm of the "living-dead" following death.[30] Moreover, just like in the parable, both the rich man and Lazarus are alive or at least, are able, in their afterlife world, to speak and communicate with the living, which suggests a porous boundary between life and the afterlife, much like the African understanding of the afterlife. Lastly, the dead can apparently consume drink, reflecting the African belief of pouring libation to the "living dead."[31]

---

26. V. Y. Mudimbe, *Parables and Fables: Exegesis, Textuality, and Politics in Central Africa* (Madison: University of Wisconsin Press, 1991), 188–91. Cf. also A. Scott Moreau, "A Critique of John Mbiti's Understanding of the African Concept of Time," *EAJET* 5, no. 2 (1986): 36–48.

27. Bujo, *African Theology in Its Social Context*, 31.

28. John Parratt, *Reinventing Christianity: African Theology Today* (Grand Rapids: Eerdmans, 1995), 124.

29. See Ch. 3, "*Schweitzer on Missionary Work and Biblical Studies.*"

30. Mbiti, *African Religions and Philosophy*, 25.

31. A. M. Mbuvi, "Christology and Cultus in 1 Peter: An African (Kenyan) Appraisal," in *Jesus Without Borders: Christology in the Majority World*, ed. G. L. Green, S. T. Perdue, and K. K Yeo (Grand Rapids: Eerdmans, 2014), 141–60.

In the Akamba cosmology, the dead are still living in the afterlife and are able to communicate and move about. And just like in the Lukan parable, there is the possibility of communicating between the world of the living and that of the departed. It is also a world where the physical traits of this world remain present. For example, being thirsty and needing to eat and drink. However, rather than appealing to these connections between Akamba (African) cosmology and the parable as a means of making the biblical message relevant to the Akamba, the western missionaries, instead, used the passage to reject what was essentially a non-existent Kamba belief. According to Mbiti, the passage appeared only as an addendum to the catechism booklet used by the missionaries among the Akamba. It was used essentially to address whether the spirits of the dead could return to "afflict" the living, deceptions concerning spirits of the dead, and whether spirits could foretell the future, all of which were rejected.[32]

Mbiti laments the exegetical incompetence of the western missionary document in understanding how the Lukan passage deals with "unbelief and lack of response by the Jews even when God's kingdom had appeared" and not simply explaining the afterlife.[33] He also notes that the document says "nothing . . . about the New Testament understanding of the subject, apart from bringing in spirits and demons."[34] And, as Mbiti also makes clear, there are complete misconceptions of the Akamba cosmological construction in these missionary documents. For example, the dead among the Akamba do not afflict but assist the living; there is no punishment in the "hereafter"; divination and sorcery are two distinct aspects with the Akamba consulting the diviner, and not the living-dead, for questions about the near future, etc. Beyond that, Mbiti highlights the confusing choice of vocabulary used to translate demons and spirits in the Ki-Kamba Bible, which created distinctions and categories that did not exist in the Akamba cosmology.[35]

10.3 A South African Liberationist Eschatology: Allan Boesak

South African anti-apartheid stalwart, pastor, and theologian Allan Boesak wrote a commentary on the book of Revelation while in solitary confinement for his activism against the colonialist apartheid government of South Africa. Titled *Comfort and Protest*, the commentary takes to task the form of western eschatology that propped the apartheid system that he calls "escapist eschatology" and which tends to advocate for a spiritualization of the message of Revelation. He rejects "the eschatological trajectory in the reception history of Revelation, because such readings lack transformative and efficacious power" in the present, to challenge

---

32. Mbiti, *New Testament Eschatology in an African Background*, 151.
33. Ibid., 152.
34. Ibid., 153.
35. Ibid., 152–3.

the racist and oppressive apartheid system.[36] Boesak, sounding much like Mbiti, maintains that in these escapist eschatologies, the "attention is not focussed [*sic*] on [the reader's] present plight and on ways to change that plight but on the mysteries of God and on the future joys of a world yet to come."[37]

For Boesak, reading Revelation as if it had no present relevance for the reader was the downside of the approaches championed by the West. These interpretive approaches perceived the events of Revelation as a historical past with no direct connection to the present, or a future awaiting fulfillment with no clear timeline. Boesak insists that the present plight of the reader is central to the book of Revelation. And not just that, he insists that because Revelation addressed a suffering and persecuted community in the first century, its readers must understand it from the vantage point of suffering and persecuted communities in the present. That to him is the only viable way of reading Revelation and what he calls the reading from the "underside." As he puts it, this is not simply a way of reading Revelation, but of interpreting the whole of biblical history: "We see and understand the events of history from the underside. . . . It is the fact that the weak and the destitute remained oppressed which provides the framework for understanding and interpreting history."[38] It is a transformative interpretation that does not relegate the biblical text to mere theory or ethereal discourse. Such an approach means that even the exegesis applied to the Bible would have to be "biblical exegesis from the underside," which aligns very much with Liberation Theologies' notion of reading from the perspective of the poor and powerless.[39]

Given Revelation's first-century political role in confronting the persecuting machinery that was the Roman Empire, Boesak finds parallel to his own South African racist apartheid situation in which the government's machinery was persecuting and killing its own people who sought justice. But this focus on South Africa does not diminish the relevance of Boesak's commentary beyond its immediate contexts, in addressing the plight of suffering and persecuted communities everywhere. As he put it, the "primary concern is the one in which God's people find themselves in this world, a situation that is caused by political, social, and economic forces which are identified and challenged, and are called to account in a unique way in this kind of literature."[40] His insistence that readers of Revelation approach the text from the "underside" and through the experience of suffering, provides the hermeneutical key to interpreting the book for those who find themselves in a similar setting of suffering, poverty, and powerlessness:

---

36. Pieter G. R. De Villiers, "Reading Revelation from the Top or the Underside," *STJ* 3, no. 2 (2017): 361–77, 370.

37. Allan Boesak, *Comfort and Protest: The Apocalypse from a South African Perspective* (Philadelphia: Westminster John Knox, 1987), 18.

38. Ibid., 25.

39. Ibid., 35.

40. Ibid., 18.

Those who do not know this suffering through oppression, who do not struggle together with God's people for the sake of the gospel, and who do not feel in their own bodies the meaning of oppression and the freedom and joy of fighting against it shall have grave difficulty in understanding this letter from Patmos.[41]

In effect, Boesak's approach challenges and undermines any self-perceived claim of Christianity by the apartheid South African government, as a pretext for its ideological white supremacist foundation. Apartheid as an oppressive system had no grounds to claim the "biblical" basis of its existence, as its premise of white supremacy contradicted the teachings of the gospel.[42] So, for Boesak, only those who struggle for justice under oppressive and repressive systems of power, like the author of Revelation and his readers, can genuinely understand the book of Revelation or make claim to a genuine Christian faith. For only the oppressed can genuinely anticipate the *comfort* that God's destruction of all oppressive systems would bring.

10.4 Ebussi Boualaga's "Christic Model"

Cameroonian philosopher and theologian, Fabian Eboussi Boulaga, reverses the western branding of African religions as "fetishes" by arguing that it was western Christianity that fetishized Christianity, through imposition of dogma or doctrine on the teachings of Jesus in the Bible.[43] Dogma, he argued, concretizes and sets up the arrogance of *certitude*, transforming teachings that were otherwise mythological and metaphorical into proclamations that demanded obedience and threatened those who refused or challenged them with violence.[44] The doctrine of Incarnation, for example, provides the potential for "imperialistic, totalitarian, and sectarian" acts that result in the exploitation of human misery.[45] Thus, "Christianity dies beneath the weight of certitudes about God's nature, plans, designs, and holy will, which each Christian may multiply to suit himself or herself."[46]

---

41. Ibid., 38.

42. Cf. The Round Table: "*Apartheid* and the Scriptures," *CJIA* 44, no. 174 (1954): 161–6, and Kevin Giles, "Justifying Injustice with the Bible: Apartheid." Available online: https://www.cbeinternational.org/blogs/justifying-injustice-bible-apartheid

43. Boulaga, *Christianity Without Fetishes*, 11: "The notion of Revelation rests on the premise there are imperially observable realities that are substantially sacred and afford direct access to God . . . . This writer fails to see in what respect a like premise differs from that of fetishism, which localizes the sacred or the divine, endows persons, affects, or things with supernatural characteristics and powers."

44. Boulaga, *Christianity Without Fetishes*, 11.

45. Ibid., 10.

46. Ibid., 145.

This is the western Christianity that promulgated missionary and colonial endeavors valuing conquest, colonization, and imperialism as the means to advance "the Kingdom of God."

> Doubtless, it was necessary for Christianity to be regionalized, localized, and tribalized in order to be really a Christianity for those of this region, this place, and this tribe . . . [However] [t]he [Christian] sects take up the pretension of each confession to be universal, to have a monopoly of the truth, and multiply it to infinity. This proliferation is their own best refutation. But it does not exorcise them of the demon of intolerance and the fund of violence it has built up.[47]

Its very strength, translatability, becomes its own Achilles' heel. With dogma, western Christianity lays the foundation for its own ruin. Because dogma is static, it is ill-suited for transference and tends to result in creating a form of religion alien to receptor communities that do not formulate dogma and do not fully understand their need.[48]

The kind of Christianity that emerges out of western Christian dogma, then, is what Boulaga calls "bourgeois Christianity." It alienates both the true teachings of the Bible and the culture and religious reality of the convert, ultimately setting itself up as a form of religion that has little to do with the teachings of Jesus or the receptor community.[49] This was what the western missionary brought to the African continent.

For Boulaga, the response to "bourgeois Christianity" is resistance via "African spirituality," "a logic that organizes attitudes of resistance to alienation and estrangement."[50] And this resistance is possible only if "African spirituality" and Christianity are *equals* as living religions, rather than one dominating the other.[51] For Boulaga, "[e]scatological activity is an operation of deconstruction and de-conditioning."[52] "Transgression of limits is one of the means of eschatological practice. The cleft between life and death is minimal and closing so rapidly that human persons now pass from the one to the other with ease."[53] This way, eschatology is one means of overcoming the "western-bourgeois Christianity," since foundationally "the eschatological principle signifies that there are no more intermediaries. God is present right here, referring men and women to the divine mystery by referring them to their own proper reality. . . . God anticipates us

---

47. Ibid., 73.

48. Ngwa, "Postwar Hermeneutics", 43–74, 59, points out that in Africa, "The Bible functions less as a book of creeds and more as a 'power' book."

49. Boulaga, *Christianity Without Fetishes*, 76.

50. Ibid., 78.

51. Ibid.

52. Ibid., 105.

53. Ibid., 106.

everywhere: indeed, God is already there."[54] In effect, Boulaga's position aligns with proponents of the *praeparatio evangelica* inbuilt in the precolonial African religious reality.

Ultimately, the establishment of an eschatological community, for Boulaga, is what Jesus sought in his teachings about love, and what he enacted in his acts of love. In such a community, no one is to lord it over another (Mt. 23:8), and the ideal is to "effect the inversion" where the greatest become the least (Mt. 23:9, 11), and power is exercised in service to all (Lk. 22:25-26).[55] Confounding Rudolph Bultmann's claims, Boulaga maintains that *demythologization* "leads to violence of an arbitrary Christianity, whose complicated sense and meaning is for only a few to enjoy, or else the counterviolence of political ideologies or liberation."[56] And so, when it comes to the issue of miracles as evidence of the eschatological irruption of "works of Christ" (Mt. 11:2), Boulaga prefers not to try and give an *apologia* for the existence of miracles but, instead, to retain the text's structure that reflects the specific worldview of the first century, with its compatibility to the African worldview.

Boulaga then points out the contradictory aspect of western Biblical Studies' emphasis on history by showing that historicity, as a method, becomes problematic in its failure to take seriously the biblical account of miracles, which undermines its very premise of taking the historical worldview of the first century seriously. If one were to put aside historical questions, "[w]hat is essential here is to realize that we are not confronted with those infamous alternatives [binaries], fact-or-fiction, veracity-or-lie, reality-or-illusion, truth-or-error. Here, fiction or illusion has a reality."[57] So the western emphasis on historicity would require the acceptance of the world of mystery, of miracles, even if, because a miracle "is singularity, situated in the order of a nonreiterative event," there is no way for historical verification.[58]

Once again, for Boulaga, the methodological choice becomes a hermeneutical constraint on the very assumptions that are maintained as historical. If the Gospels retain a "kernel of history," then outright rejection of miracles is a rejection of a first-century *historical reality* corrupting the hermeneutical starting point. Such a view undermines a connection to the gospel message for the African reality, a parallel worldview on miracles still exists: "The convergence of prophetic vocation, eschatological vocation and the power of miracles is a reality still accessible to contemporary observation, especially in Africa. . . . We are not dealing with literary genres here, but with the social logic of credence and belief."[59] Like the ancient worlds of the Greeks and Jews, the African presuppositions about such issues as miracles remain grounded in the probability of such events; they have not

54. Ibid., 107.
55. Ibid., 113.
56. Ibid., 146.
57. Ibid., 121.
58. Ibid., 119.
59. Ibid., 123.

succumbed to the western historical and scientific skepticism. This is the world of myth, where metaphor and myth, rather than historical fact as understood in western terms, concretize language. The world of the ancients was a world of metaphor and myth, just like that of Africa, which allows for theological discourse unmediated and undeviated by western dogma.

Only then does the faith become African. In Boulaga's terms, it avoids the limits of the alien dogma and unyielding presuppositions that are the foundations of western Christianity, and it finds its own expression. Using the analogy of the Samaritan woman, Boulaga expounds:

> Faith doubtless begins with the personal and collective verification of something that has transcended missionary rumor and hearsay. ("No longer does our faith depend on your story. We have heard for ourselves, and we know that this really is the Savior of the world"—John 4:42.) A "word" like this, issues from one's *experience*, one's *situation* . . . . Only then has one passed from a foreign belief to a hearing and *knowing* of one's own. . . . An immediate, "personal" rapport with Jesus and God by psychic acts transpiring within our intentionality is what we rightly call paganism, fetishism. "Personal" contact with God and Jesus can only mean a relationship expressed through and by human determination, effectuated through the work done with the materials of nature, through an encounter with other persons and with things.[60]

60. Ibid., 85–6. (emphasis original)

Chapter 11

"ORDINARY READERS" AND THE BIBLE

NON-ACADEMIC BIBLICAL INTERPRETATION

Ordinary readers . . . *are* a part of academic African biblical interpretations!
— Gerald West[1]

11.1 Who Are "Ordinary Readers"?

Patrick Kalilombe of Malawi and Gerald West of South Africa are perhaps the two individuals most closely associated with this mode of biblical interpretation in Africa.[2] Both Kalilombe and Gerald West understand their readings "with" the ordinary readers as liberationist. This approach incorporates several interpretive dimensions: the materialist reality of the poor and marginalized (South) African reader, an uncritical non-scholarly perspective (typically the poor in South Africa or Malawi), and a liberationist approach.[3] However, the method distinguishes between scholarly and "ordinary" readings but considers them equally valid. Gerald West is emphatic when he maintains that African biblical scholarship has to engage the "ordinary" readers as part of the academic interpretation of the Bible because "*they are a part of academic African biblical interpretations!*"[4]

---

1. G. West, "Unpacking the Package that is the Bible in African Biblical Scholarship," in *Global Village*, ed. J. Ukpong et al, 70. (emphasis original)

2. Patrick Kalilombe, *Doing Theology at the Grassroots: Theological Essays from Malawi* (Mzuzu, Malawi: Kachere Press, 1977); G. West, *Biblical Hermeneutics of Liberation: Modes of Reading the Bible in the South African Context* (Pietermaritzburg and Maryknoll: Cluster/ Orbis, 1995); idem, *The Academy of the Poor: Towards a Dialogical Reading of the Bible* (Sheffield: Sheffield Academic Press, 1998). Cf. also J. Ukpong, "Popular Readings of the Bible in Africa and Implications for Academic Readings: Report on the Field Research Carried Out on Oral Interpretations of the Bible in Port Harcourt Metropolis, Nigeria under the Auspices of the Bible in Africa Project, 1991–94," in *The Bible in Africa*, ed. G. West and M. W. Dube (Leiden: Brill, 2000), 582–94.

3. P. A. Kalilombe, "A Malawian Example: The Bible and the Non-literate Communities," in *Voices from the Margin*, ed. Sugirtharajah, 442–53, 443.

4. West, "Unpacking the Package that is the Bible in African Biblical Scholarship," 70. (emphasis original)

Gerald West narrowly defines the term "ordinary" as not any untrained person, but the poor and marginalized, which as critics have pointed out, eliminates middle-class people.[5] According to Gerald West, the "ordinary" reader is not without training even though they lack formal biblical training. For Gerald West, "training" becomes broader than the narrow academic constrictions: "The ordinary reader has been 'trained' by his or her primary (for example, the family) and secondary (for example, the church and school) communities."[6] Moreover, because the majority of African readers of the Bible are ordinary readers, there is a need to listen to their readings. According to Gerald West, then, "Ordinary readers of the Bible have always hovered on the edges of academic Biblical Studies, but within biblical liberation hermeneutics, they have found a more central and integral place."[7]

11.2 What Is Reading "With" versus Reading "For"?

Gerald West is convinced that literary approaches are more favorable and egalitarian when reading with "ordinary readers" than are western historical-critical approaches. The latter, he notes, tend to codify and "mythify" the biblical text and enshrine it with power, authority, and immutability that undermine the possibility of exchanges necessary in discourse with the text.[8] The reading with "ordinary readers," on the other hand, aligns with the "reader-response" approaches that prioritize the perspective of the reader (a reading "in front of the text") over historical analysis (a reading "behind the text").[9] This is not to say ordinary readers are uninterested in history, rather only in so much as history gives them a direct link to their present reality. As Gerald West explains, "It is important that the poor, the working class, and the marginalized be allowed to pose their questions" to the text and the world behind the text.[10] As a white, middle-class, South African professor, Gerald West recognizes that he does not fit the bill of "ordinary readers" who are Black South Africans; instead, he envisions his role in the interpretive process in his context as a "midwife," one who reads "with" ordinary readers to bring out their voice and perspective, while resisting reading "for" ordinary readers. Gerald West conceives the relationship of the "scholar-midwife" and the "ordinary reader" as essential, so the "scholar-midwife" can record "ordinary readers'" contributions.

---

5. West, "Constructing Critical and Contextual Readings with Ordinary Readers," 60–9, 60.

6. G. West, *Reading Other-wise: Socially Engaged Biblical Scholars Reading with Their Local Communities* (SBL Semeia Studies: Atlanta; SBL, 2007), 2.

7. G. West, "Locating 'Contextual Bible Study' within Biblical Liberation Hermeneutics and Intercultural Biblical Hermeneutics," *HTS* 70, no. 1 (2014): 1 (Accessed June 22, 2020).

8. G. West, "The Historicity of Myth and the Myth of Historicity: Locating the Ordinary African 'Reader' of the Bible in the Debate," *Neot* 38, no. 1 (2004): 127–44, 128. Cf. also idem, "Scripture as a Cite of Struggle: Literary and Sociohistorical Resources for a Prophetic Theology in a Postcolonial, Post-apartheid (Neocolonialist?) South Africa," in *Scripture and Resistance*, ed. Jione Havea and Collin Cowan (Lanham: Lexington, 2019), 149–63, 160.

9. West, *Biblical Hermeneutics of Liberation*, 45–59, 140–80.

10. West, "The Historicity of Myth and the Myth of Historicity," 130.

Gerald West advocates for "ordinary readers," yet as Godwin Akper has challenged, his use of the term "critical" (as in, scholars do critical reading while ordinary scholars do pre- or uncritical readings) is denigrating to "ordinary readers'" readings.[11] So while Gerald West makes the case for holding scholarly readings and "ordinary" readings on equal terms, his terminology may betray a bias—possibly the reason that he has since turned to describing ordinary readers as "dialogue partners," in the interpretive process.[12]

While "dialogue partners" might imply a mutual back-and-forth, the ordinary readership approach demands that the accompanying scholar put aside his or her academic views and transmit the ordinary reading as untainted as possible. However, there is still the real danger of the scholar manipulating the data to fit a certain academic structure or interest, whether intentionally or otherwise. The question of how realistic that expectation is, is daunting. Gerald West does report that the questions have to emerge "from below" (from among the "ordinary" readers) rather than from above (from researcher or scholar)—a rather unfortunate analogy that perpetuates a hierarchical relationship rather than the egalitarian one he claims to practice.[13] Even if a scholar can be a socially concerned midwife, she still appears to be a privileged conduit or benevolent transmitter of ordinary readers' views.[14]

That "ordinary readers" still need the assistance of scholars to be heard orchestrates a lopsided relationship; by implication, "ordinary readers" have no way of getting their reading transmitted except by scholars. Yet, as Gerald West and Masoga point out, for academic interpretation of the Bible to retain relevance, it needs interaction with "ordinary readers" whose interpretations of the text are not usually treated as valid.[15] Both trained readers and "ordinary readers" would mutually benefit from the exchange and, hopefully, produce readings beyond the "sanitized" scholarly readings (that lack social engagement) and the supposed unsophisticated" readings of "ordinary readers" (lacking academic rigor). Both parties would interpret the text from their social contexts, and each interpretation would be admitted as viable, resulting in what Masoga names "conversation hermeneutics."[16]

However, unless it is made clear that the "ordinary readers" ought to have their views represented, the project has the propensity by the scholar to make the "ordinary ready" a subject of analysis rather than a true conversation partner. And so, the need to heed Ukpong's warning that readings must always be "with" rather than "for," and that readings "with" must always uncritically represent fully the

11. G. I. Akper, "The Role of the 'Ordinary Reader' in Gerald West's Hermeneutics," *Scriptura* 88 (2005): 1–13, 9.

12. G. West, "The Bible and the Poor," in *Bible in Mission*, ed. Pauline Hogarth et al. (Oxford: Regnum, 2013), 159–67.

13. West, "Constructing Critical and Contextual Readings with Ordinary Readers," 64.

14. See review by Philippe Denis, "On Reading Gerald West's *The Stolen Bible*," *RSR* 44, no. 2 (2018): 155–63.

15. G. West and A. Masoga, "Redefining Power: Reading the Bible in African from the Peripheral and Central Positions," in *Global Village*, ed. J. Ukpong et al. 102, 107–8.

16. Ibid.

perspective of "ordinary readers"; not an easy task![17] This critique notwithstanding, the idea of the "ordinary reader" pushes against the regimented categories and "ivory tower" mentality of western Biblical Studies, which have resulted in the elitist and socially disengaged readings. Reading with "ordinary readers" refuses to privilege academic experts at the expense of non-academic readers, who remain the majority of Bible readers in Africa and the West. In Gerald West's words, "Biblical Studies and trained readers need 'the other,' particularly those 'others' from the margins, in our readings of the Bible. Our readings may be critical, but they are not truely [*sic*] contextual without the presence of ordinary readers."[18] The resultant reading would be fall within the "third" category discussed earlier in the book, of hybridity that retains a stance of resistance and a liberationist underpinning in refusing to be sidelined, disrupting the otherwise typically self-contained scholarly conversations of biblical interpretation.[19]

Under this approach, "ordinary readers" have become a vital reading constituency that put social concerns such as the scourge of HIV/AIDS, poverty, political oppression, patriarchy, etc., in focus for African biblical interpretation. Traditional part answers about God's care and concern are challenged by victims themselves fanning the discomfort in academic platitudes with no practical substance.[20]

An Interpretive Sample: Mark 5:21-43—Blood and Taboo

Turning now to a specific biblical text, the story of the hemorrhaging woman in Mark, who touches the hem of Jesus's clothing and is healed, has been read with different groups of "ordinary" African readers resulting in views that expose the inadequacies with Western interpretations of the passage. The primary difference is that, while western biblical scholarship tends to focus on establishing the ancient setting of the story and giving little regard to its present application, "ordinary" African readers almost exclusively seek its implications for the present. "Ordinary" African readers, as defined by Gerlad West—poor, marginalized, oppressed— immediately identify with the woman's plight as reflecting their own. While western scholarly interpreters, presuming an academic audience, analyze the text at some remove, "ordinary" African readers connect directly with the text.

In Grant LeMarquand's volume on the passage, he asserts that "African women are developing a more counter-cultural approach than many of their male counterparts . . . ," and the story of the woman with the blood issue provides a good example.[21]

17. Ukpong et al., *Global Village*, 23–4.

18. West, "Constructing Critical and Contextual Readings with Ordinary Readers," 68.

19. M. W. Dube, "Villagizing, Globalizing, and Biblical Studies," in *Global Village*, ed. J. Ukpong, 53.

20. M. W. Dube, "HIV/AIDS and Other Challenges to Theological Education in the New Millennium," in *Theological Education in Contemporary Africa*, ed. Grant LeMarquand and D. Galgalo (Eldoret, Kenya: Zapf Chancery, 2004), 105–30.

21. Grant LeMarquand, *An Issue of Relevance: A Comparative Study of the Story of the Bleeding Woman (Mk 5:25-34; Mt 9:20-22; Lk 8:43-48) in North Atlantic and African Contexts* (New York: Peter Lang, 2004), 143.

In general, this story attracts the attention especially of African feminists, and these readers tend to interpret it in light of their current affairs, as a text with potential liberative capacity.[22] These readers understand the story as empowering for its encouragement of African women to break from "dehumanizing aspects of African culture and, through Jesus, achieve a renewed role in African society."[23] Beyond the impact of African cultural taboos, deeper problems for the African woman include lack of agency in a patriarchal society that sets and imposes the taboos and that makes it difficult for the woman to survive, let alone thrive. The action of the woman in the biblical story bucks the cultural trend, as she takes charge of her situation; this act provides impetus and models a way out for the taboo-laden African woman. Jesus commends and affirms the woman, instead of issuing the audience's expected reprimand. Thus, Nigerian biblical scholar Teresa Okure pronounces that African women should strive for wholeness in life, for themselves and the larger community, just like the woman in the story, who became part of Jesus's mission.[24]

In Helen John's juxtaposition of the story with "ordinary readers" of the Namibian Iihongo peoples, their view of "blood, clothing, and shadow" interrogates the nature of the healing in the story in comparison with the Iihongo context of magic. The study provides a surprising perspective where the woman's healing narrative becomes less attributed to "magic," and more to "alternative anthropological constructs of personhood," which provides a different interpretation of the passage.[25] According to Helen John, bereft of an alternative perspective, it is western biblical interpretation of the passage that usually attributes the healing to "primitive" cultural conception of magic. For the Iihongo, the focus is less on the magic of the healing and more on the wholeness afforded the woman by Jesus. In comparison, for Helen John, the western interpretation of the text parallels Schweitzer's findings in that it reflects more of western interpreters' prejudiced perspectives about the "primitive" culture, and "illustrates more about their [western interpreters'] own contextual location than is acknowledged."[26] By focusing on issues of purity rather than the woman's health, the western interpretations obscure an understanding like the one presented by the Iihongo for whom blood, clothing and shadow are "*part* of a person" and therefore transmissible *sans* magic.[27] Unfortunately, by equating the Iihongo perspective with the "pre-Christian worldview" Helen John's own conclusion seems to revert to the very system she critiques.[28]

22. Ibid., 144.

23. Ibid.

24. Ibid., 155.

25. Hellen C. John, *Biblical Interpretation and African Traditional Religion: Cross-Cultural and Community Readings in Owamboland, Namibia* (BIS, 176: Leiden, Brill, 2019), 299.

26. Ibid.

27. Ibid.

28. Ibid., 230.

Chapter 12

GENDER, SEXUALITY, AND THE BIBLE IN AFRICA

It is rather that, both as object of colonialist historiography and as a subject of insurgency, the ideological construction of gender keeps the male dominant. If, in the context of colonial production, the subaltern has no history and cannot speak, the subaltern as female is even more deeply in shadow.

Gayatri Spivak[1]

For me, the real disease in human relationship is rooted in the perverse patriarchalization of life. The cure I propose is a good dose of woman inspired wisdom.

— Mercy. A. Oduyoye[2]

12.1 Wälättä Petros: A Proto-Colonial Model of an African Christian Woman's Encounter with European Christianity

The enablement of a feminist voice in resistance to patriarchy that both Gayatri Spivak and Mercy Oduyoye reflect in the epigraphs above is an iconic one in African Biblical Studies. African postcolonial feminist voices have been some of the most vocal in establishing a vibrant interpretive contribution in Africa, bucking the dominant cultural patriarchy. It was, therefore, important to identify an "ancestress" that would serve as a historical inspiration for this feminist contribution, and we found it in Wälättä Petros, an anti-colonial figure from the Habesha ("Abyssinia") kingdom (a precursor of the modern country of Ethiopia in East Africa). She is not only an African proto-feminist, but also a precolonial biblical interpreter in Africa with amazing faith, intelligence and courage. For most African biblical scholars, the discussion of a "proto-ancestress" usually focuses, and rightly so, on the life of Kimpa Vita (1682–1706) from the kingdom of Kongo, and her resistance to

---

1. G. Spivak, "Can the Subaltern Speak?" in *Marxism and the Interpretation of Culture*, ed. Cary Nelson and Lawrence Grossberg (London: Macmillan, 1988), 271–316, 287.
2. M. A. Oduyoye, "Feminist Theology in an African Perspective," in *Paths of African Theology*, ed. Rosino Gibellini (Maryknoll: Orbis, 1995), 166–81, 177.

European colonialism and western Christianity.[3] A contemporary of Kimpa Vita, Wälättä Petros (1592–1642) was equally a formidable figure deserving just as much attention, who helped her own *Habesha* kingdom resist and overcome the colonizing incursions of Portuguese and Catholic Jesuits.

While her life predates the African colonial period that commenced in late 1800s, it was a proto-colonial encounter between African Christianity and European Roman Catholicism in the kingdom of *Habesha,* which saw Ethiopian Orthodox Christian women play a pivotal role in resisting European colonizers. Her story is found in a hagiography, penned by her follower titled *The Life and Struggles of Wälättä Petros,* (originally written in the Ethiopic language of Ge'ez). Written between 1734 and 1735, it narrates a Christian noblewoman's story, whose pre-colonial encounter with the Portuguese proved most enlightening as an early encounter of an authentic African Christian with European Christianity.[4] It is important to remember Ethiopian Orthodox Täwaḥədo Christianity did not come from Europeans, but is indigenous African Christianity going back to the fourth century. A literate, independent, strong, and courageous leader, Wälättä Petros was a woman who stood out in the history of the *Habesha* kingdom for her devotion to God, her Christian community, her church, and her country.[5]

A member of her religious community (a monk) wrote the story of Wälättä Petros (her name translates to "Daughter of St. Peter") about thirty years after her death.[6] She was born around 1592 into a noble Ethiopian family and died in 1642, as a leader of her own religious community. She married young, as was customary, to a counselor in Emperor Susenyos's court, and all three of her children died in infancy, resulting in her joining a monastery and becoming a nun. Following the Ethiopian emperor's conversion to Roman Catholicism from Ethiopian Orthodox Christianity, orchestrated by Jesuit priests, Wälättä Petros' husband was called upon to quell an anti-Catholic uprising that followed, in 1617. Still supportive of the Ethiopian Orthodox Täwaḥədo Church, Wälättä Petros eventually left her husband and joined the fight on the side of the Ethiopian Orthodox Täwaḥədo Church.

To Wälättä Petros, the Emperor had abandoned the true homegrown Ethiopian Christianity for a "foreign" religion. Her opinions put her at cross-hairs with the

---

3. Cf. for example, M. W. Dube, "*Talitha Cum* Hermeneutics: Some African Women's Ways of Reading the Bible," in *The Bible and the Hermeneutics of Liberation,* ed. Alejandro F. Botta and Pablo R. Andiñach (*Semeia* 59: Atlanta: SBL, 2009), 13–27, and Teresia Hinga, *African, Christian, Feminist: The Enduring Search for What Matters* (Maryknoll: Orbis, 2017), xiii–xxv. "Introduction."

4. For this entire section, I am almost exclusively reliant on Galawdewos, *The Life and Struggles of Our Mother Walatta Petros: A Seventeenth-Century African Biography of an Ethiopian Woman,* trans. and ed. Wendy Laura Belcher and Michael Kleiner (Princeton: Princeton University Press, 2015). This is the most recent and most comprehensive English translation, with notes.

5. Galawdewos, *The Life and Struggles of Our Mother Walatta Petros,* 181, 184, 191.

6. Ibid., 83–4.

Emperor, but, twice, the Emperor spared her life. First, was when she was arrested in 1622 for resisting the Emperor's edict not to teach Ethiopian Orthodoxy, and was spared by the Emperor following pleas from her family. A subsequent arrest for treason, three years later, almost resulted in death again, but for her husband's pleas to the Emperor.[7] Wälättä Petros was ordered by the Emperor to undergo Jesuit "indoctrination" but remained unmoved confounding the Portuguese Jesuit priests with jest and intelligent counter-responses, and the Emperor exiled her to the modern-day region of Eastern Sudan, where her leadership and establishment of religious communities would commence.

That the Jesuits were so keen and determined to convert her implies that they viewed Wälättä Petros as a significant threat given her influence on her people, and a major threat to their own mission and political colonial machinations.[8] Eventually, she established seven religious communities that served as sanctuaries for men and women escaping Catholic conversion. After the Emperor gave up trying to convert the country to Catholicism, and with his son, as Emperor, set to eradicate Catholicism in the kingdom, Wälättä Petros's exile ended. But she remained an abbess, in charge of her community that was situated along Lake Tana; a source of the river Nile and the largest lake in the country, and an enclave of Ethiopian Orthodox monasteries.

The Jesuit position on Ethiopian Orthodox Täwaḥǝdo Christianity, an African form of Christianity active for about 1700 years (and possibly going back to the Ethiopian Eunuch in Acts 8), was that it did not constitute a legitimate form of Christianity. This was both theological and political: with respect to theology, Ethiopian Orthodox Täwaḥǝdo Christianity differs from western Christianity in matters of Christology, praxis, and calendar. Ethiopian Orthodox Täwaḥǝdo Christians do not believe in original sin, and they believe in salvation by grace, not faith. They also practice ritual circumcision, observe the Sabbath, and practice rebaptism. Concerning politics, European prejudice sought to bring in line these "errors" of the Ethiopian Orthodox Täwaḥǝdo Church under the Catholic Church. Though the period is pre-Enlightenment, European racial hubris was already taking shape in Portuguese encounters with Africans and they were establishing the race-based enslavement of Africans. So a non-western form of Christianity had to be heretical, since non-westerners were "heathens" and could not possess uncorrupt Christian truths, outside of European transmitters.

---

7. Paradoxically, her husband's reasoning before the Emperor was to blame her stubbornness on possession by an evil spirit (Cf. W. Belcher, "Sisters Debating the Jesuits: The Role of African Women in Defeating Portuguese Proto-Colonialism in Seventeenth-Century Abyssinia," *NAS* 13, no. 1 [2013]: 121–66, esp. 146–7).

8. W. A. Belcher, "Introduction to the Text," 9, in Galawdewos, *The Life and Struggles of Our Mother Walatta Petros*.

According to historian Alòs-Moner, the consensus of the Portuguese monarchy and Jesuits was that "Ethiopian Christianity was a heresy that had to be expurgated."[9] Opposing views existed , but had no political clout.[10]

To make matters worse, the Ethiopian emperor's conversion was less theological and more a political strategy, as he intended to align himself with the Portuguese to gain their military support in consolidating and expanding his kingdom.[11] While virtually all men in the royal court converted along with the Emperor, many of the royals' wives, including Wälättä Peṭros, refused to abandon their Ethiopian Orthodox Täwaḥǝdo Church. Roman Catholicism was to them a "filthy faith of the foreigners" or "the faith of the Europeans," and its priests were "false teachers."[12] They saw and understood correctly the insidious collaboration of the Jesuits and a Portuguese monarch with colonial intent.[13] Jesuit priests traversed the kingdom with the brazen accompaniment of the Portuguese military.[14] It was a "colonial effort" that the Ethiopians would eventually repel, completely expunging Roman Catholicism from the kingdom.[15]

The initial resistance was largely led by women. Her biographer Galawdewos describes Wälättä Peṭros' resistance thus:

> She argued with them [Jesuits], defeated them, and embarrassed them. Each morning other Europeans came to her, reading and explaining to her from their filthy book. Our holy mother Wälättä Pǝṭros, however, did not listen to their talk and did not accept their faith. Rather she laughed about and made fun of them.[16]

Galawdewos references and rephrases Mt. 23:8 in defense of Wälättä Peṭros's actions: "As the Gospel says, 'Therefore, you all should not call yourselves teachers

9. Andreu Martínez Alòs-Moner, "The Jesuit Patriarchate to the Preste: Between Religious Reform, Political Expansion and Colonial Adventure," *Aeth* 6 (2003): 54–69, 59: "Hence, what these mysterious silences seem to reveal is a certain complicity of the Jesuits with the dominant trend in Portugal and Rome. Instead of a compromise, both the monarchy and the order chose to take the hard line."

10. Alòs-Moner, "The Jesuit Patriarchate to the Preste," 58.

11. Belcher, "Sisters Debating the Jesuits," 123.

12. Ibid.; Galawdewos, *The Life and Struggles of Our Mother Walatta Petros*, 46, 227.

13. Alòs-Moner, "The Jesuit Patriarchate to the Preste," 58: "The spirit of reform and paternalist attitude of both the Portuguese monarchy and the religious order could in no way welcome assessments of the Ethiopian Orthodox Täwaḥǝdo Church as authentic Christianity."

14. Belcher, "Sisters Debating the Jesuits," 125–6: "Such statements suggest that both the Jesuits and the Habesha saw imperial expansion as a motive for the Jesuits' presence in the Ethiopian highlands. After a decade of bloody conflict, however, the Portuguese were routed, and Europeans did not attempt to colonize Ethiopia for the next 200 years."

15. Belcher, "Sisters Debating the Jesuits," 125.

16. Galawdewos, *The Life and Struggles of Our Mother Walatta Petros*, 45.

on this earth because your teacher is one, Christ."[17] Her hagiography celebrates her rhetorical prowess, teaching abilities, and courage. As Wendy Laura Belcher who translated the work into English intones: "The tremendous rhetorical resistance that Wälättä Peṭros showed is striking. Her hagiography is devoted to debate, to the power of language. It is an African text that celebrates the rhetorical abilities of an early modern African woman."[18]

Wälättä Peṭros was not a lone figure. She developed strong relationships, especially with other women in her religious community, and her friendship with Eheta Kristos stands out. "Throughout their entire lives," Galawdewos explains, "Wälättä Peṭros and Eheta Kristos were like our Lady Mary and Salome."[19] The comparison to the mother of Jesus and her supposed sister, Salome, derives from a Christian tradition that sought to connect them with Mary's unnamed sister in Jn 19:25, and is referenced to an early disciple of Jesus with the same name (Mk 15:40, 41; Mt. 20:20-28). Observers compared Wälättä Peṭros's piety to that of Christ and attributed to her faith the fact that God had stayed the hand of the Emperor from killing her. Even the miracles attributed to her mirror those of Jesus, such as feeding the masses, healing the sick, and calming the waters with words reminiscent of Jesus's "Oh ye of little faith!"[20] Others compared her ministry to that of Paul, as she bore her responsibility with heart.[21] Influenced by an Egyptian painting, she came to envision the image of the Virgin Mary, a central figure in Ethiopian Orthodox tradition, as an Ethiopian woman. And at the behest of a monk, she constantly read the Gospel of John and sought guidance through prayer in front of the icon of St. Mary.[22]

While functioning in a patriarchal society, ruled by an Emperor, and a Church ruled by a "Patriarch," Wälättä Peṭros nevertheless managed to exert religious and political influence on male leadership, because she had gained great influence on men, women, and children that made up her religious communities.[23] On occasion,

---

17. Ibid.

18. Ibid., 46.

19. Ibid., 157. Galawdewos (255) reports of an incident where Wälättä Peṭros witnesses a same-sex romantic encounter between two of her nuns that disturbs her, and possibly arouses her. "It was evening and I was sitting in the house, facing the gate, when I saw some young nuns pressing against each other and being lustful with each other, each with a female companion." Cf. Wendy Laura Belcher, "Same-Sex Intimacies in the Early African Text *Gädlä Wälättä Peṭros* (1672): Queer Reading an Ethiopian Woman Saint," *RAL* 47, no. 2 (2016): 20–45, for discussions of the relationship between Wälättä Peṭros and Eheta Kristos.

20. Galawdewos, *The Life and Struggles of Our Mother Walatta Petros*, 232.

21. Ibid., 207.

22. Ibid., 176, 184, 186.

23. Ibid., 187. "Many people gathered around her, grown men as well as grown women, old folks as well as children, young men as well as young women. They came from east and west, with their number increasing by the day."

she had to overcome male resistance to her leadership.[24] According to Galawdewos, she did it with love, respect, understanding, and hospitality, in line with Paul's instructions to Romans (12:20): "If your enemy is hungry, feed him, if he is thirsty, give him something to drink. If you do this, you will heap burning coals upon his head."[25] Yet, when she had a chance to visit with the Egyptian Patriarch of the Orthodox Church who was visiting the region, and had heard of and was impressed with her story and leadership, he ordained her followers, "all the men with her" into the priesthood, but he declined her ordination request.[26] The irony is uncanny—she was the leader of this group, and the Egyptian Patriarch recognized her influence and authority, but she was ineligible when it came to ordination.

Later, from among her ranks, some male theological instructors would unsuccessfully challenge her authority and leadership based on their interpretations of such texts as 1 Cor. 14:34-35 and 2 Tim. 2:12.[27] But, a favorable priest, *Abba* Fatla Sillasé defended her authority emphatically and described her as "the teacher of the entire world," by referencing Gamaliel's reproach to the Sanhedrin (Acts 4) concerning interfering in matters ordained by God.[28] Only on her death bed was she ordained, as an "archdeaconess"—not by the church, though, but by Christ.[29]

Leading by example, Wälättä Petros influenced even royal women to participate in the reconstruction of the church on Rema Island where her parents had been buried. Helping to ferry water for construction from the lake, she did what "typically [was] done by women, but normally by poor rural women or the female domestic servants or slaves of wealthy families. That [Wälättä Petros], of a noble family, takes on such work is a sign of her spiritually motivated humility."[30] Additionally, the biblical passages commonly referenced by modern feminist biblical interpreters—"There is neither Jew nor heathen, and there is neither slave nor free" (Gal. 3:28) and "Come to me, you who are weary and carry a heavy load, and I will give you rest" (Mt. 11:28)—motivated her willingness to admit anyone into her communities, irrespective of their backgrounds.[31]

On her deathbed, 144,000 saints of Bethlehem are said to have comforted Wälättä Petros: "In this past hour, the 144,000 Children of Bethlehem whom Herod killed came to me and have been playing and enjoying themselves before me! But just now, when you arrived, they departed from me and left."[32] This is a conflation of Mt. 2:16,

---

24. While the community members lived together, the nuns and monks among them lived separately, with each group, respectively, in its own monastery. Later, Wälättä Petros established strict ground rules prohibiting close interactions between nuns and monks, threatening them with death. (Ibid., 200, 204–5)

25. Galawdewos, *The Life and Struggles of Our Mother Walatta Petros*, 187.

26. Ibid., 197.

27. Ibid., 229–31.

28. Ibid., 230.

29. Ibid., 265–6.

30. Ibid., 197, n.7. Cf. also 243–5.

31. Galawdewos, *The Life and Struggles of Our Mother Walatta Petros*, 263–6.

32. Ibid., 261.

as taught in the Ethiopian Orthodox Täwaḥədo Church, and Revelation 7 and 14. The former is part of the narrative in which Herod orders the killing of infants in an attempt to kill Jesus after being outwitted by the Magi, and the latter refers to 144,000 elders of the house of Israel.[33] In this hermeneutical juxtaposition, 144,000 became the number of children killed by Herod, rather than the elders of Israel.

Wälättä Peṭros's hermeneutical approach to the Bible bears a resemblance to some of the African Biblical Studies approaches discussed in this volume. While the history of Christianity in Ethiopia may go back centuries, and depending on whom you ask, to the time of the early church, it is more likely that it begins in the fourth century with Syrian missions to the region of Aksum (modern-day Eritrea and North Eastern Ethiopia). Ethiopia was the only African country to avoid European colonization, and this may have been thanks in no small measure to the nonviolent resistance to Portuguese colonization attempts by Ethiopian Christian women like Wälättä Peṭros.[34]

Her interpretation of the Bible may seem to be proof-texting, a literalistic form of reading that entails little or no interpretation but makes a simple direct application to the reader's present reality. However, her emphasis on the present aligns with what I have argued characterizes African Biblical Studies today. No doubt her story (hagiography—"history of a saint") is embellished, nonetheless, there is strong historical evidence regarding the role that Wälättä Peṭros played in resisting the Catholic Church's incursions, her understanding of those events, and her teaching within her community. Though she was initially labeled a traitor, these acts earned her the respect and admiration of Habesha's religious and political leaders.[35] Her resistance to colonization and her rejection of the Jesuits, as a guise for Portuguese colonial interest, would foreshadow the struggles for freedom that would face the rest of Africa in the nineteenth and twentieth centuries.[36] Her unwavering defense of an authentic African Christian tradition, that today has about forty million adherents, reflects her foresight and conviction that her service was to God and Christ, within her African Christian context.

12.2 Gender and Sexuality Discourse in African Biblical Studies Today

Two primary issues have dominated the recent discourse on gender in African Biblical Studies: first, *patriarchy* (in both African cultures and the Bible) and its

33. Ibid., n.11.

34. Belcher, "Sisters Debating the Jesuits," 126–30. Belcher makes it clear that Wälättä Peṭros was one of hundreds of influential Christian women who resisted the Portuguese Jesuits' incursions into the country.

35. See "Introduction" to Galawdewos, *The Life of Walatta-Petros: A Seventeenth-Century Biography of an African Woman*, Concise Edition; trans. Wendy L. Belcher and Michael Kleiner (Princeton: Princeton University Press, 2018), vii–xix.

36. Portuguese records of these encounters betray the colonialist intent. Cf. Martínez Alòs-Moner, "The Jesuit Patriarchate to the Preste," 54–69.

oppression of women and, second, the *marginalization and silencing* of women via sexism (once again, in both African culture and the Bible) and paternalism. Albert Schweitzer so clearly exemplified these two attitudes to the degree that there is no African woman referenced in his writings.[37] His racism, patriarchalism, and sexism all contributed to erasing the presence of the African woman in his purview even as he interacted with them daily, as a medical doctor.[38] When it comes to the Bible, similarly, the European Bibles used in the translation process of African vernacular Bibles were heavily androcentric, having been men's products.[39] So, what Wälättä Pet̞ros had to deal with was a harbinger of what African women biblical scholars would still be facing over three and half centuries later. Hopefully, also as her story becomes well known in Africa, her inspiring life, her leadership, her intelligence, her innovative nonviolent resistance to a colonial incursion, and her political acumen and ability to navigate male-dominated discourses and institutions while also challenging the patriarchal systems, will serve as inspiration for the fight for gender equality and justice.

Wälättä Pet̞ros's story, while an inspiration, is still more of an exception. And so, African women biblical scholars' hermeneutical approaches tend to deliberately investigate biblical texts from the perspective of the silenced and voiceless women in the Bible, which, in turn, has become a form of resistance against the patriarchal overload in the Bible itself, in European cultures, and in African cultures.[40] Because gender itself is a social construct that manifests differently in different cultures, it is not static and fixed, but it is transferable from one culture to another for better or worse.

Within the colonial experience, there were constructs of gender and gender relations that the colonialists assumed were universal and imposed on the colonized, or simply ignored different constructs of gender in the colonized communities

---

37. His relationship with his wife Helene notwithstanding, as described by his successor in Lambarene, Walter Munz in his biographical *Albert Schweitzer dans la Mémoire des Africains* (*Schweitzerian Studies*, 5; Strasbourg: Bischwiller: AFAAS, 1994), where Helene is described as co-founder of the Lambáréré hospital, she and a majority of the European women who toiled with Schweitzer remained essentially invisible, in both his own works and the construct of his larger than life myth. Cf. Patti M. Marxsen, "Unmasking a Myth through the Art of Biography." Available online: https://www.wcwonline.org/Women-= -Books-Blog/schweitzer (accessed June 18, 2020).

38. Harris, "The Allure of Albert Schweitzer," 817: While running from the hierarchies of academia, the church, and the musical world, Schweitzer nevertheless "maintained authority in a little colony of his own making."

39. Mercy Amber Oduyoye, *Daughters of Anowa: African Women and Patriarchy* (Maryknoll: Orbis, 1995), 174.

40. See the example of a colonial imposition of gender on the otherwise gender-neutral God (*Mwari*) among the Shona of Zimbabwe, and its impact on oppressive violence against women in Dora R. Mbuwayesango, "The Bible as a Tool of Colonization: The Zimbabwean Context," in *Colonialism and the Bible*, ed. Benny Liew and Segovia, 31–42.

and imposed their own.[41] The language of colonization itself took on a gendered construction, with colonists describing the distant lands they planned to dominate as being "penetrated" (obvious sexual innuendo) and "subdued" (emphasis on masculine prowess).[42] Consequently, colonizers could lump together entire communities and construct them as one gender or another. For example, Musa Dube explains that the "use of the female gender to describe the colonized [both male and female] serves the agendas of constructing hierarchical geographical spaces, races, and cultures," while, at the same time, legitimating the specific oppression of women.[43]

Decrying the continuing neocolonial western influence on the African church, and a widespread application of literal readings of the Bible, Oduyoye laments:

> My criticism of African churches is made to challenge them to work toward redeeming Christianity from its image as a force that coerces women into accepting roles that hamper the free and full expression of their humanity. As with class and race, on issues of gender discrimination, the [African] church seems to align itself with forces that question the true humanity of "the other" and, at times, seems to actually find ways to justifying the marginalization and oppression of "the other."[44]

Like the majority of African communities, Biblical Israel was a patriarchal society that was dominated by male leadership, a legal system that favored men against women and children, and even a God that was anthropomorphized using male pronouns. Nigerian Teresa Okure puts it quite pointedly: "Jewish patriarchal society, as we know, was one in which the woman had no legal status, except insofar as she was an object of marriage and divorce . . . . In short, the woman was *de facto* if not *de jure* the property of the husband."[45] In contrast, while patriarchy dominates in most African cultures, African concepts of God usually have no clear gender constructs. And unlike Christianity with its single, male, intermediary to God (Jesus), intermediaries in many African cultures were both male and female (ancestors, mediums, shamans, medicine-men and medicine-women, etc.). Nonetheless, even in matrilineal African communities, when it came to political power and control, male dominance still prevailed.[46]

---

41. María Lugones, "Heterosexualism and the Colonial/Modern Gender System," *Hypa* 22, no. 1 (2007): 186–209.

42. Ania Loomba, *Colonialism/Postcolonialism*, 3rd ed. (London and New York: Routledge, 1998, 2015), 154. "from the beginning of the colonial period till its end (and beyond), female bodies symbolise the conquered land."

43. Dube, "Reading for Decolonization (John 4:1-42)," 75, 37–59, 42.

44. Oduyoye, *Daughters of Anowa*, 173. Cf. also, idem (Sheffield: Sheffield Academic, 2001), 11–12.

45. Okure, "Women in the Bible," in *With Passion and Compassion: Third World Women Doing Theology*, ed. V. Fabella and M. A. Oduyoye (Maryknoll: Orbis, 1988), 49–50.

46. Cf. Oduyoye, *Daughters of Anowa*.

As a result, the colonial introduction of the Bible into African communities, with their own patriarchal systems, meant that male dominance found ready-made correlations within the predominantly patriarchal African cultures in which women have little to no public voice.[47] So while methods like "Inculturation Hermeneutics" tend to focus on finding connections between the Bible and the African cultures, when it comes to gender and women's issues, these same connections turn out to be mostly negative, perpetuating oppressive paternalism. Biblical patriarchy and African patriarchy have joined hands in orchestrated suppression, oppression, and frustration of women in the African Church, building on "textual" support within both the Bible itself, and in the traditional African cultures.[48] In this way, the Bible has become a weapon against African women in the African Church. The commonly referenced biblical claim is that "The Bible says . . .," usually preceding a text from 1 Corinthians or 2 Timothy to silence women.[49] The pairing of biblical and African patriarchy, in addition to the well-engrained Evangelical notions of the Bible's infallibility and its literal readings, have allowed conservative constructs of sexuality and gender to go unchallenged (cf. 1 Cor. 14:34-35; 1 Tim. 2:11-15). This way, African women have been rendered invisible in the leadership of the Church.[50]

The African woman, as African women biblical scholars point out, finds herself twice oppressed and marginalized—by the Bible and by the culture! And if you add the colonial oppression, the African woman is *thrice* oppressed. As Dube confesses, "For me, and other Two-thirds World women, the colonial oppression was equally significant as patriarchal oppression."[51] The western colonizers, even from countries led by queens, also functioned in systems that remained patriarchal, with a missionary like Schweitzer defending this patriarchal structure on his understanding of the Bible.[52]

47. This fact does not change even when, as Ifi Amadiume has argued in *Re-Inventing Africa: Matriarchy, Religion, and Culture* (London and New York, 1997), gender constructions in precolonial Africa were not binary and there were no monolithic masculine symbols and principles.

48. Oduyoye, *Daughters of Anowa*, 174–5.

49. Ibid., 173.

50. Ibid., 189–9.

51. Dube, "Boundaries and Bridges," 145.

52. J. Paget, "Theologians Revisited," 118. Even though there were many European women missionaries in Africa, especially spinsters from Europe, they were usually relegated to teaching indigenous women and children and had to be under the supervision of male European missionaries. Elizabeth E. Prevost, *The Communion of Women: Missions and Gender in Colonial Africa and the British Metropole* (Oxford: Oxford University Press, 2010). Noting the reasons why the women suffragists agitated for equality, Prevost makes it clear that it was "women's emancipation from patriarchal systems of power" (230). Further still, "Hanson [a suffragist] drew attention to the moral and constitutional inconsistencies

Therefore, the African Christian woman has struggled with the oppressive aspects of the African cultures, colonialism and its paternalism, racism and its domination, and the Bible itself with its patriarchy and suppression of women's voices.[53] In response to these concerns, and the need to provide a Pan-African academic forum for African women to address their concerns of "exclusion and disempowerment," Ghanaian theologian Mercy Amber Oduyoye formed the *Circle of Concerned African Women Theologians* (hereafter, "Circle") in 1989.[54] The Circle started with an initial membership of about 70 scholars and now has over 500 members.[55] For over thirty years now, the Circle has published some of the most important African women theologians' works, including such important volumes as *The Will to Arise* and *Other Ways of Reading*, that transformed the landscape of biblical interpretation in Africa and beyond.[56]

Given the compromised nature of methods like inculturation hermeneutics with respect to matters of gender, African women theologians tend to favor liberationist hermeneutics, feminist interpretation, and postcolonial readings that offer more promising avenues of engaging with the Bible while addressing gender oppression in the Bible, African cultures and colonialism/imperialism. The aim, then, is to "revisit the Bible both with a *hermeneutics of suspicion* as well as a *hermeneutics of liberation, hope and healing* not only for their own sake as women but for the whole continent in dire need of liberation and healing."[57] This is because feminism does not simply focus on the plight of women, but, rather, it "emphasizes the wholeness of the community as made up of male and female beings . . . geared to liberating the human community from entrenched attitudes and structures that can only operate if dichotomies and hierarchies are maintained."[58]

The Circle, however, was reticent to use the word "feminist" in its title and pointed out certain shortcomings of the term as it related to African women.[59]

---

of preaching a gospel of equality and liberation in the mission field while keeping women in a position of political and social subjugation" (236).

53. Oduyoye, *Daughters of Anowa*, 170: In a section titled "Breaking the Silence," Oduyoye speaks of "voicing" the silenced African woman.

54. Rachel NyaGondwe Fiedler, *A History of the Circle of Concerned African Women Theologians 1989–2007* (Mzuzu, Malawi: Mzuni Press, 2017), 36.

55. M. W. Dube, "Gender and the Bible in African Christianity," in *Anthology of African Christianity*, ed. Isabel A. Phiri, Dietrich Werner, Chammah Kaunda, and Kennedy Owino (Pietermaritzburg: Cluster, 2016), 144–54, 147.

56. M. W. Dube (ed.), *Other Ways of Reading: African Women and the Bible* (Atlanta: SBL and Geneva: WCC, 2001) and M. A. Oduyoye and Musimbi Kanyoro (eds.), *The Will to Arise: Women, Tradition and the Church in Africa* (Maryknoll: Orbis, 1992).

57. Hinga, *African, Christian, Feminist*, xxiii.

58. M. A. Oduyoye, *Hearing and Knowing: Theological Reflections on Christianity in Africa* (Nairobi: Acton, 2001), 121.

59. Interestingly, several members of the Circle went on to produce volumes with "feminist" in the title, for example, Musimbi Kanyoro, "Introducing Feminist Cultural Hermeneutics: An African Perspective"; Okure, "Feminist Interpretations in Africa,"

First, because the term originated in the West, it was still part of the imperial structure and therefore did not fully incorporate the plight and issues of the African woman. For Dube, "The failure of western feminists to recognize and to subvert imperialistic cultural strategies of subjugation means that their advocacy for women's liberation has firmly retained the right of the West to dominate and exploit non-western nations."[60] Second, the word "feminist" was too restrictive a term for the kind of scholarly projects in which the Circle intended to engage. Third, the use of the term came with the fear of being trivialized, especially by African male scholars, as being marginal and focused only on women's issues and interests.[61] The Circle was convinced that its concerns were also concerns of *all*, men and women, and that they needed to be understood and addressed by *all*.

Drawing attention to suppressed African women's voices has meant that certain biblical texts have received special attention, for example, Job's wife as a voice of the suffering and oppressed;[62] Mary, the mother of Jesus;[63] the Syrophoenician/Canaanite woman's exchange with Jesus (Mt. 15:21-28, Mk 7:24-30);[64] and Mary and Martha (Lk. 10:38–42).[65] In the story of Abraham, the roles of Sarai/Sarah and Hagar are prominent, as the privilege of Sarah contrasts with the plight of Hagar, who embodies the kind of suffering many African women experience.[66] Therefore, it is most perplexing that Galatians 4 presents Hagar the Egyptian as a symbol of Israel. This juxtaposition is curious as it plays into the notion of reversal present in the parables of Jesus. Similar is the rehabilitation of the image of Rahab from

in *Searching the Scriptures*, ed. Schussler Fiorenza (London: SCM, 1993), 76–85; M. A. Oduyoye, "Feminism: A Precondition for a Christian Anthropology," in *Hearing and Knowing* (Nairobi: Acton), 120–37; Dube, *Postcolonial Feminist Interpretation*; Hinga, *African, Christian, Feminist*.

60. Dube, *Postcolonial Feminist*, 26.

61. Hinga, *African, Christian, Feminist*, 7–9.

62. Sarojini Nadar, "'*Barak* God and Die!': Women, HIV and a Theology of Suffering," in *Voices*, ed. Sugirtharajah, 189–203.

63. Cf. Godfrey Chigumira, "Mary as an Inspiration for the Empowerment of Southern African Christian Women Disproportionately Infected/Affected by HIV/AIDS," (Unpublished PhD. dissertation: University of Birmingham, 2011); Philomena Njeri Mwaura, "Alternatives to Globalization: An East African Women's Theological Response," in *The Oxford Handbook of Feminist Theology*, ed. Mary McClintock Fulkerson and Sheila Briggs (London: Oxford University Press, 2012), 250–79.

64. Nlenanya Onwu, "Jesus and the Canaanite Woman (Matt.15:21–28): Toward a Relevant Hermeneutics in African Context," *BBh* 11, no. 3 (1985): 130–43; M. W. Dube, "Readings of *Semoya*: Batswana Women's Interpretations of Matt 15:21-28," *Semeia* 73 (1996): 111–29.

65. Anne Nasimiyu-Wasike, "Christology and an African Woman's Experience," in *Jesus in African Christianity: Experimentation and Diversity in African Christology*, ed. J. N. K. Mugambi and Laurenti Magesa (Kenya: Initiatives Publishers, 1989), 126–30.

66. David Tuesday Adamo and Erivwierho Francis Eghwubare, "The African Wife of Abraham (Gen 16:1-16; 21:8-21)," *OTE* 18, no. 3 (2005): 455–71.

her portrayal simply as a prostitute and traitor to her people, to a wise and brave woman savior of lives and challenger of the powerful, who is also a victim of both colonial and patriarchal domination, reflecting her hybrid identity.[67]

As a way of highlighting Biblical Studies' contributions by African women biblical scholars, I will now analyze the works of a select number of members of the Circle.

a. T. Okure—Mission and Gender: Gospel of John.

At the inauguration of the Circle, Okure was the only member formerly trained in Biblical Studies, with a PhD in New Testament. In her dissertation, *The Johannine Approach to Mission: A Contextual Study of John 4:1-42*, published in the prestigious WUNT Series, Okure makes the case that the story of the Samaritan woman by the well is paradigmatic of mission in the entire Gospel of John and that the Samaritan woman is a *typos* ("typology"), not just for women, but for the disciples as well.[68] And the fact that the Samaritan woman is simple and not a sophisticated educated person, yet fully grasped the message of the Gospel and was able to relay it faithfully to her audience, speaks to mission's openness to even the non-scholarly African woman.[69] Such interpreters would read "by exploiting their affective nature," and biblical texts should "serv[e] as instruments that could encourage women who find themselves in degrading or less than acceptable situations," like that of the Samaritan woman.[70]

Okure bemoans how ideas of marginalized communities, including readings by women, minoritized groups, and Othered peoples, are usually ignored and sidelined, and gain currency only when members of the dominant white society take up the same ideas, repackage them, and then present them as *idée nouvelle*.[71]

In her promotion of a "hermeneutic of life," Okure proclaims that any reading of the Bible that does not have the fostering of life as its aim is not in alignment with the universal biblical will of God.[72] Thus any reading that does not actively

---

67. M. W. Dube, "Rahab is Hanging Out a Red Ribbon: One African Woman's Perspective on the Future of Feminist New Testament Scholarship," in *Feminist New Testament Studies: Religion/Culture/Critique*, ed. K. O. Wicker, A. S. Miller, and M. W. Dube (New York: Palgrave Macmillan, 2005), 177–202.

68. T. Okure, *The Johannine Approach to Mission: A Contextual Study of John 4:1-42* (Tübingen: Mohr Siebeck, 1988).

69. Ibid.

70. Jan G. Watt, "Johannine Research in Africa, Part 1: An Analytical Survey/Johannese Navorsing in Afrika, Deel 1: 'n Analitiese Oorsig van der," *IS* 49, no. 2 (2015): 1–14, 4.

71. T. Okure, "Historical Jesus Research in Global Cultural Context," in *Handbook for the Study of the Historical Jesus*, ed. Stanley E. Porter and Tom Holmén (Leiden: Brill, 2011), 953–84, 959.

72. T. Okure, *To Cast Fire upon the Earth: Bible and Mission Collaborating in Today's Multicultural Global Context* (Pietermaritzburg: Cluster, 2000).

pursue life and well-being is "suspect and should be regarded as inauthentic."[73] Reading the Bible from a woman's point of view highlights the fact that, as the giver of life, woman's prerogative is to not only give life but also to sustain it. As an example, Eve and Mary are juxtaposed as "mothers of all things"—Eve the mother of all the living, and Mary the mother of the church. Motherhood then makes the woman an exclusive "co-creator" with God, epitomized in the story of the birth of the God-man, Jesus Christ.[74]

Okure makes the case that the social construct of gender becomes dangerous when it is given a divine imprimatur, making it unchangeable. Given that the social constructs of gender are products of human beings who are sinful and imperfect, gender constructs are laden with imperfections. So the patriarchal prism of the biblical world meant that the biblical portrayal of women was predominantly negative, yet that portrayal cannot be held as immutable.[75] For this reason, the exceptions that portray women in positive terms may, in fact, reflect the suppressed balanced portrayal of women if the biblical societies were not patriarchal.

As an example, Okure points to the story of Rebecca in Genesis 27. She compares Rebecca's plan of deception against her blind husband Isaac, to get the inheritance for her younger son Jacob instead of Esau, to Abraham's and Isaac's plans of deception about their wives to Abimelech (Genesis 20 and 26). In the case of Rebecca, even the text implies hers as a negative act of deception, while God essentially excuses Abraham's and Isaac's acts, with Abimelech bearing the brunt of God's punishment. But Rachel's act does not get God's approval.[76] For Okure, this is a "patriarchal prism" of the narrator whose perspective is in the story and is not necessarily a fair and balanced presentation of Rebecca's action. And even when women are presented in positive terms, like Deborah's bravery in saving the community (Judg. 4:4-10), the text characterizes these acts as exceptions.

It is for this reason that Okure is convinced that "though woman is viewed positively in certain instances in the Bible, the negative image dominates. Earlier studies on women in the Bible showed that this negative view of woman originates from sinful humanity, not from God's created will."[77] In fact, for Okure, the diminished status of women in the Bible effectively undermines the feminine side of God of the Bible, essentially misconstruing God's image and presenting an imbalanced overall portrayal of God. Women "are indeed God's coworkers. Without them, there would not have been Moses, leader of the chosen people in the OT, or Jesus, the Son of God, Son of Mary and the Saviour of the World (John 4:42)."[78]

73. Ibid.

74. Okure, "Women in the Bible," 51: "Hence motherhood, the bearing and bringing forth of life, remains a prerogative that God shares exclusively with the woman."

75. T. Okure, "Contemporary Perspectives on Women in the Bible," *BDV* 53 (1999): 4–11.

76. Ibid., 8.

77. Ibid., 5.

78. Ibid., 10.

As a result, only the liberative instances of women in the Bible are the true reflections of the divine, while the oppressive elements are products of human fallibility. In other words, "Only when the woman is granted her full honor and dignity in society will [the biblical] God also come fully into his/her own. Then humanity will no longer be ashamed to recognize and celebrate the womanliness of God."[79] As giver of life, God would then be worshiped and embraced as the compassionate one (female), and not simply as an authoritative and powerful lawgiver (male).

Prioritizing what she identifies as a hermeneutic of "sanctity of life," Okure maintains that the African concern with sanctity and fullness of life aligns closely with the biblical notion of God as the origin of life.[80] In this reading, interpreters must read the Bible from the standpoint of sanctity and fullness of life. For example, all of Jesus's miracles were about restoring to fullness the lives of those healed. This is a life-centered hermeneutic that Okure argues must be the foundational premise upon which any biblical-theological reflection stands; since the Bible itself advocates for and champions a teaching of "fullness of life" (Jn 10:10), "life holds the key to comprehending it."[81]

Methodologically, however, Okure is very much entrenched in historical-critical interpretation even as she strives to apply elements of African culture to her interpretation of the text. The results are sometimes awkward and ill-fitting readings that do not break the mold of western interpretive outcomes. Also, Dube's feminist postcolonial construct of divinely sanctioned genocide in the Bible challenges Okure's somewhat conservative and somewhat naïve claim that "no oppressive element in the Bible can be attributed to God's will."[82] While other African feminist scholars have pointed out the shortcomings of the inculturation methods as noted earlier, Okure is still insistent on doing inculturated readings of Mary the mother of Jesus in light of a "powerful, initiative-womanhood" from an African perspective.[83]

b. Musa W. Dube—Postcolonial Feminist Hermeneutics

Among the most prolific African biblical scholars, Musa Dube has been one of the most influential spokespersons for African Biblical Studies. Dube's *oeuvre*

---

79. Okure, "Women in the Bible," 52.

80. T. Okure, "First was the Life, Not the Book," in *To Cast Fire*, ed. idem, 194–201.

81. Ibid., 197.

82. Okure, "Women in the Bible," 55. Cf. Dube, *Postcolonial Feminist Interpretation of the Bible*.

83. Okure, "Contemporary Perspectives," 8. Idem, "Historical Jesus," 963: "Indeed for the Catholic Church, it is impossible to plant the gospel firmly in any culture at any age without this process of inculturation, understood as 'the intimate transformation of authentic cultural values through their integration in Christianity and the insertion of Christianity in the various human cultures.'"

interrogates the role that race, gender, colonialism, and patriarchy have played in the interpretation of the Bible.[84] Dube's wide-ranging publications have also focused attention on the scourge of HIV/AIDS and the need for a biblical response that envisions Jesus's "people-centered mission" as a central guideline.[85] Postcolonial studies and HIV/AIDS and the Bible studies in Africa and beyond owe immense gratitude to Dube's tireless publications and activism.[86] For Dube, postcolonial feminist interpretation is always aimed at several issues that she lists as questions: 1) Does history show us that the imperial notion of universalism has been achieved through respect for various cultures? 2) If not, how can the Christian gospel interact with other cultures' perceptions of the divine? 3) A postcolonial feminist approach seeks to know who is served by the universalism of Christianity: is it the imperial centers or the subjugated?

After earning her PhD in New Testament from Vanderbilt University, she published her first monograph, converted from her doctoral dissertation, which was a groundbreaking work. Entitled *Postcolonial Feminist Interpretation of the Bible*, this work soon became a touchstone of matters postcolonial and feminist—and not always positively! Western feminists met her critique of western feminism as still embedded in the imperialistic strictures with a hue and cry.[87] She explains:

> female gender terminology was used to articulate the subjugation of the Other. Earlier feminist readers of these stories had sought to reconstruct the early Christian history as women's history, without problematizing the colonizing ideology embedded in these texts. My reading of feminist interpretations of mission texts brought me in sharp conflict with my feminist community of readers as I argued our commitment to liberation is wanting if it does not pay equal attention to imperialism and how imperialism is manifested in the texts.[88]

---

84. A cursory assessment revealed over fifty academic publications by M. W. Dube on topics ranging from Feminist interpretations, HIV/AIDS and the Bible, Postcolonialism and the Bible, Race and Gender, Globalization and the Bible, Biblical Hermeneutics, Bible and Literature, among others.

85. M. W. Dube, *Africa Praying: A Handbook of HIV/AIDS Sensitive Sermons and Liturgy* (Geneva: WCC, 2003); idem, *Grant Me Justice: HIV/AIDS and Gender Readings of the Bible* (Maryknoll: Orbis and Pietermaritzburg: Cluster, 2004); idem, *The HIV and AIDS Bible* (Scranton: University of Scranton Press, 2006).

86. Lovemore Togarasei, "Musa W. Dube and the Study of the Bible in Africa," *SHE* 34 (2008, Supplement): 55–74.

87. M. W. Dube, "Rahab is Hanging out a Red Ribbon: One African Woman's Perspective on the Future of Feminist New Testament Scholarship," in *Feminist New Testament Studies: Global and Future Perspectives*, ed. Kathleen O. Wicker, Althea s. Miller, Musa W. Dube (Basingstoke: Palgrave Macmillan, 2005), 177–202, 183–5.

88. Dube, "Boundaries and Bridges," 150.

However, others saw her critique as accurate and necessary if there was to be a broad feminist movement that was aware of the diversity in its own ranks.[89] Dube's analysis especially found support within African Americans Womanist biblical interpretation that had also identified the compromised state of the predominantly white Western feminist movement as continued beneficiaries of the racist structure that favored white people over people of color.[90]

For Dube, postcolonial feminist interpretation needs to make a clear distinction between imperialism and patriarchy, something western feminism had failed to comprehend: "To confront imperialism as a postcolonial feminist, one must, first, recognize that patriarchal oppression overlaps with but is not identical to imperialism."[91] Well-intentioned feminist discourse could still contain imperial rhetoric.

Beyond that, postcolonial feminism must also be aware of interpretive methodologies that may be compromised and may perpetuate the subjugation of the oppressed. In this regard, then, there is a need to develop a mode of resistance that highlights aspects of imperialism, whether in the biblical text or the interpretive community, to expose the culpability of colonial discourse as gender oppressive.[92] This was the danger Dube perceived in western feminist readings; because they failed to take into consideration the imperialistic nature of the biblical text, they blamed victims while hiding their own culpability in the oppression.[93]

When Dube interprets the story of the Samaritan woman in Jn 4:1-42, her perspective could not be more distinct and radical than that of Okure's. She locates it within an imperialistic framework of the Greco-Roman Empire, on the one hand, and in the competition for power between Jesus and his followers (the Johannine community) and the Pharisees, on the other.[94] Both the Johannine community and the Pharisees are trying to gain influence and make converts, and as such have the upper hand to define Jewish identity. Thus, going to the Samaritans is an attempt to win this "arms" race, an imperialist impulse of expansionism that demands going past one's borders. The construction of the Samaritans as a "passive field" betrays this imperial drive, with the text portraying the Samaritan woman in colonialist terms as ignorant and helpless (v. 10), unaware of the correct place or form of worship (v. 22), and morally repugnant (vv. 17-18).[95] Even her uncertainty after bringing the message of her encounter with Jesus to her own people ("He cannot really be the Messiah, can he?" v. 29) perpetuates her gendered ignorance,

---

89. Melissa D. Browning, "Hanging out a Red Ribbon: Listening to Musa Dube's Postcolonial Feminist Theology," *JRER* 2, no. 13 (2011): 1–27.

90. Mitzi J. Smith, *I Found God in Me: A Womanist Biblical Hermeneutics Reader* (Eugene: Cascade, 2015). See M. W. Dube, "Towards a Post-Colonial Feminist Interpretation of the Bible," *Semeia* (1997): 11–27, 18–20.

91. Dube, *Postcolonial Feminist*, 43.

92. Dube, "Towards a Post-Colonial Feminist Interpretation of the Bible," 17.

93. Dube, *Postcolonial Feminist*, 28–9.

94. Dube, "Reading for Decolonization: John 4:1-42," 46.

95. Ibid., 50.

as she is unable to understand as fully as the male disciples.[96] She represented the people and land that in colonial terms has to be penetrated—"[s]he is the point of entrance, and she is finally domesticated."[97] Thus, the reader must interrogate the biblical text, since "as a written text, the Bible can easily legitimize or underwrite gender, imperialistic, and colonizing inequalities (thus the need for different hermeneutical skills . . .)."[98]

Dube then analyzes a retelling of the story of the Samaritan by a Motswana writer, Mositi Totontle, titled *The Victims*.[99] In it, Totontle repurposes the story to have the Samaritan's interlocutor be another woman ("a prophetess") rather than the male Jesus, who announces the freedom from apartheid. This literary move, for Dube, decolonizes and reimagines the gender structure of the text; Totontle "arrests the oppressive constructions of gender, race, geography and religion."[100] By melding aspects of the African religions with the biblical text, by identifying the prophetess as both a preacher and a faith-healer, Totontle's reading places the two on an equal footing. Rather than a colonizing text for the Johannine community, we get a decolonizing reading that advocates for interdependence and upholds the role of women in mission, but in a way wholly unlike Okure's reading.

For Dube, African women biblical scholars must go beyond the feminist interrogations to have decidedly anti-colonizing readings that expose and interrogate both inherent colonialism and patriarchy. The need to be decolonizing readers, Dube explains, is necessary since "patriarchal resistance does not always translate into a decolonizing reading."[101] She proceeds:

A decolonizing reader strives to arrest the violence of an imperializing text by exposing its effect and seeking ways of perceiving and promoting difference. Put differently, a post-colonial feminist is concerned with ways of reading that counteract various forms of imperialism and gender oppression rather than bracket or perpetuate them.[102]

Beyond resistance, Dube envisages a postcolonial feminist reading that "re-envisions" mission, by proposing relationships of liberating interdependence.[103] This is the decolonizing reading that would bring liberation by respecting the Other.

---

96. Ibid.

97. Ibid., 51.

98. Emmanuel Katongole, "Embodied and Embodying Hermeneutics of Life in the Academy: Musa W. Dube's HIV/AIDS Work," *SBL Forum*, n.p. (cited March 2006). Available online: http://sbl-site.org/Article.aspx?ArticleID=510 (accessed June 23, 2020).

99. Mositi Totontle, *The Victims* (Gabarone: Bostalo, 1993).

100. Dube, "Reading for Decolonization: John 4:1-42," 53.

101. Dube, "Boundaries and Bridges," 150.

102. Dube, "Readings of *Semoya*," 123.

103. Dube, "Towards a Post-Colonial Feminist Interpretation of the Bible," 21.

Dube's interpretive moves are invigorating, exciting, and challenging. I would be hard-pressed to find a reader who is so incisive, clear, and creative in their interpretation. On one or two occasions, however, some interpretive jumps happen that merit clarification. For example, Dube makes what I think is a faulty assumption, that the notion of communality in the African cultures would have "promoted gender equality and liberation in general"; this claim presumes that community means a lack of hierarchical structures of gender and domination.[104] Even societies that value community may have structures of difference deeply engrained if they assume that such differences are integral to the culture, and these structures may have little or no bearing on the construction of community. In fact, they may have seen these structures as necessary for the construction of community in the first place.

For example, colonizers imposed Christianity on African cultures which had neither a prior concept of "sin" as constructed in the Bible nor a notion of the need for a Savior. Installation of the male person Jesus as the sole intermediary between humans and God meant erasure of traditional intermediaries, ancestors, who included men and women.[105] Yet, some positive cross-fertilization also occurred. Dube herself points out the importance of the concept of the Spirit as vital in empowering African Christian women, as the "Spirit enable[d] women to claim positions of power, to become prophets and founders of churches, and claim to have heard God's call to the office of ordination."[106] Examples of such women include Kimpa Vita of the Kingdom of Kongo and Wälättä Peṭros, presented above.

c. Madipoane Masenya – Bosadi (Womanist) Biblical Interpretation

The South African Hebrew Bible professor Madipoane Masenya (ng'wana Mphahlele) has developed a distinct form of biblical reading that she has defined as *bosadi* (womanhood) hermeneutics.[107] Inspired by feminist and then subsequently womanist interpretations, Masenya felt the need to articulate an African reading that was not labeled by a westerner, one that embraced its African origin and focus.[108] In refuting criticism that *bosadi* hermeneutics is simply inculturation hermeneutics, Masenya is emphatic:

> The *bosadi* approach is not simply a comparative analysis between the biblical text and the African culture. It critiques both cultures and texts not only in

104. Dube, "Gender and the Bible in African Christianity," 147.

105. Ibid., 149.

106. Ibid.

107. Madipoane Masenya, *How Worthy is the Woman of Worth?: Rereading Proverbs 31:10-31 in African- South Africa* (New York: Peter Lang, 2004.)

108. Madipoane Masenya (ngwana' Mphahlele), "An African Methodology for South African Biblical Sciences: Revisiting the *Bosadi* (Womanhood) Approach," *OTE* 18, no. 3 (2005): 741–51, 744.

terms of gender concerns. It also includes issues of class, "woman-as-strange," and "Africans as-strange" in their own territory. Unlike in many past black South African male theological discourses and those discourses which foreground inculturation hermeneutics, in the *bosadi* concept, the idea of the Bible as Word of God is not accepted uncritically.[109]

As an example, even in African communities that perceive the "living-dead" as retaining authority and control over the living, Masenya points out that usually the male living dead receive this status. Consequently, Masenya reads the book of Ruth in a context where biblical and African parallels are closely connected and she excoriates the continued subjugation of women in patriarchal societies that mutually support their dominating position.[110] For Masenya, both the reader's world and the biblical text must be subject to scrutiny and critique. This explains why, in the *bosadi* approach, interpreters read the biblical text side by side with African "texts" (oral narratives, proverbs, songs, etc.) as equals and mutually interrogate and critique both sources.

In her major contribution, the analysis of the woman of worth in Prov. 31:10-31, Masenya articulates how a *bosadi* reading can contribute to a liberationist reading of the text. Masenya highlights four factors that shape the experience of a Southern African woman, which are racism, classism, sexism, and African patriarchal (she prefers *kyriarchal*) cultures.[111] Beyond the racial oppression of apartheid, the systemic oppression of African women in African cultures denies them authority or a voice to be able to articulate their thoughts. A culture in which domestic life is the default for women and the church in which the construct of an obedient woman is the ideal have suppressed and oppressed women in South Africa. In this context, a *bosadi* approach seeks to prioritize the positive aspects of culture, such as humanity, family, and the like.

Contrasting the construct of "Lady Wisdom" in Proverbs 1–9, Masenya rejects the argument that Proverbs 31 represents Wisdom personified.[112] Rather, Proverbs 31 presents an "idealized picture" of a woman—she is not real—that reflects the community's expectation of women. An ideal toward which all women should strive.[113] However, given the relative well-off status of the woman and her husband's social standing in the community, she does not represent the average woman (the poor, widow, etc.), neither in antiquity nor the present. Household management

---

109. Ibid., 745.

110. Madipoane Masenya (ngwana' Mphahlele), "Who Calls the Shots in Naomi's Life? Reading the Naomi-Ruth Story within the African Religio-Cultural Context," *Acta Theol* 24 (2016): 84–96.

111. M. Masenya, "Proverbs 31:10-31 in a South African Context," *Semeia* (1997): 56–60. *Kyriachy* she defines as "domination by the master or lord," in contrast to patriarchy which is "domination by father."

112. M. Masenya, "Proverbs 31:10-31," 61.

113. Ibid., 62.

indicates a certain authority and status, while care for the needy fits well with the African *ubuntu* philosophy, and industriousness offers liberative readings of the text in the South African setting.[114]

Conclusion

African women biblical scholars take the posture of Mary, the sister of Lazarus (Lk. 8:4-15), who sat in the place of the apostle and whose position and choice Jesus defended; this forms the basis of African women's rights to be educated and to become catechists, educators, and leaders in the African church. In tandem with this role is that of Mary Magdalene, who was among the first to bear witness to the resurrection at a time when the disciples still hid behind locked doors. As she was the voice of the transmission of this good news, so should African women be the voice of the mission to bring Good News to Africa.[115] Mercy A. Oduyoye appeals to the story of the Samaritan woman in presenting her case for missions for the African woman; she suggests that the African woman's role as a missionary is to bring the message to her community, allowing it to embrace the gospel message so fully that, like the Samaritans, it would say, "It is no longer because of what you said that we believe, for we have heard for ourselves, and we know that this is truly the Savior of the world" (Jn 4:42).[116]

114. Ibid., 63–6.
115. Fabella and Oduyoye, *With Passion and Compassion*, 60–2.
116. Oduyoye, *Hearing and Knowing*, 11.

Chapter 13

CHRISTOLOGY IN AFRICA

"WHO DO YOU SAY THAT I AM?"

Christ has been presented as the answer to the questions a white man would ask, the solution to the needs that Western man would feel, the Saviour of the world of the European world-view, the object of the adoration and prayer of historic Christendom. But if Christ were to appear as the answer to the questions that Africans are asking, what would he look like?

— J. V. Taylor[1]

13.1 Introduction

In light of our earlier comments about the ancient connection of Africa to the Bible, one may want to make the case that the Christological constructs developed by such luminaries of the Church as Anthony of Egypt (*Life of Anthony*), Athanasius of Alexandria, and Augustine of Alexandria were, indeed, African Christologies, and they would be right. For my purpose, however, I focus on the colonial experience as having evidenced the largest spread of the Bible on the African continent, with a central guiding question being who Jesus is to the African, succinctly captured in James Taylor's epigraph quote. What image of Christ would have emerged in an African encounter with the Bible outside of the colonial western missionary enterprise's imposition of its presumed universally applicable theology?

When Schweitzer published *The Quest* at the turn of the twentieth century, it flipped the world of Biblical Studies upside down. Schweitzer made the case that what the previous generations had accomplished in their study of the life of Jesus was not an objective historical figuring of first-century Jesus (in contrast to the spiritual Christ), but, rather, simply a reflection of each generation's particular view of Jesus. Like looking into a well, each interpreter looked into the life of Jesus

1. J. V. Taylor, *The Primal Vision: Christian Presence Amid African Religion* (Philadelphia: Fortress, 1963), 16.

and saw his/her own reflection which he/she presented as the historical Jesus. This was Schweitzer's critique and his rejection of the purported objective historical research, though he acknowledged that this approach was necessary to make Jesus relevant: "That was, indeed, the *only* way in which it could make Him live."[2]

Though aimed at rejection of "objective" interpretive claims, Schweitzer's critique may inadvertently have set the stage for the recognition of the interpretive pluriformity embraced in African Christology. As Jaroslav Pelikan has shown in his important volume, *The Life of Jesus: His Place in the History of Culture*, the historical encounter of Jesus by different communities in different geographical locations, languages, theologies, and worldviews has resulted in different constructions of the image of Jesus. Each image is not comprehensive or self-contained, but, rather, presents what he calls a "kaleidoscopic variety" in view.[3]

13.2 Jesus in Africa

It, therefore, makes sense that Christianity's postcolonial interaction with the African reality has also elicited a constructive and diversified engagement with the person of Jesus, distinct from the western perspectives. If Pelikan is right that, we "want to see what it was that each age [of encounter] brought to its portrayal of [Jesus]," and we could add "each culture," then it would come as no surprise that the African historical, religious, cultural reality would elicit different Christological inquiries.[4] Unlike Schweitzer, what preoccupies the question of Jesus' identity in the African context is not the distinction between the historical Jesus and the spiritual Christ, but what it means for the man Jesus to be the Messiah for the African. It is possibly this focus on constructing a meaningful articulation of what Jesus means to the African person that this Christology may be the most creative, and least reactionary, aspect of African Biblical Studies. In the Synoptic Gospels, Jesus' journey toward Jerusalem culminates with a pointed question about his identity posed to the disciples (Mk 8:29; Mt. 18:13-17):

> Now when Jesus came into the district of Caesarea Philippi, he asked his disciples, "Who do people say that the Son of Man is?" And they said, "Some say John the Baptist, but others Elijah, and still others Jeremiah or one of the prophets." He said to them, *"But who do you say that I am?"* Simon Peter answered, "You are the Messiah, the Son of the living God." And Jesus answered him, "Blessed are you, Simon son of Jonah! For flesh and blood has not revealed this to you, but my Father in heaven." (*NRSV*)

2. Schweitzer, *The Quest of the Historical Jesus*, 4.
3. Pelikan, *Jesus through the Centuries*, 2.
4. Ibid.

This passage is central to the study of Christology in Africa for several reasons. First, Jesus poses a question about his identity to his followers. This question has to do with what others, aside from his followers, have to say about him. While this question does not elicit personal conviction in its responder, it opens up the possibility of multiple perspectives as to who Jesus is. The responses his disciples provide are varied, and Jesus does not reject them, as such. He simply follows up with another question that demands a personal response, thus betraying the responders' personal evaluation of the identity of Jesus.

Second, the follow-up question demands an answer that is not only personal but is also revelatory with respect to the contextual location of the responder. Therefore, for African biblical scholars, the first question and its answers evoke the plausibility of different perspectives. Yes, he is not John the Baptist or Elijah or Jeremiah, but like all of them, Jesus is a prophet. Jesus as a prophet and his actions as prophetic would not be a wrong conclusion. Jesus as a "prophet" would help explain how one could understand some of Jesus's actions *vis à vis* those of Hebrew prophets, though this would only constitute one perspective of Jesus's identity, and not a comprehensive one.

Note, however, that Jesus does not refute those other identities, he only shifts the question directly to his hearers. To the other responders, Jesus fits the bill of one of earlier prophets because there is a template for what a prophet looks like. And because he fits this mold, they give him the presumed identity based on their background knowledge of the prophet. Their background knowledge shapes their response. That some thought he was John the Baptist suggests that they saw common elements between Jesus' teaching and public ministry, and those of John's. That others thought of him as Elijah may have indicated an eschatological understanding that expected Elijah to precede the Messiah; since Jesus did not fully align with the political expectations of the Jewish Messiah, those who associated him with Elijah may have thought of him as the forerunner to the Messiah.

When Jesus turns the question to his followers, it demands a personal response—"But who do *you* say that I am?" To put it another way, Jesus is asking his followers, "Who am I to *you*? Forget what others have said about who I am, with which you may or may not agree. What is *your* answer?" African biblical scholars see the pertinence of this question as central for Christology, as they understand its implication to be, "Who am I to you, that is, in your context as an African?" Peter's affirmation of Jesus as the Messiah is qualified by Jesus—"God revealed this to you, otherwise you would not have known it." In understanding that God's revelation is available to all peoples in every generation and that God continues to communicate, African biblical scholarship holds that the response to this vital question of Jesus' identity has to be an African one. "Who is Jesus to the African person?" is the Christological question at stake in this passage.

Even after giving the acceptable answer, Peter still subsequently misunderstands its implication or interpretation and ends up being reprimanded by Jesus to "get behind me Satan!" (Mt. 16:23). Again, Peter seems to have received revelation, but this time from Satan rather than God. This should also serve as a warning to the African biblical scholar that just getting the answer right once does not mean that you will get all answers right. Rather, it is a process of discernment and negotiation. The African perspective of Jesus is just one of many perspectives, and for a given time period.

The Enlightenment produced a Europeanized Jesus that not only looked nothing like the biblical portrait of a Middle Eastern peasant but also became more of a reflection of the European ideal—a white Jesus! In the words of J. V. Taylor, it was a Jesus that fit within the Eurocentric world, met the needs of the white man, and answered their questions. By the same token, it was a Jesus that did not fit in the African world, meet African needs, or answer African questions. It was a foreign Jesus! Mercy A. Oduyoye put it this way:

> We note that the Greek Bible imagery that forms the foundations of traditional Christologies has appropriated beliefs and language from Jewish religion, as well as Græco-Roman paradigms. To talk intelligently about new experiences, one cannot but build upon what is known. African religion and culture furnish the language of Christologies that describe Jesus as an ancestor, a king or elder brother.[5]

As further explained then, "What African Christologists are engaged in is the arduous and imperative task of developing a clear conception of the person of Jesus Christ. Simply put: they seek to make Jesus Christ feel at home within the framework of the ordinary experience of African Christians."[6] It is a question of relevance, of connection, of domesticating (positively, not negatively) the person of Jesus in the African reality.

One may ask, though, if this is not essentially the exact hermeneutical move that resulted in the Europeanized Jesus. Is this not what Schweitzer decried of western Biblical Studies, that it had created a Jesus in its own image?[7] Yes and No! Yes, it is a deliberate process of making Jesus recognizable within the African religious and cultural world, and, in this regard, it is no different. As Jaroslav Pelikan has shown, each generation made Jesus suit its primary concerns, which explains the different historical phases and faces of Jesus.[8]

No, it is not the same because African Christians openly acknowledge that they are, indeed, performing this interpretive move and are not trying to claim a universal representation of Jesus. Part of Schweitzer's critique of the western

---

5. Mercy A. Oduyoye, "Jesus Christ," in *The Cambridge Companion to Feminist Theology*, ed. Susan Frank Parsons and Margaret Beaufort (Cambridge: Cambridge University Press, 2002), 152.

6. Agbonkhianmeghe E. Orobator, "The Quest for an African Christ: An Essay on Contemporary African Christology," *HekR* 11 (1994): 75–99, 81.

7. Schweitzer, *The Quest of the Historical Jesus*, 4. "It was not only each epoch that found its reflection in Jesus; each individual recreated Him in accordance with his own character."

8. Pelikan, *Jesus through the Centuries*, 2–3.

analysis of the life of Jesus was its assumption of an objective historical enterprise.[9] In contrast to the unacknowledged Europeanization of Jesus, African Christology is very clear in its aims to enable the African Christian to recognize Jesus within his/her own *Weltanschauung* and not construct a universally acknowledged image of Jesus. In answering Jesus' question, "Who do you say that I am?" the African biblical scholar is speaking from a very specific social, cultural, religious, and historical context, and openly acknowledges as much.

Additionally, African biblical scholars maintain their justification in subsuming Jesus in African religio-cultural categories, just like Greek Christianity subsumed the concept of Jesus, the Jewish Messiah, into the Greek concept of *Logos* in Johannine writing. The Jewish Messiah had to become the Hellenistic Christ for the Greco-Romans to fully embrace his identity as meaningful to them. In Pauline language, the preexistent Christ "emptied" himself of divine nature, and assumed the nature of a lowly servant (*kenosis*) in Phil. 2:5-8.[10] This was a manner of speaking that went beyond the Jewish conception of the Messiah.

An appeal to the letter to the Hebrews also makes the case for the proto-ancestor that some African Christologies have constructed. Hebrews analogizes the person of Jesus, including to inanimate objects such as the tabernacle or God's radiance, and describes Jesus as the "first-born" (*prototokos*, 1:6).[11] So what African Christology engages in is very much in keeping with the Christian mission from the beginning—a need to make the person and message of Jesus relevant to the recipient communities by fitting certain aspects into the local idiom. A critique by African women interpreters, as I will demonstrate below, exposes the continued gender concerns within this category, as these efforts have not constructed a Jesus to whom African women can relate.

The different ways in which Christology in Africa has answered Jesus' question draw connections among certain African social-cultural and religious categories that are thought to be well suited to capture the essence of the biblical Jesus in African idiom and religio-cultural symbolism. Thus, there are two categories of Christology in Africa:[12] First, those that portray a "superior" or "authoritative"

9. Schweitzer, *The Quest of the Historical Jesus*, 4.

10. Zablon Nthamburi, "Christ as Seen by an African: A Christological Quest," and Anselme Sanon, "Jesus, Master of Initiation," in *Faces of Jesus in Africa*, ed. Robert J. Schreiter (Maryknoll: Orbis, 1980), 65–9 and 85–102, respectively.

11. Bujo, *African Theology in its Social Context*, 83; Cf. also, Travis L. Myers, "Jesus as *Prototokos* in Hebrews and the African Phenomenon of Eldest Brother: An Analysis of a Potential Illustration," *JGC* 5, no. 1 (2019): np (9 pp); Peter T. N. Nyende, "Jesus the Greatest Ancestor: A Typology-Based Theological Interpretation of Hebrews' Christology in Africa," (Unpublished Ph.D. Diss., University of Edinburgh, 2005).

12. Diane Stinton, *Jesus of Africa: Voices of Contemporary Christology* (Maryknoll: Orbis, 2004). In this impressive and thorough study of African Christologies, Stinton orders them as Life-Giver, Mediator, Loved One, and Leader (see Fig. II-1, 52). But ultimately, she still wants to place them under two larger categories of inculturation and liberation, which

Jesus—Chief, Healer, and the like. This is the *Christus Victus* (Liberator model) imagery of Jesus. This model identifies Jesus as a significant communal figure that lends *gravitas* to the figure of Jesus and depicts him as able to overcome life's "crises," such as birth, initiation, death, and so on.[13] Second, there is the inculturation model that identifies Jesus with a common but important personality within the community's familial structure—for example, ancestor, guest, and so on.

a. Jesus the Ancestor—*Christus de Familia*

Why ancestors? John Pobee poses the question thus: "Why should an Akan [African] relate to Jesus of Nazareth who does not belong to his clans, family, tribe, and tradition?"[14] J. Mutiso-Mbandi explains that the ancestral role of intercession and mediation would provide a connection point for Jesus as humankind's intercessor (Jn 14:6; Rom. 8:34). Mutiso-Mbandi and Pobee argue that Jesus has to become the ancestor *par excellence*/"Greatest Ancestor" (in spiritual and human terms, having himself assumed human nature) who can fully assume the role that the African ancestors played.[15] But they do not explain how this relationship is established. Kwame Bediako, conversely, makes clear that this is a relationship of Christian adoption; though Jesus was born into a Jewish heritage, he "is not a stranger to our [African] heritage" because his universality makes him the incarnated "Saviour of all" peoples in all ages—past, present, and future (1 Cor. 15:22-23).[16] In sharing life and death, Jesus became like an African, and Africans can fittingly refer to him as an "elder brother."[17] Likewise, for Anselme Sanon of Burkina Faso, Col. 1:15-29 presents Jesus as the image of the invisible God and the firstborn in creation connected Jesus to the African ancestors.[18]

While Jesus takes over from the ancestors for Mutiso-Mbandi, Charles Nyamiti pushes the concept even further when he argues that African ancestors who died in good standing with God could become "Christian ancestors," much in the same way ancient ancestors function.[19] And François Kabasélé of DR Congo explains further that African ancestors do not "need to be painted over as 'saints' to deserve our veneration" or to play their role as intercessors.[20] In the same way that Jesus

---

were originally suggested by Raymond Moloney, "African Christology," *TS* 48 (1987): 505–15, and followed by Charles Nyamiti, *Studies In African Christian Theology*, Vol. 3 (SCMAE; Nairobi: Catholic University Press, 2007).

    13. Nyamiti, "African Christologies Today," in *Faces*, ed. Schreiter, 4.

    14. John Pobee, *Toward an African Theology* (Nashville: Abingdon, 1979), 46.

    15. J. Mutiso-Mbandi, "Anthropology and the Paschal Mystery," *Spearhead* 59 (1979).

    16. Bediako, "Jesus in African Culture," 99.

    17. Ibid., 102.

    18. Sanon, "Jesus, Master of Initiation," 85–7, 90.

    19. C. Nyamiti, *Christ as Our Ancestor: Christology from an African Perspective* (Gweru, Zimbabwe: Mambo Press, 1984).

    20. F. Kabasélé, "Christ as Ancestor and Elder Brother," in *Faces*, ed. Schreiter, 125.

did not abolish the human priesthood by becoming the high priest *par excellence* (Heb. 4:14-16), he did not abolish the role of human ancestors; instead, the role of the African ancestor-as-mediator finds its fullness in Christ.[21] The difference here, of course, is that it is through Christ, who himself became our "brother ancestor" in his death, that the Christian ancestors find their meaningful existence and function. Following Mbiti's concept of the "living-dead," Nyamiti describes Jesus as a "brother ancestor" but one who is "immeasurably perfect" and whom the Christian follower must emulate.[22]

Congolese Bénézet Bujo proposes the term "Proto-ancestor." Bujo feels strongly that "the term ancestor can only be applied to Jesus in an analogical, or eminent, way since to treat him otherwise would be to make of him only one founding ancestor among many . . . Jesus is the ultimate embodiment of all the virtues of the ancestors, the realization of the salvation for which they yearned."[23] In this way, African ancestors can only be "forerunners or images" of Jesus the Proto-ancestor.[24] For Bujo, Jesus as Proto-ancestor incorporates the other Christologies, such as Healer and Master Initiator, as well as the theology of the Incarnation. As the giver of life, Christ provides a liberative "revolutionary" dynamic that can inspire new life within this cultural concept that is part of the fabric of African communities, and which finds parallels in the Judeo-Christian heritage of honoring ancestors such as Abraham, Isaac, and Jacob.[25]

Joel Mokhoathi of South Africa, however, critiques the ancestor-Christology, pointing out that it remains a preserve of scholarly writings that have not found full expression in the ecclesial communities.[26] A YouTube interview with Charles Nyamiti, the proponent of "Christ the African Ancestor," brought home this critique. The interview takes place in a room with a life-size drawing of Jesus—a white Jesus!—as a backdrop. Even as Nyamiti made the case for ancestral Christology, the image of Jesus hovering in the background was not one of an African ancestor Christ. This makes one wonder how serious his claim was, as the image makes it look like it was simply ethereal academic discourse that had no real-life implications. For Mokhoathi, rather than identifying Jesus as the ancestor (Proto-ancestor, etc.), what needs to be encouraged is primarily veneration of African ancestors "in the name of Christ."[27]

---

21. Ibid., 126.

22. Nyamiti, "African Christologies," 5–6.

23. Bujo, *Social Context*, 80–1.

24. Ibid., 83.

25. Ibid., 88–9.

26. Joel Mokhoathi, "Jesus Christ as an Ancestor: A Critique of Ancestor Christology in Bantu Communities," *Pharos* 99 (2018). Available online: https://www.pharosjot.com /2015---2018.html (Accessed July 6, 2020).

27. Ibid.

b. Jesus the Liberator—*Christus Victor*

Western constructions of a *Christus Victor* ("Christ the Conqueror") model usually emphasize the glory of the risen Christ in atonement and in the imagery presented in Revelation 1. This is a royal Christ who rides on a white steed and who marches to wars with armies. Christ's work on earth is complete, and he now reigns with God, awaiting the second return to earth to save humankind for eternal life. This image did not sit well with African theologians who saw uncomfortable parallels between this Christ and the colonial conquest.[28]

Essentially, western missionaries saw in the colonial armies this vision of conquest in the name of Jesus and perceived it to be analogous to the arrival of the Gospel on the "dark continent." Their conception of this image conveniently positioned both the missionary and the colonizers on the side of Christ, and the colonized world as the enemy of Christ and the church, to be conquered. The hymns said as much:

> Onward Christian *soldiers*, marching as to *war*,
> With the cross of Jesus going on before.
> Forward into *battle*, see his banner go!. . .
> Like a *mighty army* moves the church of God. . .
> Glory, laud, and honor, unto Christ the *King*! (emphasis added)

In contrast, for Africans, *Christus Victor* Christology designates a powerful Christ who is able to overpower evil spirits, cure diseases, bring salvation to the oppressed, deliver humankind from death, and the like.[29] According to Bujo and Mbuvi, this Christ was able to descend into hell (1 Pet. 3:19:4:6) and emerge victorious, having proclaimed liberation to the dead (and the living-dead).[30] This is the kind of victory that African Christians envisage—not a conquest of other peoples and their cultures, but a victory over all things that wage war against the fullness of life. The focus is on Christ's ability to liberate and overcome evil (and all agents of evil including demons, malevolent spirits, and, ultimately, Satan), and to establish peace and justice for his followers.

Nigerian Victor Ezigbo, in *Re-Imagining African Christologies*, after laying out various concerns that African Christologies must address (including the overthrow of western hegemony, preservation of indigenous traditions, liberation of the

28. Gustav Aulén, *Christus Victor: An Historical Study of the Three Main Types of the Idea of Atonement*, trans. Herbert (London: SPCK, 1931), 20, possibly, in an attempt to mitigate this perspective, reinterpreted the "ransom theory" from the Church Fathers, instead, as a "victory over the powers which hold mankind in bondage: sin, death, and the devil."

29. J. S. Mbiti, "Some African Concepts of Christology," in *Christ and Younger Churches: Theological Contributions from Asia, Africa and Latin America*, ed. Georg Vicedom (London: SPCK, 1972), 51–62, 55.

30. Bujo, *African Theology in its Social Context*, 89–90; Mbuvi, "*Jesus Without Borders*," 155–9.

oppressed, protection of people from malevolent spirits, and eternal salvation), contends that most scholars' neglect of the issue of malevolent spirits creates a disconnect with the ecclesial community.[31] In contrast to Schweitzer's view of Jesus' miracles as simply expressions of Jesus' "compassion and piety" by primitive minds, Ozigbo understands miracles as power struggles between oppressed and oppressor.[32]

This is not a militaristic Christ as tends to be the portrayal in the West, but one that has the power to overcome the spiritual realities with which humans struggle. So any vestigial militaristic characterization is spiritualized so that the whole experience can be referred to as "spiritual warfare." In this context, Jesus wages war not against other peoples but against entities that seek to harm, debilitate, sicken, and cause death. This Christ does not ride on a steed but is a powerful Son of God who walks with the Christian, as he did with the disciples on the road to Emmaus (Luke 24), to aid them along their journey of faith.

c. Jesus the Healer (Nganga)—*Christus Medicus*

In a world where the idea of life as the fullest expression of humanity is most cherished, the concept of healing is a vital one that affects virtually every person in the community. And if all manner of atrocities and existential struggles—from warfare to disease to lack of functional healthcare systems—encumber that same world, as in large parts of Africa, there is an openness to possibilities of healing. To give life, in the African reality, is to be one with the vital force, and to take life unjustly means eternal erasure of one's name.[33] In such a context, the traditional healer holds one of the most vital positions in traditional African societies. Together with the chief/king and the rainmaker, the traditional healer is one of the most revered members of African communities as a bringer of abundance of life.[34]

Tanzanian theologian Laurenti Magesa has argued that the image of Jesus as "life-giver" is the most relevant for most African peoples.[35] Jesus describes himself as "the way, the truth, and the life" (Jn 14:6) and the source of abundant life ("I came that they may have life, and have it *abundantly*," Jn 10:10). For Magesa, "abundant Life" belongs in the context of healing, resulting in the appropriate

---

31. Victor Ezigbo, *Re-Imagining African Christologies: Conversing with the Interpretations and Appropriations of Jesus in African Christianity* (Eugene: Pickwick, 2010), xiii–xv.

32. Paget and Thate, *Schweitzer in Thought and Action*, 287.

33. Cécé Kolié, "Jesus the Healer?" in *Faces*, ed. Schreiter, 135: "The African's greatest fear is not so much death as 'dying badly'. . . ."

34. See, for example, Israel Kamudzandu, "The Nature and Identity of Jesus in Mark 7:24-37: A Zimbabwean Interpretation," in *Mark: Texts @ Contexts*, ed. Nicole Duran, Teresa Okure, and Daniel M. Patte (Minneapolis: Fortress Press, 2010), 5–15, who argues the case of Jesus as a traditional healer in line with the Shona tradition.

35. Laurenti Magesa, *African Religion: The Moral Traditions of Abundant Life* (Maryknoll: Orbis Books, 1997.

title of Jesus as "the Healer." In this contextualization, Jesus' own life, teaching, death, and resurrection embody the African worldview of ongoing healing and life's flourishing. The miracles of Jesus, read in this context, plug into the notion of "abundance of life," given that they provide restoration to broken lives, individuals, and communities. Healing, be it physical, spiritual, or psychological, is what Jesus does *par excellence*.

Paradoxically, it is this very power of Jesus that becomes an obstacle for Cécé Kolié of Guinea and Dube of Bostwana. Looking at the devastation of disease and suffering in their respective communities, they arrive independently at a disquiet about Jesus' healing acts in the Gospel. Given the suffering and struggles of many poor African communities and the decades of political malaise in many parts of the continent which have meant unresolved struggles against debilitating poverty and sickness, Kolié and Dube find it difficult to speak of Jesus the Healer.[36] Given that the traditional role of the healer is to provide equilibrium between the world of the living and the world of the spirits and God, Jesus' ability to overcome malady-creating spirits falls well within this spectrum.[37] However, as Dube pleadingly asks, "In the [biblical] texts, Jesus is a maverick healer . . . why can't Jesus heal us of AIDS/HIV in our nation? . . . How does one propound a theology of healing where there is no healing?"[38]

Kolié struggles with similar questions and comes up only with philosophical reasoning: "Not only does Jesus heal, but also, and especially, he gives a meaning to his cures, and consequently to suffering and evil."[39] Ultimately for Kolié, then, "The principle task of Christianity in black Africa is not so much to heal illness as it is to exorcise it, demystify it."[40] And a primary way of achieving that is to decolonize the conceptualization of African healing and medicine that colonialists and missionaries alike denigrated—the former as unscientific and charlatanic, and the latter as evil and of the devil. Redemption of this healing capacity within the African reality would affirm both the miraculous and the medical.

Dube, on the other hand, resignedly concludes that miracles seem to be absent and that what remains is a responsibility to reread the biblical text for social justice. She notes that "in this rereading of healing miracles of Jesus, I have no point of reference, save the society which is itself confronted by this situation . . . a theology of living with the contagiously sick in the society, must rise—and it can only rise if I read from, with, and for the affected and the infected people of my nation."[41] The healing miracle, for Dube, seems to emanate from the rereading of the biblical text

---

36. Kolié, "Jesus the Healer?" 128; Dube, "Rereading the Bible," 57–68.

37. Kolié, "Jesus the Healer?" 138: "The [African] healer is not content merely with detecting the causes of the disease. He or she is equally eager to stimulate the reconciliation of the principles in the conflicting relationship that lies at the origin of the illness."

38. Dube, "Rereading the Bible," 64.

39. Kolié, "Jesus the Healer?" 140.

40. Ibid., 148.

41. Dube, "Rereading the Bible," 65.

for social justice, which would, in turn, effect national relationships of coexistence rather than exploitation, and which in turn would bring about the sharing of resources that would bring healing to suffering communities.[42]

For Diane Stinton, the "Jesus the healer" motif can embrace the other Christological motifs, so that in "Jesus the healer," one can find implied the *Christus Victor*, the life-giver, the re-creator of wholeness ("abundance of life"), and a supreme conqueror who overcomes powerful spirits in their different forms—physical, mental, emotional, spiritual, and so on. Jesus as healer is also Jesus the liberator and the redeemer.[43]

d. Christ the Chief—*Christus Summum*

John Pobee espouses a royal-priestly Christology that finds parallels between the Gospel's portrayal of Jesus as "true human and true God" and the African (Akan) tradition of true humanity. Just as the Akan chief is the "judge, legislator, religious leader, head of the community, fire extinguisher (fire being the symbol of pain and disaster)," so does Jesus fit the royal model.[44] However, beyond Akan constructs, Jesus is "prince of peace," "preexistent agent of creation," and sinless. Similarly, Kabasélé makes the case for Jesus as Chief based on the positive aspects of a hero (pillar of the community), a Chief's Son/Emissary, a Chief's strength to protect, a Chief's generosity to the people, and the power to reconcile.[45] Shared aspects, for example, of the Akan chiefs of Ghana and Jesus include installment that renders the Chief sacred; the idea of not dying, but simply going "elsewhere" (the realm of the spirits and ancestors), makes for effective correlations.[46] Ultimately, the Chief is an intercessor in this life and the afterlife in ways amenable to parallels with Jesus' role.

However, these positive imageries seem to overlook some of the major concerns that Harry Sawyerr from Sierra Leone pointed out regarding the Christological use of the title "Chief"; these include the corruption of earthly chiefs, the not-so-universal allure of chiefs to their subjects, the inaccessibility of the chief to the common folk, and the self-importance of chiefs as essentially better than their subjects.[47] For Sawyerr, while there may be benevolent and kind chiefs, that is not the image that first appears to people when they hear a chief mentioned. Bediako also acknowledges this issue, especially the Ghanaian church's attack on the Akan chief's authority. However, Bediako wants to make a distinction between the chief's political function and his sacral duties—the latter cannot be compromised, while

---

42. Ibid., 66.

43. Diane Stinton, *Jesus of Africa*, 74.

44. Bediako, "Jesus in African Culture," 104.

45. F. Kabasélé, "Christ as Chief," in *Faces*, ed. Schreiter, 105–12.

46. Bediako, "Jesus in African Culture," 104.

47. H. Sawyerr, *Creative Evangelism: Toward a New Christian Encounter with Africa* (London: Lutterworth, 1968), 72–8.

the former can be corrupted.[48] Consequently, Bedaiko argues for a *desacralization* of the chief's political power by imbuing it with Christ's power that seeks to serve and not dominate.[49] For Sawyerr, a better category would be to consider Jesus as "elder Brother," given the concept of the church as a family.

13.3 Christology and Feminism

Given the paucity of material on Christology written by women in Africa, Mercy A. Oduyoye sought oral sources to arrive at an image of Jesus as understood by African women. Critiquing most of the male-dominated presentations from Africa, she points out that they tend to characterize Jesus within the model of the "Saviour myths" with emphasis on authority, power, and control of history.[50] So ubiquitous are these models that they have influenced women's perspectives too. Oduyoye's findings, instead, suggest that African women tend to favor liberative models when given the choice over inculturation models. This is because, as she argues, African women give preference to Jesus over Christ, emphasizing personal relations over the ethereal connection.[51]

In analyzing the oral interpretations of a Ghanaian woman, Afua Kuma, titled *Jesus of the Deep Forest*, Oduyoye finds that "Jesus clears the forest of all evil spirits making it safe for hunters. Imagery that is in keeping with the stilling of the storm abounds in oral Christology . . . . Other biblical images, like a good shepherd, healer, and the compassionate one, are seen together with cultural ones such as 'the mighty edifice that accommodates all corners,' while the provision of hospitality common to both serves as the very antidote to death. Whatever the situation, Jesus has the last word."[52] Anne Nasimiyu-Wasike arrives at similar results in her own oral interviews with African women.[53]

Oduyoye's observation finds support in Teresia Hinga's analysis of Christologies and African women. She classifies Christologies that the colonists brought to Africa as laden with ambivalence. On the one hand was a colonial Christ, one represented in such hymns as "Onward Christian Soldiers," and on the other was Christ the liberator, who was visible in some of the missionaries' charity work.[54] In contrast, African women perceive Jesus as a friend ("who helps them bear their grief, loneliness, and suffering"), as the embodiment of the Spirit (a pneumatic Christ

---

48. Bediako, "Jesus in African Culture," 107.

49. Ibid., 107–9.

50. Oduyoye, "Jesus Christ," 151.

51. Ibid., 155.

52. Ibid., 154.

53. Anne Nasimiyu-Wasike, "Christologies and an African Woman's Experience," in *Faces*, ed. Schreiter, 72–3.

54. T. Hinga, "Jesus Christ and the Liberation of Women in Africa," in *The Will to Arise*, ed. Oduyoye and Kanyoro, 183–94.

that is "a voice of the voiceless and power of the powerless"), and as a prophet (on the side of the oppressed).[55] They also draw together the roles of women who give life and Jesus who gave his life to provide life for the church (Jn 10:10).[56]

Going a step further, Dube argues that there is a need to construct Christologies that take gender issues more seriously—that if Jesus is the full expression of God in human terms, his maleness excludes females. She explains in response, "We women must name Christ for ourselves—beyond what is written in the Bible or what we have heard in our churches."[57] Proceeding to construct a liberationist understanding, Dube presents Jesus as a liberator of oppressive texts ("It was said to you—but I say to you," Matthew 5–6), who essentially sets up a paradigm that women can embrace in answering the Christological question, "Who do you say that I am?"[58] According to Dube, "Jesus respected scriptures (Mt. 5.17-18), but he did not spare them where they were found authorizing oppression."[59] Jesus understood his mission in terms of liberation (Lk. 4:16-22), as he freed women from ailments perceived as part of nature (10:10-17) and empowered systemically oppressed widows (21:2-5).

Appealing to the creation narrative in Genesis 1–2, Dube argues that the initial narrative is one of equality, as Gen. 1:27 reflects: "So God created humankind in God's image, in the image of God, God created them; male and female God created them"—gender neutralized (*NRSV*). The second narrative (Genesis 2), whose intent is an explanation of the "Fall," is already constructed within a "Fall" structure that emphasizes inequality and an androcentric bias.[60] And since gender is a social construct both within the Judeo-Christian culture and in the African cultures, the gender bias Jesus confronts is one constructed, as Dube calls it, "in the shadow of the Fall," and it is one that has wrought violence, disease, and death against women, in the name of inequality.[61]

For this reason, the African postcolonial feminist Christology identifies with Jesus who is a liberator–healer of gender inequality and patriarchy's oppression—a Jesus who can embody the Christological construct of "Bakerwoman, Midwife, Mother, Friend."[62] Oduyoye constructs the same premise and asserts that "[i]n the light of Christ, if Jesus is the God who has become a weakness in our context, in his identity as God-Man, Jesus takes on the condition of the African woman."[63] According to Dube, "An African woman perceives and accepts Christ as a woman

55. Ibid., 190–2.
56. Stinton, *Jesus of Africa*, 61.
57. M. W. Dube, "Who Do You Say that I Am?" *FT* 15, no. 3 (2007): 346–67.
58. Ibid., 349.
59. Ibid.
60. So, too, Okure, "Women in the Bible," 49–51.
61. Dube, "Who Do You Say that I Am?" 354.
62. Ibid., 347.
63. Oduyoye, "Jesus Christ," 160.

and as an African."[64] She envisions the "womanhood" of Jesus because "in Christ, the fullness of all that we know of perfect womanhood is revealed" [65]—Jesus is a compassionate nurturer, a servant who washes disciples' feet, the sacrificial lamb of God, the reconciler, a feeder of the crowds, and so on. In this way, "The Christ of the women of Africa upholds not only motherhood, but all who, like Jesus of Nazareth, perform 'mothering' roles of bringing out the best in all around them."[66]

While embracing the concept of *Christus Victor*, African women scholars offer a reconstitution of the title within a gender-sensitive perspective. Dube makes the case that "the Christ whom African women worship, honor and depend on is the victorious Christ, knowing that evil is a reality. Death and life-denying forces are the experience of women, and so Christ, who countered these forces and who gave back her child to the widow on Nain, is the African woman's Christ."[67] She continues that "Christ liberated women by being born to Mary, demanding that the woman bent double by gynecological disorders should stand up straight . . . . The practice of making women become silent 'beasts' of societies' burdens, bent double under racism, poverty, and lack of appreciation of what fullness of womanhood should be, has been annulled and countered in Christ."[68] While Teresa Hinga agrees with the *Christus Victus* image, she argues that the image of Christ for African women must go beyond the liberation construct. She maintains that there must be a Christology of "Reconstruction" that emphasizes Jesus the Healer, which would enable communities to find wholeness and holiness.[69]

13.4 Conclusion

While these Christological categories may be useful in understanding the variety of approaches that African biblical scholars have developed, they are not necessarily exclusive, as I have sought to demonstrate. Such notions as healer, savior, and ancestor can all be useful in analyzing a single text. Therefore, for some, these individual categories cannot stand on their own and can provide a fully conceptualized Christology only when combined. Hence, Waliggo, seeking a Christology that is relevant to suffering in Africa, wants a Christ that is not only an ancestor and elder brother but also a liberator and healer *par excellence*, who

---

64. Elizabeth Amoah and Mercy A. Oduyoye, "The Christ of African Women," in *With Passion and Compassion*, ed. Fabella and Oduyoye (Maryknoll: Orbis, 1992), 43.

65. Ibid., 42.

66. Ibid.

67. Ibid., 43. In this regard, Dube is in agreement with Mbiti's reference made by Nyamiti, "African Christologies Today."

68. Amoah and Oduyoye, "The Christ of African Women," 43

69. Hinga, *African, Christian, Feminist*, 78–80.

can heal and break bondages of physical, spiritual, or psychological suffering.[70] Emboldened by the fact of Jesus' rejection (Acts 4, 1 Cor. 3:11-13), Africans who may feel rejected should rest assured that the same God who brought Jesus back from the dead brings new life to the African church, through Christ the liberator, healer, and ancestor.

An Interpretive Sample—Christology in Hebrews

Kwame Bediako has shown that a single study (in this case his analysis of the Letter to the Hebrews) can consider various Christological categories in order to understand the different strands of Christology at play in a text.[71] The clue to understanding the letter's relevance for an African audience is its presentation of Christ, primarily as a sacrifice, priestly mediator, and ancestral figure. These concepts are rife with meaning within the African religious context: Jesus is the perfect sinless sacrifice (symbolizing human sacrifices?), the ideal mediator as the "God-man" (Heb. 1:1-3), and the one who surpasses the human ancestors (Heb. 7:25).

The connection that establishes relationship to Jesus in Hebrews is the concept of the *prototokos* (firstborn) (Heb. 1:6, 11:28, 12:23). As the firstborn from the resurrection, Jesus establishes a familial relationship with all human beings. And in a significant move, the text declares Jesus a High Priest, even though he is not from the Aaronic priestly line. It is a lineage of an outsider, that is, everyone who is not a priest. This is because Jesus' High Priestly status is not part of the human lineage that Moses established but is established when Jesus dies ("If he were on earth, he would not be a priest at all," 8:4). For Bediako, "The uniqueness of Jesus is rooted in his radical and direct significance for *every* human person and *every* human context and *every* human culture."[72]

In living and dying, Jesus became like one of us, a human being, an African (Heb. 2:14-15). But in his resurrection and ascension, Jesus enters into the realm of power, the world of the Spirit and ancestors.[73] Entering into this realm of the ancestors as a Lord—of both the living and the dead (including the living-dead)—establishes Jesus' priesthood. Christ's Lordship enables him to send the Holy Spirit to the church to be a guide and support.[74] This same lordship makes him the Chief who is greater than an earthly chief, and it makes him more efficacious than animal sacrificial victims and ancestors. Therefore, just like Hebrews' converts who have to chart a different priestly tradition, the African Christians have to chart a different ancestral tradition, given their connection to the perfect Ancestor.

---

70. John M. Waliggo, "African Christology in a Situation of Suffering," in *Faces*, ed. Schreiter, 176.

71. Bediako, "Jesus in African Culture," 93–121.

72. Ibid., 114. (emphasis original)

73. Ibid., 103.

74. Ibid., 104.

Espousing a slightly different take on the end result of the African ancestor tradition in Hebrews, Peter Nyende holds that African Christians have not abandoned the African ancestors but have fully absorbed them into the Christian tradition. For Nyende, Jesus' relationship to the African tradition is typological, by which he means African ancestors become types that point toward Christ. This is essentially the *praeparatio evangelica* approach to interpretation.[75] But in a confusing move given the typology analogy, Nyende proceeds to claim that African Christians must abandon the ancestors now that the "Greatest ancestor," Jesus Christ, has taken the role to which they pointed all along. Absorption and abandonment are two distinct responses—one recognizes the continued connection, while the other assumes a necessary disconnection.

Nyende's position of abandonment is, however, challenged by Bediako who argues that the "cloud of witnesses" in Heb. 12:1 includes the ancestors. While the ancestors may have lost their mediatory power with the arrival of Jesus, the perfect mediator between humans and God, they continue their role as part of the praising choruses of those who worship before the eternal throne. The ancestors continue, in union with Christ, to participate in mediating the gifts of life and salvation.

---

75. So too Bediako, *Christianity in Africa*, 225: "A theology of ancestors becomes, therefore, the corollary and unavoidable by-product of the continuity of God in African experience. . . . The past can be examined for its anticipations of the present, thus some who would have been considered ancestors emerge as striking confirmation that the divine initiative had, in fact, been at work in the past" (Acts 14:17). Cf. two works by Israel Kamudzandu that explore the notion of ancestor in the teachings of Paul about Abraham, as Israel's ancestor and as a spiritual ancestor to African Christians (*Abraham Our Father: Paul and Ancestors in Postcolonial Africa* [Minneapolis: Fortress Press, 2013]; idem, *Abraham as a Spiritual Ancestor: A Postcolonial Zimbabwean Reading of Romans 4* [Leiden: Brill, 2010]).

Chapter 14

CONCLUSION

Toward a Decolonized Biblical Studies

Here is the challenge plainly put: there can be no critical interpretation worthy of the name, without coming to terms with the first contact— between the West and the rest, the West and the Others—and its perduring toxic and blinding effects and consequences.

— Vincent L. Wimbush[1]

In this context, the meeting of the West with Africa takes place in the form of violence . . . [a] form of savagery that the West carries with itself from a "culture of intolerance and violence" that belongs intrinsically to it.

— Jean-Marc Ela[2]

14.1 Transforming Biblical Studies

To imagine a Biblical Studies discipline that is built on a foundation of hope, justice, and equality is essential for the future of the discipline. As Willie Jennings puts it, there has to be the eradication within western Biblical Studies of the "quest for white masculinist self-sufficient intellectual form" that has reigned supreme from its colonialist installment thereby "giving up their historical colonial positionality" as the "epistemic emperors."[3] It has to be a possibility and ideal that involves a complete realignment of the structure of the discipline from its present form. While it will not come without challenges, real and imagined, it is the only way that full transformation can take place and a truly diverse and representative discipline be realized.

---

1. Wimbush, "Interpreters," 9.
2. Jean-Marc Ela, "The Memory of the African People and the Cross of Christ," in *The Scandal of a Crucified World*, ed. YacobTesfai (Maryknoll: Orbis, 1994), 17–35, 22.
3. Willie J. Jennings, "Renouncing Completeness: The Rich Ruler and the Possibilities of Biblical Scholarship without White Masculine Self-Sufficiency," *JBL* 140, no. 4 (2021): 837–42, 842.

For Biblical Studies, as currently construed in the West, to move beyond its current state and become fully representative, diverse, and embodying of equality and justice, it has to acknowledge complicity in a racist past that it has yet to completely undo: a past that Jean-Marc Ela of Cameroon characterizes as replete with the West's "culture of intolerance and violence." For this to happen, it has to, essentially, adopt an *anti*-colonial and *anti*-racist hermeneutical stance and framework. In its current form, it does not. To achieve this there must be a collective introspection within the discipline, a public acknowledgment and denouncing of complicity in past racially constructed approaches and associated violence that retained imperialistic and colonialist presuppositions, and a restructuring of the discipline to make clear its parochial nature devoid of any pretense of universalism.

Inspiration can be drawn from several African innovations that have served to confront racism and clear a path forward for transformation—TRC and the Kairos Document of South Africa. At the end of apartheid in South Africa, there was established the Truth and Reconciliation Commission (TRC) in 1995 chaired by Rev. Desmond Tutu.[4] The commission's purpose was to provide a space for the confrontation and acknowledgment of the atrocities of the past to be addressed and promulgate a restorative justice for victims of the racist apartheid reign of terror in South Africa. Only in doing so would societal healing and restoration occur allowing for a path forward for a new community in South Africa. The notions of "confrontation and acknowledgment," and restorative justice are what western Biblical Studies must face up to if there is going to be healing and transformation in the discipline.

Identifying, uprooting, and replacing long-enmeshed colonialist and racist underpinnings and presuppositions that persist within the discipline will come at a price. But it has to be done. There will be resistance, no doubt. However, just like the treatment of life-threatening cancer may involve invasive and even life-threatening procedures, there will be a need to create the necessary discomfort and pain in order to begin to heal. For those aligned with oppressive systems, the discomfort and pain of dislodging "their history." For those oppressed by the system, an opportunity for justice and hope. But supplanting the colonialist and imperialist structure would usher in a self-aware and self-critical Biblical Studies structure that would, hopefully, transform the discipline for the better.

If taken seriously, the implication of this study's advocation of decolonization of the discipline of Biblical Studies would result in the reconstitution of at least four broad areas, beyond the importance of reckoning with the colonial and imperialist past. These include i) Language and control—definition and application of terminology as a means of control; ii) interpretive approaches and methodology—determination of what questions are considered worth addressing; iii) pedagogical structures—what is taught, how it is taught, by whom it is taught; and iv) the dynamics of power that govern the production of knowledge.

---

4. This is the link for the complete report https://www.justice.gov.za/trc/.

a. Language and Control

Naming is an act of power and control.[5] What African Biblical Studies' critique of Biblical Studies in the West reveals is that even the concept of "Biblical Studies" itself is racialized.[6] Typically, the generally unstated assumption of what Biblical Studies means when used without a modifier (African, Asian, Black, etc.) essentially refers to white Euro-American scholarship or works based on that scholarship—approaches that are built on presuppositions, methodologies, assumptions, and applications developed by Euro-American scholarship. Not only have these approaches remained dominant, but they have also assumed a universal and "objective" stature. However, as we have shown in this study, Biblical Studies without a modifier is not a reflection of universality or neutrality at all. Instead, it is a reflection of the enduring white Euro-American hegemony that retains colonialist and imperialist assumptions of being the *de facto* source of interpretive approaches. To reference Jennings again, "Modern biblical studies [in the West] exists inside white male self-sufficiency with its three dismal virtues—control, possession, and mastery."[7]

It is this western hubris that African Biblical Studies calls out. This continued lending of false credence to a systemic structure ridden with unfair and prejudicial assumptions about the Other fosters the continued holding of the so-called minoritized approaches at arm's length, as being not quite "biblical studies."[8] The resistance and undermining of this enduring colonial legacy are what unite the so-called "minoritized" groups. Challenging the historical unfairness of the system and its failure to concede its own colonizing and imperializing stance. They do so by exposing the complicity of the discipline as practiced in the West in the colonial project, and championing ways of reading, often suppressed by being named differently. Naming is just one way that language is used to control who belongs and who does not. Language is also used to impinge upon the possibility of divergent questions being posed to the biblical texts, or any push against presumed

---

5. Gabriele vom Bruck and Barbara Bodenhorn (eds.), *The Anthropology of Names and Naming* (Cambridge: Cambridge University Press, 2006); Justin Kaplan and Anne Bernays, *The Language of Names* (New York: Simon & Schuster, 1997).

6. Jennings, "Renouncing Completeness," 837: "White male self-sufficiency has been a governing image for formation and intellectual development in the Western world since the beginning of colonial modernity."

7. Jennings, "Renouncing Completeness," 837.

8. When, for example, John Barton writes of Biblical Criticism as a "common-sense" approach to reading the Bible, the unspoken assumption is that there really is a universal "common sense" (whatever that is). However, when the list of common-sense questions is narrowed to those of *origin*—"where?", *context*—"when?", and *genre*—"why?", it precludes any other possibilities of inquiry. The "why?", "how?", "really?" John Barton, "Biblical Criticism: A Common-Sense Approach to the Bible," *TheTorah.com* (2020). Available online: https://thetorah.com/article/biblical-criticism-a-common-sense-approach-to-the-bible

disciplinary boundaries. African Biblical Studies and its "minoritized" siblings have resisted any insinuations of scholarly deficiency of their contributions to the discipline and insist on crossing disciplinary boundaries.[9]

It is paramount, then, for Biblical Studies in the West to openly acknowledge that the typical application of the phrase "Biblical Studies" essentially and narrowly represents only "white Euro-American perspectives," and should be labeled as such. But as Willies Jennings reminds us, "whiteness" is not simply biology or phenotype, but "an identity achieved and sustained through alignment—social, political, economic, geographic, and intellectual—with a very successful colonial life project."[10] While language and terminology driven by certain sensibilities in public discourse may have evolved over time, occluding overt racist expressions today (think, "politically correct language") in contrast to the writings of yesteryear, racialized methods, approaches, and presuppositions built into, and bequeathed from that past, remain dominant as we have shown with Schweitzer's case in Chapter 3.[11]

So, while the recent endeavor of the biblical studies guild, SBL, for a deliberate and conscientious promotion of plurality in the discipline is welcome, without an honest introspection into the darkest aspects of the discipline's past and their continuing impact, not much headway can be made.[12] For this reason, to attain true equality, Biblical Studies in the West should assume a label of its own—"white" Biblical Studies, perhaps. Awkward as that may sound, it would be a candid renaming of what biblical studies in the West has epitomized. Renaming is one of the first things that decolonizing the discipline would call for: not only owning up to its locatedness and "local/peripheral" status, but also ceding its presumed right to control and colonize.[13] In this way, no representative group remains unnamed within the discipline (Asian, American, African American, Native American, etc.) and none retains assumed neutrality devoid of a descriptor. This also would decenter the structure of the discipline with the title "biblical studies" taking up the position of a true umbrella term that equally embodies all differently labeled groups.

---

9. Mbuvi, "An African Biblical Scholar Explores the Broadening of the Biblical Studies Landscape," 41–63.

10. Jennings, "Renouncing Completeness," 842. Cf. idem, *After Whiteness: An Education in Belonging* (Theological Education between the Times; Grand Rapids: Eerdmans, 2020), where Jennings builds the case for addressing and eradicating whiteness as an all-pervasive colonial ideological construct that pervades western Biblical Studies (he addresses theological education in general).

11. Cf. Kelley, *Racializing Jesus.*

12. I have in mind a statement like the one made by SBL following the murder of George Floyd in June, 2020 (Cf. https://www.sbl-site.org/assets/pdfs/2-June-2020_Statement_on _Black_Lives_Matter_Right_to_Protest_and_Bible_as_Prop.pdf).

13. Sugirtharajah, *Voices from the Margin,* 9.

There is also the need to address the injuries and traumas inflicted by past racist structures, assumptions, and applications on the Othered ("hermeneutic of healing"), and a complete reorienting of the discipline as a whole. To assume a position of true equality, a reckoning with the toxic historical legacy cannot be sidestepped.[14] It is not enough to simply acknowledge the racist historical reality, but measures must be taken that will completely transform the way the discipline functions going forward. That would mean a complete rethinking of the relationship between the so-called "centers" (Europe and America) and the so-called "peripheries" (Africa, Asia, South America, etc.). Without a radical restructuring of the discipline, any claims to diversity, equality, and justice remain superficial verbal diversions.

b. Approaches and Methodologies

Continued imposition and defense of approaches developed in the West, at the detriment of approaches developed elsewhere, betray the continued colonialist and imperialist structure, presuppositions, and ideology that continue to dominate Biblical Studies in the West. As Wimbush has pointed out, even seemingly innocuous propositions often transcribed as "objective" scholarship, such as the western Biblical Studies' dictum of "focusing only on the text," can be exposed for their racist underpinnings.[15] By sidestepping the cultural significance for the reader, such an interpretive approach becomes a convenient means for the predominantly white western biblical scholarship to avoid dealing with the implications of its history.

Interpretive approaches and methodologies are typically born out of the questions the reader poses to the text, and no one's questions are more important than others', more authentic than others', or universally representative of all the types of questions that can be posed. If, for example, as one critic has put it, the possibility of a better future "is to transcend the Euro-centric construct of Africa, politically, economically and equally importantly, ideologically," then what I have shown in this study is how African Biblical Studies demands an openness to the fact that different questions would result in a diversity of approaches and methodologies.[16]

This is not simply a whole cloth rejection of western biblical approaches; they have their value. However, it is the undoing of their presumed universalistic applicability that essentially remains blind to, or deliberately ignores, their colonizing and imperializing tendencies and agendas. As shown earlier, there are some African Biblical Studies practitioners whose methods and approaches

---

14. Jennings, *After Whiteness*. In the series' (Theological Education between the Times) introductory blurb for it states that "If we continue to promote whiteness and its related ideas of masculinity and individualism in our educational work, it will remain diseased and thwart our efforts to heal the church and the world.

15. Wimbush, "Interpreters," 9.

16. N. Noah Bassil, "The Legacy of Colonial Racism in Africa," *Australian Quarterly* Vol. 77, No. 4 (2005): 27–32, 27.

remained entrenched in the Eurocentric interpretive models while integrating elements of African perspectives.[17] This is not an attempt at a power swap, an intentional introversion of power by African biblical scholarship so as to dominate. Rather, it is a push for an honest acknowledgment that one's starting point in the interpretive process is a recognition of the transience and rootedness of the interpreter and interpretation. It is a deliberate resistance to the colonial project's claim to be the sole purveyor of knowledge—resistance to being defined by the West as "less than."

African Biblical Studies has already established approaches and methods that challenge the toxic elements in western Biblical Studies and in so doing, engages in constructing an alternative hermeneutic that is decidedly anti-colonialist and anti-racist.

c. Pedagogical Structures

To evidence any sense of diversification and willingness to encounter headlong the colonialist and racist legacy, Biblical Studies syllabi in the western academy *must* consciously include the teaching of non-Western biblical scholarship, not as an addendum but as an integral part of the curriculum. There must be a welcome to pedagogical approaches that encourage self-interrogation of the discipline. African academic institutions, in turn, must cease aping western biblical approaches without consideration of their colonial and imperial undercurrents. The inclusion of multiple interpretive perspectives, representing the multiple voices that engage the biblical text, must be engaged in from the vantage of equality and authenticity. Diverse contributions in the teaching of Biblical Studies is the only way to reflect the full embrace of diversity by the discipline.

This may mean orienting oneself to the different approaches already represented in the guild, to positively introduce them to students and not simply to denigrate them or expose their flaws. When, for example, I teach courses on the history of the Bible and enslavement and/or colonialism in American institutions, for many of my students, both Black and white, it is the first academic encounter with interpretations prioritizing oppressed voices. For most white students, it is usually their first direct reflection of their corporate culpability within the systemic racial structure. For most African American students, it is usually an unnerving revelation of the centrality of biblical invocation by white oppressors in defense of their oppressive enslavement structures. Not having personally been enslaved or not having enslaved others does not change how such unveiling of the historical reality resonates with the students in the present. This is a pedagogy that refuses to ignore the past or cover it up. Instead, it chooses to directly encounter it and wrestle with its ramifications.

Similarly, African Biblical Studies creates a discourse that is simultaneously *constructive/creative* (in its application of the African reality to biblical

17. Ibid.

interpretation), and *critical* (of the colonial, racist, and imperialistic foundations, practices, inclinations, ideologies, etc.). It embraces difference, while also contributing critical engagement with the discipline's past, and refuses to be silent about the undeniable continuing impact of the colonial and imperial past. In this volume, I have wrestled with the impact of the violent encounter between the "West and the rest," as characterized specifically by the missionary and colonizer in Africa, and its formative and subsequent impact on Biblical Studies as a discipline. I have striven to unearth and to lay bare the unheralded and racially blemished origins of the discipline and the persistent systemic "racialized discursive practices and politics that have defined it," and continue to impact it, even when unacknowledged.[18]

For this reason, Postcolonial African Biblical Studies proffers a pedagogical model that is a decentralized or multiple-centers model that recognizes not a single center with multiple peripheries but multiple centers with myriad peripheries. In such a model, there is no notion (verbalized or not) of a "universalized" perspective, presupposition, authority, interpretation, meaning, or text. Instead, there is (for lack of a better term) democratization of the interpretive enterprise.

d. Dynamics of Power

The colonial project set in place enduring dynamics of power that, in many respects, remain in place. Undoing them has usually involved protracted negotiations between the formerly colonized and the former colonizer, resistance (armed in some cases) when negotiations fail, leading to bloodshed from violence and wars often fought by proxies of former colonizers. This study reflects similar dynamics that African Biblical Studies has found itself engaged in—a struggle to redefine the power dynamics of the discipline as set up and practiced in the West, an exposition of this lopsided power dynamic that must be undone for there to be true equality and diversity.

Wei Hsien has proposed "an ethical commitment to the other" as a grounding necessity to move Biblical Studies forward and address its racist and colonialist past.[19] By this he means a complete reorientation of oneself toward others. Following Audre Lorde's critiques, Wei Hsien insists on the "embrace of difference," in Lorde's sense of the necessity (mere tolerance of difference is insufficient to establish a change) to determine what works and what does not. Also, having the courage to jettison that which does not work is vital, for example, the master's tools. A *nondominant interdependence* that sees difference as nonthreatening would allow for "creative chaos" from which new ways of seeing and doing would emerge.[20] Usually, this difference would threaten the "Master" and possibly the one with the most to lose and to change.

18. Wimbush, "Interpreters," 8.
19. Hsien Wan, "Re-examining the Master's Tools," 227.
20. Ibid.

Constructive a suggestion as Wei Hsien's maybe, I perceive an Achilles's heel in its seeming concession to the "master" who is left to decide whether to *accept or reject* the suggested transformation. African Biblical Studies, on the other hand, while willing to engage in *nondominant interdependence*, is quite wary of who determines the agenda. Instead, African Biblical Studies has proceeded to expose, challenge, and undermine the racialized interpretive enterprise that is western Biblical Studies. African Biblical Studies refuses to let the West determine a timetable on how the interpretive process will proceed or whether African Biblical Studies' perspectives are embraced by all.

What African Biblical Studies calls for is a hermeneutic founded on justice and liberation that undermines and seeks to undo oppressive structures and systems, while constructing a message of hope—hope, not simply in the sense of mere anticipation, but a hope that drives one to active involvement in the struggle for justice and equality.

14.2 Constructing a "Hermeneutic of Hope"

Inspiration for such hope can be drawn from the South African writing published at the height of the racist apartheid rule—the *Kairos Document*. This was clandestine writing produced in 1985, during an uprising against the white racist apartheid South African government, which advocated for resistance to the state's killing of anti-apartheid demonstrators, mostly Black South Africans. The *Document* pointed to the need not only to resist the apartheid regime's racism, brutality and oppression, but it also called for countering the regime's appropriation of the biblical text to defend its racist beliefs and violent actions, by positing a hermeneutics of justice and hope.[21]

The *Document* recognized that the result of sustained oppression of a people is the erasure of hope, and determined that to counter such loss there would need to be a concerted interrogation of biblical texts used by the racist apartheid regime to burnish terrorizing rule, much in the same way slave owners in America had done.[22] There would be the need to courageously expose the misinterpretation and fraudulent applications by seeking truth and hope—the upholding of justice, equality, and freedom as the true biblical ideals for human coexistence and antidote to racism, and in turn, showcasing a more holistic witness of the biblical teachings of love and hope.

21. *The Kairos Document*—An anonymously published document in response to the apartheid government's killing of anti-apartheid demonstrators, it is believed to have been the product of a Black and a white South African clergy. The Document gained worldwide attention, especially among religious organizations opposed to the racist South African government.
22. Callahan, *The Talking Book.*

The *Document* also called out some opponents of apartheid as superficial, and even "un-Christian," whose advocating for reconciliation with the apartheid government, failed to address issues of justice and recompense. In contrast, the *Document* called for the promotion of "truth and justice and life at all costs, even at the cost of creating conflict, disunity, and dissension along the way."[23] This response, the *Document* announced, had to be necessarily "prophetic," meaning that it had to posit the God who stands with the oppressed against oppressive political, social, and economic systems. It is this prophetic voice that would give hope to the oppressed people of South Africa, in the same way that, in the Hebrew Bible, God was on the side of the oppressed and would rescue them in the end and destroy their enemies.

To apply this prophetic hermeneutic to the discipline of Biblical Studies, with the anticipation of establishing it as diverse but inclusive, self-critical but embracing of difference, purveyor of justice, and vibrant source of hope, certain necessary overhauls have to happen. The history of the discipline must be fully interrogated, exposed, and acknowledged. Recognition and acceptance of shortcomings in our academic ancestors and their frameworks of thinking is the first step toward healing, and can only make for a much more self-conscious and self-critical discipline that is open to critique and is willing to actively respond to it. Tacit acknowledgment or defense of past scholars as simply "people of their time" is simply unacceptable. Analyzed evidence in this study shows that those who chose to be bigoted, racist, and hateful did so (and even defended their positions) with full knowledge of alternative perspectives to their prejudiced views. Rejection and condemnation of these hateful views is the only right response.

Beyond the dismantling of colonialist and imperialist power dynamics that have characterized the discipline over the last two and a half centuries or so, vigilance must be kept to avoid sliding back. I think the recent publication by David Horrell on "whiteness" and the study of Paul is a welcome example of the kind of genuine introspection that will help biblical studies find a way forward.[24] But these kinds of studies remain few and far between, eliciting little structural reconstitution of the discipline at the moment.

14.3 A Final Thought

I wrote this book during the administration of the forty-fifth president of America (2016–20—Donald Trump) whose openly racist, misogynistic, homophobic, and

---

23. *The Kairos Document.*

24. Horrell, *Ethnicity and Inclusion,* explores how his own life as a biblical scholar has been a beneficiary of whiteness, both in scholarship and in life, generally, and the impact of this on his scholarship—the role that whiteness plays in the questions he asks, the approaches he uses, the parameters he assumes in pedagogy. Cf. also Laura Nasrallah and Elizabeth Schüssler-Fiorenza, *Prejudice and Christian Beginnings: Investigating Race, Gender, and Ethnicity in Early Christian Studies* (Minneapolis: Fortress, 2009).

sexist discourse was fully embraced by half of the country, the majority of whom comprise self-identifying Christians (mainly white Evangelicals, but also white Catholics and white Protestants).[25] Even while rejecting any accusations of "being racist," such groups would claim to see no apparent conflict of biblical teachings such as "love of neighbor," (Mk 12:28-34) or the "golden rule" (Mt. 7:12; Lk. 6:31), with the hate speeches, arrogance, open lies, support of white supremacy, and perpetrated violence against minority groups (e.g., calling African countries "shithole" countries) by their candidate.[26] Such a perspective shared by, at least, half the country (based on votes cast) affirms the persistent and unaddressed issues of festering racism that continue to animate large segments of white Christian populations in America (and Europe—note the rise of white nationalism in Europe over the same period).[27]

If such a racialized Christianity remains the bedrock of the religion in the western world (at least half of it), then these historically racist views will remain deeply entrenched, even when muted, including in Biblical Studies as practiced in the West.[28] Vincent Wimbush, the first person of African descent to be elected as president of SBL, had warned in his 2010 presidential address of how the fictionalized apolitical stance of biblical studies in the West, with its insistence on "focusing on the text," continued to mask reticent "racialized discursive practices and politics that have defined [the discipline]."[29] In turn, this pervasive "meta-racism," he postulated, affects the whole enterprise, not just the white scholars.

> The challenge remains for this [biblical] Society and all collectivities of critical interpreters, in general, to engage in a persistent and protracted struggle, not symbolic or obfuscating games around methods and approaches, to come to terms with the construal of the modern ideologization of language, characterized

---

25. Up to 80 percent of Evangelicals voted for the Republican candidate in both presidential elections, in 2016 and 2020. So did about 60 percent of other white Protestant and Catholic Christians (Cf. https://www.pewresearch.org/fact-tank/).

26. "Shithole," an obviously racist remark, was said to be used in reference to "Haiti and African countries," and contrasted to the more acceptable countries "like Norway . . ." (Cf., Josh Dawsey, "Trump Derides Protections for Immigrants from 'Shithole' Countries," *WP* (January 12, 2018).

27. Neill and Wright, *The Interpretation of the New Testament 1861–1986.*

28. I am aware that SBL leadership did put out statements that rejected the racist, sexist, homophobic vitriol. When six (6) Southern Baptist Seminary presidents, all white men, signed a statement denouncing and eliminating the teaching of Critical Race Theory in their respective institutions, it is difficult to see how this is not a reflection of the embedded racism. (See—*Huff Post*, https://www.huffpost.com/entry/southern-baptist-critical-race -theory_n_5fc81c12c5b66bc574672b84).

29. Wimbush, "Interpreters," 9.

by the meta-racism that marks the relationship between Europeans and Euro-Americans and peoples of color, especially black peoples.[30]

Without directly confronting the embedded racism and colonialism in Biblical Studies, there is no hope of casting it out. Arguments about disconnecting from the past heritage, as new grounds are forged, would leave unaddressed and unresolved historical traumas, thereby failing to deal with the root of the problem. Responses such as "I am not the colonizer" or "I am not a racist" simply fail to recognize the ubiquity of the systemic racism that has undergirded the western biblical interpretive enterprise. If all interpretation is contextual, then the unacknowledged myth of universal biblical studies in the West should cease to exist. Any unwillingness to change is itself a choice and preference to retain the now exposed colonialist, imperialist, and racist structural underpinnings that currently prop up the discipline.

30. Ibid.

BIBLIOGRAPHY

Achebe, Chinua. "The Novelist as a Teacher." *New Statesman*, London, January 29, 1965: 40-6.

Achebe, Chinua. *Morning Yet on Creation Day*. London: Heinemann, 1977.

Achebe, Chinua. *Home and Exile*. New York: Anchor, 2000.

Achebe, Chinua. *The Education of a British-Protected Child: Essays*. New York: Alfred A. Knopf, 2009.

Adamo, David Tuesday. *Africa and Africans in the Old Testament*. San Francisco: International Scholars Publications, 1998.

Adamo, David Tuesday. *Explorations in African Biblical Studies*. Eugene: Wipf and Stock, 2001.

Adamo, David Tuesday. *Africa and Africans in the New Testament*. Washington: University Press of America, 2006.

Adamo, David T. and Erivwierho F. Eghwubare. "The African Wife of Abraham (Gen. 16:1-16; 21:8-21)." *OTE* 18, no. 3 (2005): 455-71.

Adewuya, J. Ayodeji. "Revisiting 1 Corinthians 11.27-34: Paul's Discussion of the Lord's Supper and African Meals." *JSNT* 30, no. 1 (2007): 95-112.

Adeyemo, Tokunboh, ed. *African Bible Commentary*. Grand Rapids: Zondervan, 2010.

Aichelle, George, Fred W. Burnett, Elizabeth A. Castelli, Robert M. Fowler, David Jobling, Stephen D. Moore, Gary A. Phillips, Tina Pippin, Regina M. Schwartz, and Wilhelm Wuellner, eds. *The Postmodern Bible: Bible & Culture Collective*. New Haven: Yale University Press, 1997.

Akper, Godwin I. "The Role of the 'Ordinary Reader' in Gerald West's Hermeneutics." *Scriptura* 88 (2005): 1–13.

Alòs-Moner, Andreu Martínez. "The Jesuit Patriarchate to the Preste: Between Religious Reform, Political Expansion and Colonial Adventure." *Aeth* 6 (2003): 54–69.

Amadiume, Ifi. *Re-Inventing Africa: Matriarchy, Religion, and Culture*. London and New York: Zed Books, 1997.

Anonby, John A. "Achebe's Novels and their Implications for Christians in Africa." *AJET* 9, no. 1 (1990): 14–23.

Anonby, John A. *The Kenyan Epic Novelist Ngugi: His Secular Reconfiguration of Biblical Themes*. Lewiston: Edwin Mellen, 2006.

Ashcroft, Bill, G. Griffiths, and H. Tiffin, eds. *The Empire Writes Back*. 2nd ed. Abingdon, Oxon and New York: Routledge, 1991.

Aulén, Gustav. *Christus Victor: An Historical Study of the Three Main Types of the Idea of Atonement*. Translated by A. G. Herbert. London: SPCK, 1931.

Ayandele, E. A. "Review: *Christianity in Tropical Africa*. Edited by C. C. Baëta. Oxford University Press, 1968. *JAH* 10, no. 2 (1969): 336–40.

Baëta, C. C., ed. *Christianity in Tropical Africa*. London: Oxford University Press, 1968.

Bailey, Randall, ed. *Yet with a Steady Beat: Contemporary U. S. Afrocentric Biblical Interpretation*. Atlanta: SBL, 2003.

Baldwin, James. "Letter from a Region in My Mind." *The New Yorker*, November 9, 1962. Available online: https://www.newyorker.com/magazine/1962/11/17/letter-from-a -region-in-my-mind.

Banana, Canaan. *The Gospel According to the Ghetto.* Gwelo, Zimbabwe: Mambo Press, 1981.

Banana, Canaan. *The Case for a New Bible.* In *"Rewriting" the Bible: The Real Issues: Perspectives from within Biblical and Religious Studies in Zimbabwe*, edited by Isabel Mukonyora, James L. Cox, and Frans J. Verstraelen, 17–32. Gweru, Malawi: Mambo Press, 1993. Kindle Edition, 2019.

Barrett, David. *Schism and Renewals: Analysis of Six Thousand Contemporary Religious Movements.* Nairobi: Oxford University Press, 1968.

Barrett, C. K. "Albert Schweitzer and the New Testament: A Lecture Given in Atlanta on 10th April, 1975 as Part of the Albert Schweitzer Centenary Celebration." *ET* 87, no. 1 (1975): 4–10.

Barton, John. "Biblical Criticism: A Common-Sense Approach to the Bible." *TheTorah .com*, 2020. Available online: https://thetorah.com/article/biblical-criticism-a-common -sense-approach-to-the-bible.

Bassil, N. Noah. "The Legacy of Colonial Racism in Africa." *AQ* 77, no. 4 (2005): 27–40.

Bediako, Kwame. *Christianity in Africa: The Renewal of a Non-Western Religion.* Edinburgh and Maryknoll: Edinburgh University Press and Orbis, 1995.

Belcher, Wendy L. "Sisters Debating the Jesuits: The Role of African Women in Defeating Portuguese Proto-Colonialism in Seventeenth-Century Abyssinia." *NAS* 13, no. 1 (2013): 121–66.

Belcher, Wendy L. "Same-Sex Intimacies in the Early African Text *Gädlä Wälättä Ṗeṭros i* (1672): Queer Reading an Ethiopian Woman Saint." *RAL* 47, no. 2 (2016): 20–45.

Belcher, Wendy L. "Introduction." In *The Life of Walatta-Petros: A Seventeenth-Century Biography of an African Woman*, edited by Galawdewos, Concise edition, translated by Wendy L. Belcher and Michael Kleiner. Princeton: Princeton University Press, 2018.

Benny Liew, Tat-siong and Fernando F. Segovia, eds. *Colonialism and the Bible: Contemporary Reflections from the Global South.* Lanham: Lexington, 2018.

Berman, Nina. *Impossible Missions? German Economic, Military, and Humanitarian Efforts in Africa.* Lincoln: University of Nebraska Press. 2004.

Bernal, Martin. *Black Athena.* New Brunswick: Rutgers University Press, 1987.

Bhabha, Homi. "Signs Taken for Wonders: Questions of Ambivalence and Authority Under a Tree Outside Delhi, May 1817." *CI* 12 (1985): 144–65.

Boesak, Allan. *Comfort and Protest: The Apocalypse from a South African Perspective.* Philadelphia: Westminster John Knox, 1987.

British and Foreign Bible Society. *The Book Above Every Book: A Popular Illustrated Report of the British and Foreign Bible Society, 1908–1909.* London: The Bible House, 1909.

British and Foreign Bible Society. *The Book of God's Kingdom: A Popular Illustrated Report of the British and Foreign Bible Society, 1901–2.* London: The Bible House, 1902.

Botta, Alejandro F. and Pablo R. Andiñach, eds. *The Bible and the Hermeneutics of Liberation.* Semeia 59. Atlanta: SBL, 2009.

Boulaga, Fabian Ebousi. *Christianity without Fetishes.* Maryknoll: Orbis, 1981.

Bozeman, Adda Bruemmer. *Conflict in Africa: Concepts and Realities.* Princeton: Princeton University Press, 1976.

Browning, Melissa D. "Hanging out a Red Ribbon: Listening to Musa Dube's Postcolonial Feminist Theology." *JRER* 2, no. 13 (2011): 1–27.

Bruck, Gabriele vom, and Barbara Bodenhorn, eds. *The Anthropology of Names and Naming*. Cambridge: Cambridge University Press, 2006.

Bruel, Wolfgang. *Migration and Religion: Christian Transatlantic Missions, Islamic Migration To Germany*. Amsterdam and New York: Rodopi, 2012.

Bujo, Bénézet. *African Theology in Its Social Context*. Maryknoll: Orbis, 1992.

Bultmann, Rudolph. *New Testament & Mythology and Other Basic Writings*. Philadelphia: Fortress, 1984.

Burris, John P. *Exhibiting Religion: Colonialism and Spectacle at International Expositions, 1851–1893*. Charlottesville: University of Virginia Press, 2001.

Burton, Keith A. *The Blessing of Africa: The Bible and African Christianity*. Downers Grove: InterVarsity, 2007.

Buxton, Thomas F. *The African Slave Trade and Its Remedy*. London: John Murray, 1840.

Callahan, Allen D. *The Talking Book: African Americans and the Bible*. New Haven: Yale University Press, 2006.

Camara, Babacar. "The Falsity of Hegel's Theses on Africa." *JBS* 36, no. 1 (2005): 82–96.

Carter, J. Cameron. *Race: A Theological Account*. Oxford: Oxford University Press, 2008.

Césaire, Aimé. "Book Review." P. Tempels. *Bantoue Philosophie*. Available online: https://plato.stanford.edu/archives/spr2014/entries/negritude/.

Chidester, David. *Savage Systems: Colonialism and Comparative Religion in Southern Africa*. Charlottesville: University of Virginia Press, 1996.

Chigumira, Godfrey. "Mary as an Inspiration for the Empowerment of Southern African Christian Women Disproportionately Infected/Affected by HIV/AIDS." Unpublished PhD Dissertation, University of Birmingham, 2011.

Codere, Helen. "Book Review: C. C. Baëta (ed.), *Christianity in Tropical Africa*." *JAAS* 4, no. 3 (1969): 233–4.

Colenso, John W. *Ten Weeks in Natal: A Journal of a First Tour of Visitation Among the Colonists and Zulu Kafirs of Natal*. Cambridge: Macmillan, 1855.

Colenso, John W. *Paul's Epistle to the Romans: Newly Translated, and Explained from a Missionary Point of View*. Bishopstowe: Natal, 1861.

Colenso, John W. *The Pentateuch and Book of Joshua Critically Examined*. London: Longman, Green, Longman, Roberts & Green, 1862–79.

Colenso, John W. *Three Native Accounts of the Visit of the Bishop of Natal in September and October, 1859, To Umpande, King Of The Zulus*. Translated by J. W. Colenso. Pietermaritzburg, 1901.

Court, Franklin E. *Institutionalizing English Literature: The Culture and Politics of Literary Study, 1750–1900*. Stanford: Stanford University Press, 1992.

da Silva, José Antunes. "African Independent Churches: Origin and Development." *Anthropos* 88, no. 4/6 (1993): 393–402.

Davenport, Manuel M. "The Moral Paternalism of Albert Schweitzer." *Ethics* 84, no. 2 (1974): 116–27.

Dawsey, Josh. "Trump Derides Protections for Immigrants from 'Shithole' Countries." *WT*—Digital Edition, January 12, 2018.

Deji, Valentin. *Reconstruction and Renewal in Africa in Christian Theology*. Nairobi: Acton Publishers, 2003.

Denis, Philippe. "On Reading Gerald West's *The Stolen Bible*." *RSR* 44, no. 2 (2018): 155–63.

De Villiers, Pieter G. R. "Reading Revelation from the Top or the Underside." *STJ* 3, no. 2 (2017): 361–77.

Diagne, Souleymane Bachir. "Négritude." In *The Stanford Encyclopedia of Philosophy*, edited by Edward N. Zalta, Summer 2018 ed. Available online: https://plato.stanford .edu/archives/sum2018/entries/negritude/.

Diarra, Pierre. "Des Prêtres Noirs S'interrogent." *HMC* 1, no. 1 (2007): 156–60.

Dickson, Kwesi. "Continuity and Discontinuity between the Old Testament and African Life Thought." *BTA* 1, no. 2 (1979): 179–93.

Dickson, Kwesi. *Uncompleted Mission: Christianity and Exclusivism*. Nairobi: Acton, 2000.

Du Bois, W. E. B. "The Black Man and Albert Schweitzer." In *The Albert Schweitzer Jubilee Book*, edited by A. A. Roback, 121–8. Cambridge: Sci-Art Publishers, 1945.

Dube, Musa W. "Readings of *Semoya*: Batswana Women's Interpretations of Matt 15:21-28." *Semeia* 73 (1996a): 111–29.

Dube, Musa W. "Reading for Decolonization (John 4:1-42)." *Semeia* 75 (1996b): 37–59.

Dube, Musa W. "Towards a Post-Colonial Feminist Interpretation of the Bible." *Semeia* 78 (1997): 11–27.

Dube, Musa W. "Consuming a Colonial Cultural Bomb: Translating *Badimo* into 'Demons' in the Setswana Bible (Matthew 8.28-34; 15.22; 10.8)." *JSNT* 21, no. 73 (1999): 33–59.

Dube, Musa W. *Postcolonial Feminist Interpretation of the Bible*. St. Louis: Chalice, 2000.

Dube, Musa W., ed. *Other Ways of Reading: African Women and the Bible*. Atlanta: SBL; Geneva: WCC, 2001.

Dube, Musa W. *Africa Praying: A Handbook of HIV/AIDS Sensitive Sermons and Liturgy*. Geneva: WCC, 2003.

Dube, Musa W. *Grant Me Justice: HIV/AIDS and Gender Readings of the Bible*. Maryknoll: Orbis; Pietermaritzburg: Cluster, 2004.

Dube, Musa W. *The HIV and AIDS Bible*. Scranton: University of Scranton Press, 2006.

Dube, Musa W. "Who Do You Say that I Am?" *FT* 15, no. 3 (2007): 346–67.

Dube, Musa W. "Boundaries and Bridges: Journeys of a Postcolonial Feminist Biblical Scholar." *JESWTR* 22 (2014): 139–56.

Dube, Musa W., Andrew M. Mbuvi, and Dora R. Mbuwayesango, eds. *Postcolonial Perspectives in African Biblical Interpretations*. Atlanta: SBL, 2012.

Dube, Musa W., and J. Staley, eds. *John and Postcolonialism: Travel, Space, and Power*. Sheffield: Sheffield Academic Press, 2002.

Dyrness, William, ed. *Emerging Voices in Global Christian Theology*. Grand Rapids: Zondervan, 1999.

Ela, Jean-Marc. *Cri de l'homme Africain*. Paris: L'Harmattan, 1980; Trans. *African Cry!* Maryknoll: Orbis, 1986.

Ela, Jean-Marc. *My Faith as an African*. Maryknoll: Orbis, 1988.

Ela, Jean-Marc. "The Memory of the African People and the Cross of Christ." In *The Scandal of a Crucified World*, edited by Yacob Tesfai, 17–35. Maryknoll: Orbis, 1994.

England, Emma and William John Lyons, eds. *Reception History and Biblical Studies: Theory and Practice*. London and New York: Bloomsbury, 2015.

Equiano, Olaudah. *The Interesting Narrative of the Life of Olaudah Equiano, or Gustavus Vassa, The African*. London: Printed for and sold by the Author, No. 10, Union-Street, Middlesex Hospital, 1789. <The Project Gutenberg E-Book>

Eze, Emmanuel C. *Race and the Enlightenment*. Malden and Oxford: Blackwell, 1997.

Ezigbo, Victor. *Re-Imagining African Christologies: Conversing with the Interpretations and Appropriations of Jesus in African Christianity*. Eugene: Pickwick, 2010.

Fabella, Virginia, and Mercy A. Oduyoye, eds. *Passion and Compassion*. Maryknoll: Orbis, 1992.

Fanon, Frantz. *The Wretched of the Earth*. Translated by Richard Philcox. New York: Grove, 1963.

Farisani, Elelwani. "The Use of Ezra-Nehemiah in a Quest for a Theology of Renewal, Transformation and Reconstruction in the (South) African Context." Unpublished PhD Dissertation, University of Natal, Durban, 2002.

Felder, Cain H., ed. *Stony the Road we Trod: African American Biblical Interpretation*. Minneapolis: Fortress, 1991.

Fetterley, Judith. *Resisting Reader: A Feminist Approach to American Fiction*. Bloomington and London: Indiana University Press, 1978.

Fiedler, Rachel NyaGondwe. *A History of the Circle of Concerned African Women Theologians, 1989–2007*. Mzuzu, Malawi: Mzuni Press, 2017.

Fiensy, David. "Using the Nuer Culture of Africa in Understanding the Old Testament: An Evaluation." *JSOT* 38 (1987): 73–83.

Figueira, Dorothy. *Aryans, Jews, Brahmins: Theorizing Authority through Myths of Identity*. New York: SUNY, 2002.

Fiske, Edward B. "African Christians are Developing their Own Distinctive Theologies." *NYT* (March 12, 1971): 10.

Freire, Paolo. *Pedagogy of the Oppressed*. New York: Continuum, 1988.

Forrow, Lachlan. *"Foreword" to Albert Schweitzer's African Notebook*. Translated by C. E. B. Russell. New York: Syracuse University Press Edition, 2002 (1936).

Foster, Elizabeth A. *African Catholic: Decolonization and the Transformation of the Church*. Cambridge, MA: Harvard University Press, 2019.

Fuze, Magema Magwaza. *Abantu Abamnyama Lapa Bavela Ngakona*. Translated as *The Black People and Whence They Came*, edited by A. T. Cope and translated by H. C. Lugg. Pietermaritzburg: University of Natal, 1979.

Gadamer, Hans-Georg. *Truth and Method*. London: Sheed and Ward, 1975.

Galawdewos. *The Life and Struggles of Our Mother Walatta Petros: A Seventeenth-Century African Biography of an Ethiopian Woman*. Translated and edited by Wendy Laura Belcher and Michael Kleiner: Princeton: University Press, 2015.

Galbraith, Deane. "The Perpetuation of Racial Assumptions in Biblical Studies." In *History, Politics and the Bible from the Iron Age to the Media Age: Essays in Honour of Keith W. Whitelam*, edited by James G. Crossley and Jim West, 116–34. London: Bloomsbury T&T Clark, 2017.

Gale, Thomson. "African Religions: Mythic Themes." *Encyclopedia of Religion 2005*. Encyclopedia.com (accessed June 24, 2019).

Gallagher, Susan V. *Postcolonial Literature and the Biblical Call for Justice*. Jackson: University Press of Mississippi, 1994.

Gani, Jasmine. "The Erasure of Race: Cosmopolitanism and the Illusion of Kantian Hospitality." *Mill* 45, no. 3 (2017): 425–46.

Gerner, Matthias. "Why Worldwide Bible Translation Grows Exponentially." *JRH* 42, no. 2 (2018): 145–80.

Getui, Mary, T. S. Maluleke, and J. Ukpong, eds. *Interpreting the New Testament in Africa*. Nairobi: Acton Publishers, 2001.

Gifford, Paul. "The Vanguard of Colonialism: Missionaries and the Frontier in Southern Africa in the Nineteenth Century." *Constellations* 3, no. 2 (2012): 165–74 . Available online: https://journals.library.ualberta.ca/constellations/index.php/constellations/article/view/17204 (accessed June 20, 2019).

Giles, Kevin. "Justifying Injustice with the Bible: Apartheid." Available online: https://www.cbeinternational.org/blogs/justifying-injustice-bible-apartheid.

Goldberg, David Theo. *Racist Culture: Philosophy and the Politics of Meaning.* Cambridge: Blackwell, 1993.

Goldberg, David Theo. "Call and Response." *POP* 44, no. 1 (2010): 89–106.

Grässer, Erich. *Albert Schweitzer als Theologe.* BZHT. Tübingen: Mohr Siebeck, 1979.

Gray, Richard. "Christianity and Religious Change in Africa." *AA* 77, no. 306 (1978): 89–100.

Green, T. H. and T. H. Grose, eds. *The Philosophical Works.* London, 1882; repr. Darmstadt, 1964.

Gunda, Masiiwa R. *On the Public Role of the Bible in Zimbabwe: Unpacking Banana's "Re-writing" Call for a Socially and Contextually Relevant Biblical Studies.* BiAS 18. Bamberg: University of Bamberg Press, 2015.

Gunda, Masiiwa R. and Joachim Kügler, eds. *The Bible and Politics in Africa.* BiAS 7; Bamberg, Germany: University of Bamberg Press, 2012.

Harris, Ruth. "The Allure of Albert Schweitzer." *HEI* 40 (2014): 804–25.

Harris, Ruth. "Schweitzer and Africa." *HJ* 59, no. 4 (2016): 1107–32.

Harris, Ruth. "Book Review: Albert Schweitzer in Thought and Action: A Life in Parts." *JEH* 69, no. 1 (2018): 215–17.

Hatch, William P. "The Primitive Christian Message." *JBL* 58, no. 1 (1939): 1–13.

Heaney, Robert S. *From Historical to Critical Post-Colonial Theology: The Contribution of John S. Mbiti and Jesse N. K. Mugambi.* Oregon: Pickwick, 2015.

Hegel, G. W. F. *Philosophy of History.* Buffalo: Prometheus, 1892, 1991.

Hinchliff, Peter. "Ethics, Evolution and Biblical Criticism in the Thought of Benjamin Jowett and John William Colenso." *JEH* 37, no. 1 (1986): 91–110.

Hinga, Teresia. "Jesus Christ and the Liberation of Women in Africa." In *The Will to Arise,* edited by Mercy A. Oduyoye and Musimbi Kanyoro, 183–94. Maryknoll: Orbis, 1992.

Hinga, Teresia. *African, Christian, Feminist: The Enduring Search for What Matters.* Maryknoll: Orbis, 2017.

Hochschild, Adam. *King Leopold's Ghost: A Story of Greed, Terror, and Heroism in Colonial Africa.* New York: Houghton Mifflin Harcourt, 1998.

Hockey Katherine M. and David G. Horrell, eds. *Ethnicity, Race, and Religion: Identities and Ideologies in Early Jewish and Christian Texts, and in Modern Biblical Interpretation.* London and New York: T&T Clark, 2018.

Horrell, David G. *Ethnicity and Inclusion: Religion, Race, and Whiteness in Constructions of Jewish and Christian Identities.* Grand Rapids: Eerdmans, 2020.

Huber, Hugo. "Anthropological Approaches to the Study of Myth: African Variants of the Separation of Heaven and Earth." *URM* 10, no. 1 (1987): 54–66.

Idowu, Bolaji. *Olodumare: God in Yoruba Belief.* London: Longmans, 1962.

Immerwahr, John. "Hume's Revised Racism." *JHI* 53, no. 3 (1992): 481–6.

Isizoh, Chidi Denis. "The Resurrected Jesus Preached in Athens: The Areopagus Speech (Acts17,16-34)—An Inquiry into the Reasons for the Greek Reaction to the Speech and a Reading of the Text from the African Traditional Religious Perspective." Unpublished PhD Dissertation, Pontificia Universitas Gregoriana, Rome, 1996.

Isizoh, Chidi Denis. "African Traditional Religious Perspective of the 'Areopagus Speech' (Acts 17, 22-31)." *ACS* (1998): 1–25.

Jean-Baptiste, Rachel. "'A Black Girl Should Not Be with a White Man': Sex, Race, and African Women's Social and Legal Status in Colonial Gabon, c. 1900-1946." *JWH* 22, no. 2 (2010): 56–82.

Jenkins, Paul, ed. *The Recovery of the West African Past: African Pastors and African History in the Nineteenth Century: C.C. Reindorf & Samuel Johnson.* Basel, Switzerland: Basler Afrika Bibliographien, 1998.

Jenkins, Phillip. "The Power of the Bible in the Global South." *CE* July 11 (2006a): 22–6. Available online: http://www.religion-online.org/article/the-power-of-the-bible-in-the -global-south/.

Jenkins, Phillip. *The New Faces of Christianity: Believing the Bible in the Global South.* Oxford: Oxford University Press, 2006b.

Jenkins, Phillip. *The Next Christendom: The Coming Global Christianity.* Oxford and New York: Oxford University Press, 2011.

Jennings, Willie. *The Christian Imagination: Theology and the Origins of Race.* New Haven: Yale University Press, 2010.

Jennings, Willie. *After Whiteness: An Education in Belonging. Theological Education Between the Times.* Grand Rapids: Eerdmans, 2020.

Jennings, Willie. "Renouncing Completeness: The Rich Ruler and the Possibilities of Biblical Scholarship Without White Masculine Self-Sufficiency." *JBL* 140, no. 4 (2021): 837–42.

Jipp, Joshua W. "Paul's Areopagus Speech of Acts 17:16-34 as Both Critique and Propaganda." *JBL* 131, no. 3 (2012): 567–88.

John, Helen C. *Biblical Interpretation and African Traditional Religion: Cross-Cultural and Community Readings in Owamboland, Namibia.* BIS, 176. Leiden, Brill, 2019.

Johnson, G. Wesley. "Book Review." *AHR* 78, no. 2 (1973): 469.

Joy, Charles R. *The Spiritual Life: Selected Writings of Albert Schweitzer.* Boston: Beacon, 1947.

Kairos, Theologians. *The Kairos Document Challenge to the Church: A Theological Comment on the Political Crisis in South Africa.* Braamfontein: Skotaville Publishers, 1986.

Kalilombe, Patrick. *Doing Theology at the Grassroots: Theological Essays from Malawi.* Mzuzu, Malawi: Kachere Press, 1977.

Kamudzandu, Israel. "The Nature and Identity of Jesus in Mark 7: 24–37: A Zimbabwean Interpretation." In *Mark: Texts @ Contexts,* edited by Nicole Duran, Teresa Okure, and Daniel M. Patte, 5–15. Minneapolis: Fortress Press, 2010a.

Kamudzandu, Israel. *Abraham as a Spiritual Ancestor: A Postcolonial Zimbabwean Reading of Romans 4.* Leiden: Brill, 2010b.

Kamudzandu, Israel. *Abraham Our Father: Paul and Ancestors in Postcolonial Africa.* Minneapolis: Fortress, 2013.

Kant, Emmanuel. *Observations on the Feeling of the Beautiful and Sublime and Other Writings.* Translated by John T. Goldthwait. Berkeley: University of California Press, 1981.

Kanyoro, Musimbi. *Introducing Feminist Cultural Hermeneutics: An African Perspective.* Cleveland: Pilgrim Press, 2002.

Kaplan, Justin, and Anne Bernays. *The Language of Names,* New York: Simon & Schuster, 1997.

Katongole, Emmanuel, ed. *African Theology Today.* Scranton: University of Scranton Press, 2002.

Katongole, Emmanuel. "Embodied and Embodying Hermeneutics of Life in the Academy: Musa W. Dube's HIV/AIDS Work." *SBL Forum,* n.p. [cited March 2006]. Available online: http://sbl-site.org/Article.aspx?ArticleID=510 (accessed June 23, 2020).

Kelley, Shawn. *Racializing Jesus: Race, Ideology and the Formation of Modern Biblical Scholarship.* London and New York: Routledge, 2002.

Kenya National Archives [Digital Access]—*Kenya National Assembly House of Representatives Report.* "Kenya National Committee Minutes: Motion—Kenya National Funds." July 30, 1963, column 1475.

Kidd, Colin. *The Forging of Races: Race and Scripture in the Protestant Atlantic World, 1600–2000*. Cambridge: University Press, 2006.

Kimuhu, Johnson M. *Leviticus: The Priestly Laws and Prohibitions from the Perspective of Ancient Near East and Africa*. New York: Peter Lang, 2008.

Kincheloe, Joe L., Shirley R. Steinberg, Nelson M. Rodriguez, and Ronald E. Chennault, eds. *White Reign: Deploying Whiteness in America*. New York: St. Martins Griffith, 1998.

Kleingeld, Pauline. "Kant's Second Thoughts on Race," *PQ* 57, no. 229 (2007): 573–92.

Legaspi, Michael. *The Death of Scripture and the Rise of Biblical Studies*. New York: Oxford University Press, 2010.

LeMarquand, Grant. *An Issue of Relevance: A Comparative Study of the Story of the Bleeding Woman (Mk 5:25-34; Mt 9:20-22; Lk 8:43-48) in North Atlantic and African Contexts*. New York: Peter Lang, 2004.

LeMarquand, Grant and D. Galgalo, eds. *Theological Education in Contemporary Africa*. Eldoret, Kenya: Zapf Chancery, 2004.

Loomba, Ania. *Colonialism/Postcolonialism*. 3rd ed. London and New York: Routledge, 1998, 2015.

Lorde, Audre. *Sister Outsider: Essays and Speeches*. Berkeley: Crossing Press, 1984.

Lovesey, Oliver. "The Postcolonial 'Crisis of Reception' and Ngugi wa Thiong'o's Religious Allegory." In *And the Birds Began to Sing: Religion and Literature in Post-colonial Cultures*, edited by Jamie S. Scott, 181–94. Amsterdam and Atlanta: Rodopi, 1996.

Lugones, María. "Heterosexualism and the Colonial/Modern Gender System." *Hypa* 22, no. 1 (2007): 186–209.

Magesa, Laurenti. *African Religion: The Moral Traditions of Abundant Life*. Maryknoll: Orbis Books, 1997.

Mahfood, Sebastian. *Radical Eschatologies: Embracing the Eschaton in the Works of Ngugi Wa Thiong'o, Nuruddin Farah, and Ayi Kwei Armah*. Moldova: Lambert Academic, 2009.

Maluleke, Tinyiko. "Half a Century of African Christian Theologies: Elements of the Emerging Agenda for the Twenty-First Century." *JTSA* 99 (1997): 4–23.

Mana, K. Kä. *Eglises Africaines et Théologie de la Reconstruction*. Genève: Protestant, 1994.

Manus, Ukachukwu Chris. *Intercultural Hermeneutics in Africa: Methods and Approaches*. Nairobi: Acton, 2003.

Marxsen, Patti M. "Unmasking a Myth through the Art of Biography." Available online: https://www.wcwonline.org/Women-=-Books-Blog/schweitzer (accessed June 18, 2020).

Marzouk, Safwat. "Interrogating Identity: A Christian Egyptian Reading of the Hagar-Ishmael Traditions." In *Colonialism and the Bible*, edited by Tat-siong Benny Liew and Fernando F. Segovia, 3–30. Lanham: Lexington Books, 2018.

Masenya, Madipoane. "Proverbs 31:10-31 in a South African Context." *Semeia* 78 (1997): 56–60.

Masenya, Madipoane. *How Worthy is the Woman of Worth?: Rereading Proverbs 31:10-31 in African-South Africa*. New York: Peter Lang, 2004.

Masenya, Madipoane. "An African Methodology for South African Biblical Sciences: Revisiting the *Bosadi* (Womanhood) Approach." *OTE* 18, no. 3 (2005): 741–51.

Masenya, Madipoane. "Who Calls the Shots in Naomi's Life? Reading the Naomi-Ruth Story within the African Religio-Cultural Context." *Acta Theol* 24 (2016): 84–96.

Mazrui, Ali A. "Review: Dr. Schweitzer's Racism." *Transition* 53 (1991): 96–102.

Mutiso-Mbandi, J. "Anthropology and the Paschal Mystery." *Spearhead* 59 (1979): 25–45.

Mbiti, J. S. *African Religions and Philosophy*. London: Heinemann, 1969.

Mbiti, J. S. "Christianity and Traditional Religions in Africa." *IRM* (1970): 430–40.

Mbiti, J. S. *The Concepts of God in Africa*. London: SPCK, 1970.

Mbiti, J. S. "Christianity and Traditional Religions in Africa." *IRM* 59, no. 236 (1970): 430–40,

Mbiti, J. S. *New Testament Eschatology in an African Background: A Study of the Encounter between New Testament Theology and African Traditional Concepts*. London: Oxford, 1971.

Mbiti, J. S. "Some African Concepts of Christology." In *Christ and Younger Churches: Theological Contributions from Asia, Africa and Latin America*, edited by Georg Vicedom, 51–62. London: SPCK, 1972.

Mbuvi, Andrew M. "African Novels as Resource for Socially Engaged Gospel?" *SBL Forum*, 2006. Available online: https://www.sbl-site.org/publications/article.aspx ?ArticleId=527 (accessed June 23, 2020).

Mbuvi, Andrew M. "Missionary Acts, Things Fall Apart: Modeling Mission in Acts 17:15–34 and a Concern for Dialogue in Chinua Achebe's Things Fall Apart." *Ex Auditu* 23, (2007): 140–56.

Mbuvi, Andrew M. "Christology and Cultures in 1 Peter: An African (Kenyan) Appraisal." In *Jesus Without Borders: Christology in the Majority World*, edited by Gene L. Green, S. T. Perdue, and K. K Yeo, 141–60. Grand Rapids: Eerdmans, 2014.

Mbuvi, Andrew M. "African Biblical Studies: An Introduction to an Emerging Discipline." *CBR* 15/2, (2017): 149–78.

Mbuvi, Andrew M. "An African Biblical Scholar Explores the Broadening of the Biblical Studies Landscape." *JTSA* 168, (2020): 41–63.

Mbuvi, Andrew M. "Revisiting Translation and Interpretation Issues in the Story of the African Royal Official ("Ethiopian Eunuch") in Acts 8:26–40: The Hebrew Bible (LXX) Background." *OTE* 34, no. 2 (2021): 474–84.

Mbuwayesango, Dora. "The Bible as a Tool of Colonization: The Zimbabwean Context." In *Colonialism and the Bible*, edited by Tat-siong Benny Liew and Fernando F. Segovia, 31–42. Lanham: Lexington Books, 2018.

Mbuwayesango, Dora. "Childlessness and Woman-to-Woman Relationships in Genesis and in African Patriarchal Society: Sarah and Hagar from a Zimbabwean Woman's Perspective (Gen. 16:1-16; 21:8-21)." *Semeia* 78 (1997): 27–36.

McFall, E. A. *Approaching the Nuer of Africa Through the Old Testament*. South Pasadena: William Carey Library, 1970.

McGrane, Barnard. *Beyond Anthropology: Society and the Other*. New York: Columbia University Press, 1989.

Memmi, Albert. *The Colonizer and the Colonized*. Boston: Beacon, 1957.

Mofokeng, Takatso. "Black Christians, the Bible and Liberation." *JBTSA* 2, no. 1 (1988): 34–42.

Mokhoathi, Joel. "Jesus Christ as an Ancestor: A Critique of Ancestor Christology in Bantu Communities." *Pharos* 99 (2018). Available online: https://www.pharosjot.com /2015---2018.html (accessed July 6, 2020).

Moloney, Raymond. "African Christology." *TS* 48 (1987): 505–15.

Montesquieu, M. De Secondat Baron De. *The Spirit of Laws*. Vol. 11. Translated Thomas Nugent. Cincinnati: Robert and Clarke, 1863.

Moreau, A. Scott. "A Critique of John Mbiti's Understanding of the African Concept of Time." *EAJEA* 5, no. 2 (1986): 36–48.

Mosala, Itumeleng. *Biblical Hermeneutics and Black Theology in South Africa*. Grand Rapids: Wm. B. Eerdmans, 1989.

Moses, Michael Valdez. "Caliban and his Precursors: The Poetics of Literary History and the Third World." In *Theoretical Issues in Literary History*, edited by David Perkins, 206–26. Cambridge, MA: Harvard University Press, 1991.

Mrozcek, Eva. *The Literary Imagination in Jewish Antiquity*. Oxford: Oxford University Press, 2016.

Mudimbe, V. Y. *Parables and Fables: Exegesis, Textuality, and Politics in Central Africa*. Madison: University of Wisconsin Press, 1991.

Mudimbe, V. Y. *The Idea of Africa*. Indianapolis: Indiana University Press, 1994.

Mudimbe, V. Y. *Tales of Faith: Religion as Political Performance in Central Africa*. London and Atlantic Is: Athlone, 1997.

Mugambi, J. N. K. *From Liberation to Reconstruction: African Christian Theology After the Cold War*. Nairobi: East African Publishing House, 1995.

Mugambi, J. N. K. *Christian Theology and Social Reconstruction*. Nairobi: Acton, 2003.

Muilenburg, James. "Form Criticism and Beyond." *JBL* 88, no. 1 (1969): 1–18.

Mukonyora, Isabel, James L. Cox, and F. J. Verstraelen, eds. *Rewriting the Bible: The Real Issues: Perspectives from Within Biblical and Religious Studies in Zimbabwe*. Gweru, Zimbabwe: Mambo Press, 1993.

Munz, Walter. *Albert Schweitzer dans la Mémoire des Africains*. Etude Schweitzerian: N. P., 1993.

Musodza, Archford. "'Rewriting' The Bible: Its Canonical Implications and Meaning for Anglicans in the City of Harare." Unpublished MPhil Thesis, University of Zimbabwe, 2003.

Mwangi, E. Maina. *Translation in African Contexts: Postcolonial Texts, Queer Sexuality, and Cosmopolitan Fluency*. Kent: The Kent State University Press, 2017.

Mwaura, Philomena Njeri. "Alternatives to Globalization: An East African Women's Theological Response." In *The Oxford Handbook of Feminist Theology*, edited by Mary McClintock Fulkerson and Sheila Briggs, 250–79. London: Oxford University Press, 2012.

Mwikisa, Peter. "Politics and the Religious Unconscious in Ngugi wa Thiong'o's *A Grain of Wheat* and His Other Works." *Scriptura* 92 (2006): 248–64.

Myers, Travis L. "Jesus as *Prototokos* in Hebrews and the African Phenomenon of Eldest Brother: An Analysis of a Potential Illustration." *JGC* 5, no. 1 (2019): 9.

Nasimiyu-Wasike, Anne. "Christology and an African Woman's Experience." In *Jesus in African Christianity: Experimentation and Diversity in African Christology*, edited by J. N. K. Mugambi and Laurenti Magesa, 126–30. Kenya: Initiatives Publishers, 1989.

Nasrallah, Laura, and Elizabeth Schüssler-Fiorenza, eds. *Prejudice and Christian Beginnings: Investigating Race, Gender, and Ethnicity in Early Christian Studies*. Minneapolis: Fortress, 2009.

Neill, Stephen. *The Story of the Indian Church in India and Pakistan: 1707–1858*. London: SPCK, 1970.

Neill, Stephen, and Tom Wright, eds. *The Interpretation of the New Testament, 1861–1986*. 2nd ed. Oxford: Oxford University Press, 1988.

Ngewa, Samuel. *1 & 2 Timothy* and Titus. Hippo/Africa Bible Commentary Series. Grand Rapids: Zondervan Academic, 2009.

Ngewa, Samuel. *Galatians*. Hippo/Africa Bible Commentary Series. Grand Rapids: Zondervan Academic, 2010.

Ngwa, Kenneth. "Postwar Hermeneutics: Bible and Colony-Related Necropolitics." In *Colonialism and the Bible*, edited by Tat-siong Benny Liew and Fernando F. Segovia, 43–74. Lanham: Lexington Books, 2018.

Nichols, Ashton. "'If there is One God, Fine, there will be Others': Dialogical Theology in the Novels of Chinua Achebe." In *And the Birds Began to Sing: Religion and Literature in Post-colonial Cultures*, edited by Jamie S. Scott, 159–69. Amsterdam and Atlanta: Rodopi, 1996.

Nyamiti, Charles. *Christ as Our Ancestor: Christology from an African Perspective*. Gweru, Zimbabwe: Mambo Press, 1984.

Nyamiti, Charles. *Studies in African Christian Theology*. Vol. 3 (Some Contemporary Models of African Ecclesiology). Nairobi: Catholic University Press, 2007.

Nyende, Peter T. N. "Jesus the Greatest Ancestor: A Typology-Based Theological Interpretation of Hebrews' Christology in Africa." Unpublished PhD Dissertation, University of Edinburgh, 2005.

Nyiawung, Mbengu D. "Contextualising Biblical Exegesis: What is the African Biblical Hermeneutic Approach?." *HTS* 69, no. 1 (2013): Art. No. 2011, 9 pages.

Obeng, Emmanuel. "Use of Biblical Critical Methods in Rooting the Scripture in Africa." In *The Bible in African Christianity*, edited by Hannah Kinoti and John Waliggo, 8–24. Nairobi: Acton, 1997.

Oduyoye, Mercy Amber. "Feminist Theology in an African Perspective." In *Paths of African Theology*, edited by Rosino Gibellini, 166–8. Maryknoll: Orbis, 1995a.

Oduyoye, Mercy Amber. *Daughters of Anowa: African Women and Patriarchy*. Maryknoll: Orbis, 1995b.

Oduyoye, Mercy Amber. *Hearing and Knowing: Theological Reflections on Christianity in Africa*. Maryknoll: Orbis, 1986; repr. Nairobi: Acton, 2000.

Oduyoye, Mercy Amber. *Introducing African Women's Theology*. Sheffield: Sheffield Academic, 2001.

Oduyoye, Mercy Amber. "Jesus Christ." In *The Cambridge Companion to Feminist Theology*, edited by Susan Frank Parsons and Margaret Beaufort. Cambridge: Cambridge University Press, 2002.

Oduyoye, Mercy Amber and Musimbi Kanyoro, eds. *The Will to Arise: Women, Tradition, and the Church in Africa*. Maryknoll: Orbis, 1992.

Oermann, Nils Ole. *Albert Schweitzer, 1875–1965: Eine Biographie*. Munich: C. H. Beck, 2009.

Okure, Teresa. "Women in the Bible." In *Passion and Compassion: Third World Women Doing Theology*, edited by V. Fabella and M. A. Oduyoye, 49–50. Maryknoll: Orbis, 1988a.

Okure, Teresa. *The Johannine Approach to Mission: A Contextual Study of John 4:1- 42*. Tübingen: Mohr Siebeck, 1988b.

Okure, Teresa. "Feminist Interpretations in Africa." In *Searching the Scriptures*, edited by Schussler Fiorenza, 76–85. London: SCM, 1993.

Okure, Teresa. "Contemporary Perspectives on Women in the Bible." *BDV* 53 (1999): 4–11.

Okure, Teresa, ed. *To Cast First Upon the Earth: Bible and Mission Collaborating in Today's Multicultural Global Context*. Pietermaritzburg: Cluster, 2000.

Okure, Teresa. "Historical Jesus Research in Global Cultural Context." In *Handbook for the Study of the Historical Jesus*, edited by Stanley E. Porter and Tom Holmén, 953–84. Leiden: Brill, 2011.

Olusegun, Berekiah O. "African Biblical Studies in Retrospect and Prospect: A Reflection on the Practice and Praxis of Biblical Studies in Africa." In *The Present State and the Future of Biblical Studies in Africa: Essays in Honour of Samuel O. Abogunrin*, edited by J. D. Gwamna, A. O. Dada, and Hope Amolo, 70–87. Ibadan, Nigeria: NABIS, 2017.

Onwu, Nlenanya. "Jesus and the Canaanite Woman (Matt.15:21–28): Toward a Relevant Hermeneutics in African Context." *Bible Bhashyam* 11 (1985): 130–43.

Orobator, Agbonkhianmeghe E. "The Quest for an African Christ: An Essay on Contemporary African Christology." *HekR* 11 (1994): 75–99.

Osterhammel, Jürgen. *Colonialism: A Theoretical Overview*. Trans. Shelly Frisch. Princeton: Marcus Weiner, 1997.

Paget, Henry. "Between Hume and Cugoano: Race, Ethnicity and Philosophical Entrapment." *JSP* 18, no. 2 (2004): 129–48.

Paget, James C. "Theologians Revisited: Albert Schweitzer." *JEH* 62, no. 1 (2011a): 113–20.

Paget, James C. "Schweitzer and Paul." *JNTS* 33, no. 3 (2011b): 223–56.

Paget, James C. and Michale J. Thate. *Albert Schweitzer in Thought and Action: A Life in Parts*. New York: Syracuse University Press, 2016.

Pallister, Janis L. "Leopold Sedar Senghor: A Catholic Sensibility?" *FR* LIII, no. 5 (1980): 670–79.

Parratt, John. *Reinventing Christianity: African Theology Today*. Grand Rapids: Eerdmanns, 1995.

Pauw, C. M. "African Independent Churches as a "People's Response" to the Christian Message." *JSR* 8, no. 1 (1995): 3–25.

Pawliková-Vilhanová, Viera. "Christian Missions in Africa and their Role in the Transformation of African Societies." *AAS* 16, no. 2 (2007): 249–60.

Pelikan, Jaroslav. *Jesus Through the Centuries: His Place in the History of Culture*. New Haven: Yale University Press, 1985.

Phiri Isabel, A., Dietrich Werner, Chammah Kaunda, and Kennedy Owino, eds. *Anthology of African Christianity*. Pietermaritzburg: Cluster, 2016.

Pitt, Andrew. "Albert Schweitzer: A Jewish-Apocalyptic Approach to Christian Origins." In *Pillars of Biblical Interpretation*, edited by Stanley E. Porter and Sean A. Adams. Vol. 1: BCB 1980, 211–38. Eugene: Wipf and Stock, 2016.

Pobee, John. *Toward an African Theology*. Nashville: Abingdon, 1979.

Prevost, Elizabeth E. *The Communion of Women: Missions and Gender in Colonial Africa and the British Metropole*. Oxford: Oxford University Press, 2010.

Proceedings of the Conference on Foreign Missions. London: Mildmay Park, October 5th to 7th, 1886.

Prothero, Stephen. "Thomas Jefferson's Cut-and-Paste Bible: Our Third President Sought to Separate the Words of Jesus from the 'Corruptions' of his Followers." *WSJ*, March 25, 2011.

Ptolemy, Claudius (90–168 CE), *Tetrabiblos*. Loeb Classical Library, No. 435, Harvard University Press, 1940.

Punt, Jeremy. "Postcolonial Biblical Criticism in South Africa: Some Mind and Road Mapping." *Neot* 37, no. 1 (2003): 66.

Reed, David A. "Acts 17:16-34 in an African Context (An Assessment from a N. Atlantic/Western Perspective." *AJET* 22, no. 1 (2003): 87–101.

Renan, Ernst. *The Future of Science*. London: Chapman & Hall, 1891.

Reventlow, H. G., and W. Farmer, eds. *Biblical Studies and the Shifting of Paradigms, 1850–1914*. JSOT Series 192. Sheffield: Sheffield Academic, 1994.

Richard, H. L. "Religious Syncretism as a Syncretistic Concept: The Inadequacy of the 'World Religions' Paradigm in Cross-Cultural Encounter." *IJFM* 31, no. 4 (2014): 209–15.

Rittner, Carol, ed. *Genocide in Rwanda: Complicity of the Churches*. Paragon House Books on Genocide and the Holocaust. St. Paul: Paragon House, 2004.

Round Table, The. "*Apartheid* and the Scriptures." *CJIA* 44, no. 174 (1954): 161–6.

Rukundwa, Lazare S. "Postcolonial Theory as a Hermeneutical Tool for Biblical Reading." *HTS* 64, no. 1 (2008): 339–51.

Sæbø, Magne, ed. *Hebrew Bible/Old Testament: The History of Its Interpretation, II: From the Renaissance to the Enlightenment*. Göttingen: Vandenhoeck & Ruprecht, 2008.

Said, Edward. *Culture and Imperialism*. New York: Vintage, 1993.

Sanneh, Lamin. "Christian Missions and the Western Guilt Complex." *CC* 104, no. 24 (1987): 331–4.

Sanneh, Lamin. *Translating the Message: The Missionary Impact on Culture*. Maryknoll: Orbis, 1989.

Sawyerr, Harry. *Creative Evangelism: Toward a New Christian Encounter with Africa*. London: Lutterworth, 1968.

Schreiter, Robert J., ed. *Faces of Jesus in Africa*. Maryknoll: Orbis, 1992.

Schweitzer, Albert. *Die Religionsphilosophie Kants: Von der Kritik der reinen Vernunft bis zur Religion innerhalb der Grenzen der bloßen Vernunft*. Leipzig and Tubingen: J. C. B. Mohr Siebeck, 1899.

Schweitzer, Albert. *Von Reimarus zu Wrede: Geschichte der Leben-Jesu-Forschung*. Tübingen: Mohr Siebeck, 1906.

Schweitzer, Albert. *The Quest of the Historical Jesus: A Critical Study of its Progress from Reimarus to Wrede*. Translated by W. Montgomery. London: Unwin Brothers, 1910.

Schweitzer, Albert. *The Mystery of the Kingdom of God*. New York: Dodd, Mead & Co., 1914.

Schweitzer, Albert. *On the Edge of the Primeval Forest: Experiences and Observations of a Doctor in Equatorial Africa*. London: A & C Black, 1924.

Schweitzer, Albert. "The Relations of the White and Coloured Races." *CR* CXXXIII, no. 745 (1928): 65–70.

Schweitzer, Albert. *Die Mystik des Apostels Paulus*. Tubingen: Mohr Siebeck, 1930.

Schweitzer, Albert. *The Mysticism of Paul the Apostle*. Translated by W. Montgomery. New York: Macmillan, 1931.

Schweitzer, Albert. "Religion and Modern Civilization." *Christian Century* 51, no. 47 (1934): 1519–21.

Schweitzer, Albert. *Christianity and Religions of the World*. New York: Henry Holt, 1939a.

Schweitzer, Albert. *My African Notebook*. Translated by C. E. B. Russell. New York: Holt, Rinehart and Winston, 1939b.

Schweitzer, Albert. *Out of My Life and Thought*. New York: Henry Holt & Co., 1948a.

Schweitzer, Albert. *The Forest Hospital at Lambaréné*. Trans. by C. T. Campion; NY: Macmillan, 1948b.

Schweitzer, Albert. "Our Task in Colonial Africa." In *The Africa of Albert Schweitzer*, edited by C. K. Joy and Melvin Arnold, 145–50. New York: Harper & Bros, 1948c.

Schweitzer, Albert. *On the Edge of the Primeval Forest*. French edition, 1952; Trans. by Fitzgerald, 1964.

Segovia, Fernando and R. S. Sugirtharajah, eds. *A Postcolonial Commentary on the New Testament*. London and New York: T&T Clark, 2009.

Senghor, Leopold. "Book Review" of P. Tempels. *Bantoue Philosophie*. Available online: https://plato.stanford.edu/archives/spr2014/entries/negritude/.

Sheehan, Jonathan. *The Enlightenment Bible: Translation, Scholarship, Culture*. Princeton: Princeton University Press, 2013.

Shifman, Arie. "'A Scent' of the Spirit: Exegesis of an Enigmatic Verse (Isaiah 11:3)." *JBL* 131, no. 2 (2012): 241–9.

Shorter, Aylward. *African Christian Theology—Adaptation or Incarnation?* Maryknoll: Orbis, 1977.

Simon, Christian. "History of a Case-Study of the Relationship between University Professors and the State in Germany." In *Biblical Studies and the Shifting of Paradigms, 1850–1914*, edited by H. G. Reventlow and W. Farmer, 168–96. Sheffield: Sheffield Academic Press, 1995.

Smalley, William A. *Translation as Mission: Bible Translation in the Modern Missionary Movement*. Macon: Mercer University Press, 1991.

Smith, Justin E. H. "The Enlightenment's 'Race' Problem, and Ours." *NYT Opinionator*, February 10, 2013. Available online: https://opinionator.blogs.nytimes.com/2013/02/10 /why-has-race-survived/ (accessed July 11, 2019).

Smith, Linda Tuhiwai. *Decolonizing Methodologies: Research and Indigenous People*. London and New York: Zed Books, 1999.

Smith, Mitzi J. *I Found God in Me: A Womanist Biblical Hermeneutics Reader*. Eugene: Cascade, 2015.

Smith, Mitzi J., and Jayachitra Lalitha, eds. *Teaching All Nations: Interrogating the Matthean Great Commission*. Minneapolis: Fortress, 2014.

Spangenberg, Izak and Christina Landman, eds. *The Legacies of Albert Schweitzer Reconsidered*. SHEB Series, 1. Cape Town: AOSIS, 2016. *Stanford Encyclopaedia of Philosophy* (May 9, 2006). Available online: https://plato.stanford.edu/entries/ colonialism/.

Spivak, Gayatri C. "Can the Subaltern Speak?" In *Marxism and the Interpretation of Culture*, edited by Cary Nelson and Lawrence Grossberg, 271–316. London: Macmillan, 1988.

Sprinkle, Joe. "Literary Approaches to the Old Testament: A Survey of Recent Scholarship." *JETS* 32, no. 3 (1989): 299–310.

Stanley, Brian, ed. *Christian Missions and the Enlightenment*. Grand Rapids: Eerdmans, 2001.

Stanley, Henry W. *Into the Dark Continent or the Sources of the Nile Around the Great Lakes of Equatorial Africa and Down the Livingstone River to the Atlantic Ocean*. Vols. 1 & 2. New York: Harper and Brothers, 1878.

Stewart, James. *Dawn in the Dark Continent: Africa and Its Missions: The Duff Missionary Lecture for 1902*. New York: Young People's Missionary Movement, 1902.

Stine, Philip C., ed. *Bible Translation and the Spread of the Church: The Last 200 Years*. Leiden: Brill, 1990.

Stinton, Diane. *Jesus of Africa: Voices of Contemporary Christology*. Maryknoll: Orbis, 2004.

Sugirtharajah, R. S., ed. *The Postcolonial Bible*. Bible and Postcolonialism. Sheffield: Sheffield Academic, 1998.

Sugirtharajah, R. S. *The Bible and the Third World: Precolonial, Colonial and Postcolonial Encounters*. Cambridge: Cambridge University Press, 2001a.

Sugirtharajah, R. S. *The Bible in the Third World*. Cambridge: Cambridge University Press, 2001b.

Sugirtharajah, R. S. *Postcolonial Criticism and Biblical Interpretation*. Oxford: Oxford University Press, 2002.

Sugirtharajah, R. S., ed. *Voices from the Margin: Interpreting the Bible in the Third World.* Maryknoll: Orbis, 2006.

Sundkler, Bengt G. M. *Bantu Prophets in South Africa.* Cambridge: James Clarke & Co., 2004 (1948).

Taylor, J. V. *The Primal Vision: Christian Presence amid African Religion.* Philadelphia: Fortress, 1963.

Tempels, Placide. *La Philosophie Bantoue.* Paris: Presence Africaine, 1945.

Thackeray, H. St. J. *The Letter of Aristeas.* London: SPCK, 1917.

Togarasei, Lovemore. "Musa W. Dube and the Study of the Bible in Africa." *SHE* 34 (2008): 55–74.

Togarasei, Lovemore. "The Prophet and Divine Manifestation: On the Translation of the Word "Prophet" in the Shona Union Bible." *OTE* 30, no. 33 (2017): 821–34.

Totontle, Mositi. *The Victims.* Gabarone: Bostalo, 1993.

Tigay, Jeffrey H. *Jewish Publication Society Torah Commentary: Deuteronomy.* Philadelphia: JPS, 1996.

Trevelyan, C. *The 35th Report of the British and Foreign Bible Society.* N.P., 1939, 59.

Ukpong, Justin S. "Rereading the Bible with African Eyes: Inculturation and Hermeneutics." *JTSA* 91 (1995): 3–14.

Ukpong, Justin S. "The Parable of the Shrewd Manager (Luke 16:1–13: An Essay in Inculturation Biblical Hermeneutic." *Semeia* 73 (1996): 189–210.

Ukpong, Justin S. "Popular Readings of the Bible in Africa and Implications for Academic Readings: Report on the Field Research Carried Out on Oral Interpretations of the Bible in Port Harcourt Metropolis, Nigeria, under the Auspices of the Bible in Africa Project, 1991–94." In *The Bible in Africa,* edited by G. West and M. W. Dube, 582–94. Leiden: Brill, 2000.

Ukpong, Justin, Musa W. Dube, Gerald O. West, and Alpheus Masoga. *Reading the Bible in the Global Village: Cape Town.* GPBS. Atlanta: SBL, 2002.

Vander Stichele, C., and T. C Penner, eds. *Her Master's Tools?: Feminist and Postcolonial Engagements of Historical-Critical Discourse.* Leiden: Brill, 2005.

van Vuuren, Marijke. "Kihika's Bible: The Recontextualisation of the Gospel in Ngugi's *A Grain of Wheat.*" *Koers* 65, no. 1 (2000): 1–16.

Vermes, Geza. *Scripture and Tradition in Judaism.* Leiden: Brill, 1961.

Villa-Vicencio, Charles, ed. *Theology and Violence: The South African Debate.* Johannesburg: Skotaville, 1987: 15–30.

Villa-Vicencio, Charles. *A Theology of Reconstruction: Nation-building and Human Rights.* Cambridge: University Press, 1992.

Wachege, P. N. "Curses and Cursing among the Agĩkũyũ: Socio-Cultural and Religious Benefits." Unpublished article available on author's website. Available online: https://profiles.uonbi.ac.ke/patrickwachege/ (accessed July 28, 2020).

Wagner, Gunter. *The Bantu of North Kavirondo.* Abingdon. Vol. 1, AESTC. Oxon: Routledge, 2018 (IAI: Oxford University Press, 1949).

Warren, M. A. C. *Caesar the Beloved Enemy: Three Studies in the Relation of Church and State.* London: SCM Press; Chicago: Alec R. Allenson, 1955.

wa Thiong'o, Ngũgĩ. *Weep not, Child.* African Writers Series. London: Heinemann, 1967a.

wa Thiong'o, Ngũgĩ. *A Grain of Wheat.* African Writers Series. London: Heinemann, 1967b.

wa Thiong'o, Ngũgĩ. *Petals of Blood.* African Writers Series. London: Heinemann, 1977.

wa Thiong'o, Ngũgĩ. *Caitaani Mutharabaini.* Translated by author: *Devil on the Cross.* African Writers Series. London: Heinemann, 1980.

wa Thiong'o, Ngũgĩ. *Decolonising the Mind: the Politics of Language in African Literature*. African Writers Series. London: Heinemann, 1986a.

wa Thiong'o, Ngũgĩ. *Decolonizing the Mind: The Politics of Language in African Literature*. Nairobi: East African Education Press, 1986b.

wa Thiong'o, Ngũgĩ. *Matigari ma Njiruungi*. African Writers Series. London: Heinemann, 1998.

wa Thiong'o, Ngũgĩ. *Murogi was Kagogo*. Translated by author: *Wizard of the Crow*. New York: Anchor Books, 2006.

wa Thiong'o, Ngũgĩ and Ngũgĩ wa Mĩriĩ. *Ngaahika Ndeenda*. Nairobi: N. P., 1977. Translated by authors: *I Will Marry When I Want*. African Writers Series. London: Heinemann,1977.

Watt, Jan G. "Johannine Research in Africa, Part 1: An Analytical Survey/Johannese Navorsing in Afrika, Deel 1: 'n Analitiese Oorsig van der." *In die Skriflig* 49, no. 2 (2015): 1–14, 4.

West, Gerald O. "The Relationship between Different Modes of Reading (the Bible) and the Ordinary Reader." *Scriptura* 9 (1991): 87–110.

West, Gerald O. *Biblical Hermeneutics of Liberation: Modes of Reading the Bible in the South African Context*. Pietermaritzburg; Maryknoll: Cluster and Orbis, 1995a.

West, Gerald O. "Constructing Critical and Contextual Readings with Ordinary Readers: Mark 5:21-6:1." *JTSA* 92 (1995b): 60–9.

West, Gerald O. "On the Eve of an African Biblical Studies: Trajectories and Trends." *JTSA* 99 (1997): 99–115.

West, Gerald O. *The Academy of the Poor: Towards a Dialogical Reading of the Bible*. Sheffield: Sheffield Academic Press, 1998.

West, Gerald O. "The Historicity of Myth and the Myth of Historicity: Locating the Ordinary African 'Reader' of the Bible in the Debate." *Neot* 38, no. 1 (2004): 127–44.

West, Gerald O., ed. *Reading Other-wise: Socially Engaged Biblical Scholars Reading with Their Local Communities*. Semeia Studies. Atlanta: SBL, 2007.

West, Gerald O. "The Beginning of African Biblical Interpretation: The Bible among the BaTlhaping." *Acta Theol* 12, no. 1 (2009): 33–47.

West, Gerald O. "The Bible and the Poor." In *Bible in Mission*, edited by Pauline Hogarth, Fergus MacDonald, Bill Mitchell, and Knud Jørgensen, 159–67. Oxford: Regnum, 2013.

West, Gerald O. "Locating 'Contextual Bible Study' within Biblical Liberation Hermeneutics and Intercultural Biblical Hermeneutics." *HTS* 70, no. 1 (2014): 1. Available online: http://dx.doi.org/10.4102/hts.v70i1.2641 (accessed June 22, 2020).

West, Gerald O. *The Stolen Bible: From Tool of Imperialism to African Icon*. Leiden and Pietermaritzburg: Brill and Cluster, 2016.

West, Gerald O. "African Biblical Scholarship as Post-colonial, Tri-Polar, and a Site-of-Struggle." In *Present and Future of Biblical Studies: Celebrating 25 Years of Brill's Biblical Interpretation*, edited by Tat-siong Benny Liew, 240–73. Leiden and Boston: Brill, 2018.

West, Gerald O. "Scripture as a Site of Struggle: Literary and Socio-historical Resources for a Prophetic Theology in a Postcolonial, Post-apartheid (Neocolonialist?) South Africa." In *Scripture and Resistance*, edited by Jione Havea and Collin Cowan, 149–63. Lanham: Lexington, 2019.

Wicker, K. O., A. S. Miller, and M. W. Dube, eds. *Feminist New Testament Studies: Religion/Culture/Critique*. New York: Palgrave Macmillan, 2005.

Wimbush, Vincent L. "Interpreters—Enslaving/ Enslaved/Runagate." *JBL* 130, no. 1 (2011): 5–24.

Wimbush, Vincent L. "#BlackScholarsMatter: Visions and Struggles." SBL
 BlackScholarsMatter Symposium, August 13, 2020. Available online: https://sbl-site.org
 /meetings/blackscholarsmatter.aspx.
Woodberry, Robert D. "The Missionary Roots of Liberal Democracy." *APSR* 106, no. 2
 (2012): 244–74.
Yamauchi, Edwin. *The Bible and Africa*. Grand Rapids: Baker Academic, 2006.
Young, J. C. *Postcolonialism: A Very Short Introduction*. Oxford: Oxford University Press,
 2003.

NAME AND SUBJECT INDEX

Achebe, Chinua   111–18, 122
Adamo, David Tuesday   74–8, 104–6,
　165 n.66
Adewuya, J. Ayodeji   82–3
Adeyemo, Tokunboh   105 n.7
African Biblical Studies
　defining   3–12, 103–10
　on gender   160–75
Aichelle, et al. *Postmodern Bible*   56 n.163
Akper, G. I.   151
Alòs-Moner, Andreu Martínez   157,
　160 n.36
Amadiume, Ifi   162 n.47
Anonby, John A.   114–20
anti-colonialist biblical
　interpretation   70–8, 84–102,
　139–48, 160–201
apocalyptic/apocalypticism   31, 36–7,
　136
　European missionary   24, 80, 87,
　136–45
Ashcroft, Griffiths, Tiffin, *Empire Writes
　Back*   1 n.2, 3, 61, 87 n.12, 125
Aulén, Gustav   182 n.28
Ayandele, E. A.   96

Baëta, C. C.   20 n.28, 93, 96–7, 108
Bailey, Randall   3 n.4
Baldwin, James   17 n.15, 85 n.6
Banana, Canaan   129–32
Barrett, C. K.   35
Barrett, David.   80 n.5, 91 n.20
Barton, John   193 n.8
Bassil, N. Noah   195 n.16, 196 n.17
Bediako, Kwame   8 n.25, 30, 96, 110 n.23,
　180, 185–6, 189–90
Belcher, Wendy L.   155 n.4, 156 nn.7–8,
　157 n.11, 157 nn.14–15, 158,
　160 nn.34–5
Benny-Liew   6 n.13, 77 n.78, 107 n.15,
　161 n.40

Berman, Nina   34 n.50
Bernal, Martin   77 n.76
Bernays, Anne   193 n.5
Bhabha, Homi   6, 91–2
Biblical Studies in the West   3–12
　and colonial project   6–8
　origins   4, 7–12, 95, 194, 200
　and SBL   12, 200
Boesak, Allan   143–5
Boulaga, Fabian Ebousi   1 n.1, 18–19, 41,
　48 n.120, 49 n.128, 76–7, 84 n.4,
　131, 145–8
Bozeman, Adda Bruemmer   100 n.58
*British and Foreign Bible Society
　(BFBS)*   17, 64
Browning, Melissa D.   170 n.89
Bruck, Gabriele vom   193 n.5
Bruel, Wolfgang   22 n.36
Bujo, Bénézet   95, 140, 142, 179 n.11,
　181–2
Bultmann, Rudolph   31, 130, 147
Burris, John P.   45 n.102, 45 n.104
Burton, Keith A.   103 n.2
Buxton, Thomas F.   17, 33 n.46, 63 n.15,
　64 n.19

Callahan, Allen D.   78 n.81, 109 n.21,
　198 n.21
Camara, Babacar   54 n.153, 87
Carter, J. Cameron   32 n.37
"center" and "periphery"   4–8, 13, 50
Césaire, Aimé   86, 138 n.8
Chidester, David   15 n.2, 16 n.8, 18 n.20,
　19–20, 33, 40 n.78
Chigumira, Godfrey   165 n.63
Christology, African   14, 142 n.31, 156,
　165 n.65, 175–90
Codere, Helen   96
Colenso, John W.   39–40, 43, 46, 50–1,
　82, 90, 95 n.37
Colonial Bible   15–16, 119, 121, 125

Colonial Project, The   4–7, 13–14, 18, 21,
    23, 25–32, 41 n.88, 49 n.131, 50, 63,
    67, 71, 75–6, 86, 109–10, 112, 114,
    120–1, 136, 138 n.7, 193, 197
colonization   4, 20–4, 32–4, 47, 74, 115,
    121, 160
    Ethiopian resistance to   155–60
    language and   74–8, 161–4
    resisting   12, 160
    Schweitzer, European missionaries
        and   14, 18, 20–4, 33–4, 40–2,
        97 n.46, 145
colonized, The   4, 7 nn.20–1, 12–13, 19,
    20 n.27, 21 n.34, 22, 26, 30, 33, 48,
    49, 59, 61–9, 74, 80, 85, 90, 92 n.27,
    97 n.46, 106, 110, 125–35, 161–2,
    182, 197
Court, Franklin E.   28 n.21

da Silva, José Antunes   90 n.19
Davenport, Manuel M.   41 n.84, 50 n.132
Dawsey, Josh   200 n.26
De Villiers, Pieter G. R.   144 n.36
decolonization/decolonizing   12, 13 n.45,
    14, 26, 32 n.36, 34 n.48, 41 n.88,
    59, 62, 70, 88 n.13, 101, 103–10,
    117 n.20, 119, 121, 125, 129, 133,
    171, 184, 192, 194
Deji, Valentin   132 n.37
Denis, Philippe   151 n.14
Diagne, Souleymane Bachir   86 n.8
Diarra, Pierre   88
Dickson, Kwesi   12 n.40, 80 n.3, 81 n.8,
    82
Du Bois, W. E. B.   41
Dube, Musa W.   5 n.10, 12 n.42, 21–2,
    32 n.36, 33–4, 61–2, 63 n.16, 65–7,
    69, 91, 101, 106, 109–10, 133 n.39,
    149 n.2, 152 nn.19–20, 155 n.3,
    162–6, 168–72, 184, 187–8
Dyrness, William   96 n.45, 110 n.23

Ela, Jean-Marc   97, 191–2
England, Emma   3 n.3
Enlightenment   4 n.5, 6, 14, 25–33,
    55 n.157, 55, 63, 69, 71 n.51, 72,
    74–7, 108, 128, 136–42, 156, 178
    colonization and   15–30
Equiano, Olaudah   22–3

eschatology   24, 34, 37, 80, 104
    African (cyclical) *vs.* western (linear)
        |136–47
    "escapist"   143–4
    political eschatology   120
    radical liberationist   120, 143–5
    realized   120
    Schweitzer's "thoroughgoing"   37
Ethiopia/Aethiopia/Abyssinia/Habesha
    74–8, 103, 154–60
    Orthodox Täwaḥǝdo Church   155–9
Eze, Emmanuel C.   55 n.157
Ezigbo, Victor   182–4

Fanon, Frantz   18 n.19, 19, 86 n.7, 101,
    103, 125
Farisani, Elelwani   133 n.39
Farmer, W.   1, 26–8, 55 n.162
Felder, Cain H.   3 n.4
feminist/womanist interpretations
    121 n.34, 154, 160–6, 169, 170,
    178
    Achebe, *Anthills of the Savanah*   116
    African proto-feminist   154–60
    Christology   186–9
    postcolonial feminist   5 n.10, 9 n.26,
        22 n.35, 91 n.24, 168–72
Fetterley, Judith   121 n.34
Fiedler, Rachel NyaGondwe   164 n.54
Fiensy, David   137 n.7
Figueira, Dorothy   6
Fiske, Edward B.   93 n.31, 94 n.34
Forrow, Lachlan   55 n.159
Foster, Elizabeth A.   88 n.13
Freire, Paolo   80 n.4
Fuze, Magema Magwaza   50 n.133

Gadamer, Hans-Georg   35 n.55
Galawdewos   155 nn.4–5, 156 n.8,
    157–60
Galbraith, Deane   9–10, 16
Gale, Thomson   95 n.35
Gallagher, Susan V.   111, 112
gender and sexuality in African cultures
    and in the Bible   14, 70 n.45,
    154–74, 186–8
Gerner, Matthias   62 n.10
Getui, Maluleke, Ukpong, *Interpreting the
    New Testament in Africa*   66 n.34

Gifford, Paul 136
Giles, Kevin 145 n.42
Goldberg, David Theo 6 n.17, 10
Grässer, Erich 35 n.53
Gray, Richard 136-7
Green, Gene 142 n.31
Green and Grose, *Philosophical Works* 53 n.149
Gunda, Masiiwa R. 129 n.23

hagiography 159-60
Harris, Ruth 34 n.49, 38 n.67, 39 nn.71-2, 44 n.99, 48 n.123, 49, 161 n.38
Hatch, William P. 95
Heaney, Robert S. 95 n.39
Hegel, G. W. F. 43, 47-8, 49 n.125, 52-7, 87-8, 92-3
hermeneutics
    African biblical 9, 85, 93, 103, 105-7
    Black biblical 127-32
    comparative 105
    conversion 152
    culturally sensitive 40, 105
    vs. exegesis 105, 108
    feminist 164 n.59, 168-72
    inculturation 81 n.7, 97-8, 105, 133-5, 162, 164
    intercultural 97, 105
    of justice and hope 198
    liberationist 88, 149 n.2, 150-2, 164
    Postwar 146 n.48
    reader-response 94, 121
    reconstruction 132-3
    of suspicion 164
    "Talitha Cum" 154 n.3
    vernacular 70-3
    Womanist/Womanhood/*Bosadi* 172-4
Hinchliff, Peter 39 n.75
Hinga, Teresia 155 n.3, 164 n.57, 164 n.59, 165 n.61, 186, 188
Hochschild, Adam 20 n.28, 21 n.31
Hockey Katherine M. 10 n.28, 63 n.16
Horrell, David G. 10 n.28, 32 n.37, 63 n.16, 199
Huber, Hugo 95 n.36

Idowu, Bolaji 79, 93, 97
Immerwahr, John 53 n.149

imperialism, European 4-5, 7, 8, 10-13, 18, 26, 30, 34, 41 n.88, 47, 50 n.135, 55 n.158, 62, 65 n.26, 72-3, 106, 112, 115, 117 nn.20-1, 129, 145, 157 n.14, 164-5, 169-71, 192-3, 195-7
"Imperial Diet" 22 n.36
"scriptural" 63
Isizoh, Chidi Denis 122 nn.36-8, 124

Jean-Baptiste, Rachel 42 n.90
Jenkins, Paul 62 n.10
Jenkins, Phillip 8 nn.24-5, 9 n.26, 20 n.29
Jennings, Willie 39 n.73, 40 n.79, 46, 50 nn.134-5, 191, 193-5
Jipp, Joshua, W. 123
John, Helen C. 153
Johnson, G. Wesley. 139
Joy, Charles R. 35 n.52

Kabasele, François 180 n.20
Kairos Document 192, 198-9
Kalilombe, Patrick 149-50
Kamudzandu, Israel 183 n.34, 190 n.75
Kant, Emmanuel 38, 52-5, 88
Kanyoro, Musimbi 9 n.26, 73 n.65, 164 n.56, 164 n.59
Kaplan, Justin 193 n.5
Katongole, Emmanuel 106 n.13, 171 n.98
Kelley, Shawn 32 n.41, 194 n.11
Kidd, Colin 6-7, 20 n.30
Kimuhu, Johnson M. 99
Kincheloe, et al 11 n.32
Kush 75-6

Landman, Christina 33 n.44
Legaspi, Michael 16, 28, 30
LeMarquand, Grant 152-3
Liberation Theology, African 125-8, 143-51
literature, Bible and African 111-24
Loomba, Ania 162 n.42
Lorde, Audre 12 n.40, 197
Lovesey, Oliver 119 n.26, 119 n.29
Lugones, María 161 n.41

McFall, E. A. 138 n.7
McGrane, Barnard 15, 16, 22 n.38, 23, 33 n.43, 40 n.82

Magesa, Laurenti   165 n.65, 183–4
Mahfood, Sebastian   120 n.32
Maluleke, Tinyiko   66 n.34, 103–5
Mana, K. Kä   132
Manus, Ukachukwu Chris   97 n.49,
   122 n.36, 124
Marxsen, Patti M.   161 n.37
Marzouk, Safwat   77–8
Masenya, Madipoane   172–4
Mazrui, Ali A.   49
Mbiti, J. S.   20 n.28, 66 n.32, 79, 89 n.16,
   91–5, 97, 104, 122, 137 n.6, 139–43,
   181, 182 n.29, 188 n.67
Mbuvi, Andrew M.   12 n.42, 62 n.6,
   78 n.83, 89 n.15, 104, 105, 108 n.18,
   110 n.25, 111 n.3, 113 n.8, 122 n.37,
   133 n.39, 142 n.31, 182, 194 n.9
Mbuwayesango, Dora   12 n.42, 62 n.6,
   78 n.82, 133 n.39, 161 n.40
Memmi, Albert   20 n.27, 21 n.34, 48–9,
   59, 61, 63 n.14, 92 n.27, 97 n.46
Mofokeng, Takatso   96 n.43, 126–7
Mokhoathi, Joel   181
Moloney, Raymond   180 n.12
Montesquieu, M. De Secondat Baron
   50 n.137
Moreau, A. Scott   142 n.26
Mosala, Itumeleng   127–9
Moses, Michael Valdez   117 n.21
Mrozcek, Eva   126 n.3
Mudimbe, V. Y.   6 n.13, 21, 26–7, 30 n.30,
   57, 66, 142
Mugambi, J. N. K.   95 n.39, 132, 165 n.65
Muilenburg, James   108–9
Mukonyora, Isabel, et al   130 n.26,
   131 n.31
Munz, Walter   160 n.37
Musodza, Archford   131 n.29
Mutiso-Mbandi, J.   180
Mwangi, E. Maina   70, 73 nn.60–1
Mwaura, Philomena Njeri   165 n.63
Mwikisa, Peter   117 n.20
Myers, Travis L.   179 n.11

Nasimiyu-Wasike, Anne   165 n.65,
   186
Nasrallah, Laura   199 n.23
négritude/negritude   85–8, 105, 138
Neill, Stephen   17 n.12, 36 n.56, 200 n.26

Ngewa, Samuel   105 n.7
Ngũgĩ wa Thiong'o   110, 112, 116–20
Ngwa, Kenneth   6 n.13, 146 n.48
Nichols, Ashton   112, 115 n.15
Nthamburi, Zablon   179 n.10
Nyamiti, Charles   180–1
Nyende, Peter T. N.   179 n.11, 190
Nyiawung, Mbengu D.   104

Obeng, Emmanuel   67 n.39
Oduyoye, Mercy Amber   73 n.65, 154,
   161 n.39, 162–4, 174, 178, 186–8
Oermann, Nils Ole   33, 38
Okure, Teresa   103 n.1, 153, 162,
   164 n.59, 166–8
Olusegun, Berekiah, O.   104
Onwu, Nlenanya   165 n.64
"ordinary readers," The Bible and   107,
   134, 149–53
Orobator, Agbonkhianmeghe E.   178 n.6
Osterhammel, Jürgen   29 n.25

Paget, Henry   52 n.146
Paget, James C.   33 n.45, 36 n.58, 38 n.70,
   39 n.72, 41 n.88, 47 n.118, 51 n.140,
   73 n.65, 163 n.52, 183 n.32,
Pallister, Janis L.   87 n.11
Parratt, John.   142
Pauw, C. M.   89 n.19
Pawliková-Vilhanová, Viera   18, 84 n.3
Pelikan, Jaroslav   25, 30, 55 n.161, 176,
   178
Penner, T. C.   12 n.40
Peṭros, Wälättä (1592–1642)   155–61,
   163, 173
Phiri, Isabel   164 n.55
Pitt, Andrew   31 n.35
Pobee, John   180, 185
postcolonial/postcolonialism   3, 6,
   12–14, 21, 31, 56, 57, 70–3, 84–5,
   91 n.22, 89, 91–2, 98, 101, 103–7,
   109, 111–21, 133 n.39, 134 n.43,
   139, 150 n.8, 161 n.42, 164,
   168 n.84, 176, 190 n.75, 187, 197
   feminist biblical interpretation
      168–71
   feminist Christology   187
   pre-colonial African "womanist" biblical
      interpretation, a sample of   154–9

presence, African 74–6
Prevost, Elizabeth E. 163 n.52
Prothero, Stephen 130 n.24
Ptolemy, Claudius 75 n.71
Punt, Jeremy 106

race/racism/racist 10–11, 14, 20–7,
    61–9, 76, 88, 103–10, 113, 126–7,
    136–48, 162, 168, 169 n.84, 170–1
  among German biblical scholars 28
  racially based social-evolution approach
    44
  Schweitzer and 32–5, 38–40, 44–57
  structures and systemic 27–30,
    191–201
racism and Christian Mission in
    Africa 10–11, 20–59, 86–9,
    126–7, 136–48, 191–201
Reed, David A. 122 n.36
rehabilitation, hermeneutic of 14, 78,
    85–6, 92–102, 105, 113, 165
religious reality, African 12, 14, 19, 23–4,
    31, 39, 46–7, 63, 66, 69, 79–86,
    90–8, 110–15, 118, 123, 124, 136–9,
    141, 146–7, 176, 178, 183–4, 189,
    196
Renan, Ernst 32
Revelation, the book of 159, 181
  A South African interpretation
    143–5
Reventlow, H. G. 1, 26 n.5, 27–8
Re-Written Bible, The 125–35
Richard, H. L. 97 n.47
Rittner, Carol 112 n.4
Round Table, The 145 n.42
Rukundwa, Lazare S. 12 n.40

Sæbø, Magne 4 n.6
Said, Edward 5 n.8, 12 n.41, 13 n.43, 59,
    70 n.48
Sanneh, Lamin 30, 62–3, 71, 74 n.66,
    97 n.15
Sanon, Anselme 179 n.10
Sawyerr, Harry 185–6
Schreiter, Robert J. 179 n.10, 180 n.13,
    180 n.20, 183 n.33, 185 n.45,
    186 n.53, 189 n.70
Schüssler-Fiorenza 164 n.59, 199 n.23

Schweitzer, Albert 14, 20, 26 n.9, 31–57,
    88, 113–14, 137, 142, 160–1, 163,
    175–6, 178, 179 n.9, 183 n.31
  Jesus of history and Christ of faith
    37–8
  "thoroughgoing skepticism" 37
Segovia, Fernando 3 n.2, 6 n.13, 77 n.79,
    146 n.48, 161 n.40
Senghor, Leopold 86–7, 138 n.8
Sheehan, Jonathan 15–16, 26, 28,
    32 n.40, 63, 71 n.51
Shifman, Arie 69–70
Shorter, Aylward 94 n.33
Simon, Christian 27
Smalley, William A. 62 n.7
Smith, Justin E. H. 54 n.155
Smith, Linda Tuhiwai 25–6
Smith, Mitzi J. 121 n.35, 170 n.90
Spangenberg, Izak 33 n.44
Spivak, Gayatri C. 154
Sprinkle, Joe 108 n.20
Stanley, Brian 16 n.4, 20 n.30
Stanley, Henry W. 21 n.34
Stewart, James 30
Stine, Philip C. 62 n.7
Stinton, Diane 179 n.12, 185, 187 n.61
Sugirtharajah, R. S. 3, 5 n.9, 6, 8 n.23,
    13 n.45, 16 n.7, 17 n.11, 18 n.17,
    20 n.26, 21, 25, 29, 30 n.34, 33 n.46,
    40 n.80, 50 n.134, 50 n.136,
    56 n.163, 61, 63 n.12, 63 n.15,
    64 n.18, 65 n.24, 67, 69–70, 71 n.52,
    72–3, 84–5, 91–2, 97, 101, 105 n.10,
    107, 134 n.43, 149 n.3, 165 n.62,
    194 n.13
Sundkler, Bengt G. M. 89 n.17, 90 n.19

Taylor, J. V. 175, 178
Tempels, Placide 51, 138
Thackeray, H. St. J. 62 n.8
Tigay, Jeffrey H. 11 n.37
Togarasei, Lovemore 66–9, 169 n.86
Totontle, Mositi 171
translation/vernacular 61–77
Trevelyan, C. 67 n.35

Ukpong, Justin S. 66 n.34, 81–2, 98,
    105 n.11, 133–5, 149 nn.1–2, 151–2

van Vuuren, Marijke   118 n.25
Vander Stichele, C.   12 n.40
Vermes, Geza   126 n.3
Villa-Vicencio, Charles   22 n.37, 132

Wachege, P. N.   100 n.60
Wagner, Gunter   100 n.59
Warren, M. A. C.   31 n.34
Watt, Jan G.   166 n.70

West, Gerald O.   62 n.9, 65, 89 n.17,
    104–7, 149–52
West/western   7 n.21
Wimbush, Vincent L.   4, 11, 191, 195,
    197, 200
Woodberry, Robert D.   29 n.27

Yamauchi, Edwin   78 n.83, 99 n.55
Young, J. C.   4 n.7, 12 n.39, 91 n.22

BIBLICAL INDEX

Genesis
1	130
1–2	95, 187
1:26-28	116
1:27	187
2	187
2–3	94
9	99
9:24	99
9–10	76, 99–100
10	76
10:1-10	99
12:37-50	77
16	78
16:1-16	11, 78 n.82, 165 n.66
17:7-8	130
20	167
21:8-21	11, 78 n.82, 165 n.66
26	167
27	167
41:45	78

Exodus
| 20:2 | 77 |

Leviticus
| 18:7-16 | 99 |
| 20:11-21 | 99 |

Numbers
12:1	78
13–14	11
13:33	11

Deuteronomy
2:10, 21	11
6:5	68–9
9:2	11
8:14	77
13:6-10	130

Judges
| 4:4-10 | 167 |

1 Kings
| 8 | 133 |
| 11 | 77 |

Esther
| 1:1 | 76 n.74 |
| 8:9 | 76 n.74 |

Psalms
| 68:31 | 76, 78 n.79 |
| 72:4, 12 | 120 |

Proverbs
| 1–9 | 173 |
| 31:10-31 | 172 n.107, 173–4 |

Ecclesiastes
| 1:4-11 | 140 |
| 3:1-8 | 140 |

Isaiah
11:3	69–70
18:1-6	75
19:25	77
20:3-5	76
37:9	76
43:3	76
45:14	76
63:1	78 n.79

Jeremiah
| 13:23 | 75 |
| 40–42 | 77 |

Ezekiel
| 18:20 | 100 |
| 29 | 77 |

30:4	76
32	77
38:5	76

Micah

1–2	128–9

Nahum

3:9	76

Zephaniah

1:1	78
3:10	75

Matthew

2:16	159
5–6	187
5–7	48
5.17-18	187
6:5	68
7:12	200
8:4-15	174
8:28-34	65–6
9:20-22	153 n.21, 210
10–11	36
10:8	65
11:2	147
11:28	159
15:21-28	165
15:22	65
16:23	177
18:13-17	176
20:20-28	158
23:8	146, 157
23:9, 11	146
28:19	46
28:19-20	5, 22, 121, 138

Mark

5	153
5:21-43	152–3
5:21-6:1	107 n.17
5:25-34	153 n.21
7:24-30	165
7:24-37	183 n.34
8:29	176
12:28-34	200
15:40, 41	158

Luke

1–2	128–9
4	128
4:16-22	187
4:16-28	13 n.42
6:31	200
8:4-15	174
8:43-48	153 n.21
9:25-19:27	135
10:10-17	187
10:38-42	165
12:13-41	135
15	134
16	133
16:1-13	133–5
16:19-31	43, 135, 142–5
19:1-10	135
21:2-5	187
22:25-26	147
24	120, 183

John

1:1-4	123
3:16	68
4:1-42	32 n.36, 34 n.48, 162 n.43, 166, 170, 171 n.100
4:10	170
4:17-18	170
4:22	170
4:29	170
4:42	148, 167, 174
10:10	168, 183, 187
12:24	118
14:6	180, 183
19:25	158
21	120
21:15-17	68

Acts

1:8	124
4	159, 189
8	78 n.83, 156
8:26-39	78
8:26-40	78 n.83
10	91
10:14-16	91
14:17	190 n.75

17   121–4
17:15-34   113 n.8
22:22-23:11   124
22–31   122 n.36

Romans
4   190 n.75
8:34   180
15:2   123
12:10   68
12:20   158

1 Corinthians
1:15-29   180
3:11-13   189
5   83
6   83
7   68
9:22   123
10:15-22   122
11:20-22   83
11:27-34   82–3
14:34-35   130, 159, 163
15   94
15:22-23   180

2 Corinthians
5   94

Galatians
3:28   159
4   78, 165
4:8-11   122

Philippians
2:5-8   179

Colossians
1:15-29   180

1 Thessalonians
1:9   122
4:16   24, 80
5:1-11   140

1 Timothy
2:11-15   163

2 Timothy
2:12   159

Hebrews
1:6   179, 189
2:14-15   189
4:14-16   181
7:5   189
8:4   189
11:28   189
12:1   82, 190
12:23   189

1 Peter
3:19:4:6   182

Revelation
1   182
7   159
14   159

Lightning Source UK Ltd.
Milton Keynes UK
UKHW020345071122
411622UK00022B/33